INVENTORY 98

INVENTORY 1985

3/14/75

NAPOLEON AND HIS BRITISH CAPTIVES

TOWN AND
CITADEL OF
BITCHE
*From a
relief-map*

MICHAEL LEWIS

C.B.E., M.A., F.S.A., F.R.HIST.S.

Late Professor of History, Royal Naval College, Greenwich
President of the Society for Nautical Research

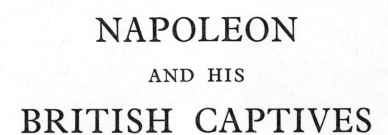

NAPOLEON

AND HIS

BRITISH CAPTIVES

London

GEORGE ALLEN & UNWIN LTD

RUSKIN HOUSE MUSEUM STREET

FIRST PUBLISHED IN 1962

PRINTED IN GREAT BRITAIN
in 10 *pt. Plantin type*
BY UNWIN BROTHERS LIMITED
WOKING AND LONDON

ACKNOWLEDGMENTS

My thanks are due to the Trustees and Director of the National Maritime Museum for their permission to reproduce their miniature of Captain Jahleel Brenton. The photographs from which plates Nos. 2, 3, 10 and 11 and the frontispiece are reproduced were provided by the French Archives Photographiques (Caisse Nationale des Monuments Historiques, Paris). I am greatly indebted once again to Lieutenant-Commander George Naish, RNVR, for calling my attention to contemporary prisoner-literature, and even providing a good deal of it from his remarkable library. To Mr Richard Ollard I owe a debt which has now almost become a standing one. As ever, he continues to put his great historical and critical gifts most ungrudgingly at my disposal. Last, I must record with gratitude the unstinted help afforded by my son, M. J. T. Lewis, who has not only read the whole book in typescript—much of it twice—and put his beautiful penmanship to such good use in map and plan, but also discovered new and valuable material, and made many most fruitful suggestions.

CONTENTS

ILLUSTRATIONS

INTRODUCTION
THE NEW AND THE OLD

This book is about those subjects of King George III who fell into the hands of the French during the great conflict of 1803–14 known in this country as 'The Napoleonic War': only these—not even the Frenchmen who at the same time fell into ours, nor of the British who fell into French hands in other wars.

An oddly small slice, it may seem, of a not particularly large cake? In terms of numbers alone, certainly, or even in terms of the individual worth and quality of the people concerned: but not so small if this book be thought of, as I think of it, as a chapter in the history, not primarily of Captivity, but of War itself; especially of War as it developed in our part of the world—Western Europe. In that context, I believe, this comparatively insignificant band of comparatively unimportant people is immensely significant. It is not selected at random, still less as being typical of all captives in all ages; but as—in the history of war in Western Europe—a group of people who, quite inadvertently, made history.

These British captives of Napoleon were of two types, overlapping sometimes but always distinct. One type was old, old as recorded history. They were fighting men taken by the enemy after the outbreak of hostilities. 'Prisoners of War'—p.o.w.s for short—is, and has long been, the name by which they are known. The other type was new, in its own day alarmingly new. It was composed, mostly but not necessarily, of civilians—'non-belligerents' as we should say. The man who, at a stroke of the pen, invented the class called them '*ôtages*'—hostages—but the common French name was '*détenus*', the detained ones. The twentieth century calls them 'internees'.

Both types loom large in the story of Western War; and in this book—this chapter of Western War—they are in a manner of speaking its twin heroes, though not necessarily in themselves heroic. Sometimes we shall be able to discuss them together because, at times, their physical fortunes were closely intermingled. Yet, to start with, the types must be examined separately because their history, their origin and their legal standing differed so radically. Here the new phenomenon, the *Détenu*, shall have the first turn: then the p.o.w. shall have his.

CHAPTER I

DÉTENU

In the civilization of Christian Europe, even then passing its noon, there was a world of difference between the treatment accorded to, and expected by, the gentle and the lowly. (This applies in both Britain and France: not surprisingly in this country, where the gentleman still had almost all the fun that was going in all departments of life, but rather more unexpectedly in France, where 'Equality and the Rights of Man' was still, in 1803, supposed to be by law established.) Indeed there had been times, still vivid in the memories even of the young, when 'all men are born free and equal' had meant nearly all it said, and when 'privileged' heads had been falling like leaves, lopped off by Madame Guillotine simply because they were privileged.) But the new France of the First Consul, already rapidly evolving, was not at all like that. Even if the aristocracy of birth was still in the shadows, other aristocracies were not, notably those of reflected power and of money. (Already a certain pseudo-gentility could readily be earned by judiciously backing the right horse, or by simple purchase, if one had the cash: and long before Napoleon fell there was a very solid neo-aristocracy of wealth and power, even though its members were not *ancien régime.*)

So, from the start of the war, and throughout its course, gentility —British gentility anyway—was recognized in France, in theory if not always in fact. In true p.o.w. circles this meant that the older custom of civilization—a sharp distinction between the relative treatments of officers and men—still held good, in theory always, in practice often; because, then as before, the convention still held that every officer, of both services and, oddly enough, of both nations, was a gentleman: every officer, that is, who enjoyed his office by virtue of a commission given him by his Sovereign, whether that dignitary called himself King, Prince Regent, First Consul or Emperor.

It happened that in France in this period, and especially in the early days of the war, the proportion of gentlemen to non-gentlemen among the captives was unusually high: not because the ratio of officer-prisoners to 'other rank' prisoners was higher than usual, but because most of the new class of captives, the *détenus*, came under the head of gentle: gentle, that is, in the wide and general sense then accepted in France. They were not necessarily titled or landed, for there were among them a goodly sprinkling of people on a sensibly lower plane of gentility than this; but still people of substance and good repute at home: those for instance who counted in the worlds of politics, the law, medicine and the Church, as well as in literature, the arts, or even the sciences. Most *détenus*, therefore, came from one or other of these upper social layers, though not by any means all, as is now to be seen, when the trend of events and the reasons why they became *détenus* at all are investigated.

During that brief, year-and-a-half interlude between the signing of the treaty of Amiens in October 1801, and the renewal of hostilities in May 1803, there had been a tremendous exodus, of all classes, from England to France. It was indeed a cross-section of British social life which made the journey: not only the types just named, but also business men keen to reknit contacts severed by the first war; merchants in a big way, tradesmen in a small way, engineers, mechanics, artisans, servants, grooms, jockeys; even crooks, leaving their country for their country's good—and their own—at the first available moment. Few of these last named, of course, claimed gentility and its privileges. But they were the minority. Let us then take a look at the majority— those whose main motive for their journey was pleasure.

The British upper class, then as at almost any time during the last three centuries, were inveterate travellers (That was the word then: now, when the luxury is no longer the monopoly of that class but is shared by us all, we call ourselves 'tourists'.) 'Travelling Gentlemen', even in an age which had not yet descended to calling everything by its initials, were already commonly known, both to one another and to those who catered for their comfort, as 'T.G.s' and they were among the commonest, and by no means least welcomed, of continental phenomena.) With them it had long been the fashion, amounting by now to an ingrained habit, to consider 'travel' essential for the acquisition of good breeding and *ton* a kind of social cachet: a keeping up with those Joneses who were already at the top, or near it.) It was not mere snobbery either. For many years, before the 1789 Revolution spoiled it, French *culture* had been a very real thing, and in many aspects of civilized life the French really were the leaders.

(Ever since the days of *le Grand Monarque*, indeed, such Britons as were civilized enough to realize how relatively skin-deep their civilization was, had yearned, secretly or openly, to catch something of the French *élégance, esprit* and *savoir faire.*) They were even, many of them, eager to secure such benefits for their children while they were still of impressionable age; and, (long ago, things had reached such a point that the noble or upper-class youth, on leaving school or university, was not considered 'finished' until he had done the Grand Tour, visiting Paris, Vienna, Florence and Rome with his 'bear-leader' or tutor:)or, if the parental purse could not run to Austria or Italy, there was always Paris, the one capital never omitted from the itinerary.

It was all very pleasant and comfortable. The best people, for instance, would take their own coaches or carriages with them, complete with full staff of coachman, footmen, body-servants and lady's maids. Moreover, full and by they were very popular as they rolled majestically along: they spent liberally, and were received accordingly with bows and smiles wherever they went: shamelessly rooked too, as often as not, because (being British) they seldom troubled to master the French language, hiring instead experienced *couriers* whose conception of the business was to have a foot in both camps. To the ordinary Frenchman, under-privileged and over-taxed, these colourful 'T.G.s' were a gift indeed: gullible as geese—but not so colourful as the eggs they so freely laid.

Nor—up to 1789 anyway—did the existence of a state of war seem to make much difference. For War itself, till then, was a comparatively gentlemanly affair, waged, in the eyes of all civilized belligerents, not between states but between sovereigns. Thus 'Britain' was not conceived of as being at war with 'France', and, emphatically, the individual Briton did not regard himself as at war with the individual Frenchman: and he did not hate him: he was not expected to. It was just King George who had unfortunately fallen out with King Louis. Yet, naturally, King George expected his loyal subjects to back him up; was indeed at some pains to convince them of Louis' wrongheadedness and his own rightness, and therefore that his loyal subjects *ought* to back him. Meanwhile—naturally—King Louis was taking precisely the same line with his loyal Frenchmen. So, inevitably, a certain amount of synthetic ill-will was sometimes generated: and this sometimes led to an appreciable slackening in the Dover–Calais bookings. There was also another, and more prosaic, cause for this fall-off—a natural deterioration in the standards of travelling comfort across the Channel: local food-shortages arising indirectly from hostilities, neglected roads, troop-movements, or even, now and then, an inconvenient battle in the neighbourhood. These, however, were mere incidentals. It was very seldom indeed that anyone interfered directly with the British visitor: that was bad form. It was considered bad business too, especially by the French who, in common with their government, rightly regarded 'Milord' and his equipage as a very worthwhile goose, with a handsome golden egg to lay: one who should be encouraged to lay it comfortably—in France.

How little ordinary Anglo-French relations were disrupted by a state of war, even as late as 1778, is illustrated by the fact that the Dover–Calais (and of course the Calais–Dover) packet service ran uninterrupted for more than a year after the War of American Independence had started.[1] It was then suspended; not, however, through any feeling of hostility between the rank and file of the nations but because, at that moment, there was hatching a full-scale Franco-Spanish invasion scheme, and the enemy, wishing naturally to keep its objects from us, felt that here was too obvious a hole in 'security' arrangements. Throughout the war, however, there existed in most of the provincial towns of France regular colonies of British residents leading normal and pleasant lives, untouched, apparently, by the harsh breath of war. Even in Paris itself such a community flourished, enjoying all its normal social amenities, including a weekly engagement to dine at the hospitable table of de Biron, *Maréchal de France*.

It is only right to record, however, that this essentially friendly atmosphere was sadly polluted by the events of 1789 and subsequent years. The reasons are only too obvious—the abhorrence which all upper-class Britons felt towards French republican principles in general, and sansculottism in particular; and, even more perhaps, the very violent views, and actions, of the French mobs. On their side, too, the Republicans, at every level, were far from sympathetic to aristocratic Britons, who reminded them all too unpleasantly of their own aristos whose heads they were after. To them 'privilege', whether British or French, was not to be countenanced. In addition there were now the physical dangers inherent in all sea-travel, even across the Dover Straits. For the French, having virtually ceased to dispute sea-supremacy with our battle-fleets, were already concentrating their

[1] A. Temple Patterson, *The Other Armada*, London, 1960, p. 106.

18

principal efforts on an intensive *guerre de course*, waged against the non-naval shipping of their enemy. So the regular cross-channel service, already faltering before the execution of Louis XVI and the declaration of war which followed it, ceased altogether during the years of 'red' government, and ordinary tourist-traffic dried up of its own accord. Yet, though it was never properly reconstituted, no sort of precedent was set up because, when the Convention gave way to the Directory, the marked anglophobia of the first-named gave place to a reactionary anglomania; and, from 1795 onwards, at least one cross-channel ship (the American *Two Friends*, Captain Gilbert) made so many trips, both ways, as almost to constitute a 'service'.

So far, then, the interruption of intercourse between the peoples had been almost entirely a social matter, and not one of war and peace at all. The travel-urge of wealthy Britons had dried up because they no longer wanted, or found it pleasurable, to travel. When war broke out again in 1803, things were to be incomparably worse, but also basically quite different. Before we see what those things were, however, let us consider what the otherway traffic had been like, when ideological antagonisms had not yet bedevilled social relations.

In those happy days a Frenchman was equally free to travel in Britain at all times—if he wanted to. Normally, however, he did not exercise his privilege to anything like the same extent: not because we were more than usually rude to him in wartime, but because we were apt to be rude to all foreigners always. He was not usually, therefore, so welcome: nor was he so eager to come. He was not so congenital a globe-trotter. His *jeunesse dorée*, too, did not so often favour us with inclusion in its *grand tour*, our best society being (it held) less polite, less gracious than its own. Besides, where to us Paris was on the road to Vienna or Rome, for the Frenchman the road to London might almost be said to stop there. Between the two countries, therefore, peace or war, the tourist-traffic had been very one-sided. There were practically no French equivalents to our T.G.s, or to our bear-led grand-tourers.

Such facts, always true, were even truer than usual in 1801. When the great rush of that year suddenly developed it was largely one-way. For, this time, a much more humdrum reason operated. A dozen years of political and economic chaos had violently changed the distribution of French wealth. Many of those who in the old days would have liked to come to England, *had* come, but as refugees, beggared and supplicant. Those who could now afford to come were, for the most part, those who did not particularly want to.

The British, on the other hand, had no such difficulties or inhibitions. The war was over. The well-born were as well-born and privileged as before: the wealthy were, if anything, wealthier. They had been starved of their wanderlust for ten long years, and now, they knew, sansculottism in its more virulent forms had gone to earth. Off they went in their hundreds: and the French, almost all of them, were more than ready to welcome them. They had missed the golden eggs. Indeed, the travellers could hardly wait. The treaty was signed at Amiens on October 1, 1801, but the cross-channel rush began in September. And, for quality, what a rush it was! The French called their visitors 'milords', and it was no misnomer. It is estimated that among the British who arrived during this halcyon period were five dukes, three marquises, thirty-seven earls and countesses, eight viscounts, seventeen barons and forty-one elder sons and other heirs —all but one-third of the then House of Lords.[1]

Then, literally overnight, the knife fell, neatly guillotining not only the poor goose, but the whole civilized convention which had begotten and nurtured it; killing it for ever. On May 23, 1803, the edict went forth to detain every male Briton between the ages of 18 and 60 then on French soil, whether 'service' or 'civilian'. No exceptions were made. It is indeed symbolic that the Dover packet, *Prince of Wales*, Captain Sutton, lying in Calais harbour with a full freight of homeward-bound T.G.s, was not allowed to sail. Even Captain Sutton, with all his officers and men, was arrested: and for the next eleven years not a single packet crossed the Channel.

For all practical purposes, it is reasonable to pin upon the First Consul the sole responsibility for ending for ever a whole phase in the history of war. But, in human affairs, few actions are entirely without precedent. In the poison-gas attack at Ypres in 1915 the gas was new, not the poison: arrows and wells had been poisoned for countless centuries. When the atom-bomb was dropped on Hiroshima in 1945, thousands of bombs, though not atomic ones, had fallen on hundreds of cities. Yet April 22, 1915, and August 6, 1945, are regarded—and for general purposes rightly regarded—as key-days in the story of war. So must May 23, 1803, be regarded here, even though there were pale

[1] J. G. Alger, *Napoleon's British Visitors and Captives*, London, 1904.

precedents for Napoleon's action: analogies faintly colourable though basically false. There were two.

The first dated from 1746. While the fate of the Young Pretender, fleeing from Culloden, was still unknown in Paris, the French Government gave way to panic and arrested the whole British colony there, perhaps in order to have something substantial to set against his possible capture, trial and execution. But he escaped, and the prisoners were at once released, with due apologies. Again, in October 1793, there had been a rather more serious case. When Lord Hood entered Toulon at the request of the French royalists, the Convention, soon to inaugurate the Terror, caused the arrest of all Britons in France—all civilians by then, of course, as the war had been in progress for five months. But this was the action of the reddest of the red French governments, upon whose shocking irresponsibility the First Consul himself had indirectly come to power, and whose conduct he never tried to defend. Moreover, even the Convention, in its debates on the subject, had allowed a glimpse of the old and conservative to peep out oddly from the new and iconoclastic. In his speech, St Just could still say, 'Make your children swear eternal hatred to that Carthage, the Court of London, not to the English people'; while Robespierre himself, though supporting the motion, stressed the injustice to individuals, and the hardship it would inflict on the innocent. This affair seems to have been something of a panic measure too, occasioned by the report—quite erroneous—that the British had hanged the local deputy. By the time the British had left Toulon and the mistake was discovered, the Terror was at its height and in the subsequent confusion the captives were for a while over-looked. It was only in February 1795 that the Directory, now in power, rescinded the order and released them. Even so, the exigencies of war made repatriation difficult and uncertain: and it was not until the *Two Friends* was informally plying that many of those who wished to leave France could do so. But, after early 1795, British visitors were not officially molested again.

Here then were possible analogies to the arrests of May 1803. But neither furnished a true precedent, because there was one essential difference. The detentions of 1746 and 1793 had been ordered in mid-war; but those of 1803 appeared to be a piece of calculated policy coinciding with the opening of hostilities. Indeed, there is every reason to think that Napoleon himself regarded the Amiens interlude as a mere half-time in the intricate game he was playing. The French team, he realized, was blown by its exertions in the first half, and needed the interval. So, he knew, did the British team: so blown, he thought, that with luck it would not want a second half at all: and, just possibly, it would not have insisted upon one, had he been a little less impatient in revealing his intentions. As it was, however, he contrived in all sorts of ways to betray his object—which was to have a second half, but to blow the whistle for it at his own time, thus securing the maximum tactical advantage for his side.

He miscalculated. September 1803 seems to have been his choice. But Britain, watchful for once, began from the very beginning of the year to put a brake on her demobilization, and, by March, was showing open distrust of the First Consul and his manœuvres. Evidently she would insist upon that second half, and upon starting it at once, unless he mended his ways. But he could not bring himself to believe that Britain would have the nerve to blow the whistle herself; and he was therefore more than normally furious with her when, on May 12th, she withdraw her ambassador, and, six days later, declared war. All his schemes were in mid-air: he was not nearly ready. Nor, it is true, was Britain, but that mattered the less because he, not Britain, was the aggressor, the man who was weaving schemes.

He was certainly very angry: so angry, it has been asserted, that his immediate reaction—nothing less than the fatal decree of May 23rd—stemmed largely not from careful calculation but from sheer rage. This may be true: but it may be a serious over-simplification. The anger was there right enough; but probably it was only one contributing factor. In his later years, when illness had undermined his constitution and success his character, he might perhaps have yielded to such a passing passion, regardless of costs. But the Napoleon of 1803 was in his prime, and a great prime it was. We should look further for causes.

Let us first see—without necessarily believing—the reasons that he himself gave. His stated pretext was the seizure by British cruisers of two French ships in Audierne Bay near Brest, which (he alleged) took place before the British Government declared war. What justification had he?

Admittedly it was a close call. The timetable was this. Lord Whitworth, our ambassador, left Paris on May 12th, thereby giving notice that Britain intended war, though the act of leaving was not in itself a declaration of war. For various reasons (one of which was the suspicious reluctance of the port authorities to let his suite depart) he reached London only on the 20th. In that week several things happened. On the 17th Britain ordered the detention of French and Dutch ships in British waters, and issued letters of marque: both more or less certain indications of war, but not, at that day, war itself. This she declared formally on the 18th; and, on the 19th, seized the Audierne ships—small craft carrying timber and salt. As the captures took place in French home waters, this, of course, was an act of war, though a perfectly justifiable one, we having by then been at war with France for a whole day, or at least a whole night. Meanwhile Napoleon, though he did his utmost to hush the fact up, had himself committed what (when we did it) he called an 'aggression'. Indeed, he forestalled us in doing it by four clear days. On the 13th, he had issued orders to detain the British ships in Holland, Genoa and Tuscany.

It was on the 23rd that the fatal *détenu* order was signed: and, for obvious reasons, published only after it had been executed. In its original form, it ordered the detention of all persons liable to service in the British Militia between the ages of 18 and 60. The actual wording of it, and the significance of introducing the Militia into it will be discussed later. Here it is sufficient to note that, from the first, it really meant the arrest of every male Briton, not only of 'militia' age (18–60), but also if he were a few years younger or several older. In fact, the only exceptions when the time came were mere children and those patently approaching second childhood. For, whether by Napoleon's secret order or in their zeal to allow no eligible Briton to escape the net, the executant authorities everywhere insisted upon written proof of age—and this in a day when official birth-certificates were virtually unknown, and certainly no part of a tourist's luggage. Thus many a sturdy lad of 15 or thereabouts, and many a hearty old fellow who *might* be under 60 but was not, went into the bag, and stayed there.

Exactitude about dates, ages and qualifications, however, fades almost into insignificance when set against the principle which was at issue. Napoleon's very order, in its impact upon the world of that day, was infinitely more mischievous than any *ad hoc* irregularity could be, even if Britain could have been proved to have committed it: and he must have known that the whole civilized world would so regard it. He called his victims, at first, *ôtages*—hostages, presumably to balance the persons of the few French seamen taken in the captured ships. But for so violent a departure from all previous custom he realized that a better legal pretext was needed. Hence his reference to the British Militia; and the necessity, here, to explain the nature of that venerable institution.

It is best viewed as the descendant and heir of the Old English *fyrd*: and, in Saxon days, every male between the ages of 16 and 60 was legally obliged to serve in it when called up for home defence. In those far-off days, indeed, it was the only state-controlled military organization that existed in England. But this was very ancient history, and all that was now left of it was the general obligation of all men between these ages to turn out to defend the country *if invaded*. 'The Militia', in this sense, had been called out in 1588, when Philip II was known to be sending an army to land in England. Since then, however, the British Army had come into existence—a state service under the Crown, officered by more or less whole-time professional soldiers who held their authority by virtue of the King's commission; legally the King's servants, paid by him, and bound by their contract with him to serve him anywhere, at home or abroad, whenever and wherever he sent them. The same applied to the 'other ranks' who, though they had not the continuity of the officers, had yet legally accepted the same conditions upon their taking the 'King's Shilling'.

This does not mean that the Militia was dead. It still existed, and, as legally as ever, could still be called out, though, as before, only to fight at home. Naturally, if assembled, it would need officers who would, of course, perform the duties, and assume the titles, of Lieutenant, Captain, Major or Colonel. It was therefore possible to make *some* sort of case for maintaining that, since all Britons had a legal obligation to defend their homes, all were potential soldiers: and that all the British 'gentle' class (who if called up would inevitably become the militia lieutenants, captains, etc.) were potentially military officers. Indeed, had mid-twentieth century ideas prevailed in Napoleon's day, such a view would have been no pretence at all. For now, in the great emergency of war, National Service by law established has swallowed all older formations like Militia, Fencibles, Volunteers or Territorials, and nullified all reservations about home-defence and foreign service. And the whole modern institution of Internment is largely a corollary of National Service. Now every British male of military age, however 'civilian' he may be in peace-time, is indeed a potential sailor, soldier or airman when war comes:

and, if caught in an enemy country, he is interned in order to prevent the potentiality becoming an inevitable reality.

But this is the present situation, wherein war involves all the resources, human and material, of all the belligerents. It was by no means so in Napoleon's day. It has been computed, by what methods or with what accuracy I do not know, that barely one Briton in every ten actually engaged in our war against him, while something like 80 per cent of Britain's man- (and woman-) power was 'in war-work' of some sort in 1939–45. Both figures, no doubt, are 'round', and readily disputable in detail. But the fact behind them is not. The Second World War, in all its aspects (including manpower), was 'total'. The Napoleonic War was essentially 'limited'. In the eighteenth-century mind, in fact, the very concept of 'totality' had no place at all; for 'war' was still the concern only of the Heads of States and their 'private' armies and navies. It is true that the republican governments of France in the 1790s had gone some way towards leaving this concept behind them, when they inaugurated, by conscription, the first 'national' army. But, when they did it, they took the rest of Europe by surprise, and, even in the 1803–14 war, Britain for one still held fast to the old theory of 'private' armies. As things actually were in Britain, therefore, the gulf was abysmal between a 'regular' officer, wielding authority by virtue of his Sovereign's commission, and a 'militia' officer, universally regarded as little more than a civilian gentleman decked out in uniform for a special occasion. No one had, for centuries, ever dreamt of equating the two. This, however, was just what Napoleon was doing now; and, in so doing, was taking a long, irreversible step towards total war. Nor can it be urged in his defence—as it could be nowadays—that he was only ensuring that potential officers did not fight against him. It is quite wrong to suppose that these unfortunate *détenus*, if not detained, would have rushed home and straightway 'joined up'. They would have done no such thing. War was for His Majesty's Forces, not for them—they (or most of them) were civilians. A picturesque but convincing proof that this is substantially true may be culled from the charming but essentially peaceful pages of Jane Austen. Who could guess, simply by reading them, that all her novels are set in an England engaged in the largest and fiercest war she had ever fought?

We can now, perhaps, view these unhappy *détenus* in their proper historical perspective. They are not particularly interesting or deserving in themselves. But they are the first of a class: the class of Internees which, though not present in all wars since then, has evidently come to stay. It was their detention which established the precedent for Internment: and the precedent is the important thing. Its rightness or wrongness, mankind being what it is, is seldom either here or there in history. There are, of course, many reasons why the 'limited' (or 'private') war of the eighteenth century degenerated into the all-out or 'total' war of the twentieth. One of them was the French National Army, which was so successful that France's enemies were constrained to imitate it; and other reasons will emerge later. Here, the only point to be stressed is that the precedent for the internment of non-combatants is one very prominent and obvious factor in that degeneration: obvious because, *ipso facto*, it swells the numbers of 'belligerents' from hundreds of thousands to, in the wars we know and deplore, hundreds of millions. The precedent for this most lamentable extension of war is the French decree of May 23, 1803; and the precedent's creator was one man—Bonaparte, the First Consul.

This is the decree, so heavy with future sorrow for untold millions. But, here, it is preserved in its original frame—one of the many missives delivered to individual Britons over the length and breadth of France; simultaneously lest some should take fright and make a bolt for it. This particular missive was one of those penned by the prefect of the Somme department.[1] In those from other departments the frame would vary slightly, but the import would be identical. The part of it—Napoleon's part—which would be common to all is the portion here printed in italics. It reveals to perfection what the First Consul was intending—and pretending.

The Prefect of the Department of the Somme, to M. S. . . ., Englishman at Amiens.

I inform you, Sir, of the Decree of the Government of the Republic dated the 2nd Prairial, 11th year of the Republic, of which a copy is below:

Copy.

St. Cloud, 2nd Prairial, 11th Year of the Republic.
All the English enrolled in the Militia, from the age of 18 to 60, holding a commission from his Britannic Majesty, who are at present in France, shall be made Prisoners of War, to answer for the Citizens

[1] From Admiral Sir William Dillon's *Narrative*, MS. Vol. III, pp. 195–6. In this book all references to this important source are to the *manuscript* in the author's possession, and not to the published version (2 vols., Navy Records Society, 1953 and 1958) which does not contain most of the p.o.w. material.

of the Republic who have been arrested by the vessels or subjects of his Britannic Majesty before the declaration of war. The Ministers, each as far as concerns him, are charged with the execution of the present Decree.

Buonaparte, the First Consul
B. Marot, the Secretary of State.

Consequently, within the space of 24 hours from the present notification, you will please to constitute yourself a Prisoner of War at the house of the Town Major of the City of Amiens. I tell you beforehand that no pretext, no excuse, can exclude you, as, according to the British laws, none can dispense you from serving in the Militia. After having made this declaration within 24 hours, you will be permitted to remain a prisoner upon Parole. In case you have not made your declaration within 24 hours, you will no longer be allowed to give your Parole, but will be conducted to the control point of the military division that will be fixed upon by the Minister of War.

I salute you.

To appreciate the subtlety of this precious document, the two parts must be read together. How harmoniously the First Consul and the Prefect were working in harness! The Consul introduces the Commission, the existence of which alone gives legal colour to his order, and only then by stretching legality to its utmost limit. The Prefect then takes up the running, and blandly explains what he chooses to consider his powers under the Act, knowing full well that, if he confines himself to the strict powers given to him therein, he will make only a very small catch, since very few of his prey actually hold any commission at all. He therefore retreats immediately from actualities and takes his stand upon potentialities. 'It is no good arguing', he says in effect. 'If you will not sign away your liberty of your own free will and at once, you will simply be thrown into prison. And you cannot get out of it by objecting that you hold no commission in the Militia, because, by your own laws, you cannot escape the liability to hold one.'

It was clever, because it was specious: but that did not do away with its two underlying fallacies: first, that a militia commission could be equated with a King's commission: and second that most of the *détenus* were, or were going to be, militia officers. In Britain as she then was, both these assumptions were demonstrably wrong.

The British, government and people alike, naturally regarded the whole thing as a bare-faced breach, not only of international law, but also of common decency and the hitherto unchallenged obligations of

27

hosts to guests. Dillon puts his finger on the really sore spot when he writes, 'They had been detained while travelling upon the faith of the passports granted to them by the French Government'.[1] That, among civilized peoples, should have been sufficient, as it had always been before. It was many years, therefore, before the British, either government or people, would allow the validity of the arrests: nor would they fall in with Napoleon's constant endeavours to equate *détenus* with prisoners of war. This refusal to countenance what, in British eyes, amounted to compounding a felony was to have widespread repercussions, nullifying, as we shall see, all negotiations about all captives.

They had another reason, too, for regarding Napoleon's 'militia' argument as a mere subterfuge. He was not even consistent to his own decree. Even were it tenable as an argument, it overstepped its own limits, again and again, in its implementation. We have already seen his servants ignoring the age-limits at both ends, though no one, not even Napoleon, denied the facts, still less attempted to remedy them. But this was not all. When a *détenu* in his late 50's reached 60, there was no talk of releasing him. Not a single case is on record of anyone being allowed to go home on the score of age alone. Again, liability to militia service in England was not universal. Certain classes were expressly exempted—the clergy, for instance, always, and medical men usually. Yet parsons and doctors were nabbed with all the rest, and there was never any talk of releasing them, as classes. Indeed Napoleon was here adding further fuel to the flame of our wrath. In the good old days of 'gentlemanly' warfare, exemption from captivity extended to the surgeons and chaplains even of the fighting forces: in fact, to all individuals other than the actual fighting men. In British eyes, therefore, the detention of such people, being civilians, seemed a double act of shame.

On the other hand, among the *détenus* there were some real serving officers, holders of King George's commission. With them Napoleon had a better case. They were taking a risk by being in France at all in such uncertain times, and knew it. Yet, until quite recently, commissioned officers, even senior ones, had been safe from molestation. An outstanding case of this had occurred during the American War, when Sir George Rodney, one of our leading admirals, found himself in Paris at the outbreak of hostilities. He was detained, however, not because he was an Englishman, but because he was a debtor; and he

[1] Dillon, op. cit., III, p. 157.

28

was instantly released when the gallant and kindly Maréchal de Biron stepped in and paid his debts: whereupon he repaid the maréchal, ironically enough, by thrashing the French fleet off the Saints islands, and saving the war for Britain. De Biron's action was in the best tradition. But it was never to happen again; and indeed, knowing how the Revolution had undermined the old amenities, the officer-visitors of 1803 did not look for any such generosity now. A number of them, warned in time from home, made a dash for it, and crossed the Channel with, or ahead of, Lord Whitworth. Those who did not were detained.

There were fortunate—or long-sighted—*détenus* also, in spite of the fact that the state-inspired French press tried hard to lull them into a sense of false security. Foremost among such journals was the English-language paper, the *Argus*, edited by the renegade Lewis Goldsmith. It did its best to allay natural fears by laughing at them, expatiating on France's well-known notions of honour and civilization. For all that, some made good their escape—more, certainly, than Napoleon bargained for. Others, quite a numerous band, were actually taken at Calais; even in the unhappy *Prince of Wales*. There were others, too, who were arrested but, in the early confusion, contrived to slip away. For confusion there was, even on the French side —'operations' as new as this one was are always apt to reveal gaps in essential staff-work. Clearly not all the actors cast for the various roles had been sufficiently briefed. Thus two *détenus* named Smyth and Jodrell, both men of good standing, signed their parole-forms at once, as, no doubt, the better of two evils. But, having second thoughts, they secured an interview with the military governor of Valenciennes, where they were confined, and, while overloading him with polite if meaningless compliments, deliberately handed their paroles back to him. The general, a simple, elderly soul whom, evidently, no one had thought of briefing, quite failed to grasp what they were after. But Dillon,[1] who happened to be visiting the governor on quite different business, saw well enough, and contrived to engage the old man in bright talk for nearly two hours: and when he left, found, as he expected, that Messrs Smyth and Jodrell had left too. They were not overtaken. The affair caused some stir. The official *Moniteur Universel*—outstanding pioneer of that 'controlled press', since become part and parcel of the Dictator's paraphernalia—took up the incident with relish, and published

[1] Dillon, op. cit., III, p. 160.

29

a violent article describing them individually as a Colonel and Major of the Militia who had violated every principle of honour by breaking their Parole, after having experience every attention due to their station in life . . .

. . . and so on: this generation will have no difficulty in recognizing the technique. The British Government even went to the length of denying the main point of the attack, stating categorically that the gentlemen in question were neither militia officers nor the holders of any official positions whatever.[1]

The long and short of it was that Napoleon, who hoped to catch some thousands, succeeded in detaining only from seven to eight hundred. Yet these were no mean prize, because quite half of them were Milords and T.G.s. There are hints, too, that he captured, and then released, some of the very wealthiest and most influential. For money was talking very loud in France just then: and Influence, though more quietly, was talking too. Needless to say, people released in such ways were by no means a dead loss to Napoleon: the price of bought or engineered freedom would obviously be very high. Others, somewhat less lucky—or wealthy—failed to get home but still bought a measure of exceptional comfort by being permitted to choose their own place of residence in France. Verdun was the official domicile for all 'gentle' British prisoners, but a few certainly never turned up there. Dillon, who lived in Verdun for four years, says that there were never more than 300 of the wealthy sort: and he may well be right. But the full tally of wealthy *détenus* must have been nearer 400.

It may well be that, in stressing the wealth of this 400, we are approaching the real motive for Napoleon's uncivilized behaviour. Gold, he knew very well, was a necessary sinew of war: and he very likely argued somewhat along these lines: 'These wealthy fools who are so free with their sterling in France, are aiding both French economy and my own war effort. We must not let them depart, to spend their money in aiding the enemy's economy. But, when war comes, that is what they will almost certainly do: so we must prevent them forcibly.'

Unfortunately, if this was indeed his aim, Bonaparte was sizing up his victims with considerable acumen. They were not on the whole

---

[1] It is regrettably possible that a splash of the tar from the *Moniteur's* brush had crossed the Channel and alighted upon the British Government. One of the pair *may* have held a militia post at the time.

the sort of people who would voluntarily forgo their luxuries and pleasures and, in the event, they did not: in fact, they played right into his hand. They continued, in captivity, to live well; how extraordinarily well we shall learn later: and it is significant that, in spite of a few protective manœuvres to mask his real game, he never interfered seriously with their arrangements to transfer their wealth from England. They were not being consciously disloyal, and little serious criticism of their extravagance appears in English papers—there was more, oddly enough, on the French side. They were just running true to the form they had always shown. They were generous too, according to their own lights, spending a great deal in relieving the distress of poorer British captives. But that they were unconsciously helping the enemy there is no doubt.

Contemporary writers tend naturally to concentrate on these rich and relatively important captives. These were the *détenus* of everyday parlance. But the humbler sort must not be neglected, if only because, whatever they were called, they were all, strictly, *detained*. No Briton in France was permitted simply to pack up and depart. Not all, however, were arrested. Settled up and down the country were many genuine British residents, long established as component parts of French life: and some of them were too valuable as cogs in the French economic machine to be lightly disturbed. We shall have more to say of some of these. Here we must look, briefly, at those non-resident *détenus* who were also non-gentle. Napoleon seems to have displayed comparatively little interest in them, and never to have formulated any very precise policy to regulate their lives and movements. They were not treated as 'gentle', nor yet as the non-gentle 'other ranks' of the armed forces, whose lot, as we shall see, consisted of close incarceration in various fortresses. They mostly settled down wherever they could, wherever they happened to be, or wherever they could best use their respective skills to earn their bread. They were not sent *en masse* to Verdun with the gentlemen, yet it is clear that many of them turned up there.

Those who did so may be divided, roughly, into two classes. The first consisted of such people as, in Britain, normally made their living by attending to the wants or comforts of the rich—shopkeepers, valets, grooms, etc. At Verdun they were bound to find employment, for there resided their natural clients and masters. Some, especially the tradesmen, did quite well for themselves, particularly in the first years of the captivity. Until then, Verdun had been a mean provincial town; poor, unfashionable, and served by the meanest provincial shops. Now it blossomed forth into a reflection, if a little pale, of Bath or Tunbridge Wells. Instead of the poky little *épiceries* and *tabacs* there appeared *maisons* showing signs like ANDERSON, GROCER AND TEA-DEALER FROM LONDON, or STUCKEY, TAILOR AND LADIES' HABIT-MAKER FROM LONDON. Nor did these signs lie. Messrs Anderson and Stuckey were just as they described themselves— London tradesmen who had been unlucky enough to be travelling in France in May 1803.

The second non-gentle element which gravitated to Verdun was much less desirable: yet it arrived for much the same reason. Milords demanded not only necessaries like food and clothing (good food and fashionable clothes, naturally): not only—to them—near-necessities like servants. They also wanted their customary entertainments: their clubs, their horse-racing and hunting; their gambling, their baser sexual relaxations. It is the old story of supply and demand. Like magic they all appeared—club-managers and waiters, vets, horse-copers, touts and tipsters, proprietors of doubtful gaming-halls; even courtesans—British ones, too. These, or most of them, accustomed in England to swarm about the honeypots, had no difficulty in nosing them out in France.

There was one other feature about this curious Verdun settlement, this little enclave of English high-life buried in the heart of an alien and hostile land, which made it, probably, unique. Many of the original victims, interned because they might possibly become militia officers, were accompanied by persons who could not possibly become such—their wives, maids, daughters and, occasionally, mistresses. What the official attitude towards such people was is not always clear: but it seems certain that the French Government very seldom detained them, officially. Yet many of them chose to remain with their menfolk, and were allowed to do so: the more cheerfully, no doubt, because their presence certainly envisaged more and larger golden eggs. Nor, by parity of reasoning, was any obstruction usually placed in the way of those devoted people—mostly wives, but occasionally children and even courtesans—who wished to share their men's captivity. Many such heroines arrived to form a novel and interesting class of (if the oxymoron may be permitted) *détenues volontaires*. It need hardly be stressed that the presence of these women and children, in considerable numbers, made for a very different type of society and social life than was usual in wartime prison camps. By virtue of their very presence existence became more normal, more civilized. They helped enormously to relieve the tedium, tension and frustration which are the common ills of captives. There were other results, too. Their presence was obviously the making of Messrs Anderson and Stuckey: and it added a new activity altogether to the preoccupations of the *détenus*—education.

Though the subject of schools for captives concerns others beside *détenus*, it is convenient to treat it here. At most of the places where British prisoners were collected there were children, though from widely differing homes and classes. There were, first, the *détenus'* young families at Verdun. Second—a good many of them at Verdun —were the youngest of the true combatant prisoners of war, both officers and men and almost all from the Royal Navy. It seems strange to find mere children in the forefront of battle, but such was the oddness of contemporary naval recruitment that would-be officers of 11 and serving seamen-boys of 13 could be taken to sea, legally too. But the reality was even more astonishing. The minimum legal ages, fantastic as they were, were widely disregarded, and it was perfectly possible for boys of an even more tender age to turn up at Verdun, legitimate prisoners of war. One such was a certain Henry Leworthy who was 10 when he arrived there: and there were doubtless a few who were younger still. The youngest seaman-boy known to me was Alexander Stewart, aged 14; but we shall hear (p. 254) of a mere infant of 5. There was a third category, too, constantly being recruited throughout the war—children captured in British merchant-men. The French authorities usually thought fit to keep them, presum-ably because they too might, in due time, become militiamen.

The *détenus* and officer-prisoners at Verdun faced the problem like men, and started schools both there and in some of the other prison-depots. The money was found largely by the wealthy civilians, aided by the Patriotic Fund, established by Lloyds for this and other war-purposes. To administer them, the captives appointed a Standing Charitable Committee consisting of seven members and two treasurers. The names of the first committee, established in 1804, are worthy to be recorded, for they rendered arduous and devoted service. There were two soldiers (*both détenus*), General Scott and Colonel Aber-cromby, son of the great Sir Ralph and later distinguished in his own right; Captain Gerrard, captain of an East Indiaman and also a *détenu*; Dr Thomas Grey, an ex-naval surgeon, afterwards a successful physician and a knight; a Mr Sevright, our agent of packets

B 33

at Helvoetsluys, a *détenu*, but with more reason for detention than most, since he had been detected sending information to the British Government; and two of the wrongfully detained clergy, the Rev. Launcelot Lee and the Rev. William Gorden, Vicar of Gunstew. The treasurers were a *détenu* named Stephen Wilson and the Rev. Robert Wolfe. The last-named, a man cast in the heroic mould, left after a while for Givet, where we shall meet him again. He was succeeded by Mr Gorden, who remained treasurer throughout the war, and won the love and admiration of countless captives. The Committee's task, and especially the treasurer's, was no sinecure, for the number of pupils, and of schools, was growing steadily. By 1805 there were four larger ones and several small ones, all with their own staffs of Britons, mostly *détenus*. The Verdun school, with (in 1804) 65 boys and 11 girls, was actually the smallest of the principal four. Givet (140 pupils), Valenciennes (120) and Sarrelibre (119—the Sarrelouis of pre-revolution days) were detention-fortresses for non-gentle service men and merchant-masters, and all held many more prisoners than Verdun. The 45 pupils in smaller schools brought the 1804 total to 500.[1] Others followed—at Arras, for instance, in 1806 and later Cambrai. The effort did great credit to all concerned: and indeed it was typical of this little-Britain-beyond-the-seas. Papa's—and even Mamma's—activities might not always bear too close an investigation: but for the children—well, that was another matter. Says Dillon,

> It was a pleasing sight to behold the little boys, chiefly taken upon the ocean, walking in their neat blue jackets and white trousers (which did honour to the benevolent) to Church every Sunday.

Not all the ladies lasted out the war, and when they wished to go permission was usually given. So, what with that and a fairly constant movement the other way, there was a good deal of coming and going: and this sometimes led to problems which we should now group under the general heading of 'Security'. Now that total war has become the norm, security, of course, has become the norm also, and no modern state would dream of countenancing so obvious a channel for leakages. But, for all Napoleon's strides towards total war, his security seems to have lagged far behind, and there was certainly some illicit traffic in contraband of war, whether in the form of articles, letters or information. Such transactions, if undiscovered then, are even less

[1] Dillon, op. cit., III, p. 228. By faulty addition he makes the total 400.

likely to be discovered now: but Dillon notes several little successes of his own in these matters, unimportant in themselves yet most unlikely to have been unique. In February 1804, he was anxious to make contact with the then First Lord, though for private reasons which had nothing to do with espionage. Casting about for ways and means, he had a stroke of luck:

> Sir Thomas Wallace, with whom I was on most friendly terms, was obliged to send his kept mistress home, on urgent affairs. She kindly took charge of all the letters relating to me, undertaking to deliver them, herself, at the Admiralty. That task she performed with the strictest punctuality.

And this unconventional intermediary was not the only one he used. In 1806 he got another letter through, this time to his patron, Admiral Gambier, carried on the person of a clerical *détenu* then released; and yet another in 1807 to the Minister of Agriculture, Mr Arthur Young. This time he does not reveal the channel used. Later that year he secured his own release, and finally left France with several clandestine papers—routine secret-service stuff relating to troop-movements— sewn into the collar of his coat. There were, of course, similar secret channels from France to England. With these we are not greatly concerned here; nor with the regular secret service avenues. All that seems to emerge is that there was really not much difficulty or danger in communicating, either way. Indeed, the French on their side were probably not trying very hard to close their captives' avenues, for the reason already hinted at—that a very considerable percentage of what passed through them from England to France consisted of what they were only too pleased to wink at, remittances of British cash.

At first, the *détenus* loomed very large in the story of British captives. They were the centres of brisk and acrimonious controversy; and they had no rivals, because there were no prisoners. As the war grew older, however, the emphasis, both of importance and of numbers, gradually and radically changed. The acrimony perforce waned with age—after ten years even the *Moniteur* had exhausted its vituperation —and, all the time, the victims of the 1803 internment were decreasing in numbers through various causes like release, escape and natural death. Nor were they ever substantially recruited.[1] On the other hand,

---

[1] The only exceptions were a few captured in merchantmen and a few, later in the war, detained in places like Hamburg or Berlin when overrun by the French Army. In no previous war would such people have been molested: but this time they were sent into France and kept there.

the regular prisoners were steadily, though never quickly, flowing in, and long before the end their numbers quite swamped the *détenus'*. The question of p.o.w. numbers will be discussed later. Here, an attempt can be made to assess—but only roughly—the number of *détenus* left towards the close of the war, and how they were then distributed. A paper in the Public Record Office[1] purports to name all surviving civilians and the places where they were then residing. Its information is unexpected, as regards both numbers and localities. Evidently, somehow or other, more of them than we should have guessed had disappeared altogether, and more had secured that limited freedom of being allowed to choose their own domicile within France. At Verdun itself, the compiler of the list can find only 47 male civilians, 11 of whom still have wives or families with them. By now, however, there were nearly twice that number scattered in 14 other named towns. Paris, for instance, had 37; Valenciennes 13; Tours 7; Sarrelibre 5; St Germain, Versailles, and Malines 3 each; Gorgnon, Moulins, Givet, Cambrai and Orleans 2 each; St Quentin and Nancy 1. This makes 130 in all, most (but not quite all) of whom were 'gentle' victims of the original internment. So drastic a fall-away of numbers is admittedly surprising, but not quite so surprising when it is realized that Captain Fane's list almost certainly does not include the 'non-gentle' elements. In other words, the number of *détenus* has fallen to 130, not from the 700–800, the accepted total of all detained civilians, but only from the 400-odd 'gentle' ones.

It would seem from these figures that it cannot have been exceptionally difficult, in the later days anyway, for a gentle civilian to secure his release, if he really set about it in earnest. If so many, one is tempted to ask, why not all? There are probably two answers to this. Some would not have the means, in terms of either 'interest' or cash, or both. But, on examining more closely the names in Fane's paper, one is tempted to suspect that many, if not most, of their bearers could have surmounted such difficulties if they had had the will to do so. Here perhaps is the true answer in many cases. They did not want to go. Sometimes this would be due to that natural apathy and loss of initiative which is one of the commonest maladies that long-term prisoners have to face. Sometimes, no doubt, they had grown to love their chains for other reasons—because, perhaps, they had fitted themselves

[1] Admiralty, 103. 468. 'List of Officers, etc. copied from the Memorandum Book of Captain Fane, 17.7.1811.'

snugly into the social life of their chosen town, or married a French-woman and reared a French family. But sometimes also—a more down-to-earth reason—they had learnt that a fixed income would buy for them a higher standard of comfort in France than it would in Britain, where prices were soaring. It was for this reason that, soon after the war, an appreciable stream began to flow the other way. Not a few genteel though penurious British civilians began to find their way back, together with many equally genteel, and even more penurious, service officers of the lower ranks, especially of the Navy. These, unemployed because there were very few ships in commission, and often dependent upon quite inadequate half-pay, found that it went further in France, where appearances had not to be kept up to the same extent. Soon there appeared once more not a few little British communities, sad and faintly shabby, in the towns where the *détenus* had been; detained now, not by force but by economic necessity.

Far otherwise were the fortunes of the wealthy *ex-détenus*. The Milords and globe-trotting T.G.s were back in France and Belgium in no time, and in their hundreds, even before the Hundred Days of 1815 began—and then there was a wild scramble to get out again. But this was only temporary. Immediately after Waterloo, Paris drew upper-class Britons like a magnet; and, when the excitements of treaty-making had faded, the old habits returned to stay. There they were, the Nobility and Gentry, their sons and their bear-leaders, their carriages, flunkeys and couriers; welcomed—and fleeced—as of old by their late enemies, and apparently quite undeterred by the ex-Emperor's uncouth experiments in total war. For was not Boney safe in St Helena? And was not poor old Louis XVIII, whatever his other shortcomings—a gentleman?

For all that, however, things were not the same. It is beyond man's wit to restore its pristine beauty to a damaged cobweb. The old trust was gone. For ever afterwards, whenever revolution looked to be lurking round the corner, or France and Britain drifting towards war, Milords were taking no risks. Standing orders were—'Post for Calais!'

It is not the intention of this book to record the story of French captives in Britain. But, in so far as the detention of French civilians is concerned, the tale is so short that, for the sake of contrast, it is worth telling. A number of French agents, spies and smugglers were caught and punished: and, like the French, we kept the officers, and most of the men, of the merchant service, when taken in the ordinary course of the naval war. Otherwise, there is nothing to tell. In the sense in which the word *détenu* has been used in this chapter, there were none at all.

CHAPTER II

PRISONER OF WAR

The *Détenu*, that historical novelty, was aggrieved at captivity; but the p.o.w., a hoary feature of war as old almost as war itself, expected it. Yet his lot, at the dawn of the nineteenth century, was incomparably better than it had once been; and we must see, first, how this came to be so. That, however, is not enough because, once more, the element of gentility obtrudes, cleanly cutting the prisoners into those 'two nations' common to all walks of contemporary society. In the services, they even had their distinctive names: the gentle were 'Officers', the lowly, 'Men'. First, then, we will examine the history and status of prisoners of war in general: then we will see how, and why, the officer benefited by his gentility, and contrived to enjoy substantially preferential treatment.

A. ALL PRISONERS

Among entirely uncivilized people, in really barbarous times, there was not a great deal to choose between captivity and death. Indeed, death was often preferable, since captivity all too often implied horrors like torture or starvation first, with death to follow. Very early in the progress of civilization, however, there began to emerge certain ameliorations of the captive's lot. So long as the acquisition of food was man's first and most pressing occupation—when it was hard enough anyway to keep himself at subsistence-level—the captor was apt to think of a captive merely as a mouth to be fed, and therefore better dead than alive. But as the captor gradually passed from hunter to husbandman, and his own food-supply became more secure, certain new considerations began to modify this entirely primitive view. Once he found that he could feed his captive without the risk of starving himself, he discovered that living prisoners had certain advantages to himself which dead ones did not possess.

First, if the captor had tiresome or dirty work to be done, which he disliked doing himself or making his own folk do, why not make his

39

prisoner do it? He would have to give him enough food to keep him alive; but that was all. He need not pay him wages, or any such equivalent as his own free people would expect. Here, of course, is one origin of the institution called Slavery: and if, dispassionately, we follow the history of that institution along just one line—that of the treatment and status of prisoners of war—we shall find (and, let us hope, blush in the finding) that, here in the twentieth century, there still exist horrible survivals of both the barbarous equations 'Captivity equals Death' and 'Prisoner of war equals Slave'. The first is seen in gas-chambers and liquidation-camps, the second in labour-camps and forced work of all sorts. Yet such things, if we would not despair of humanity, we must regard as sad backslidings in man's long struggle upwards. They are by no means the highest point he has ever reached. Even by Napoleon's day—indeed, many centuries earlier—the 'Prisoner equals Slave' concept had ousted the 'Prisoner equals Corpse' idea, and had advanced since then steadily and far, giving place to something much more civilized. The whole theory of the relation between captor and captive had, in fact, reached a peak untrodden either before or since, in the 'Age of Enlightenment'; during the 'gentlemanly' wars between the Crowns of Western Europe. How high that peak was is well revealed by a famous international lawyer, writing in 1758 when an Anglo-French war was actually in progress:

> As soon as your enemy has laid down his arms and surrendered his body, you have no longer any right over his life. A Prisoner may be secured, and for this purpose may be put into confinement, and even fettered if there is reason to apprehend that he will rise on his captors or attempt to escape. But he is not to be treated harshly unless personally guilty of some crime against those in whose power he is.[1]

Here indeed is a tremendous philosophic advance, and Vattel is careful to point it out, declaring that states which behave like this—and both France and Britain are mentioned by name—are in the forefront of civilization:

> We praise the English and French. Our hearts glow with love for them when we hear of how prisoners of war, on both sides, are treated by these generous nations.

What, perhaps more than anything else, made such liberal ideas possible just then was the view that it was crowns, not peoples, who

[1] Emeric de Vattel, *Les Droits des Gens*, Bk. III, p. 3 (sect. 49).

were quarrelling; because this meant that sovereigns like Louis and George, who flattered themselves on their general benevolence, though prepared to go to great lengths against each other, had no special grudge against lesser fry. They were therefore not averse to measures which might lighten the lot of those who (not quarrelling themselves) had become involved in their sovereigns' quarrels; and the most important institution, perhaps, which sprang from this amiable attitude was 'Exchange'. Simplified, the mental process by which each government came to favour it must have gone something like this. 'Loss of personal freedom is very grievous to the ordinary man, be he French or English. Is there no way round detaining prisoners, thereby making so many so unhappy? I might, of course, release all my captives as I capture them. That would indulge my benevolence: but I can hardly afford it. After all, war is war, and while I hold them they are as lost to my enemy's war effort as though they were dead. But, since his dilemma is precisely the same as mine, there seems only one logical thing to do. Let us arrange a *pro rata* swap. Let us mutually agree to liberate general against general, captain against captain, private against private, always in equal numbers. Then without either securing any advantage over the other, the sheer weight of accumulated unhappiness stemming from loss of liberty will be drastically reduced. As we stand at present, if I have X prisoners and he has Y, the sufferers total $X + Y$. On a basis of equal exchange they will total $X - Y$.'

Already, by Vattel's day, this simple and sensible scheme was in full operation; indeed working very smoothly just then because it happened that—very roughly speaking—the values of X and Y were equal. So 'flags of truce' could be sent in at fairly regular intervals, and 'cartels' arranged ceremoniously, with tremendous benefits to all concerned. Many regained freedom quickly who would otherwise have languished long in captivity, while the less immediately fortunate yet retained that first necessity of all prisoners—hope: hope that their names would figure in the next cartel. Further—and from a practical point of view quite as important—there was seldom, on either side, a real 'prisoner problem'—how to accommodate, guard, clothe and feed large numbers of essentially unprofitable bodies and mouths.

In the eyes of the liberal mid-century governments who favoured the arrangement and made it work, there was probably no reason why it should not continue to do so. Yet time was soon to show that there was a reason.

The whole thing was in the nature of a game which, like all games, must have mutually agreed rules: and both sides must keep them. Anything else would be fatal. For suppose that George and Louis arrange a cartel—a mutual exchange of, say, 1,000 men of similar and agreed grades. Suppose that George cheats, and sends only 950, or that Louis includes only 50 sergeants among his 1,000 when he has promised 100. What is the remedy? The injured party cannot take the ordinary remedy of an aggrieved state: he cannot declare war to enforce his rights, because war, the ultimate arbiter, is already declared. He is at once angry and impotent. No one likes being cheated; and the chances are that the whole scheme goes by default. In the event, neither George nor Louis defaulted: to the last they played to the rules. Not so Napoleon Bonaparte. We have watched him flouting the whole code as it concerned civilians. We are soon to see him doing essentially the same mischievous thing with the service prisoners, and to view the grievous results.

'Exchange' covered all prisoners: but in practice the officers benefited from it more than the men; at least, more surely and more quickly. The men almost always had to wait for cartels; and batches or shiploads, often of many hundreds, had to be assembled and forwarded. We can see the good old game at its best when we can watch the officers playing it. If one of these was lucky, his term of captivity might be remarkably short, since it could end as soon as a similar-ranking 'exchange' was forthcoming. Thus, as late as 1797, Lieutenant Thomas Masterman Hardy could be captured in a prize in January and be back, an entirely free man, in February. Lord Cochrane did even better in 1801. Taken in the *Speedy* on July 3rd, by the 14th he was officially exchanged and once more entirely his own master. But then the officer always had a better deal than the man: and it is time we sought the reasons for it. His story, in his capacity of prisoner, we shall find, had long been developing differently from that of the seaman or private soldier; mainly because, at a very early date, another element altogether had been introduced into it.

B. OFFICER-PRISONERS

It has been shown how the lot of all captives improved when the captor discovered a use for them—as slaves. Some time later, however, (but still very early in history) he discovered a second use for some of them—that is, for those destined to become the 'officer class'. We are back now in the days when the social cleavage between the leader and the led was enormous: when the leader was (to borrow the generic term we have been using) 'gentle', perhaps noble, while his men were—*his* men, his vassals and dependants. This meant another big difference—here is generalization, but the essential fact is there. The leader was well-off; the led were not: and the captor was not slow to realize the difference which that fact made. Captivity, slavery, death are unpleasant things; and if wealth can buy a man's release from them, assuredly he will buy it. He does, and there is Ransom; a second amelioration of captivity, but only for those who can afford it.

The complex process which gradually turned ransom into exchange cannot be elaborated here. It was part of that larger process which turned the self-supporting feudal vassal of his overlord (the King) into a professional paid servant of his Head of State (the Crown). This was the economic side of it; but it had its social side, too, and here there was no comparable change, even by mid-eighteenth century. The privileged feudal baron, knight or squire was still privileged, though he was now a general officer, a flag officer or a commissioned officer. The essential difference was merely that, now, the rival crowns were responsible for ransom as well as pay; and, by mutual agreement, could—and did—set off rival ransom-claims against each other. Perhaps this was sometimes a mixed blessing to the officer: though it saved his pocket, he might have to wait a little while for his freedom. But for the man the blessing was unmixed. Where, before, he was very seldom freed at all, he might now hope to be, even though, for him, the delay would be longer than for his privileged leader. All in all, however, it was certainly a considerable advance in the history of captives, and it was virtually complete by Vattel's day.

Yet ancient institutions seldom perish utterly; and ransom did not. Faint though unmistakable traces of it survive even into Napoleon's war, in so many ways iconoclastic. Thus when an order from Paris suddenly reached Verdun to the effect that Lord Yarmouth was to be released—just like that: 'released', not 'exchanged'—what had almost certainly happened was that his father, the wealthy and powerful Marquis of Hertford, had retrieved his son by arranging to pay a *ransom* for him. By that time, however, no one called it by that name: indeed, it was done so secretly that it is doubtful whether anyone now knows how much Lord Yarmouth was worth in contemporary currency. But this was only an obsolete recrudescence. Exchange had long been the norm: and, unfortunately, exchange itself was on the way out. Just why and how it went will be discussed later. First, however, must be introduced another institution altogether, of prime importance to officers, but not even available to ordinary men. It is the *Parole d'Honneur*.

The syllogism upon which the parole was based is easily told:

> An attribute common to all gentlemen is that they keep promises.
> All officers are gentlemen,
> Therefore every officer can be trusted to keep his promise:

a fallacy, alas: yet a minor one compared with the very unkind corollary which invariably flowed from it:

> A common man, not being a gentleman, can *not* be trusted to keep his promise:

and he very seldom was. This may be very unjust, and very poor logic, but it explains a great deal. Once more the officer enjoys the ha'pence while the man has all the kicks.

That halfpenny was worth having, too. Let us paraphrase King George again (remembering, of course, that we are also paraphrasing King Louis):

'At the moment, it seems, King Louis has no British officer to exchange for his Captain X, now in my possession. It's a pity: but there is no reason why Captain X (who is no personal enemy of mine) should suffer from this fortuitous circumstance. So I will ask him to promise not to serve against me again until his master can produce his British equivalent. If he makes this promise, he will of course keep it—he is an officer and a gentleman. Let him go, therefore, where he will and do what he likes. Let him live in London, the Bath or the Wells, for his pleasure or his health: or, even, let him return to France, where probably he'll be happiest of all.'

This is no pretty invention: no exaggeration—in the sunny heyday of exchange and parole so soon to cloud over. Let Vattel, the Swiss-German neutral, bear witness again:

> By a custom which reveals at once the honour and humanity of Europeans, an officer, when taken prisoner, is released on his parole, and enjoys the comfort of spending the time of his captivity in his own country, surrounded by his own family: and the side which has released him remains as perfectly sure of him as if it held him confined in chains.[1]

Such then was the *Parole d'Honneur* at its shining best; a surprisingly

[1] Vattel, op. cit., ib.

perfect flower to be blooming in the otherwise very imperfect meadow of eighteenth-century Western Europe. But, like so many fair flowers, it was delicate: all too easy a prey to foul winds or dirty weather; indeed, a certain victim to them. This, however, makes it the more pleasant to contemplate while it still bloomed unspoiled. It speaks so eloquently for those who cultivated it, the governments who had planted it, the gentry who tended it. These were not the people who compassed its destruction. The game, on both sides, was played in strict accordance with the rules, and with punctilious care. Cases of broken parole —before 1793 anyway—are extremely rare: and, when they do occur, the crowning proof of the average player's good faith is that the rule-breaker was almost universally condemned by public opinion, on both sides. Once convicted, he ran the grave risk of complete social ostracism. Here indeed is perhaps the secret of why there were so few parole-breakers. It would be a grave mistake to overrate the morality of *all* concerned. Many, no doubt, kept their word because of deep moral conviction or general moral rectitude: but it is not cynical to suppose that many more kept it because of the unpleasantness which would accrue—from their own people—if they broke it.

In France, the Revolution changed all this. Many of the revolutionary leaders, and perhaps even more of the new revolutionary officers, were avowedly not Gentlemen in a 'parole' sense: indeed, perhaps, not in any sense at all. Worse still, many of them were somewhat blatantly proud of the fact, deliberately trying to stamp out the whole breed of Gentry, and the whole concept of Gentility. Yet parole did not wholly perish, partly because in Britain its rules were still scrupulously respected, partly because there remained on the other side a number of individuals who, if not *ancien régime* themselves, were still capable of being shamed into preserving the old decencies: or—perhaps more likely—who realized their material value to themselves, seeing that they too might some day become captives. It was the survival of such people which, as late as 1801, enabled Lord Cochrane, whose rapid exchange we have already described, to secure complete freedom so soon. His case is an excellent example of how the systems of both exchange and parole worked when at their best. He was, we saw, a 'prisoner of war' for only eleven days. But he was in enemy hands for only four. Taken on July 3rd, he was back in Gibraltar on the 7th—on parole. Freedom to serve again was achieved a week later, when he was formally exchanged. But the end

45

was now near. Two years later this could not have happened: not, at least, if he had been captured—as he was—by the French.

At no stage was it the British leaders who spoilt things. With a persistence which does credit to their hearts, if not their heads, they continued playing the old game to the old rules right into the Napoleonic War, and would not give up even when it became obvious that they were being grossly imposed upon: when, almost openly, the First Consul was mocking them for being such simpletons, and even their own people—especially the sufferers—were crying for a change. Later on, we shall have to discuss the various moral problems which confronted would-be British escapers, handicapped on the one hand by the physical difficulties of evasion, but also by the knowledge of the frigid reception awaiting them at home if parole-breaking was suspected. This aspect of their story is only apposite here, as illustrating the determination of the British authorities to keep to rules growing ever more obsolete. Let us see what did happen to those exceptional officers—for exceptions there were—who were adjudged parole-breakers.

The constant, almost routine, working of a sort of court of honour is discernible throughout the war. It was held at the Board of Transport, the body charged with all p.o.w. affairs. On reaching England, all escaped prisoners had to report themselves there, to undergo a strict inquisition as to their status at the moment of escape. The key question always was, 'Were you or were you not "on parole" at that moment?' And, now and again, there are entries like 'Henry Conn, Lieutenant; decided a parole-breaker'. This was in 1812. What action was taken in this case is not known: but the inference is that the adverse report was a serious black mark against him. He was not dismissed the service, but was never employed again and never promoted, though he was living, still a lieutenant, nearly 40 years later. A commoner entry in the records is, 'Owen, Lieutenant RN; escaped from *la maison de force* [Paris], from a dungeon'. This passed muster: physical duress was, as we shall see, rightly held to cancel the obligation of parole.

There was a particularly bad case in 1806. A youth named Temple, wealthy and of good family but a specious young rogue—not, by the way, a commissioned officer but only the next best thing, a midshipman—got clear of Verdun without taking any steps to cancel his parole: and, worse if possible, leaving behind him debts amounting to some £4,000. He reached Russia, whence he obtained a passage home in H.M. brig *Childers*, in which ship his cheerfulness and exciting adventure-stories made him very popular. Meanwhile, however, a true account of his doings had reached home via the Senior Naval Officer at Verdun and the French Ministry of Marine, and a shock was in store for him. His friends cut him dead; he was evicted from his club; the Board did not pass him, and there was talk of sending him back to France. His family—he was, or so he said, a relative of Lord Palmerston—had just influence enough to prevent that; but he was expelled from the Navy with infamy and never allowed in again. Moreover, to the very end, the government itself held out, behaving with almost unbelievable punctiliousness. The climax came when, late in 1813, a certain Roger Sheehy, lieutenant in the 89th Foot, broke his parole at Verdun under circumstances nearly as bad as Temple's. After going through the usual mill, he was reported to the Commander-in-Chief, who sent him back to France under arrest. As it was now March 1814, he soon secured automatic release: but this did not help him much. He was never allowed to rejoin his regiment.

Another odd case is that of William Graham, an ensign of the 4th Foot. He receives two notices in the surviving records. The first, a Transport Board paper, shows that he reported at that office in September 1812, but 'was decided a Parole Breaker by the Admiralty'. The second is more mysterious. His name appears in a straight list (of French origin) of captured army officers, and against it is a note, in English, 'Returned from France 7 Oct. 1812, being arrested for debt'. The purport of this note is not very clear. It might mean that Graham had committed the offence of escaping with his bills unpaid, for which, when he arrived home, he was arrested and confined *in England*. In that case, however, it is not easy to see how his confinement would help his French creditors—unless, of course, we are to assume that, when or if he disgorged what he owed, the British Government transmitted the money to France: and, from all we know of the general British attitude to the subject, this must be regarded as a distinct possibility. More likely, however, the note means that he made his escape while locked up (for debt) in a French prison; but that, in the eyes of British authorities, was not excuse enough, because they condemned escapes *either* while parole was operative *or* while debts were unpaid. Yet there is evidence that, while both such courses were frowned upon, the first offence was regarded as the more serious of the two. Thus we know that Graham, like Conn, though

47

he failed to pass the court of honour, was not dismissed the service —he even received modest promotion, dying (7.4.1825) a captain. So it may well be that both of them broke only the debt convention, where Temple (certainly) and Sheehy (probably, for he was punished even more severely than Temple) broke both, for which they suffered the supreme ignominy of expulsion from their respective services. Whatever the truth may be, however, the treatment accorded to all four of them reveals clearly that the official British attitude towards all breaches of honour was a very real thing. If only the official French attitude had even approximated to it, all might have been well.

But it was not to be. We are to see parole whittled down to a mere shadow, and exchange itself virtually abandoned. But, first, certain conditions peculiar to the Napoleonic War must be examined: for it was these which induced a climate in which parole could not flourish and exchange could not survive.

C. SPECIAL CONDITIONS IN THE NAPOLEONIC WAR

The war had two unusual features which should be noted at once. Both concern relative numbers, the first of French prisoners in British hands compared with British prisoners in French hands; the second of British sailors compared with British soldiers caught by the French.

(1) At the start, naturally, neither side held prisoners at all. But, almost at once, the British began to take more than the French took, and throughout hostilities this trend continued; indeed grew more and more pronounced. By 1814, in round numbers, the British held —or, more accurately, had held—some 122,000 enemy officers and men. The number of Britons held by the French has never been exactly determined, and that vexed question must not detain us here. We will assume (as, after examination, we conclude on page 266) that there were 16,000 of them. Not all our 122,000 captives were Frenchmen, however: only about two-thirds of them. So there were, roughly, 80,000 French prisoners to set against 16,000 British ones: that is, about five British-held Frenchmen for every French-held Briton. This fact, we shall see, was to prove very important to both sides.

(2) Of the Frenchmen held in Britain an overwhelming majority consisted of soldiers. But of Britons held captive in France the reverse was the case. Something like three out of every four were sailors— about 75 per cent of them all—and this fact cannot fail to affect profoundly the proportions of this book, for it is unlikely that there will

48

be so much to record about 4,000 as there is about 12,000. Nor is this merely a matter of sheer numbers. It is partly due to what looks very like pure chance. The evidence of contemporary writers happens to be overwhelmingly naval:[1] and, as a result, this book concerns itself far more with the Navy than the Army.

To account for these unusual features, the excess both of French over British prisoners and of British seamen over British soldiers, the impact of war upon both sides and both services must be examined.

(a) Soldiers

The British Army was not seriously engaged upon the Continent until the war was more than half over: it could not, therefore, lose many prisoners. A list of officer-captives in the Public Record Office,[2] showing the numbers, names and places of capture, strikingly confirms this fact. Of the 128 in the list, only 29 were taken between 1803 and 1808 inclusive, and nearly half of these were wrecked in one transport off Gravelines in the winter of 1805. It is only after the start of the Peninsular War that prisoners begin to appear in appreciable numbers; and even then, compared with French officer-losses, they are inconsiderable. The list shows that Talavera, fought in 1809, was by far the most expensive action to us: no less than 52 have 'Talavera' against their names; and this leaves only 47 officers to be taken in all other actions up to July 1811. Such insignificant numbers were due, mainly, to the fact that we almost always remained masters of the many battlefields, and that we were fighting in a friendly countryside where our wounded and stragglers, when taken, were often retaken by the guerrillas and returned to us. The French position was, of course, worse in every way. In addition to what they lost in the battles themselves, or left wounded on the field, they scarcely ever retook a prisoner once captured. Another prolific, and one-sided, French loss in soldier-prisoners occurred at sea, either when we took their transports or, more often than is generally supposed, when they were taken, in quantity too, while serving in warships. The endemic shortage of French seamen was such that the authorities were often compelled to make it up with army drafts. At Trafalgar, for instance, there were at least 4,000 soldiers serving, well over half of them in ships which were captured.

[1] See Appendix I.
[2] Admiralty, 103. 468. 'Military Officers held prisoner of war in July, 1811.'

(b) Sailors

This brings us to the sea-war and captured British sailors. Here again the French lost more than we did, though not so many more. Our captives can be divided into two groups, 'Royal Navy' and 'Merchant Navy'. Where officers were concerned, the distinction was radical, as will soon be seen. With the men, however, it is barely worth making because, in this as in former wars, both 'ratings' and 'hands' were still drawn from one common reservoir, the one and only pool of British seamen—all British seamen, whether 'royal', 'merchant' or fishermen. Indeed, the category in which he happened to be at the moment of his capture depended upon what luck he had had with the press-gangs. In peacetime, normally, he would be 'merchant'; but in wartime, especially, in a long war, he would think himself very fortunate indeed if he was not 'royal' for at least part of the time. Were it possible, however, to discover how many were taken in merchantmen and how many in warships, we should probably find the numbers about equal.

Assuming he had to be taken, he was rather luckier if he could show himself to be a naval seaman. Then he received from his captors an allowance, minute though it was, as an acknowledged 'belligerent' p.o.w. If only a merchant seaman he did not receive it, though, later in the war, the British Government gave him one. It must not be supposed, however, that he was compensated for not being a belligerent by being allowed to go free. His status in international law was far from clear, but in practice that made very little difference because the invariable custom of both French and British was to hold him when they caught him. It is not surprising, or even blameworthy, seeing that 'men' were the people who manned ships, merchant and war indifferently. To detain merchant seamen, then, was not regarded, even by us, as a crime against society. It bore no relation to the holding of *détenus*. These last, in all probability, were never going to become belligerents: the seamen, sooner or later, almost inevitably were.

With the officers there is a very different story to tell. In Britain there was all the difference in the world between a naval captain or lieutenant and a merchant master or his mate. It was the old story. The one pair held the King's commission, the other did not. They were gentle, the others were not. Yet, in Britain, the merchant officer's status was much higher than the seaman's, even than the naval seaman's. In the crucial matter of 'pressing', for instance, he ranked with the naval officer in that he could not normally be taken, so long as he could prove that he was actually working in a merchant ship. Napoleon, too, quite ready to play the gentleman game when it suited him, made a marked distinction between 'naval' and 'merchant'. Whereas all naval officers were sent to, and allowed to remain at, Verdun, the depot reserved for the gentle, only a very few of the merchant officers were permitted to live there, and to enjoy officer conditions. The great majority went to detention depots established for the men. The French method of deciding which should stay and which should go is not always clear. There seems to have been a rule, on paper, that masters of large ships were allowed parole, and those from smaller were not. But there were so many exceptions that it is tempting to think that the real criterion was very different. The distinction was probably made, in fact, on individual social merits, or even social appearance. Given this basic principle of 'treatment according to class', there was much sense in this. There really was a considerable social gulf between, say, the officer of an East Indiaman and that of a small coaster. The one looked gentle, the other did not: the one commanded, probably, a certain amount of money, the other had little or none. It is entirely in keeping with the spirit of the age, as manifested on both sides, that such things should make all the difference.

Yet the 'privileged' merchant officers were not so well off as might appear. To live at Verdun without cash of one's own might mean near-starvation. As officers on parole, privileged to lodge out in the town, they had to pay all their board and lodging out of their prison allowance, which was—for those, mark, who enjoyed the highest allowance—the half-pay of a midshipman RN: about £1 5s od a month. As a result, they had to make both ends meet by hiring themselves out to their wealthier compatriots in the far from genteel callings of 'stable-keepers, coach-washers, shoeblacks, knife-cleaners, etc.'.[1] What happened to the really small-ship officers, both in treatment and allowances, will be told later. The point to be made here is that even these were not reduced to the level of the ordinary sailors, but classed with another category of officer whose status gave the French much trouble, because they did not really understand it—the midshipman of the Royal Navy.

This grade—one of the most important in our story—was something of an anomaly even in Britain. The Admiralty regarded him,

[1] James Choyce, *The Log of a Jack Tar*, London, 1905.

51

though he held no commission, as an 'officer', for two reasons: first, because he was on his way to becoming one, and, second, because he he was usually (socially speaking) a gentleman. Indeed, Young Gentleman was his official service name. But the French were not quite so certain of his 'gentle' status, treating him often as a sort of borderline case. Sometimes he received modified officer-status, though more closely watched than officers, and more likely to forfeit the privileges. More often, however, their solution was to bracket him with the humbler merchant officers. Both groups will receive much more attention later—especially the midshipmen. We leave them for the time being, a good deal less comfortable than commissioned officers, yet a good deal more so than ordinary men.

12,000 seamen is not, perhaps, a great number to be taken by the French in eleven years. Yet, given our great sea predominance over them, how, it may be asked, did we come to lose even 12,000? The first thing to notice is that singularly few fell to the enemy in stand-up fights. A few (but very few) of our ships of frigate size and under had to surrender in single-ship actions: but throughout the war we lost no ship of the line in action. Our main losses stemmed, not from battle, but, oddly enough, from the French refusal to meet us in battle. Their substitute for inter-fleet fighting was a continuous and intensive *guerre de course*—attack upon our sea-borne trade. Nor was it possible, for all our very real control of the seas, to protect, all the time and everywhere, our far-flung trade and fisheries, conducted by thousands of ships of all sizes, but mostly very small and sparsely armed. Thus, inevitably, considerable numbers of our merchant seamen fell to French raiders and privateers. Such captures took place all over the world, from eastern waters where the occasional East Indiaman was unlucky enough to bump into a French raiding squadron, right into the heart of home waters. Indeed, with Britannia ruling the waves as effectively as she did, it comes as something of a shock to read how easily fickle fate might sometimes turn against the poor mariner. One illustration, out of many hundreds, must suffice. In January 1805 a small Sunderland coaster rounded Beachy Head, and was running quite close in with the Sussex shore when, as she was opposite Brighton, a swift lugger came up, apparently from nowhere. The north-country master took alarm, and scurried inshore: but he had not quite reached the cover of Brighton Battery when he was boarded, taken, and carried to France and captivity with all his crew. Among the number was little Alexander Stewart, cabin-boy, who remained a prisoner for nine years; and all because the guns of Brighton Battery would not carry a few more yards.[1]

This same overall British supremacy was indirectly responsible, too, for nearly all our naval prisoners, both officers and men. Our blockade of the European coast was continuous from start to finish. Hosts of our frigates, sloops, brigs and corvettes were constantly cruising off enemy shores, even entering their bays and estuaries: in all weathers, in all seasons and (where France was concerned) almost always on a lee shore, with Atlantic winds and waves driving them in. No wonder that, for all the practised seamanship of officers and men, there was a steady toll of shipwreck. Then, of course, some of the crew would drown, but a majority could usually scramble ashore, to find themselves prisoners of war. Such people formed, by a little, the largest category of British prisoners.

D. 'FIRST-CLASS' PRISONERS

If now we widen our view to include French prisoner policy, not only as it touched British captives but also as it concerned all their opponents, we shall find ourselves looking at a very different scene. If, from first to last, we brought some 80,000 Frenchmen into Britain, Napoleon brought into France, at the very least, half a million prisoners: of whom, let us recall, only some 16,000 were British. The number of Frenchmen whom Napoleon left as captives in other lands is not known: but it was not, probably, very great—not indeed nearly so great as it should have been had some states of Europe been more civilized then they were. For there can be little doubt that an appalling number of those left behind as prisoners very soon became corpses, ceasing thereby to be part of this story. This is particularly true in Spain, where the Spanish irregulars seldom took prisoners: they shot them, not altogether surprisingly, seeing that the French often treated the guerrillas in the same way. It was true too in Russia in 1812 where the French stragglers died in their thousands from cold and exposure, or, if they survived these, from hunger: again not very surprisingly because, where food is desperately short, no prisoner is likely to receive his fair share. The final tally of French prisoners surviving in Russian hands was minute.

Thus it fell out that, in sharp contrast to the Anglo-French position, Napoleon had a very long numerical lead in 'continental' captives held. In fact, we may safely reverse our former ratio, and more. If

[1] Alexander Stewart, *Life of*, O.U.P., 1947.

there were five Frenchmen in Britain to every Briton in France, there were probably at least ten 'continental' captives in France— Austrian, Prussian, Russian, Spanish, etc.—for every one Frenchman in continental hands. Moreover, these numbers are very large: so large that, long before the end, Napoleon found himself faced with a major prisoner problem. We, with our smaller, though by no means negligible, numbers, had this kind of problem too, and solved it, as will be shown later, by no means creditably to ourselves. But Napoleon's problem was quite four times as big—half a million against 122,000. He was not the man to let humanity override material advantage, however, and, beyond all doubt, he treated his continental prisoners with extraordinary ruthlessness. For this he has been condemned, and rightly. Yet it is only fair to record that he had a problem. Nor, in the light of subsequent and similar problems, is it surprising that he failed to find an equitable answer. Here again we are in the face of a new phenomenon; one of the many which stem directly from total war, with its massed, conscripted 'total' armies. Since his day international lawyers have tried hard to bring humanity into what must be at best an inhuman business. They have succeeded in part, but how imperfectly!

Napoleon's problems and policy, however, are mentioned here merely to show why he did not treat his British prisoners as he treated his continental ones. The reason is plain. He could—or thought he could—afford to maltreat the latter because of his ten-to-one advantage. But, in face of our five-to-one advantage, he could not run the risk of goading our government into wholesale reprisals. Therefore, realist and cold calculator that he was, he formulated a policy, quite openly. There would be two classes of p.o.w., first-class, and the rest. The British prisoner, and he alone, was first class for only Britain held the whiphand of him in this matter:

> The English prisoners of war belong, without exception, to the first class category, and are to be allowed, daily, 1 lb. bread, one ration vegetables and salt, $7\frac{1}{2}$ centimes in cash. . . . The prisoners of all other nations belong to the second class category, and are to receive only one half of the pay of the privates of the French Army, and one ration of bread each. . . .

He meant it to appear that he was being particularly generous to his first-class prisoners. He was giving them, in food and pay, exactly what he gave to his own *poilus*. He was careful, too, to have down in black and white how he was clothing them and ministering to their other bare necessities. There were to be provided, per man,

> One knitted waistcoat and pantaloons, one waggoner's frock, one hat . . . one blanket and one palliasse for every two men, if they can be provided from the public stores: if not, straw, 5 kilograms per man, to be renewed every 15 days.

All this was fair enough—on paper. It put the p.o.w. on a level with the *poilu* in all but clothes, or nearly. It was enough to keep him alive if not really enough to keep him in health. But two facts, not on paper, instantly falsify any worthwhile prisoner-*poilu* comparison. First, the French private, as is well known, had seldom actually to live on his basic ration. On active service anyway he was always allowed, indeed expected, to augment it from what he could find in the country around him—a privilege or right which obviously could not be conceded to a prisoner. Second, these orders which look so well in print seldom if ever materialized in practice. It is notorious that legislation is by no means the same thing as administration. Legislation does not as a rule lend itself to petty malpractices; administration, unfortunately, often does. Moreover, the lower one descends the administrative scale, though the little cheats and subterfuges become the pettier, still they become the more common, until they sometimes become the norm. There is ample evidence from the surviving accounts of various prisoners that their gaolers, from the lowest grades up to depot commandants, often made fortunes of various sizes by such elementary wickednesses as intercepting prisoners' pay or deliberately giving them short measure in rations. It is true that, theoretically to balance the *poilu's* ability to live off the country, Napoleon's 'generous' law ordained that, in suitable cases, the British captive might supplement his allowance by following his trade in the neighbourhood in which he was incarcerated: but in fact he was usually imprisoned in areas where the local people were too poor to buy the prisoners' products. Often, too, where he was cheated of his pittance of pay, he had not the wherewithal to buy the materials for his pitiful little products: while, so far as one can see, quite as often as not the order was ignored altogether, and he was allowed neither to make anything in the depot nor to go out of it to work.

Certainly the average p.o.w. was in practice badly treated, though not necessarily by the French Government; and, though he seldom starved, he lived as a rule at bare subsistence level. What, then, of the unhappy second-class prisoners, doomed—even officially—to try to survive on approximately half the Britons' fare? The answer unquestionably is that some of them managed it—the experience of modern prison-camps is that some do manage to live on their own will to survive and little else. Moreover the continental captive often had another way out. He could buy better terms for himself by enlisting in the various corps and regiments established for the purpose. He could fight for the enemy: and some of them did, though thereby losing their present self-respect and their future chance of rehabilitation. Others were put to work on public projects like building canals, draining swamps, repairing roads, or in the fields to help on the land. Napoleon maintained, more than once, that all these were only voluntary labours; that no one was ever forced to do them. With first-class prisoners there was a certain amount of truth in this claim: but with the second-class, there was really none because, if a choice were ever given, it was between the offered work and the withholding of rations, or even, in several known cases, service as *forçats*—galley-slaves, recruited otherwise entirely from the convict-prisons of France.

It is to be feared, however, that the majority of all continental prisoners survived neither by will-power nor by working for the enemy. They did not survive at all.

E. COMPARISONS

Did the British do better than that with their prisoners?

So long as *all* prisoners are under review the answer must be an emphatic 'Yes'. Indeed, it has probably never been disputed that Frenchmen in Britain suffered less than continental prisoners in France—i.e. an overwhelming majority of all French-held captives. On the narrower comparison, however, between French in Britain and Britons in France, there has been no little debate, sometimes acrimonious.

(1) *The Men*

In such a question sheer numbers must once more loom large, because all prisoners must be accommodated. At first sight it might seem that, since we had five Frenchmen to house for every one Briton in France, our accommodation problem should have been five times as hard. This, however, was not so. It was much harder than that—perhaps (though here of course figures can only be exceedingly 'round') ten times as hard—and this for what might be called a 'local' reason. It chanced that, just then, France had available for the housing of prisoners a large number of suitable buildings nearly ready for use, and not wanted just then for other purposes. These were the strong places, both fortresses and walled towns, strung all along the east and north-east borders of France, and used for centuries to guard her vulnerable land-frontiers. Now, thanks to the outward thrust of the revolutionary and Napoleonic armies, they were no longer needed for their original purposes. The frontiers were far beyond them, defended in depth. They had been designed, it is true, to keep people out: but walls are walls, and can be readily adapted for keeping people in. They were therefore obvious receptacles for prisoners in the bulk, being now, as it were, 'to let'; and even 'with vacant possession', because the living and sleeping quarters of the former garrisons were almost unoccupied. All the principal depots for British prisoners of war were of this sort.[1]

Of such ready-made prisons Britain had hardly any. Everywhere our frontier was the sea, and, though we still had a few coast-defences guarding our main ports, these were still required for defence, and so not available for prisoners, even if they had been large enough. Elsewhere, a fortress was a curiosity, if not a picturesque ruin, while a long tradition of orderly government had allowed such town-walls as once existed to crumble away. There were, it is true, one or two exceptions, of which much the best known was Portchester Castle. No longer a necessity to the defence of Portsmouth, it had actually been used in several past wars as a prison-depot. Such exceptions, however, did not begin to solve our problem of housing prisoners.

From the start that problem grew with alarming rapidity. The government was slow to face up to it, hoping for a while—against hope, as we now know—that the old 'exchange' formula which turned 'X + Y' into 'X − Y' would become operative again. When it failed to operate, however, there was really only one answer. If there were no suitable buildings in existence, special ones must be erected. But this, in those days, was no light task; much harder and more expensive than it would be now. Ask any modern p.o.w. what is his most abiding physical impression of captivity His instinctive answer, most likely, will be 'barbed wire'. But this useful commodity—together with all its sinister wartime implications—was not yet invented, so that the captives' detention-places had to be much more

[1] See map, p. 84.

57

permanent and expensive buildings than is now necessary. Solid stone masonry, or, at cheapest, brick-and-mortar, was deemed essential.

It is no part of this story to describe in detail the great establishments which arose on Dartmoor, at Perth, or, on a smaller scale, at Stapleton and Valleyfield. The first-named, built of local granite, was of such a permanence as still to be with us: but, started only in 1805, it was not ready for occupation until May 1809. Perth began to function even later, in August 1812. One big one, however, was an exception, in two respects. The establishment at Norman Cross in Huntingdonshire had been built in 1797, the product of a similar, though smaller, problem in the Revolutionary War: and the living quarters were constructed mainly of wood, though it had surrounding walls of masonry and brick. Being available, then, in 1803, it bore the first brunt of the prisoner torrent, along with castles like Portchester, and Stapleton near Bristol,[1] which existed already as an ordinary prison, having been built originally for captives in the American War. But Norman Cross and Stapleton together housed only some 10,000 souls, and were soon filled to overflowing. Indeed, from 1805 up to the very end, demand invariably exceeded supply. Even at Dartmoor and Perth, all accommodation was earmarked before they were opened. And still the flood rolled in, until the grotesque point was reached at which the government had to order its generals to send no more prisoners home—an order so odd as not always to be obeyed. In 1811–12, for instance, an incredulous Duke of Wellington sent over 20,000 more when expressly told not to do so.

In the end, it was near-desperation which impelled us to fall back upon the expedient which, above all others, has earned the condemnation of posterity, and especially of the French people. It was certainly dire necessity, though partly engendered by lack of forethought, which drove us to it: and we could—and did—argue truthfully that we were only treating our French prisoners of war as we were treating our own prisoner population. That, however, is but a poor excuse because, after all, prisoners were not convicts, and both sides, in theory, always acknowledged it. But there it was. Ever since 1776 we had been sending the overspill of our own gaols, filled to bursting by a ferocious penal code, into the 'hulks'; old warships moored in creeks and out-of-the-way corners of harbours: and we always, hopefully, referred to them as 'temporary measures'.[2] We were still doing so some thirty

[1] See *Bristol and Gloucester Arch. Soc. Trans.*, 1956, LXXV, p. 134.
[2] W. Branch-Johnson, *The English Prison Hulks*, London, 1957, p. 3 et seq.

years later when—as a temporary measure only, of course—we decided
to use them for prisoners of war. It was the easy way out: it solved the
problem, though discreditably. The backwaters in British harbours
were inexhaustible, and so was the supply of worn-out warships.

Apart from the one great inhumanity implicit in the use for human
habitation of ships always intolerably damp and sometimes positively
rotting, many if not most of the cruelties inflicted in these sorry places
stemmed from two causes, the general one of overcrowding, and the
more particular one of the kind of gaoler provided. Overcrowded the
ships certainly were, even though, before the end, the Admiralty had
provided more than sixty of them. Yet it is not necessary to believe
that they were quite so packed, pestiferous or death-dealing as certain
Frenchmen (mostly the sufferers in them) have made out. This is
only to be expected; and the same doubtless applies to a good deal
that we hear—and shall hear in this book—from the lips of unwilling
British residents in French fortresses. It is perhaps too much to
expect any sufferer to be strictly fair to the authors of his suffering.
But another thing, too often forgotten in the heat of angry polemics,
is the fact that, for a great deal of the hulks' career as prison-ships,
the inhabitants were what the French called, on their side, *mauvais
sujets*: men who had actually committed crimes, or—and this too was
regarded as a crime in wartime—men who had tried to escape and
failed; or men who had broken parole. It was only at the crests of the
prisoner wave (mainly before Dartmoor and Perth were ready and
during the last year or two) that the prisoner who had committed no
crime found himself in a hulk. A list exists[1] which gives the whereabouts of enemy prisoners in Britain in 1810 and 1811. The second
of these years was a very crucial moment, marking one of the crises,
when the flow was rising fast and when Perth was not quite ready.
The numbers in the principal land prisons were:

Norman Cross	5,951
Dartmoor	6,329
Portchester	5,850
Stapleton	4,546
Valleyfield	2,425
Three small ones	295
Total	25,396

[1] In T. J. Walker's invaluable book *The Depot for Prisoners of War at
Norman Cross*, London, 1913, Appendix E.

The prisoners at Chatham numbered 3,863; at Plymouth, 6,918; at Portsmouth, 9,760. Total, 20,541. But not all the prisoners at the three ports were hulk-borne, especially at Portsmouth, where Forton[1] took a considerable number. So, of a total of 45,937, even in this bad year, much more than half were imprisoned on land; while if we add the 3,193 people on parole, none of whom were in the hulks, we reach a grand total of 49,130, of whom, roughly, two-thirds were in land prisons. Moreover, of the one-third in the hulks, perhaps one-third was earmarked for Perth, and another third was 'under punishment'. In fact, for the purpose of a study in relative misery, it would be fairer to set the hulk prisoners against, not the British in ordinary French prison depots, but those in the penal depots of Sarrelibre, Sedan and the abhorred Bitche.

The second—the particular—cause of the many cruelties, real and alleged, was not confined to one side only. Many of the gaolers employed in the hulks were undoubtedly bad. But so were the French gaolers similarly employed. It is not altogether surprising. No state is likely to detail its best officers or men to act as prison-camp warders. Rather, it will tend to appoint for the job its passed-over officers and elderly third-grade men. Evidently both sides did this, and thereby show much the same degree of blameworthiness. The British gaolers we are not called upon to study—fortunately, because that story is far from appetizing. We shall have plenty of chances, however, of seeing that the French gaolers were clearly not the pick of the *Grande Armée*. It is indeed in anticipation of this part of our study that some account of prisoner conditions in Britain has been given here. They will not be discussed again: but now, as we read what happened across the Channel, we shall at least know that there is something to be said on both sides.

Yet the wider comparison cannot fairly be left just there. The prime cause which made the prisoner problem of our war differ so radically from that of preceding wars was a matter of sheer numbers. It was because prisoners no longer numbered $X - Y$ but, once more, $X + Y$. And this, for certain, was the fault, not of Great Britain but of the Great Corsican. It was one of the first fruits of his fatal transition from private to total war. We are soon to see how this came about: how the principles of Exchange and Parole, the two great safeguards against an overwhelming wave of captives, crumbled before its pressure.

[1] In Gosport: established 1777, originally as a prison for captives accused of high treason.

(2) The Officers

In previous wars parole, swiftly followed by exchange and freedom, had been at once the officer's right and his fate. We must now see how, in this war, the rival camps chose to interpret parole.

On our side the principle was accepted throughout, in (with minor exceptions) much the same spirit as before. The French, too, paid lip-service to it, but with new limiting provisos, all of them unpleasant to the officers concerned. In both countries, of course, it was still only the gentleman whose parole was accepted. In France this meant parole for the gentleman-*détenu* also; but, rather more unexpectedly, for the other members of that novel class, though for gentlemen's servants their masters themselves had to answer, and were made responsible for their defection. There was, however, no *détenu* problem in Britain, because there were no *détenus* in the least corresponding to Napoleon's original ones. It is true that, after a time and as a reprisal, the British sometimes detained civilians taken at sea. This was a different matter, and infinitely less treacherous. At least we had captured them in the ordinary course of war, and not by simply ignoring the validity of peacetime passports underwritten by ourselves.

In Britain, then, the parole convention was honoured in essentials. Once admitted to it, the French officer was able to enjoy three of its four basic freedoms. First, freedom of domicile: he was not herded in with other prisoners, but could make his own living arrangements; could even have his own house if he could afford it. Second, freedom of choice of location: within very wide limits he could choose the place in which he would reside. Third—a more cherished privilege still—freedom from physical restraint: he was not locked up, either by day or by night. Even the fourth and most enlightened freedom of all—to go back to France with nothing but his honour to bind him —was never expressly ruled out; and it was certainly allowed to a few lucky ones, principally to those who could show special cause why it was important for them to be at home. It must be admitted, however, that this supreme concession was not so freely given as formerly; and, for reasons which will soon become all too clear, it grew ever rarer as the war went on.

Indeed, the regulations governing all these freedoms were gradually growing stricter. Freedom of domicile suffered least. Unless he forfeited it by violation of regulations the French officer always retained it. His right to live in the place of his choice was limited a little, but not much. He had always been obliged to keep the British authorities informed as to where he was, and to notify them of any change. But the very magnitude of numbers now made a little more administrative interference inevitable. He had now, for instance, to obtain leave before he went to a new locality, and he had, at fixed intervals, to report to an accredited government agent. This was, partly at least, in his own interest. His reporting himself was the occasion for the payment, by the agent, of the allowances due to him from his own and the British Governments. Undoubtedly this hampered his freedom of movement because the number of agents was necessarily limited. Obviously we could not undertake to have one in or near every town, village or hamlet in the country. He must, therefore, arrange to live somewhere near an agent, if he would avoid incessant travelling. For all that, however, his scope remained very wide. Walker[1] gives a list of no less than ninety-two 'places where French prisoners were allowed on parole at different periods of the war'. It embraces all sorts of localities, from London and Edinburgh down to little-known villages. But it is not comprehensive, omitting certain well-known towns, like Bath and Tunbridge Wells, where prisoners are known to have lived. There must have been at least 100 places favoured by them: and it is fair to believe that the factor which prevented an even longer list was the limited number of agents rather than the intention of the government to interfere with the officers' freedom of choice.

The third great privilege, the cardinal one of freedom from duress under lock and key, was not touched, save when a prisoner himself forfeited it by breach of rules. Yet clearly some of the old absolute trust in a gentleman's word was beginning to wear thin. This is exemplified by two new regulations which former British Governments would have thought shame to impose. First, the parole-officer was no longer allowed to go, without leave, outside a fixed radius from his domicile. The length of that radius varied. Sometimes is was disagreeably short; even (as, for instance, with officers residing near the Norman Cross depot) only one mile: sometimes it was as much as six. Yet it was always there, and it constitutes a sad sign that all was not well with the essence of the parole contract, mutual trust. The second regulation points just the same way. The intervals between the statutory visits to the agent were reduced, sometimes drastically: and there could be but the one reason for this. The principal responsibility

[1] Op. cit., pp. 192–3.

for this deterioration cannot be foisted on the British Government. The regrettable fact, of course, was that the parole syllogism, under the new social conditions of France, was becoming false. 'Gentlemen keep their promises'—yes. But 'all officers are gentlemen'—alas, no: not after the Revolution, not in Napoleonic France. No one denies that the number of French officers—on parole, too—who escaped or attempted to do so was very large. Napoleon himself did not deny it. But the difference was this: where by implication and example he condoned breach of parole—there was nothing in France which even remotely resembled the Transport Board's scrutiny—our government systematically condemned it to the last.

In France the story starts in much the same way as in Britain. Our officer-prisoners, for a very brief period, enjoyed the same three basic freedoms that the French enjoyed in Britain—though, in France, there was never any talk at all about being allowed to return home. But, very soon, there came a drastic whittling-down of nearly all the privileges. It makes sad reading. Freedom of domicile, modified extensively by the docking of the other freedoms, remained otherwise intact. Any officer who could pay for it could 'live out' at Verdun. It was freedom of choice of locality which was the first to suffer gravely; indeed virtually to fade out. Yet at the beginning all seemed well. The captives—all of them *détenus* at first—were allowed to live where they liked, which was usually at the places where they had been caught. The same applied, too, to the earliest service-officer prisoners. One of the very first of them—if we may call him by the name which he himself so strenuously rejected—was Lieutenant Dillon, taken at Helvoetsluys. Thereafter, for some six months he visited many towns, at first almost at will but gradually more and more at the whim of his captors—Rotterdam, Breda, Antwerp, Brussels, Valenciennes, Lunéville, Verdun, Metz, Thionville, Metz again, and Nancy. Then, however, the blow fell which sent the British and French parole stories off along entirely different paths. In November 1803, came the peremptory order that 'all the English under the denomination of gentlemen be concentrated at Verdun'. The only reason ever given was probably the true one, though exaggerated. Too many of the prisoners, still almost all *détenus*, were on the run; and to appoint adequate guardians to watch over them in all the towns and villages of France was an economic impossibility. Napoleon—and the *Moniteur*—shed pathetic tears of grief at the thought of so many 'gentlemen' so far prostituting their honour as to break parole: and it is true enough that some of them had given it, out-and-out imprisonment being the alternative—though some (like Jodrell and Smyth) had withdrawn theirs before bolting. Yet Napoleon was hardly the proper person to criticize broken pledges, seeing that the whole body of *détenus* were only in his hands because he had broken his.

If we would understand the collapse of the parole convention in France we must begin by admitting that a good many *détenus*—some of them 'gentle', too—broke their paroles. From that fact the rest of the story springs. But, though it did not suit Napoleon's convenience to admit it, a *détenu's* parole was not, in fact, at all the same thing as a serving officer's. There was one deep-seated difference. The commissioned officer, a professional, accepted capture and captivity as all in the day's work: and he regarded the parole system, not only as a thoroughly beneficial thing to himself personally, but also as an integral part of service discipline. It was his military duty, if captured, to give his parole, because that was the quickest and surest way of getting back to work, and starting to earn his pay again. By the same token, he must keep his parole once given because, if he failed to do so, these desired results would not eventuate. Breach of parole was, therefore, a breach of discipline; and punishable as such. That Transport Board court was in fact quite as much a court martial as a court of honour: and like any other court martial it had its ascending scale of sentences—acquittal, reprimand, loss of promotion, dismissal from the service, even return to prison.

The *détenu*, on the other hand, if a gentleman, recognized the value, and the moral obligation, of keeping his word: but in his case, nothing like service discipline came into it. His conscience might prevent him from breaking it, but not his oath of allegiance, his service pride or his inbred habit of obeying orders. Add to this two undoubted facts: first, that, while no possible material benefit could accrue to him from the strict keeping of his promise, no material or widespread harm could arise from his breaking it. Second, *his* parole, in sharp contrast to the serving officer's, was a completely one-sided bargain: one, even, which had been wrongfully extorted from him, seeing that his very arrest constituted the breach of a promise quite as fundamental as any which he could give. At that moment, too, he was consumed with natural and pardonable wrath against the perpetrator of what he regarded as a gross breach of faith, and therefore, being human, all the more prone to repay his oppressor in his own

2. VERDUN
*From a
relief-map*

1. Citadel
2. Place de
   la Roche
3. Porte
   Chaussée

3. PORTE NOTRE-DAME, CAMBRAI

coin. The greater wonder is, not that most service officers kept their paroles, but that more *détenus* did not break theirs.

It is not surprising that both governments took a very serious view of an enemy officer who broke parole. If they retook him, both deprived him ruthlessly of all officer privileges and packed him off to a penal depot: and, though the sufferers themselves, on either side, often complained, there is nothing to choose here between the two governments. Of the two, in fact, the British were perhaps the sterner because they had stricter views about the general sacrosanctity of paroles, and were prepared to punish all offenders, whether French or British.

The service officers, of course, knew this, and what galled them perhaps more than anything else was the knowledge that the French were equating their paroles with *détenu*-paroles, punishing the officers who seldom if ever broke them because the *détenus* sometimes did. That punishment, cumulative but inevitable, amounted to loss of those basic freedoms which parole had always implied—freedom of choice of residence—it was to be Verdun for all now—and personal exemption from confinement behind locked doors. We shall see later how these losses confronted all officers with a new, and very difficult, problem in ethics—at what point was liberty so curtailed as to cancel the contract of parole? For only when they had decided that that point had been reached, did the majority of them feel justified in departing from their side of the contract: that is, in trying to escape. We shall see, also, how this point was more easily reached by junior than by senior officers, because the juniors suffered so many more curtailments of liberty. For example: frequency of attendance at roll-call was geared solely to seniority. Hence the laconic summary of an aggrieved midshipman:—

> Captains of the Navy and Field Officers once a month: lieutenants every five days: midshipmen twice a day (thus calculating the word of a midshipman as equal only to one-sixtieth part of that of a field officer).[1]

[1] Edward Boys, *Narrative of a Captivity, Escape and Adventures in France*, London, 1827.

CHAPTER III

THE BREAKDOWN OF EXCHANGE

So much for parole, reduced to a mockery. What was in store for exchange?

British prisoners of war from wrecked ships began to arrive in France almost at once. It is instructive, if pathetic, to note their first reactions to captivity. All our witnesses, thinking naturally in terms of previous wars, say in effect: 'Well, it's bad luck, and it may retard my promotion. But, thank goodness, it won't last long. Any day a cartel will be arranged, either a local one like that which, only a year or two ago, came Cochrane's way, or, failing that, a governmental agreement and a general exchange.' This hope, amounting to a near-certainty, so buoyed them up that they scarcely even considered the only alternative open to high-spirited men—escape. Here speaks Midshipman Edward Boys, escape-minded if anyone ever was.[1] He had been taken off Toulon on August 4, 1803, when prize-master of a captured settee, and marched, with indignity amounting to sheer cruelty, to Nîmes. There he found some English *détenus* who befriended his little party, and these well-meaning people

> considerably allayed the ennui and mortification of captivity by confidently assuring us that an exchange of prisoners had been arranged between the two governments, and that in six weeks we might rest satisfied of a happy return to the service of our country.

Two days later, finding themselves lodged for the night in the ruined citadel of Montpellier,

> we might have decamped with little difficulty: the subject was mentioned to me, but my hope of an early exchange, in which the right of being included was then understood to be forfeited by an attempt to escape . . . induced me to think it undesirable. Could I have foreseen what followed, I should have decided differently.[1]

No doubt he would, poor lad! He was not six weeks from liberty, but

[1] Boys, op. cit., p. 19.

six years: years of indignity, discomfort and danger, but of superb perseverance and pluck.

Meanwhile his late captain (of the *Phoenix*) was also playing to pre-1803 rules. In a sporting effort to secure the release of his young officers, he stood right in with Toulon and

> made repeated proposals for an exchange of prisoners. But unfortunately the enemy were too well satisfied with having in their prisoners such a living proof of their naval prowess to accede to them.[1]

This may have been part of the reason—the lads were ostentatiously marched around several times—but, much more likely, Gantheaume, the Toulon C.-in-C., had already received from Paris a copy of Napoleon's amended rules. Anyway, he refused point blank.

Dillon (whose very special case will shortly be considered) also subordinated all thoughts of escape to his desire to get among his fellow-officers who were captives, being quite sure that, once there, he would be in the first normal cartel. He, too, could almost certainly have escaped, because no less a person than the military governor of Valenciennes virtually invited him to try. The incident illustrates again, very clearly, how Napoleon's new policy took even Frenchmen by surprise, especially if the Frenchman concerned happened to be 'a fine old gentleman of the Ancien Régime'—General de Boubers, that same simple old man who let Jodrell and Smyth escape. Dillon was to be sent to Lunéville, and asked to be allowed to travel unescorted, not because he wanted to run, but because he resented the presence of an armed gendarme whose expenses he had to pay and who expected to share his table, if not his bedroom.

> The Governor agreed to allow me to travel alone, but he insisted upon my signing a document which he drew out with his own hand, specifying that whilst on my road to Lunéville, if I made off for England, that agreement was to be transmitted to the British Government, to claim the release of a French officer of equal rank. In fact, this document was the equivalent of an exchange, and could I have foreseen that I should have to remain so many years a captive in France, I should have acted upon it at all risks.[2]

The old governor's action, of course, was pure eighteenth century: so was Dillon's, and so would have been the British Government's, had Dillon turned up in London and presented that document to the

[1] Boys, Op. cit., p. 11.
[2] Dillon, op. cit. III., p. 167.

Admiralty. A French lieutenant would have been returned without quibble or delay.

Already, however, the damage was done: not by the de Boubers or even the Gantheaumes, but by the man who had the *détenus* arrested—Napoleon. That step he could not—or thought he could not—retract without loss of face, the one thing which no dictator can afford. This instantly poisoned the whole exchange problem. To justify the unjustifiable, he found himself committed to acts and claims even less justified. The detention of the civilians instantly led to a wrangle at government level: and, in that quarrel—however objective we may try to be, remembering that, in wartime, the enemy often has more to say for himself than we may care to admit—we can only conclude that our government was completely in the right. Let us see why. Twice in 1803 and three times in 1804 it suggested a transparently fair system based upon pre-1803 conventions. All came to nothing, and the reason is clear. The First Consul's interpretation of the very term prisoner of war was obviously quite different from ours: quite new, not only to us but to all western Europeans and, naturally therefore, quite unacceptable. For Napoleon, having seized people who were admittedly non-combatant, must either acknowledge that he was wrong in doing so, or put forward the view that every non-combatant was imprisonable and, therefore, logically exchangeable. Moreover, to an unscrupulous opportunist like Napoleon, bent on squeezing every conceivable advantage from every conceivable situation, it was an almost imperceptible step towards saying, not only 'exchangeable' but also 'exchangeable on equal terms'.

Whole classes of people were affected immediately. Almost as the war opened, for instance, French troops had occupied Hanover, whole and without difficulty. The Hanoverian troops were disarmed and sent to their homes. The chance to use this circumstance in the exchange argument was too good for Napoleon to miss. All these men, he asserted, being subjects of the Elector of Hanover (*alias* the King of England), are prisoners of war; and not only that, they are, for purposes of exchange, *English* prisoners of war, exchangeable each according to his rank against French prisoners. This was preposterous; a mere quibble which he must have known the British would not accept. The primary object of exchange was to get back men so that they could fight again; and had we agreed, France would have got them. But we should have got none at all, because the Hanoverians, now demobilized and back on the land, would never have left home and country to fight for us, even if we had wanted them. Besides, *de facto*, they were no longer the subjects of the Elector of Hanover, still less of the King of England.

This claim was cool enough. A second was even cooler: at any rate it riled us even more. Napoleon applied exactly the same argument to the *détenus*. They were potential officers and therefore prisoners of war—we need not repeat the argument—and they were to be exchanged, again rank for rank, with captured French officers: and that though, in fact, scarcely any of them had any rank, even in the Militia. To every Briton this was merely adding insult to injury. The injury lay in arresting in the first place persons whom, by all known standards, it was illegal to arrest at all. The insult lay in the inference, unwarrantable in fact, that these untrained and essentially unmilitary people were the natural military equals, not only of the French service officers but also of ours. We indignantly refused and, in our turn, insisted upon the repatriation of the *détenus* as a preliminary to any exchange. We can hardly wonder at that condition when we recall the ordinary eighteenth-century theory of war—that only crowns were at war, and that only the crowns' armed and paid forces were fighting. A modern analogy may serve to show how monstrously the suggestion struck men of the Old School. To them the 'armed forces' were 'the teams' (of professionals too), and all the rest, including the *détenus*, were 'the spectators'. It was as though the French were coolly demanding back their star centre-forward in exchange for any old British spectator from the half-crown stands.

The First Consul refused to release a single *détenu*, and negotiations ceased. The British Government, however, would not take that 'no' as final, and returned to the attack. In their first 1804 attempt they appealed (how forlornly they did not yet realize) to Napoleon's sporting instincts, 'Look,' they said in effect, 'ever since you detained our civilians we have been releasing yours, whether they were guests in Britain or since taken in merchantmen at sea. So far we have released 526 of them unconditionally, and doubtless we shall catch —and release—many more. What about a reciprocal gesture?'

There was no gesture whatever.

The second attempt in 1804 came, more privately, from Nelson, watching off Toulon. He sent in a flag of truce to his opposite number, now Latouche Tréville, suggesting a local exchange. Whether the French admiral, left to himself, would have responded favourably it is impossible to say. But, as he felt bound to forward the message to

Paris, the answer which he received from the great man himself will cause no surprise:

> Inform him [Nelson] that all exchange is impossible. The King of England has shown that he wants none, by persisting in making conditions which are arbitrary and quite contrary to established custom.

Since Napoleon's day the world has grown all too familiar with this 'dictator' technique—to describe with some accuracy one's own discreditable action, but to impute it to the enemy.

In the third attempt of that year, in August, the British, though insisting upon the return of the *détenus* as the basis of any general exchange, took up individual cases. There were three in particular which seemed to them too flagrant to be passed over in silence. They all concerned naval officers, Captain Jahleel Brenton, Lieutenant William Dillon and Commander Wesley Wright. The first two involved illegal detention, the third—they suspected—murder.

Brenton was in several ways a key figure in the story of British prisoners of war, and we shall return to him again. Here only the story of his exchange will be told. Soon after his capture in July 1803, negotiations covering only himself and a French officer of equivalent rank had been—or so we thought—successful. So our authorities, still innocent as babes, selected, and dispatched to France, a captain of equal seniority named Jurien. And, for one whole year, that was all they heard of it. No Brenton turned up in Britain: indeed, we now know that the first he heard of the whole transaction was in January 1805, when, as Senior Prisoner-Officer at Verdun, he received a copy of the British Government's protest concerning him, sent in August 1804. The French Government, perhaps, had good reason not to keep him posted, seeing that they were, and intended to remain, 'one up' on the transaction. Meanwhile, another most significant thing was happening. Captain Jurien, who was evidently a gentleman, was so ashamed when he heard that Brenton was still a prisoner that he applied to return to England. Napoleon refused permission: but not only that. The officer, honourably enough (but still only playing to the old rules) had refrained from applying for an appointment until his full exchange was effected. Hearing this, Napoleon curtly ordered him to rejoin a ship.

Almost two years later, Brenton did regain his liberty, and by exchange. But the lucky French officer was not Jurien. It was a certain

Captain Infernet, captured only at Trafalgar. This is significant too. Upon examination we find that almost all of the few successful exchanges were due to personal influences on the French side. This was no exception. Infernet was the nephew of Masséna, who pestered his imperial master until he gave way. Still, Napoleon remained 'one up'.

The Dillon case was worse. It struck at the heart of a convention which was supposed, even in France, to be basic to civilized warfare —the Flag of Truce. Dillon, first lieutenant of the *Africaine*, was sent into Helvoetsluys in an unarmed six-oar cutter with a communication from his captain to the Dutch Government. The officer who received him behaved correctly enough: he dispatched the letter to headquarters and, when the answer came back, released Dillon and his men. Before he could make sail, however, an armed French launch arrived, boarded him, took possession of the boat, flag of truce and all, and brought the whole party as prisoners to the French frigate *Furieuse*. The facts were never denied. The Dutch naval authorities hurriedly dissociated themselves from the outrage: the Dutch Government itself expostulated. But all their protests went for nothing. There had to be excuses, however, and the local Dutch commodore was told to fabricate a countercharge, which he did with transparent reluctance. Dillon, he said, had only come to spy on the shipping in the port. The weakness of this charge was, of course, that, had it been true, he would not have let Dillon go at the time. The captain of the *Furieuse*, who no doubt had orders to 'shoot the official line', unfortunately chose quite a different one. The French Government, he declared, had notified ours that it would receive flags of truce only through the port of Morlaix in Brittany. This was true; but it had two fatal flaws as an argument. First, the flag in question had not been sent to the French at all but to the Dutch, who naturally had no such rule. Second, he had to admit when pressed that the French ship carrying their message to Britain had passed Dillon's *Africaine* off Helvoetsluys—under a flag of truce respected by that ship—only a few hours before Dillon left it. He was, therefore, a prisoner in the French frigate, almost certainly before the French communication reached an English port, and certainly long before the news it contained could be transmitted back to the *Africaine*.

Fortunately this particular brand of infamy was all but unique. It is not even clear why it was perpetrated. Compared with hundreds of British globe-trotters, oozing money, a single British lieutenant

71

was poor fry indeed. Napoleon himself must probably be acquitted of any original share in it. But it became something of a *cause célèbre*, and he found himself at once in his old dilemma. The Dictator can do no wrong—at least, cannot own up to it—and Napoleon never did. The worst sufferer was poor Dillon himself, because he found himself in an unfortunate minority of one. According to the French, as a serving commissioned officer he was an ordinary prisoner of war. According to the British, not having been taken in action he was illegally detained—i.e. a *détenu*, a person for whose exchange we would not negotiate. This hit him financially. The French, unable by hypothesis to regard him as other than a service officer, had to give him the p.o.w. pay, scaled according to rank: but the British authorities, who also made an allowance (of half-pay) to their officers in captivity, refused it to him for a long time, on the grounds that he was a *détenu* for whose keep they were not responsible, and that, if they paid him an officer's half-pay, they would, tacitly, be admitting the legality of his arrest. As a result, the unfortunate young man had to sell a small estate which he owned in Ireland: and this, pardonably, made him rather bitter, against one government for holding him illegally, against the other for refusing to admit his officer status. After a time, however, the British Government relented, making his a personal, 'compassionate' case while still maintaining to the French authorities that he was not exchangeable for a French officer. After this he was much better off, especially when, first, he was allowed his share of the famous Patriotic Fund, and second, when the Admiralty took the unusual step of promoting him while still in captivity to the rank of commander, thus increasing his allowances from both French and English sources. Finally our authorities, obviously sorry for him, sacrificed even the general principle, and consented to exchange him —on extravagant terms, as we shall see—for a serving French officer.

The last of the special cases taken up by the British Government in August 1804 was that of Commander John Wesley Wright. This was very different, because Wright, though a professional naval officer, clearly had some connection, never precisely traced, with the Foreign Office. He spoke several languages like a native—French, Spanish, Russian—and was a protégé of Sir William Sidney Smith, himself much mixed up in diplomacy. Both had been captured during the Revolutionary War, and confined, close prisoners, in the Temple prison in Paris. They had escaped, Smith to pursue his brilliant if erratic course in the Eastern Mediterranean and elsewhere, Wright, apparently, to a more humdrum naval career. But he was unlucky. On May 8, 1804, while commanding the brig *Vincejo*, he was captured again in Quiberon Bay. He was carted off to Paris, again lodged in the Temple, in the same room as before, and rigorously cross-examined. The object of this, said the French, was to discover whether he had landed a number of French royalist traitors. They threatened him with ill-usage, but got nothing out of him—at least, that was their story.

At about the time of our government's protest, the other officers of his ship arrived at Verdun, having, for a while, been with him in the Temple, but now allowed parole. No parole, however, was granted to Wright, and no Briton ever saw him again. James Wallis, his first lieutenant, had an odd tale to tell the Verdun prisoners. His captain, he said, had informed his officers before they left that, whatever happened, nothing would induce him to commit suicide.

> 'Therefore,' said he, 'if you hear of my death, depend upon it I shall have been murdered. I make this statement to you that you may expect it should you hear of my having quitted this life.'[1]

It was just what they did hear. Over a year later, the *Moniteur* announced that, on the night of October 27, 1805, Commander Wright had committed suicide. It even gave the reason for the tragedy—that, after reading the bulletin announcing Mack's surrender at Ulm, he could not bear the flood of ill-tidings, and, in a fit of depression, cut his throat with a razor. As there is reason to think that Wright had also just heard of the victory off Cape Trafalgar (fought the day before Ulm)—and a true version of it, not the *Moniteur's* famous travesty—the evidence of that truth-loving journal hardly carries conviction.

With one accord Napoleon's enemies cried 'Murder!' And it may have been so. After the war Sir Sidney Smith conducted a searching, though unofficial, investigation in Paris, and produced damning evidence from what he had found. The body, it seems, was discovered in a bed whose sheets were pulled up round the chin. The throat was cut to the bone, but the razor, also found, was clasped in the dead man's down-stretched hand, up against his thigh: and there was no blood on the sheet, though there was some elsewhere in the room. It seems clear, too, that his letters at no time showed suicidal tendencies: indeed, the reverse. He remained in postal touch

[1] Dillon, op. cit., III, p. 317.

73

with Wallis until nearly the end. Extracts from one such letter are given in Appendix II. It was written only some seven weeks before the tragedy, and the reader may judge for himself about suicidal inclinations. In the present author's view there are, emphatically, none, though the letter does seem to reveal the writer's pessimism about his own survival. Assuming that his 'Translator in Office' was the censoring officer, we shall appreciate how careful he had to be in his wording. He could not possibly say outright that he feared he was going to be executed or murdered; but his rather arbitrary dragging in of the *Moniteur* and his immunity against its falsehoods certainly makes the French explanation of the cause of his suicide sound thinner than ever. It looks as if the message he was trying to send Wallis was, 'Don't be afraid of my succumbing to their lies: I simply shan't believe them!' His touching solicitude towards his 'own three boys' tells the same way. In a rather earlier letter to the French Minister of War he had asked to be allowed to join his officers at Verdun, giving as his first reason his anxiety to be looking after these lads. In both letters this appears as his prime desire. It would surely not make sense that, with his own hand, he should make that desire impossible of achievement. His earnest request to Wallis to act as foster-father to them does seem to show that he had not much hope of getting to Verdun himself: but this certainly does not prove that he had no *intention* to get there (i.e. that he contemplated suicide). Rather, it reveals his fear of what the French Government might be going to do to him, and his attempt to make certain that, if the worst happened, the boys would have the best possible chance.

Suicide, then, seems a most improbable verdict. But there are unsatisfactory features about the theory of murder, too. For that crime the investigator must seek a motive, and it is hard to find a reasonable one. Still less is there any evidence that Napoleon had any hand in it. Years afterwards, at St Helena, he ridiculed the idea, making the telling point that, had he wanted Wright's life, he could have had him tried, and shot not as a naval officer but as a spy. It remains possible that someone on a lower level had a grudge against him and had him killed: but this is pure conjecture. So is another theory—that he was destroyed neither by his own hand nor anyone else's, but that he died a natural death: upon which some warped, over-subtle mind concluded that propaganda value might be gleaned from the incident if it were made to appear that Wright took his own life in despair for his country. Indeed this theory, more than

74

any other, accounts for the known facts, even the evidence of the sheets and the bloodstains. But it is mere supposition, and the mystery remains unsolved.

None of these three cases had the least effect upon Napoleon. Not only did he ignore them: he counter-attacked again, and from a new angle altogether. The British, he declared, were detaining numerous French garrisons taken in the West Indies, contrary to the terms of capitulation: they must be returned unconditionally before he would talk at all. The rights and wrongs of this charge have never, so far as I know, been established either way: but, if it is like all the others, it should not be taken too seriously. Anyway, the British flatly refused to disgorge these prisoners; whereupon Napoleon closed all negotiations.

When Pitt died two years later, Britain tried again. Fox regarded himself, and was widely regarded, as much more sympathetic to Napoleon than Pitt had ever been, and he began well. Hearing of a plot to assassinate the Emperor, he wrote and warned him, thereby earning his gratitude. Lord Yarmouth, newly released from Verdun, was sent back to Paris to negotiate, and he was followed by the even more influential Lord Lauderdale. Lengthy talks now took place, in which prisoners of war loomed large. Our envoy began, apparently, with yet another appeal to the Emperor's sense of fair play. 'I have put into the hands of the French Government', he wrote to an anxiously-waiting *détenu* in Verdun, 'a list of 150 officers to whom we have given leave to return to France, and have only received eight in exchange."[1] This approach met with no response whatever, at any rate in securing anything like the general exchanges of previous wars. On a tiny plane, however, it did not fail entirely. It secured the freedom of a few privileged or lucky people whose release did not require the surrender of either side's basic principles. One fortunate beneficiary on this occasion was Thomas Bruce, Seventh Earl of Elgin. He had been on his way home from Greece in 1803, without the famous Greek marbles which were coming by sea—where they had adventures of their own. His case was regarded by the British as a peculiarly gross piece of French treachery because, before entering France from Italy, he had taken the trouble to inquire whether it

[1] Lauderdale to Captain Gerrard, September 21, 1806, quoted verbatim by Dillon (op. cit., III, p. 382). Most of these 150 had not, probably, been released outright: they were the officers returned to France on parole, our tribute to the good old days.

75

was safe to proceed, and had been assured that it was. But this did not avail him: for three whole years he had been a *détenu*. There were also a very few service exchanges at this time. Captain Brenton, now a sick man, was one, and another was Colonel Phillips of the Marines, the officer in whose presence Cook had been slain at Hawaii. This officer had the luck to be a great friend of Sir Joseph Banks, whose immense international influence will be described later.

Dillon also expected great things from Yarmouth, as he knew him very well. For weeks, his portmanteau ready packed, he remained in hope of a passport to take him home. It did not come: he was still the odd man out. Yet the precedent of occasional individual exchanges inaugurated by Yarmouth did in the end cover him. Like Brenton, he was kept in ignorance of what was happening; but from the beginning of 1807, as he afterwards discovered, the Transport Board was busy corresponding with the French Ministry of Marine—and, characteristically, being completely bamboozled. Dillon gives part of the correspondence, but not quite enough to reveal all that happened. Still, much is clear. The British Government had at last relinquished its original stand, and was prepared to regard him as an ordinary service-prisoner. They then, very generously, offered in exchange for him a French captain named Millius; and, innocents as they still were, they assumed that France could not possibly refuse so very favourable a deal: for, though Dillon had just been made a commander, Millius was a full captain of some seniority. (That gentleman, by the way, was one of the lucky 150, already in France.) In their letter to M. Rivière, the Secretary of the Ministry of Marine, therefore, they fondly committed two cardinal blunders: they enclosed Captain Millius' parole, and they added that, if Rivière preferred any other officer to Millius, would he kindly let them know?

A long pause ensued, in which the Board waited hopefully for Dillon to arrive in England. But he did not arrive—indeed, knew nothing at all about the matter. At last, however, a most polite letter arrived from M. Rivière, not mentioning Millius' cancelled parole, but informing the Board that he would like to avail himself of its kind offer. Could he please, instead of Millius (whom he already had, complete with cancelled parole), have a certain Captain Soleil, a good deal senior to Millius—indeed, an acting commodore? There was, however, one difference this time. Soleil was in England, so that the earlier trick was not quite so easy to repeat. Yet the trustful Board scorned to take advantage of that fact. They replied 'By all means', and sent Soleil over, cancelled parole and all! Really they deserved to be cheated again: but this time they were not. Dillon was duly dispatched—only the fourteenth naval officer, he tells us, to be exchanged in the first $4\frac{1}{2}$ years of war. None the less, the ingenious Monsieur Rivière had not done too badly. He had recovered two genuine prisoners—a full captain and a commodore—in exchange for one very junior commander who, in equity and international law alike, had never been a prisoner at all.

Another man caught in a position not unlike Dillon's was Colonel (afterwards General Sir John) Abercromby, son of the famous Sir Ralph. In his person, of course, he was good p.o.w. material, but he had not been taken in war. He was a *détenu*, and therefore, from his government's point of view, an 'unexchangeable'. That he missed the limited 1806 exchange (even though he was Yarmouth's uncle) is not quite so surprising as it sounds. He was not only, in our view, unexchangeable: he was a real trump in the exchange game, especially when, a little thoughtlessly perhaps, the government promoted him major-general in captivity. This made him, for the moment, senior to any French officer that we held. But he got away as soon as we caught one—General Brennier, taken by Wellington at Vimiero in 1808. This was because we wanted Abercromby and Napoleon wanted Brennier. That kind of hard criterion was usually successful, on both sides.

As for a general cartel, the 1806 negotiations failed as completely as their predecessors; and for the next four years, discouraged, the British Government made no further overtures. By 1810, however, the Peninsular War was in full swing, the spate of prisoners already rising, and the problem of where to put them growing. Exchange was obviously what we wanted, because that would please everybody— the government by easing its problem, the prisoners by restoring them to freedom, their relatives (constantly pressing the government to act) by restoring their loved ones. So we began again; and Napoleon, at first, seemed inclined to agree. This, however, was chiefly because our government began by conceding a major point.

The Emperor's claims were as high as ever, if not actually higher. Our *détenus* must still rank as the equals of his soldiers and sailors, man for man—even woman for man, child for man and over-60's for under-60's. Every Briton in France was to count. It was a cool manœuvre, unlikely at first sight to succeed. But Napoleon was a good psychologist, and very well-informed on the trend of opinion in Britain. He thought the gamble worth while, and he was right. It came off. The British Government consented in principle, and talks started in earnest. After some stiff bargaining (in which the Emperor almost always won) a regular 'tariff' was hammered out. It looked like this:

British	to be exchanged for	French
Peers		*Admirals and Generals (highest ranks first)*
Peers' Sons and Privy Counsellors		*Naval Captains and Colonels*
Baronets and Knights		*Commanders, Lieutenant-Colonels and Majors*
Gentlemen with no social title		*Naval Lieutenants and Army Captains*
'Petite bourgeoisie', valets, servants, etc., and all others detained, male and female		*Men of both Services not holding commissions, from W.O.s down to seamen and private soldiers*

It was further agreed that, though all 'straight' exchanges should take place first (e.g. a knight against a commander), if the supply of any particular category gave out on one side before the corresponding individuals on the other could be exchanged, then the unlucky residue should be exchanged for a fixed (and larger) number from the next category which had any left in it, or a still larger number from the one after that, every category having a numerical value attached to it for this purpose. Even so, it was found when the sum was worked out that there remained many thousand Frenchmen, mostly simple *poilus*, when all the British seamen, privates and *détenus* had gone home. Again the British Government proved generous. The residue of French captives should be set against Spanish prisoners in French hands. These should be returned to Spain in such numbers as would allow the last Frenchman to leave Britain.

Then, however, the trouble began. Knowing our man by now, we were insisting that the exchanges should take place simultaneously. Napoleon appeared to agree; but when his missive was carefully studied it was found to mean that, when he sent over every Briton whom he held, we were to send over every Frenchman in Britain: and that then—later, but with no time specified—he would send back the Spaniards. Our reply was brusque. We threatened to break off negotiations. To leave our unfortunate allies to the mercy of such a man was unthinkable. Indeed, it is as certain as such things can be that he never intended to send any Spaniards back at all; and it is impossible not to suspect that he had a sinister reason for it. So far, the terms were so entirely in his favour that it is hard to see why he did not accept them without, for once, trying to obtain more. But what if he did not have enough Spaniards in his hands? No doubt we knew, roughly, how many Spaniards had surrendered to his forces; and the total was very large. What, very likely, we did not know then was how many the French had slaughtered on the spot, or at best let die. We do not know that number now: we only know that it was very large. Perhaps Napoleon did not hold enough to quit the bill—but, naturally, dared not say so.

This time, then, his bluff was called. But he was far from done. With another sudden twist, he made a completely fresh proposal; one on an altogether larger scale and, could he but be trusted, a thoroughly humane one. He suggested nothing less than a total and comprehensive exchange of all captives. The agreement was to include:

> all British, Spaniards, Portuguese, Sicilians, Hanoverians and other persons, subjects of or in the service of Great Britain; and all French, Italians and other persons subjects of or in the service of France and Italy, all Dutch and Neapolitans and all others, subjects of or in the service of the Powers allied with France shall be released without exception.

All were to be returned in simultaneous batches of 1,000: first the British in France against the same number of French in Britain; then all the other categories in turn, all simultaneously, until there would be no prisoners left anywhere. At last it looked like the real thing.

But no. This time it was the amiability of the British that ruined it all. Once more they made the astonishing mistake of trusting the Emperor. The barometer seemed to be standing so firmly at set fair that they allowed a considerable contingent of high-ranking Frenchmen to return to France, on the understanding, of course, that the British for whom they were being exchanged would turn up at once in England. Not one arrived: and when a sharp reminder was sent to him, the Emperor, with crowning effrontery, replied that he did not propose to count as exchangeable any Frenchman who was already in France! And that was that.

79

Now and again, however, Napoleon as an individual stands revealed as quite a different person from Napoleon the scheming head of state: and perhaps the best illustration of this occurred, oddly enough, almost simultaneously with the breakdown of the 1810 talks. Appealed to as a man, he sometimes showed clemency, and even a fleeting generosity. We shall meet with several examples of this welcome trait, but here is a specific and unusual one. On December 27, 1810, the Indian country-ship *Elizabeth*, Captain Robert Eastwick, drifted on to a shoal off Dunkirk in a terrific gale. Of a total complement of 380, only twenty-two, including Eastwick, braved the appalling surf, and reached the shore more dead than alive. They were instantly carted off to the town gaol and locked, white officers and lascar seamen together, in a foul *cachot*. But the Dunkirkers, who were known to have secret sympathies with the British, were, openly for once, furious. Having watched with their own eyes the survivors' long and desperate fight for life, and having spontaneously cared for them and revived them with the most solicitous kindness, they were scandalized that they should thus be hauled off to a dungeon: and their rage and shame were further increased when it came out that one of the survivors had been foully murdered. Edward Tench, a lieutenant in a Ceylon regiment, was a passenger. He was not with Eastwick in the boat, but had somehow managed to swim ashore alone. There, exhausted, he was found by a soldier and a customs officer, who promptly dispatched him for the sake of the money he carried. This was too much. With one voice they appealed to Caesar, the commandant himself leading.

The Emperor, just then, was in the throes of his argument with the British Government; squirming, wriggling, cheating right and left, and loudly proclaiming in public that he would not give way an inch to the utterly unreasonable demands of the enemy. Not a single Englishman would be exchanged until their rulers mended their vile ways. In fact, the *Moniteur* had only just printed a message from the imperial pen declaring as much. Add to this the well-known fact that His Majesty did not like Dunkirkers, who, as he knew very well, did not like him. Save perhaps for the Bretons, they were the last people whom he would willingly oblige. None the less—and to everyone's surprise, including Eastwick's—he sent for the petition as soon as he heard of its arrival, read carefully the account of the shipwreck, and, with that same hand which had written so recently to the *Moniteur*, signed an order for the immediate and unconditional release of the whole party, the French Government to bear all expenses. He did not demand, or even hint at, any exchange.

But of course he got one. Before he left for home, the grateful and far-sighted Eastwick held a consultation with the leading Dunkirkers, who presented him with a list of 150 of their townsmen who were prisoners in England; and the first thing he did on reaching London was to visit the Transport Board, where he told his story. Instantly twenty-two Dunkirkers departed for France, and they were the ones picked by their own folk as being the most deserving of release.

This episode has most interesting features. It was, so far as I know, unique, and it illustrates two things to perfection: first (which we were morally sure of already) that the British Government not only wanted to play the exchange game, but also was determined to play it fairly: and second, that here was a thing which might have happened throughout the war as a matter of everyday routine—if Napoleon would have allowed it. Indeed, it was singularly like what had happened before Napoleon came along and spoilt it.[1]

Eastwick thought, or appeared to think, that Napoleon's action stemmed from pure generosity. There is a possibility, however, that Napoleon the Man was not quite so far removed from Napoleon the Emperor as Eastwick thought: and it should be mentioned even if, here, the great man be given the benefit of the doubt. Was it just an innocent coincidence that the commandant at Dunkirk, General O'Mara, the man who signed, sponsored and forwarded the petition, was the brother-in-law of General Clarke, French Minister of War, a man high in Napoleon's favour and one who (as will be seen later) had liberal views about British prisoners? Indeed, this story of Eastwick and Napoleon—and of Generals O'Mara and Clarke—is very apposite here, as serving to introduce the final chapter of the exchange fiasco.

The abortive negotiations of 1810 were the last British attempt at negotiating a mass exchange, and for that no blame can be attached to our government. There was, however, one more reversion to the only sort of exchange which had, so far, shown any result whatever— the individual mutual-influence sort tried in 1806: the sort in which Masséna, Talleyrand—or Clarke—took a hand: in which, indeed, Napoleon himself joined, when it suited him. Such was the case in 1812, when the very last talks took place. By then, Frenchmen

[1] Eastwick himself recorded the story in full in his *A Master Mariner* (London, 1891).

taken in Spain were becoming an intolerable nuisance to us. But some of them were of very high rank. One in particular was the Prince d'Aremburg, embarrassingly high for Napoleon, who was related to him by marriage. By an almost private arrangement, therefore, d'Aremburg and a few more were set against high-up Britons, some serving officers but mostly *détenus*. That was all.

A sparse handful of *détenus*, then, and a smaller consignment of professional officers, mostly high in rank and in ones and twos, were the only people to secure their freedom by exchange.[1] To the last there was no general exchange for the more junior officers or for any of the men. From beginning to end there was no single cartel ship. All in these groups who got away—and, to their credit, many did— won their liberty the hard way. They escaped.

[1] To be absolutely accurate, we should add a few—a very few—sick men, over whom, incidentally, Napoleon cheated again (see p. 155). Affairs like Eastwick's, and the unprecedented happenings at Auxonne (p. 157) and at Givet (p. 167) were not exchanges but sporadic, unnegotiated 'releases'.

CHAPTER IV

THE ROAD TO VERDUN

We have dealt so far with the general: we turn now to the particular. What happened to the British captive from the moment he was caught to the moment of his release, however that happy event came about? To this there is no short answer, because there is no such thing as a 'typical' case. Some were treated well, some moderately, some monstrously. By this stage of our story, indeed, nothing else is to be expected. Here, as at every other point, a gentleman may expect, and will usually get, one standard of treatment, and a non-gentleman a very different one. A general will be in luxury compared with a private, a naval captain compared with a ship's boy. And this, as a generalization, will prove to be true, though we shall find a surprising number of exceptions.

In this chapter we are to see what happened in the first stage of captivity, the journey from place of capture to place of incarceration; and the most convenient setting for that story is the road to Verdun, because this fortress town was not only itself a prison depot, but also the distribution centre of almost all prisoners. Some stayed there, more passed on; but almost all arrived. Since, however, there is no 'typical' captive, it will be necessary to select from the considerable number of surviving narratives a few representative ones. We will begin at the top.

I. THE GENERAL OFFICER

No story of a flag-officer's journey is available: from first to last the French never caught one. They did, however, catch a general or two: to be exact, three, all in Spain—Lord John Murray, Sir Edward Paget, and the officer whose fortunes are here to be followed. Major-General Andrew Lord Blayney, an Irish peer from Co. Monaghan, was taken with all his men when he landed with a small force near Malaga in 1810; and the worst moment of his whole captivity was the first. He

83

FRANCE, 1803–1814

84

was all but killed before a French officer rode up and extricated him from his immediate captors.

Thereafter things went very pleasantly on the whole. Such a high-ranking prisoner was so rare a bird that the French, in their delight at securing a living specimen, were prepared to treat him with real courtesy, so long as he did not object to being exposed for show like a wing-clipt eagle. Blayney was usually wise enough to acquiesce: indeed, his own narrative[1] leaves one uncertain whether he really did object much, or even as much as became him. He had many of his countrymen's proverbial qualities: a facile tongue, plenty of blarney, and much of the soldier of fortune's resignation when that fickle lady turns against him. He certainly cuts no heroic figure, even in his own story. The officers captured with him were, in marked contrast to himself, treated very cavalierly, and his attempts to better their lot seem somehow half-hearted. His own progress, on the other hand, smacks of a triumph.

He was passed up the whole length of Spain from general to general, dining with them in turn and invited to participate in any social functions that were going; attending balls and bull-fights and hunting excursions with his hosts. He rode all the way on good horses provided by his captors, with a train of baggage-animals to carry his gear. On the road he often overtook other British prisoners in various states of misery, and, though he spoke up for them, he never claims to have secured them any substantial concessions. In fact, the more one studies the stories of other captive British officers, the lower falls one's opinion of Lord Blayney. There are records of several of them, some of not much inferior rank—we shall shortly meet one of them —who, finding their own treatment infinitely better than their subordinates', deliberately handed back their paroles and went to share the burdens of their own officers and men: and, in doing so, quite often materially helped them. No hint of this admirable spirit shows itself in the rather self-complaisant story of Blayney.

The progress was not quite 'roses, roses all the way'. Occasionally the major-general overstepped the limits. His principal object seems to have been to postpone for as long as possible his arrival at Verdun; and, as most of the French generals he met did not seem to mind how

[1] *A Narrative of a Forced Journey through Spain and France as a Prisoner of War in the years 1810–14*, London, 1814. The book achieved considerable, and deserved, success and is important to social historians; but the subject-matter is, I think, much more attractive than the author.

long he took, he loitered along, sometimes even being found in a town after having been told to leave it. One rather curmudgeonly general, Beliard, suspected that he was plotting to escape with the aid of guerrillas, and actually confined him for a while: but, to do him justice, the suspicion was quite groundless. He had no intention of breaking his parole nor was he the kind of man to whom the dangers and discomforts of escaping would appeal. He possessed, however, much outward charm, and always contrived to talk himself out of his scrapes. After leaving Spain, and as he neared Paris, he seems to have attracted more and more suspicion. This he did little to allay: indeed, entered Paris itself, without leave, took a room at one of the best hotels and proceeded to do the sights of the capital at leisure. But the police were watching him more closely than he knew. He was rudely arrested, and even locked up for a while after an official grilling intimidating even to him. Once more he talked his way out, and was allowed to leave Paris, though under arrest and accompanied by a gendarme: no longer indeed mounted upon a dashing steed, yet still in a chaise-and-pair. He was not made to walk a step of the way —as were his own officers whom he overtook on the road. So at length he reached Verdun. He had been captured in July: he entered the town in the following April. The distance, by the road he took, is some 1,200 miles, and the ordinary time allowed for prisoners— on foot—was said to be three months. Blayney, horse-borne or horse-drawn throughout, had taken nine: not bad going if one's object was dawdling.

II. CAPTAIN, RN

The general's story is, of course, far from typical. So is our next, that of a naval post captain, one of the ten who fell into French hands. Here the standard of treatment is below the norm for that rank, thought not so far below it as Blayney's was above that of his. The deterioration is marked, and sharp. Captain (later Vice-Admiral Sir) Jahleel Brenton was the first of his rank to be taken when his frigate, the *Minerve*, went aground off Cherbourg on July 2, 1803. The French authorities—the local ones anyway—had no sort of routine for handling prisoners; which meant, in effect, that the captives' fate depended almost entirely upon the whim of the commanding officer in whose district they found themselves.

No two men could be more different in character and outlook than Blayney and Brenton: the general insouciant and self-centred, the captain conscientious, responsible, intelligent, far-sighted. The general made his travels as easy as possible: the captain consistently made his harder than they might have been, because he never thought of himself. He journeyed some 600 miles between early July and mid-December—from Cherbourg to Epinal in the Vosges, thence to Phalsbourg near Strasbourg and only then to Verdun; and, characteristically, he has very little to say of his own discomforts though a great deal about those of his people. He was not allowed to travel with his men: on the first and longest leg of the journey they were one day's march ahead, and on the other two a day's march behind: only his officers were with him. This, however, did not prevent one half of his active mind from leaping forward (or later backward) plotting and planning for those who needed him most, while the other half watched the interests of his immediate comrades. He had no time left for self-pity. Even at Verdun, when he reached it, he seldom if ever complained on his own behalf, though as we have seen he had plenty of cause. He was still too occupied with the welfare of others; for, as the first senior officer of prisoners in France, this fine officer, more than any other man, was responsible for most of those sad little indulgences which at last came the way of the seamen and the younger officers.

There was no fine horse for Brenton: no horse at all, no luggage-train, not even any distinction between post captain, lieutenant and midshipman. All were marched off together on foot, the near-fifty of them guarded by three gendarmes. Nor had these worthies the least cause for alarm, because Brenton had given his parole for all his party, and the word of such a man, had they realized it, made any surveillance unnecessary.

The first thing they discovered was that France, for police and security purposes, was divided into squares, from 10 to 15 miles in extent, and each had a different officer in command. The commandant of the first square had a 'de' before his name—it was de la Gorge. They were soon to appreciate the significance of those two little letters, and to dread their absence. They usually implied *ancien régime*, so that their owners, having been born gentlemen, were apt to treat gentlemen in adversity with sympathy. Every British prisoner on every weary road to Verdun very soon made this discovery, and every one comments upon it. De la Gorge was true to type. He had the captain and his first lieutenant to dinner and, next morning, personally saw them off his territory with a sincere wish for their speedy exchange: indeed, 'Kissed me at parting, to the high amusement of the officers and midshipmen'.

The next commandant, however, had no 'de'. He added a file of cavalry to the escort: he made the party, including the captain, line up in ranks instead of (as before) being allowed to walk at ease and as they liked: he even forbade talking. A number of captured merchant captains were now added to the column, and all were urged forward by the mounted guard as fast as they could walk, or faster. Anyone in the least familiar with the almost god-like stature of a post captain of the Royal Navy *vis-à-vis* even his most senior assistant, let alone his midshipmen, will appreciate what Brenton must have felt. But he will not discover it from Brenton, who did not once demand that special treatment to himself to which he was undoubtedly entitled. Yet his silence was clearly not due to complaisancy, still less to pusillanimity: for his protests, always dignified and forceful, against any unworthy treatment of prisoners, were never lacking, and often successful. At Caen, his quiet firmness silenced the gratuitous insults of the commandant (no 'de'),[1] and, at the next halt, when the whole party was locked into one room, he induced the captain in charge, by mere force of personality, to find reasonable billets for them in defiance of written orders.

A little later, thanks entirely to Brenton's foresight, remittances of cash reached the marching column. Some of the midshipmen in their youthful exuberance hired carriages with their new-found wealth. So did Brenton: but with this difference—the midshipmen rode in theirs: the captain sent his on to take up the lame and shoeless men in the column ahead. Thereupon the midshipmen leapt out of theirs, and did the same.

So it went on for 600 miles. Undoubtedly, had he made a fuss, he could have ridden, or been driven, almost all the way: but—though he would be the last person to call attention to the fact—it is certain that he walked every yard of the distance, step for step with his commissioned officers, his warrant officers and his Young Gentlemen. It would be interesting to know whether General Lord Blayney ever read Captain Jahleel Brenton's letters; and, if he did, whether he had the grace to blush.

---

[1] *The General:* 'Je me moque de votre parole d'honneur. Je ne sais pas ce que c'est, moi!'
   The Captain: 'I will tell you, Sir: it is for a British officer stronger than any of your prisons.'

III. COMMANDER, RN

Frederick Hoffman, captain of the *Appelles* but only commander by rank, was wrecked in a fog off Etaples in May 1812. Before the mist cleared (to reveal an enormous fort-battery a few yards away) he had sent off all his crew except himself, surgeon, one midshipman and sixteen ratings for whom there was no room in the boats. He was boarded by a disorderly rabble which plundered his ship, stole all his personal possessions and hustled them all off, very roughly, to the common gaol at Boulogne. Sitting in their filthy cell, Hoffman and his surgeon felt down-hearted, and quite uncertain about their immediate future. Nothing had been said about parole: indeed there had been few words of any kind; only kicks and blows. Suddenly the cell-door opened and in walked a richly-caparisoned flunkey bearing an invitation to Hoffman to dine that very afternoon with the commandant of Boulogne, a full general and a count as well.

The commander hesitated, as well he might, having no clothes but the rumpled uniform he was wearing. On the doctor's persuasion, however, he went, though feeling quite out of place in the brilliant star-coated company which surrounded the great man. He was kindly received and treated as an equal, and thereupon assumed, naturally enough, that he was to be allowed parole. Two French naval officers paid him particularly friendly attentions all the evening and, when it was time to go, offered to see him home. He gratefully accepted, supposing they were bound for a decent hotel. But no: they took him back to the town gaol where they 'wished me a good night, and I wished them to the devil!'[1]

He was kept in gaol for ten days, mainly because certain pamphlets had been found hidden in the *Appelles*, intended apparently for distribution in France. He thought at first that they were going to try him as a spy; but his ignorance of the pamphlets' existence seems to have been genuine, and he contrived to convince his judges that the papers bore dates prior to the date of his commission to the ship. At length, therefore, they sent him off to Verdun; but the treatment he received was so poor, for an officer of his standing, that perhaps they were not really satisfied of his innocence. No parole was allowed and, though he asked for a carriage, having the money to pay for it, his request was refused. He was made to march with the men, guarded

[1] *A Sailor of King George*, London, 1901, p. 303.

by mounted gendarmes, and lodged with them in common gaols. The possession of cash eased his lot, but he was shamelessly soaked by turnkeys and others, and, in common with all British prisoners, was forced to share with his guardian gendarmes even his dearly-bought food.

In this condition he reached Arras, a regular p.o.w. depot. Here he was befriended by a lieutenant left in charge of the British prisoners, who succeeded in procuring parole for him, his surgeon and his midshipman. Thereafter their lot improved vastly: they were even allowed a carriage, though at an exorbitant price. The affair of the pamphlets may be the reason for his early treatment: but again it may not. There are several cases on record of apparently arbitrary harshness, even to senior officers. Thus Brenton cites the case (without, however, giving either names or dates) of a naval captain, a major of Marines and a wealthy Bermudan planter, who, captured in a merchantman, were treated all the way to Verdun as common seamen, and once actually guarded, and threatened, all night by a ferocious mastiff. There is no clue to what their captors had against them.

IV. LIEUTENANT, RN

Some of the experiences of one lieutenant—Dillon—have already been described. They were above the norm of comfort, but there were several reasons for this. His earlier journeyings were not in France, but in Holland and Belgium, where the attitude to Britain was much more friendly. Next, he possessed several friends, and even relatives, in some of the towns he visited: and last, he had been educated in France as a child, and spoke the language well enough to be taken for a Frenchman. None the less, it is instructive to watch the regulations being tightened against him as Verdun draws nearer. He too suffered from those twin trials common to all officer-prisoners—the bearishness of parvenu republican officers, and the obligation to live with, to feed, and even to pay his unwanted guards. But he was never seriously molested; nor did he have to walk a yard of the way. The worst he had to endure—and, being a rather vain, fastidious young man, he complained of it a good deal—was an occasional ride in a public diligence, and once, when his chaise broke down, in a farm cart. He had not to concern himself with his men, because he was separated from them from the start, and thereafter travelled alone.

Another case, again not normal, but tending this time to over-harsh-ness, was that of Lieutenant George Vernon Jackson.[1] It has several unusual features. His journey to Verdun was longer than any of those already described or to be described, whether measured in miles or in months. He was taken in the West Indies, off Guadeloupe, in the *Junon* frigate on December 13, 1809, but the summer of 1811 was near at hand before he entered Verdun. The French ship which brought him to Europe was nearly taken by a British cruiser. It reached Brest, however, and, with a fellow-lieutenant and two of the *Junon's* midshipmen, he was sent for quarantine to the hospital there. In both ship and hospital the captives were treated exceedingly well. Before they took the road, the officer commanding the squadron which had captured them presented the two lieutenants with £25 apiece, a remarkable act of generosity. But the generosity of another captain, who had brought one of the midshipmen over, was even more remarkable. He gave him three presents—£25, a map of Brest and its surroundings, and a box of opium pills.

Why? There would seem to be only one reasonable answer—that the Frenchmen concerned actually wanted these British officers to escape. If there are two things on earth which runaway prisoners pine for, they are ready cash and a map. As for the opium pills—well, we shall see. What is the explanation? Perhaps the likeliest is that these enemy officers were Bretons, notoriously hostile to the imperial régime, and apt at all times to be partial to British sailors. There is a subsidiary possibility too, which, granted some such pre-disposition in the hearts of Bretons, may help to explain why they favoured this particular quartet. In the close contacts of a long voyage together, they must have come to know them very well, and may well have come to love them. For three of them at least seem to have been more than ordinarly attractive young men. The other lieutenant, Henry Conn, was perhaps an exception, though it would not be fair to condemn him out of hand because the Admiralty did not approve of his subsequent method of escape (see p. 46): but Jackson himself was a real character, enterprising and determined; a born escaper who would never let failure daunt him. Though he had been at sea for eight years, he was only 22, and had just been made a lieutenant. Of the midshipmen, one, William Thomas, was probably a mere boy, having been at sea for only a year and a midshipman for only

[1] Admiral G. V. Jackson, *Perilous Adventures and Vicissitudes of a Naval Officer, 1801–12*, London, 1927.

three months: but he was, as Jackson says, 'a particularly well-favoured specimen of a handsome youth'.

The other midshipman, Frederick Whitehurst, earns his place in this book in his own right. He was a young man of magnificent physique, six foot two in height and broad to match: strong as a horse, clumsy as a colt, and evidently greatly loved by everybody. Yet he was more than ordinarily unlucky in war. He had already been a prisoner for nearly five years. He had then escaped, after spending a gruelling six months as a hunted fugitive, only to be taken again in another ship seven months later. We shall meet him again twice, although, from his point of view, in the wrong order. We shall see him making his first weary journey to Verdun in 1804, and then escaping from Valenciennes in 1808–9. Now it was 1810, and all was to do again; for it was he, apparently so placid and easy-going, who was to plot with Jackson, the live wire, to run for it as soon as they took the road. Perhaps the French captain's strange gifts fired him, for it was to him that they had been given. The Verdun party consisted of the four of them and five newly-captured merchant masters: nine captives, escorted by nine gendarmes.

The escape scheme was ingenious but simple. They began at once to study the mentality of their guards, and they found them to be cheerful fellows, responding to cheerfulness in others. At the first night's halt they were billeted in an inn, all eighteen of them, two to a bed in one large room. Before turning in, the conspirators used some of the French captains' cash to order a generous supply of mulled wine, which they shared equally all round, prisoners and gaolers alike: and all turned in, apparently hilariously happy. Next night precisely the same programme was followed with, however, one difference. Whitehurst mixed the last round of drinks, and quietly dropped his opium pills into every glass except his own and Jackson's. All went to bed, and sixteen of them were soon snoring. The other two, who were occupying one bed, now opened the window and simply dropped out. Evidently the pills were potent, because, true to form, 'Whitehurst moved about more like an elephant than a human being', and (in making the necessary jump of 12 feet) 'came of course to the ground like the animal above-mentioned'. But all was well. No gendarme stirred and none followed.

They made for Granville, the little port at the base of the Cotentin peninsula. There Jackson had a friend. In the hospital at Brest they had met a certain Danish 'captain', a member of that odd profession which had sprung directly from Napoleon's Berlin Decrees and the consequent British Orders in Council. He was a sort of licensed smuggler, winked at by both belligerents. He had taken a fancy to Jackson, and had promised to help him if he could get as far as Granville. Here he would either take him on board his own ship or find some other ship for him. Unfortunately, however, he had taken an unreasoning dislike to Whitehurst who, with the best will in the world, was always putting his foot in it. For him the 'captain' vowed he would do nothing.

They reached Granville after some days, aided by two circumstances which may as well be explained at once, because they applied to almost all British escapers. First, they found a widespread disposition on the part of the countryfolk to help them, partly out of sheer pity, partly because, unlike Napoleon, the peasants had never learnt to hate individual Britons, but also, partly, because—especially in out-lying provinces—they had not much use for Napoleon and what he stood for. This friendly disposition of the land-workers was, of course, much more apparent in some parts than in others. It was especially valuable to our fugitives in the Straits area, still more in Normandy, and even more still in Brittany: also in the north-eastern fringes of the 'new' France, and, naturally, in overrun countries like Holland.

The second circumstance which was to prove, again and again, the salvation of our fugitives was the French Conscription Law, whereby recruits for Napoleon's armies were, at fixed periods, selected by ballot, the lucky ones escaping for the time, the unlucky ones instantly marched off. That ballot, especially in anti-Napoleonic areas, was quite the most abhorred institution in France: and, once their names were drawn, a very large number of the wretched conscripts thought of little but running for it at the first possible moment. There were always, therefore, many deserters about; youths for the most part whom the ordinary peasants pitied, and cherished almost as though they were their own relatives, as indeed they well might be. These poor creatures, frightened, hunted, hungry, were to be found all over the country, in such numbers that, when a countryman saw a furtive, suspicious figure creeping along a hedge or lurking in his barn, he leapt to the conclusion that it was a conscript on the run, and, whenever he dared (for it was a serious crime to harbour a deserter) protected, fed and concealed him as best he could. Our runaways soon discovered this, since they were themselves so often mistaken for them: and they were not slow to keep up the pretence.

It even solved to some extent the problem of the language. If in the west, the escaper could explain his odd accent by saying that he hailed from German-speaking Alsace: if in Alsace, that he came from the deep south. In the present case, however, this last advantage did not assist our escapers so much because Whitehurst had not been five years a prisoner for nothing, and spoke French, Jackson says, as well as, if not better than, he spoke English.

On reaching the smuggler's house, Jackson went in alone, and found the smuggler in bed, suffering from dropsy. He still vowed he would do nothing for Whitehurst, but Jackson returned next day with the midshipman, on his best behaviour and eager to conciliate the sick man. There ensued a minor tragedy. The Dane asked Jackson to empty his slop-pail, but Whitehurst, seeing a chance to curry favour, seized the utensil and, without looking out, flung the contents through the window. They landed on the head of the governor of Granville who chanced to be passing—at least, so Jackson says; but he is always partial to a good story. Anyway, the episode ended their chances with the 'captain', who turned them out of the house.

That night they slid down the walls of Granville on a rope and reached Avranches next day. Here they were befriended by two elderly school-mistresses who passed them on to a male friend at Caen. From here it might seem a simple matter to find, if necessary to steal, a boat and make a dash for England. But it was not. The French Government, they learned, was wise to that move: and well it might be since boat-stealing was much the commonest method used by its own prisoners escaping from England. A very close watch, therefore, was kept on all vessels, and not even natives were allowed to sleep on board. So our officers, after many fruitless attempts, just went to earth in the house of their friend in Caen, and remained there fourteen months. Only twice during that time did Jackson venture out; once when Napoleon came to Caen, and he mingled with the welcoming crowd; once when they persuaded the skipper of a small coaster to take them on a trip to Dieppe and back. They were very near freedom then. If only they had encountered a British ship of any kind! But no. 'Our good genius was absent, and no English vessel was even seen.'

As the spring of 1811 began to stir, Jackson's patience gave out. Whitehurst—the linguist—was sent out to reconnoitre, and he returned with the news of several fair-sized fishing-boats lying some way out, and still unoccupied at night. Waiting therefore only for a favourable wind and tide, they walked by night nine miles to the place, stripped, and swam to a tiny flat-bottomed boat anchored fairly close inshore. In this they rowed as quietly as possible to one of the larger vessels. But poor Whitehurst lived up to his reputation once more, and contrived to ram it violently: whereupon up jumped six lusty fishermen who grabbed them, dragged them roughly ashore, half-naked, and handed them over to the authorities: a sad end to a gallant adventure.

Now their faces were set for Verdun again—and farther than Verdun. To avoid travelling there in chains, they had to admit that they were not French deserters, whose fate was always such. But it was a choice of evils because by law—the same in France as in Britain —the recaptured prisoner had no rights at all. If an officer, he forfeited all his officer privileges: he could not be given parole, and he would be sent in England to the hulks, in France to one of the punishment fortresses. Nor, though they escaped the indignity of chains, could they expect a comfortable journey. Their road-mates were convicts fettered together. With them, every night, they were thrown into common gaols—large single rooms, filthy, crowded to suffocation, with one heavily padlocked door and one window, high up and barred. Here they fed, and slept on benches covered with a thin layer of straw and (as Jackson minutely describes) with a rather thicker layer of lice. (In the more luxurious billets like tumbledown barns the lice gave place to armies of fleas.) The food, thin slushy soup, was served out of doors in large kids, and there were never nearly enough spoons—sometimes, indeed, only one. 'I never see', is Jackson's comment, 'a number of hungry pigs being fed now, but the spectacle recalls to my mind the scene in the prison yard.'

The journey took two months, the travellers being sometimes so weak that long halts were necessary. Rather surprisingly, he acquits the gendarmes of calculated brutality. Under no circumstance was any prisoner on the road allowed to lie down: but that, one of the guards told him, was because they knew he would never get up again. They reached Verdun at last: and, taken before the authorities, Jackson had the greatest difficulty in convincing them that he was an officer. 'My boots were toeless; my trousers had broken into instalments; my shirt was a curiosity; my coat a model of good ventilation.'

It was as they expected. They were doomed for a further journey— to Bitche, seven days' march on through hilly country. But before they started, the incorrigible Jackson actually made three separate attempts to get away. In one of them he was at large for two days: but they knew him by now, and he really had no chance. So off they went once more, the column consisting exclusively of *mauvais sujets*, runaways who had failed. The authorities were taking no risks with this batch. All were handcuffed in pairs, the cuffs (he says) being particularly small and painful; and a long chain was passed through each pair of cuffs to keep them all together. Escape was impossible, even for Jackson.

So they reached Bitche. We shall hear of both our officers again: of Jackson in the future, but of Whitehurst only of his past. His bids for freedom were over; and who can wonder? He had now spent nearly two years in being hunted, not to mentioned nearly five in captivity. During his sojourn at Bitche he had one consolation. The Admiralty, by special promotion, made him a lieutenant. But he remained a captive to the end.

Jackson, on the other hand, was quite untamed and, after several attempts, got clean away from Bitche itself, and from France, by a device as ingenious and as simple as opium pills, yet demanding much greater nerve.

V. MASTER'S MATE

The men who, in the Royal Navy, went by the name of Master's Mates were a peculiarly British anomaly. They might be one of two kinds: first, the assistants (i.e. mates) of the navigating officer (i.e. master); comparatively humble characters on board, seeing that the master himself was not a commissioned officer. More often than not in Napoleon's war, however, our master's mates were senior midshipmen occupying posts intermediate between midshipmen and commissioned lieutenants. Indeed, but for the fact that they held no commission, they were the equivalents of our modern sub-lieutenants: that is, personages of some mark in their ships, and of recognized officer status. Unfortunately for them, however, they were not known or recognized by the French, who had in their service only the equivalents of our inferior sort. These they regarded, rightly too, as inferior petty officers of lower-deck status, equivalent to an army corporal, and as such entitled to no officer status at all. This was very hard on our senior sort who, though they regarded themselves as super-midshipmen, found themselves treated, when captured, as mere seamen.

This was the principal grievance of young Donat Henchy O'Brien,

4. CAPTAIN JAHLEEL BRENTON, RN
From miniature attributed to Smith of Barbados

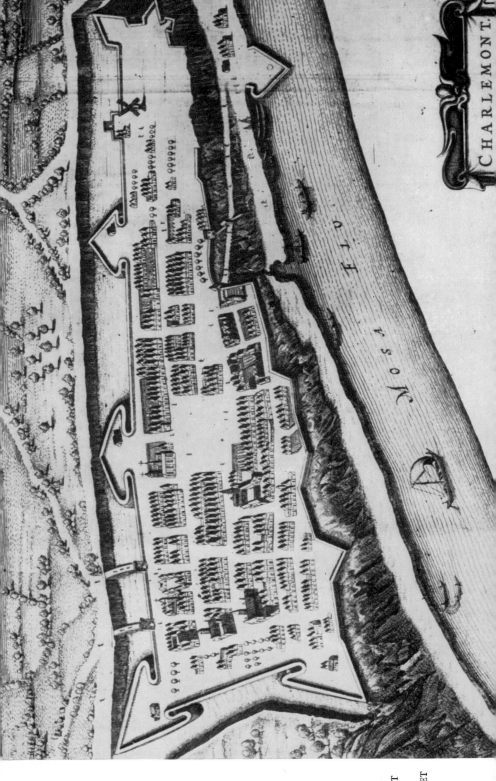

CHARLEMONT.

Flu. Moss.

master's mate of the *Hussar*, wrecked near Ushant on February 8, 1804. The captain (Philip Wilkinson), with more than doubtful propriety, went off in the only seaworthy boat and got clean away: but the rest of the ship's company, by a magnificent feat of seamanship on the part of the boat commanders (of whom O'Brien was one), made Brest harbour in rickety fishing-smacks, and, exhausted, surrendered to the warships lying there.

Three accounts of their journey to captivity survive, and all bear witness to the fact, already noted in Jackson's story, that the ordinary French naval officer could still behave like a gentleman, even if, in our British sense, he was not one. Arriving half-drowned and numb with cold, both officers and men were received with marked humanity, on board the French ships and in the hospital: and they were sent on their way well fitted out with clothes and cash. When mustered for the road, however, they were separated. The officers, including the midshipmen and even the first-class volunteers—as we should say naval cadets—were sent off direct for Verdun, and seem to have suffered no special hardships and no unbearable insults.

It was far otherwise with Donat O'Brien and a fellow master's mate named Mahoney. They were separated from the officers and marched off with the men. They protested: so did the first lieutenant, left in charge by the captain's defection. But it was no use. They were, the guard maintained, *adjutants; sous-officiers*, the equivalents of corporals, or at best sergeants. So off they had to go.

This was no real hardship, it may be thought. Officers should share their men's discomforts. This is true; but it needs no great effort of imagination to understand the feelings of Mr O'Brien and Mr Mahoney. They were young, ambitious, and accustomed to the tight precedence of ship life. In that closed shop they were somebodies, being the little lords of the midshipmen's mess. And there was young Sutton, only rated reefer the other day: there was that dog's-body Mascal, the captain's clerk: and yes—believe it or not—there was even that lowest form of marine life, the newly-joined Volunteer Hopkinson— all trotting off with the lieutenants! And here were they, master's mates, no less; men who might any day ship the white lapels, treated as ordinary seamen and boys, and marched off, not even to Verdun where all the officers went, but to Givet, the men's depot. It was, we may be quite sure, much more than the prospect of greater hardship which hurt O'Brien. Before we are through with him we shall find that he could take almost anything that was given him in the way of hardship, and without complaining. What he was suffering from now was the outrage to his boyish pride: after all, he was only 19.[1]

For the first few days the two parties followed the same road, and the mates were allowed, as a favour, to walk with the officers. But even this was gall to them because, when the day's stint was done,

> the *officers* were allowed to go to a tavern, and *we . . .* as *adjutants*, were conducted with the ship's company to the common gaol. . . . We were placed among criminals and malefactors of every description, where we found ourselves covered with vermin in spight of every effort used to avoid it.

After Laval, the parties separated, the officers for Verdun, the men, with the protesting *adjutants*, for Rouen, en route for the fortress of Charlemont overlooking Givet. At Rouen, again in the common gaol, they were allowed to order food from outside, and the old woman who brought it had the effrontery to demand—and to get—rent for the use of her spoons! Indeed, they were constantly put upon. Money would buy things, as it will the world over. But it was demoralizing to be cheated and yet to have no remedy. Thus, also at Rouen, the gaoler offered them a night's rest outside the gaol, and they had it, but only by paying for two nights' lodging. At this rate their purses soon became very light. Moreover, though allowed 11 sous (5½d) travelling money ('and the youngest mid had 50!') they often did not see even that because, at the end of a stage, the departing guard would make off with it, and the new one would know nothing about it. At Amiens they were cheated again; this time, with shame it must be recorded, by an Englishwoman whose husband, a Mr S. Pratt, kept an eating-house nearby. Coming to see them, she '*shed tears* at seeing the distressed condition of her poor countrymen', promising to procure them, at once, '*poor dear creatures*', a lovely dinner. It consisted, when it arrived an hour later, of a minute leg of mutton, with no garnishings whatever. She had promised to return next morning to visit her '*dear, dear countrymen*'; but, instead, there appeared her manservant who demanded payment on a scale exceeding even that of the French thieves: and they had to pay.

On the other hand, it must be recorded that the officer in charge of

---

[1] This officer's escape record is one of the most stirring of the whole war, and one of the best known. It was written by himself, first as a series of 'naval bulletins' in the *Naval Chronicle* (Vol. 28, p. 338, to Vol. 31, p. 389), then in book form under the title *My Adventures during the Late War*, London, 1814: reprinted and enlarged in two vols., 1839. Extracts quoted here are mostly from the original 'bulletins'.

them on this part of their march was a humane man. Just before he left them, he gave them a slap-up breakfast at Albert. But at Bapaume he had to go, and, genuinely affected, 'literally shed tears'. The mates all but did the same, and with better reason. O'Brien gives him no name, but surely it began with 'de'.

So they journeyed on, usually lodged in gaols, but occasionally billeted out—and cheated. At Cambrai, itself a prison-depot, the men were put in the *souterrains*—the dungeons—but not the mates. At length, through bad weather and over shocking roads, they reached the ship's company's destination, Charlemont, the stronghold of Givet. They were all exhausted. They had been marching for thirty-eight days—'near 700 miles from Brest', says O'Brien. No doubt it seemed all that to the weary, dispirited lads. But, sitting in an easy chair and measuring the distance on a mere map, I make it, by the route they took, a bare 500.

Here they remained for nearly four months. They were allowed to rent cheap rooms in the town, but their finances were becoming desperate. Their fivepence-halfpenny travelling allowance ceased as soon as they were off the road, and, they discovered to their horror, their anomalous status of master's mate, while it served to keep them from actually quartering with the men, also meant that they could not draw the men's daily ration of a pound of meat, and that their allowance was—like the men's—a penny-halfpenny a day.

Though they did not know it at first, however, they had a champion, working indefatigably for them. Hearing at Verdun of their plight, Captain Brenton first secured for them their right to the men's ration: then, though not without a prolonged and tedious struggle, persuaded the commandant at Verdun that master's mates were indeed officers, and therefore entitled to such welcome as Verdun could afford. They heard the good news on July 16th, and instantly set out: but what made them happy beyond words was that they were described on their *feuille de route* as 'officers of high rank on parole'; and they were treated accordingly. So, after another week of the usual rooking by landladies and hoteliers—which seemed almost fun, since there was now no talk of gaols—they passed through the gates of Verdun on July 23rd, and 'were received by Captain Brenton, our officers and countrymen in the most handsome manner'. The other *Hussar* officers had been there four months.

VI. MIDSHIPMAN

The outraged *amour propre* of our master's mate did not, perhaps, make him a very good travelling companion. Fortunately, we shall meet him again, when he is not brooding upon his wrongs; and then we shall be able to correct any prejudice we may have formed against him. Meanwhile, we turn to three midshipmen, not rated master's mate and so free of the inhibitions which preyed upon O'Brien: in fact, three lads singularly free of any inhibitions at all. One, whose narrative enables us to follow their fortunes, was Edward Boys, whose capture in August 1803 and early treatment have already been noticed (pp. 66-7). Another was one John Murray, about whom little is known beyond what Boys tells us. The third, however, was that same Frederick Whitehurst whose later adventures have already been described: but a younger Whitehurst than the one we met before, less war-weary, less travel-stained, with less experience of life's hardships and fortune's tricks: already a handsome, lovable, colt-like youth, but with all youth's unspoilt freshness. It is impossible not to sympathize with these obviously attractive lads: tough, healthy, resilient and refusing to be down-hearted or cowed: simple-minded, philosophic, cheerful in spite of their misfortunes: ever determined to see the bright side of things if there was one, and, if there was not, to manufacture one.

Though ill-treated at first, and (without undue complaint) made to suffer the hardships of their men, they soon reached a district where the French commandant was *ancien régime*. This worthy gentleman expressed surprise that they were not used as officers and, on his own responsibility, gave them a sort of temporary parole, accepting their word, without anything written, that they would not attempt to escape. At this early date there was no talk of Verdun: in fact, they set off in the opposite direction and, after a while, reached Toulouse. Here another gentleman held command, and he confirmed their parole; indeed, improved it, and that in a most gentlemanly way which instantly won their hearts:

> The General, on being asked if our paroles were to be signed, replied, 'No: a British officer values his honour too much to render his signature necessary'.

He was a good psychologist. The midshipmen were delighted, not so much at securing officer privileges, few of which they actually obtained, as at being regarded as officers, and trusted. 'With what feelings of pride', Boys goes on, 'His Britannic Majesty's midshipmen resolved to merit the eulogium of the enemy!'

How they merited it only confirms our respect for them; for they were, on the whole, badly treated. All was well while they remained at Toulouse. They were given the 25-sous allowance (about one shilling) instead of the penny-halfpenny upon which the ratings were expected to subsist—indeed, he tells us, the men suffered so much at Toulouse that many tried to run. But none succeeded in getting clear away, save one. Truly, virtue is not always its own reward. This man, seeking some time before to elude the press-gangs, had fraudulently acquired an old American passport; and it was this which now enabled him to escape.

Their next move was not even yet for Verdun, but for the little town of Auch, forty miles to the west. Their party was now eleven strong, all but one of them midshipmen, and all on parole. Such was the surviving influence of the *ancien régime* in these remote southern provinces that they travelled from Toulouse with no guard at all: and they took no advantage whatever of the privilege. At Auch, too, they were happy, the midshipmen lodging with a 'ci-devant nobleman . . . who possessed all the distinguishing qualities of the gentleman'. Here they were allowed to ramble over the countryside at will: it was pretty oasis in the arid desert of Napoleonic France.

Then, on December 11th, came the order for Verdun. Instantly the oasis became a mirage, and vanished. A heavy escort was provided: every effort was made to remind them that they were prisoners.

> The next day, reaching Montauban after a tedious march, we were drawn up in line in front of the town-hall and formally inspected by the commissary who, with a studied politeness, enticed us into a prison by the most artful piece of duplicity intended no doubt to wound our feelings. He was, however, disappointed of his hopes of annoyance, for we could not refrain from a general burst of laughter at the simple manner in which we had been entrapped.

Here is the true 'Boys' touch—since we have got to take what comes, let us take it with a smile. What came that time, however, was not exactly a smiling matter:

> On entering the room, which had been formed by the spade, we found the barred windows but a few feet above the surface of the water; it was only on one side that we had either light or air, and this attended by the refreshing vapours of the river, and the cooling dampness of the surrounding earth, oozing saltpetre from every pore.

They complained, but were informed that this was a special order from the local commandant who, having been confined in Portchester Castle during the late war, 'had sworn to retaliate'. They were kept in this hole for two nights.

They reached Cahors on December 15th, and next morning there began an interlude which only showed the wisdom of that *ancien régime* general who had put the Young Gentlemen on their honour. When the time came to start, the whole guard was dead drunk. The party therefore set out without them, and for the next five days proceeded entirely alone. They were then overtaken by a very scared posse of gendarmes who 'from a state of consternation on account of the loss of their prisoners, became as much elated when they found we were all present'. This after their experience in the water-logged hole at Montauban where, by every known convention of warfare, no officer on parole should be incarcerated! Surely, in the eyes of all but the most honourable and punctilious of gentlemen, this could have been held to cancel any parole contract previously made. But Boys and his friends were just that—truth-respecting Young Gentlemen who had told the dear old boy at Auch that he could trust them. It would have taken much worse places than that to induce them to let him down.

So the relentless journey continued, in very cold weather. They kept in wonderful spirits; and, though they made no attempt to escape, it must be admitted that they were sometimes a bit of a handful to their rather pedestrian keepers, whose brand of humour (if it existed) was noticeably different from that of his Britannic Majesty's midshipmen. One thoughtless prank bade fair to land them in serious trouble. Once, when they were being cheated as usual over the price of food and some of them were vainly protesting,

> I entered an adjoining bedroom, and observing on the mantelpiece various little images in plaster of Paris, in the midst of which was the bust of the adored Buonaparte, and no one being near, I could not resist the temptation of placing its head downwards in a vessel which was no ornament to a mantelpiece.

Nothing happened for the moment: but, ten days later and some hundreds of miles farther on, they were suddenly, and rudely, thrown into prison in earnest. On inquiring the reason, they were informed that a fully-accredited *courier de la République* had been galloping after them day and night with an official order for their instant arrest. And why?

'You are in prison by a counter-order lately received for having put Buonaparte's head in a *pot-de-chambre.*' A silent gaze of astonishment was followed by sudden gusts of laughter which so thundered through the prison as to drown the voice of the incensed orator. . . . The louder he spoke the more boisterous was our mirth until, frantic with rage, he drew his sword, rushed forward and thrust it through the grated hole in the door, stamped, and swore in such a foaming passion that, when the storm of derision was over, he could scarcely articulate.

On nearing Paris, they were informed that it was too great a privilege for people like them to enter it, and they were sent on a wide detour before resuming their way to Verdun. Many times on the road their various guards tried to insist upon eating meals with them, and upon them paying for the 'privilege' of being escorted. But these bright boys simply, and quite bluntly, refused to do either, and always won their point: why it is hard to say, since these things were certainly customary. Everybody knew that British midshipmen were notoriously poor, and simply could not pay. But it is tempting to think, also, that it would have taken an exceptionally inhuman creature to proceed to extremities with people like Boys and Whitehurst, and that their wonderful carriage in adversity touched an unaccustomed chord in the hearts of many of their guardians.

At last, on January 21, 1804, five and a half months after capture, they reached their goal. There, coming under the protection of the ever-vigilant Brenton, they were granted the modified parole reserved for their class. Since leaving Toulon they had walked, Boys reckons, 950 miles—much nearer the mark than O'Brien's 700 from Brest. Like the master's mate they arrived cheerful: but with this difference —they had been cheerful all the way.

One more midshipman's journey to Verdun must be briefly recorded: and, if excuse be needed for so stressing these 'gun-room officers', it may be recalled that nearly two out of every three naval-officer prisoners came out of midshipmen's messes. This one's name was Robert Bastard James, and, when we meet him, he was just 16. He had been put in charge of a small and crank prize, with a crew of five very poor-grade men and one boy, but without any navigational instruments at all. With all his men drunk, he was caught in a gale off the mouth of the Loire, had to run before it, and hit shoal-water. With the crew of another retaken prize, he and his men were put into a *chasse-marée* to be taken by river to Nantes. His narrative[1] throughout is conspicuous for its modesty; yet he must have been no ordinary lad, even for those days of early development and responsibility at sea. Though still half-drowned, and guarded by a dozen veteran soldiers, he had not been afloat an hour before he had contrived to surprise and disarm the guard, and to make for the open sea. Such initiative deserved a better fate: but it failed. A French privateer spied what was happening, overtook them and brought them back.

His march into bondage, therefore, began under the worst auspices. He was a *mauvais sujet*, and could look for no privileges. What made things even worse was that his men, arrived (as they thought) in the land where all men were free and equal, refused to obey him and decided, when approached by the French, to desert to them. Young James, hearing of it just in time, ran straight into the office of the general commanding at Nantes, and not only told the men, most forcibly, what he thought of them, but also, quite fearlessly, told General Dumuy what he thought of him, for trying to tamper with the men's loyalty. Surprisingly, perhaps, he won both his battles. The men went back to their chains: the general, clearly impressed by the courage and stinging words of such a stripling, acquiesced.

The horrors of the long march will not be told in detail. Suffice it to record that they were worse than any yet recounted. At Melun, in the darkness of a fetid gaol, they found themselves engaged in a pitched battle with the criminal occupants who demanded a 'footing' from them. James was not the lad to cave in, and a tremendous fight ensued, the weapons being wooden sabots and stones tied in handkerchiefs. There were twelve Britons to twice as many Frenchmen; but again this resolute young officer won, helped, this time, by a stroke of luck. When things were looking at their blackest, the door opened and nine more British prisoners entered: and the day was his.

Hustled on through a violent heat-wave, the boy's strength at last gave out, and he reached Verdun dumped like a sack at the bottom of a farm-cart. But still, at the cart's tail, trudged five sullen seamen and one boy, still, apparently, preferring their chains to the lash of a 16-year-old's tongue.

[1] MS. BM. Add. 38,886. Much of it is printed in Edward Fraser's *Napoleon the Gaoler*, London, 1914.

THE ROAD TO VERDUN

VII. MERCHANT SERVICE OFFICER

We are through with commissioned officers and aspiring commissioned officers, but not quite with 'officers'. There remain the stories of two merchant skippers, a strongly contrasted pair.

The first was Peter Bussell,[1] and he was master and part-owner of the *Dove of Weymouth*, an unarmed trading-sloop of 61 tons and a crew of two besides himself. He was 32 years old. He was hugging the south coast when caught off the Needles by the French lugger *Deux Frères*, a privateer from Boulogne armed with four carriage-guns and with a crew of sixty men. So there could be no argument. To follow his journey would be to anticipate much of what is to come concerning the tribulations of ordinary seamen: for, on the road anyway, he was treated as though he were one. There is never a word about officer treatment, no talk of parole: indeed no hint that he ever expected either. It must be admitted, too, that Peter was not a very colourful character. Compared with people like Jackson or O'Brien, Boys or James, he is almost cowlike in his placidity, a man of peace if ever there was one. 'It is all very tiresome', is his invariable philosophy, 'but there it is. I must grin [not laugh like Boys] and bear it [not end it like Jackson].' So throughout his captivity, which lasted from 1806 to the end, he made no effort to escape: he did not even contemplate it, but actually turned a disapproving eye upon any prisoner who did. This attitude, in one of Bussell's kidney, is quite natural. To him the escaper was simply a nuisance who only succeeded in depriving him of his own small privileges.

Yet his story fills an important gap in ours, because it reveals the kind of life led by that very large group of captives, the merchant-navy officers. These, he makes clear, fell into three classes. The first, numerically small, consisted of a few masters of big ships like East Indiamen. They were often people of considerable substance, and even of social account; and they were treated accordingly. They had officer privileges, were allowed parole, and permitted to reside at Verdun. The rest were much more numerous and divided about equally. All depended upon the tonnage of their vessel; and the magic number was 80. 'Over-80's' and 'under-80's' are his constant theme, and no wonder. Poor Bussell was only a '61', and therefore, where prisoner benefits were concerned, nothing at all. He began to feel the

[1] *The Diary of Peter Bussell*, Ed. G. A. Turner (his great-grandson), London, 1931.

pinch at once when he discovered that the over-80's were allowed

> 25 livres (£1 4s 2d) per month, while all those that are under that
> tonnage receive no more than the smallest lad in the depot. I am
> sorry to say that I am one of the unfortunate number whose pay
> is the small sum of one sol and a half (three farthings) per diem.[1]

That is, is 10½d a month!

If the under-80's were nobodies, the over-80's (as opposed to the
top-grade few) were clearly of little more account. He never makes it
very clear what their position was in regard to parole, but he does
show that, in fact, they did obtain a limited type of it. Their relative
affluence enabled them, once at their depot, to take outside lodgings
(in places where that privilege was allowed): and, of course, before
they were permitted to do that, they had to sign a promise that they
would not attempt to run—one, it must be admitted, which sat but
lightly on many of them. Actually, however, Bussell also was
often accorded the same privilege, when he could afford it. In this
respect, then, there was not perhaps so much difference after
all. But the difference between £1 4s 2d and is 10½d was real
enough.

We shall meet this long-suffering little man again: and, for all his
placidity, he will have important testimony to bear. Let us leave him
for the moment trudging patiently along the 334-mile road from
Cherbourg to Arras through bleak March weather; often wet through
and foot-sore, but not chained; often 'hungry as half-starved hounds'
and always grossly overcharged, but not complaining unduly.
When driven along in a manner obviously brutal, he comments
sadly,

> Our new guard did not behave with that humanity which they
> ought to do.

The other merchant skipper, a striking contrast to Bussell, was
Seacombe Ellison, master and part-owner of the brig *Rachel* of
Liverpool, of 240 tons and carrying 16 guns and 35 men: an over-80
man therefore, by a wide margin, enjoying his 30-sous travelling
money and his £1 4s 2d (he says £1 5s 0d) monthly allowance.
Socially, too, he was much above Bussell, consorting in captivity not
only with his fellows of 'Verdun' status, but with midshipmen—
Boys was a great friend of his—and even lieutenants RN. In fine, he
was a top-class merchant captain. He was also as lively and enter-

[1] Bussell, op. cit., p. 29.

prising as poor Bussell was meek and lethargic; and he had, before he had done, a fine escape record.[1]

On December 2, 1803, homeward bound from Honduras, with most of her best men pressed out of her, and battered by violent gales, the *Rachel* entered the Channel, and ran right into the arms of the French privateer *Vaillant*, Captain Etienne of Bordeaux, carrying thirty guns and 300 men. This powerful vessel had recently taken the *Sir Edward Hamilton* East Indiaman, bringing home (though he himself escaped) no less a person than General Sir David Baird. For the *Rachel* resistance was out of the question.

Ellison was well treated, both by his captor and almost all the way to Verdun. The only exceptional moment was his first night ashore, when he and his fellow-prisoners (five masters and thirteen mates) were lodged in a filthy gaol. But, here as ever, money could buy relaxations, and Ellison was not short of it. They were put on their parole, given a cart for their baggage, and sent on their way on foot, but with very few guards: often indeed only one. Nor were they hurried, reaching Verdun on January 28, 1804, after thirty-six days' march. Once there, still granted parole, apparently without question, they were given good lodgings in the town. The variations in the treatment accorded to captives was clearly great, but not, probably, quite fortuitous. This party, of course, had the luck to fall into the hands of kindly guards. But also they had plenty of cash; and, unlike most of the prouder naval officers, who always stood up for their rights, they were prepared to spend their money on securing their comforts without too close an inquiry into the rights of the case. More important still, most, if not all, of this group from the *Rachel* and, still more, from the East Indiaman, were the *élite* of the merchant service; substantial, well-turned-out men who *looked* gentlemanly: and that was so often a passport to gentle treatment.

VIII. CIVILIAN

Unlike all our previous companions on the road to Verdun, John Spencer Stanhope was not a service man at all, and certainly not a merchant skipper, though possibly, at home, a militia officer, since in his baggage there was a full suit of regimentals for use on formal

[1] He tells his own story in *Prison Scenes*, London, 1838, a work at once exciting and thought-provoking. He has, however, the regrettable habit of calling many of his characters by the first letters of their names only—'K - - -', 'W - - -' or 'B - - -'.

occasions. (This, it would seem, was the uniform of a major, or lieutenant-colonel, of Yeomanry, but the vexed 'militia' question is never broached, by either party.) But though he was not an officer and gentleman, he was certainly a gentleman: a survivor of the class 'T.G.': 23 years old, well-off and of very good family, and an enthusiastic amateur archaeologist. In January 1810, for all that the war was already seven years old, he set out from England simply to travel and enjoy himself, as though there were no such thing as war at all. Having ambled around Spain for some time, he decided to make his way to Greece, and, as a first step, somewhat imprudently took a passage for Palma in Majorca with a villainous-looking Gibraltar privateer captain. His friends warned him of the risks he ran; and their advice (which he did not take) proved sound. In the coolest way imaginable Captain Constantine proceeded to sail with him, not to British-held Palma but straight to French-held Barcelona, at which port Stanhope landed still fully under the conviction that he was in Majorca. The French military authorities, almost as surprised as he was, promptly arrested and gaoled him, not believing his explanation, which must have sounded fantastic indeed. In fact, they took him for a spy.

T.G.s, however, were still oddly privileged people; and Stanhope had influential friends, not only in Britain but also in Spain and France. Not liking his Spanish prison at all, he demanded release and, when it was refused, asked to be sent to France. To this they agreed, and off he went, escorted by an army some 10,000 strong which happened just then to be going home. Its commander willingly allowed him parole and, on the road, treated him well: exactly, in fact, as he treated his own officers. But, while in Spain, he had to walk most of the way because the cart provided for him would not accommodate both himself and his luggage. No T.G. ever dreamed of travelling light. Once in France, however, he went more or less as he liked, sometimes on foot, sometimes by diligence.

One has the impression—and he had it too—that the French military authorities were indifferent as to whether he escaped or not. On countless occasions it would have been easy. The Commander-in-Chief in Catalonia, the Scot-descended Marshal Macdonald, clearly expected him to run: indeed, practically arranged it for him. But young Stanhope, civilian though he was, had an exalted sense of what was due from him, and a veneration for his parole which no service man could have bettered. So, though various people kept on tempting him, making flight ridiculously easy, he steadfastly refused. It was a long trek from Barcelona to Verdun, but he could take his time. Besides, he was young and strong, and rather fond of walking. He fed well as a rule and slept well too, so that, by and large, he enjoyed the experience, though he resented his loss of freedom. He reached Verdun in January 1811, and, of course, resided where he liked.[1]

IX. SEAMAN (OLD SHELLBACK)

It is a very far cry from Stanhope the Travelling Gentleman to James Choyce, a hard-boiled sailorman with eleven exceedingly chequered years of sea-life behind him. In 1804 he was, it is true, only 27 years old: but he had already seen enough adventure, mostly very unpleasant, to satisfy a dozen ordinary men. His career illustrates the futility, already mentioned, of trying to distinguish between merchant and naval seamen. He had been both, and was to be both again: and that not only in British ships but in enemy ships too. He had been captured quite half a dozen times, and just as often escaped, from Spanish gaols and Spanish and British warships. He knew Spanish so well that, for all his flaming red hair, he could pass for one anywhere, and no questions asked. Such a career does not conduce to refinement, but it does breed a kind of stoical philosophy without which no human being could have survived experiences which were everyday occurrences to Choyce. His book,[2] however, reveals a basically sound man, with a natural flair for writing, though he and his ten brothers and sisters only had, as he says, 'A.B.C. for our education and the wide world for our inheritance'.

It would not be in order to outline his earlier experiences. We must begin with his capture in the West Atlantic on March 4, 1804. He was then a hand on board a South Atlantic whaler, the *Diana*, homeward bound. Her captor was the French privateer *Blonde* of Bordeaux, whose haul, in this one cruise, serves to show how formidable was the enemy's threat to our shipping, and why so many merchant-service people were prisoners. When she reached home she had on board (including Choyce) the crews of five British merchantmen, two privateers and one naval escort. She tried to disgorge her accumulation of captives at Passages. But the Spaniards, not yet in the war, refused to allow them to be marched overland to France. All the prisoners, therefore, officers RN and MN and all their men

---

[1] Much of his lively *Journal* is edited by his daughter, A. M. W. Pickering, and incorporated in her *Memoirs*, London, 1903.

[2] *The Log of a Jack Tar*, London, 1905.

—over 200 of them—were thrust into the hold of one exceedingly small schooner, and escorted by French gunboats to St Jean de Luz. That trip rivals the horrors of the Black Hole. In their fight against the intolerable, airless heat, the unfortunates stripped stark naked. But still, when unpacked on arrival, twenty-six of them were unconscious and apparently lifeless. Mercifully, however, the trip had been short, and all revived.

The journey which followed, for all that it is recounted without a trace of hyperbole or self-pity, makes ghastly reading. Once, soon after the start, Choyce and two others, Jerseymen, made a bold bid for freedom. They were still near the Pyrenees, and reckoned that, could they but cross them, they could go to earth in Spain. It was brave to the verge of foolhardiness, and it nearly came off. Posing (as usual) as French deserters, they received intermittent aid from the country-folk on the northern slopes of the mountains and, though in imminent danger of death by exposure, succeeded in reaching the highest crest of the Pyrenees, after sinking several times up to their armpits in soft snow. Exhausted, they dragged themselves to what they thought was the frontier. But it was the last French military post; and 'here ended our delusive hopes of liberty'.

They were hurried back to rejoin their party. In just one wry sense they were luckier than officers: they could not expiate the crime of running by being put into chains. In common with the whole party they had been in chains all the time. Every night they were thrown into the local *cachots*, crawling with vermin. At a place called Souillac, one of his comrades was stricken with fever and could not go on. The rest implored the guard to send him to hospital, but the only answer was that hospitals were not for *canaille* like him. He was therefore placed, chained, in the middle of the procession and dragged along by the others. After one more march, the wretch could not even get up, and was beaten as he lay with the flat of a gendarme's sword, until even that worthy had to admit that he was not shamming. A cart was then procured and he was thrown into it, his companions pulling it along.

Though hailing from no very exalted layer of society, and treated like beasts, these men still showed in their own fashion a quite remarkable spirit. Indeed, though a native of Finchley can hardly hear the Bow bells, Choyce was near enough to cockneydom to display the more endearing characteristics with which that breed notoriously faces adversity. After a while, to alleviate the monotony of suffering, they began to 'amuse themselves' by 'calling Buonaparte a brigand, a robber and other hard names'. It was a great success. The guard rose beautifully, threatening all sorts of condign punishment. But Choyce's reasoning was sound enough: they could not be worse treated than they were: so why not have a little fun? At the next night's halt, it is true, three of them were chained to the posts supporting the roof. But as there were only three posts, the rest had their little amusement gratis.

Yet Choyce can be bitter at times; and no wonder. Nor is his criticism levelled only at the French. At Orleans a certain Mr Hewitson, a naval (or perhaps an ex-naval) surgeon, was 'commissary' of the British captives there. He came to the gaol to see Choyce's party, and gave them a shirt and a pair of shoes apiece. He escapes the worst of Choyce's vituperation: but Lord Elgin, whom he brought with him, does not. He is violently accused of coming merely to gape at the sufferers, omitting not only to open his purse but even to let drop a word of sympathy. It would be wrong, however, to convict Lord Elgin of heartlessness merely upon this evidence, if only because of another not dissimilar barb which Choyce lets fly, and which we know to be false. He alleges that Captain Brenton, who (he does not deny it) came to see them as soon as they reached Verdun—that Captain Brenton, of all people, deliberately withheld from them the arrears of their miserable travel-money; which, fobbing them off with false promises, he never paid. This of course is quite untrue; and Choyce would have been the first to admit it had he known the facts. He was not uncharitable by nature. What happened, almost certainly, is that Brenton did promise the money and did send it; but that it disappeared into some rapacious pocket before it could reach the prisoners. For it had to be forwarded from Verdun, which was not the place for Choyce and his likes—Verdun, where he met the *détenus'* curricles and *calèches* spanking past him to the races, and was not amused. They went on to Sarrelibre. Indeed, Choyce himself stresses the likelihood of the money disappearing somewhere between Verdun and Sarrelibre, recording that, as a matter of course, every French official conspired to take his pickings of the poor seaman's pittance: no doubt an over-generalization, but unfortunately based on particular facts.

He makes his itinerary 1,089 miles, 'on a diet of bread and water'. It is a little too much, perhaps. But with such light fare within and such heavy chains without, who will complain?

We have not heard the last of Choyce either. He too escaped; ingeniously enough, but by a method unlikely to appeal to the Transport Board's court of honour. But, as he was no officer, that kind of honour was hardly his concern.

X. SEAMAN (YOUNG)

Next, though briefly told, comes the story of another seaman, not a shellback like Choyce, but one fairly recently impressed: and—the warning is necessary at the outset—quite unusually prejudiced in tone. His name was John Wetherell, and his ship—again—the *Hussar*, Captain Wilkinson. It is chiefly because this was his ship that his story is worth including here, because it means that his land-journey to Givet is identical with O'Brien's. Its interest lies in the remarkable contrast between the two accounts, due to the entirely different mental outlooks of the narrators. The master's mate, happy in his ship, was the angry young man ashore, with pride grievously wounded: everything therefore was wrong. The young seaman had had a miserable time in the *Hussar*, and hated his captain ferociously—perhaps (though no doubt he greatly exaggerated) with reason. To him, in fact, life on board was so foul that any other life would be paradise by comparison,[1] so that the discomforts of his winter march are shrugged off like water from a duck's back. O'Brien, accustomed to the best, was experiencing something infinitely worse: Wetherell, to whom the *Hussar* represented the worst, was finding—or, which comes to the same thing, thought he was finding—something very much better. Everyone cheated O'Brien of the little he had: no one cheated Wetherell because he had nothing to be cheated of. External evidence proves that both are describing the same journey: but we should never guess it from what they say.

It has been suggested that Wetherell's original story has been doctored in its modern version. This may or may not be so; but, anyway, its obvious prejudice makes it untrustworthy, even to the verge of untruth. Its author so clearly has an eye to good story-telling, and, for that reason, often seems prepared to sacrifice History upon the altar of Fiction.

XI. SHIP'S BOY

The last involuntary journey to be described was made by the youngest and most junior of our travellers—that same Alexander Stewart who

[1] *The Adventures of John Wetherell*, London, 1954.

was picked up off Brighton beach in January 1805.[1] He had been at
sea for a year or two, but was still only 14. This fact, however, availed
him nothing. He was treated just like the rest: landed at Gravelines,
lodged in the gaol on dirty straw, given bread and water and nothing
else: paraded through the town for the townsfolk to admire his
captors' prowess: marched off to Dunkirk roped to his fellows with
strong cord (not chains this time), and preceded by drummers beating
the Rogues' March: paraded again and lodged in gaol again. Here the
skipper and mate were separated from the crew, and given better
treatment. On the fourth day at Dunkirk, the straw in the cell accidentally caught fire, ignited by the carelessness of their convict companions.
For a long time the gaolers would not open the door, and did so only
when the boy had fainted—a minor incident, no doubt, but one which
serves to bring home to us what a mere child was being called upon
to suffer.

Their road led through Valenciennes, where they found the prisoner
depot full to overflowing, and thence by St Quentin, Rheims and
Chalons to Verdun, *en route* for Sarrelibre. Their treatment was like
Choyce's at first, though never quite so bad: and after the fourth day
they were untied while marching. They had their 3-sous allowance
and a daily pound and a half of coarse bread. Yet the life must have
been cruelly hard for a boy of 14. Twenty-five miles was the normal
stage, their lodging always a gaol with at best a wooden bench to
sleep on and, at worst, the verminous straw on the floor. Long before
the end their shoes had worn out, and for several days they went
barefoot until, as they neared Verdun, replenishments arrived. Who
sent them he does not say; but it must have been the Verdun Relief
Committee or the poor prisoners' guardian angel. None of them
probably, had ever heard of Captain Brenton: yet, somehow, a rumour
passed down the marching line. Something was to happen—something
to be looked forward to—when they reached that (to them) 'expectant
paradise', where they hoped to meet British officers again, get some
money, and help in explaining themselves. 'In none of these respects
were we disappointed.' They were scarcely through the gates before
one of his attendant officers appeared: and before night fell, there he
was himself—Captain Jahleel Brenton, no less.

This new glimpse of that good man must confirm our belief in the
falseness of Choyce's evidence. Already the senior officer had worked
wonders. Among other things he had persuaded the authorities to

[1] See pages 52–3.

113

segregate the boys from the rest, and had established a school for them under trusted petty officers of his own. As soon as he learned that a lad was of the party, he claimed Stewart, as one too young for Sarrelibre. He was successful. The boy was instantly taken from the gaol and sent to join the other boys ('in whose welfare Capt. B. took great interest') in special barracks allotted for the purpose. Here, though supervised with a thoroughness to which he was not accustomed —this was his first experience of the naval petty officers' discipline— he was very happy, especially at being put to school. He was a good, serious-minded boy, and evidently knew what was good for him. Unfortunately, however, some of his school-mates did not, with disastrous results. Either they abused their comparative freedom, or else Brenton fell out with the commandant. He does not know which: but, when we come to a better acquaintance with that commandant, we shall be in a better position to guess. Anyway, the establishment was suddenly broken up after Stewart had been there for only three months, and the lad found himself on the road again—to Sarrelibre, seven days' march away, and, says Alexander, 500 from Gravelines: anyway, cruelly far for a half-starved 14-year-old.

A CONTRAST

Our footsore witnesses often note the mileage from port to prison. What of French captives landed in Britain? There can be no comparison here: only contrast. Verdun is thrice as far from salt water as the most inland spot in the British Isles, and at least a dozen times as far as were any of our principal prison-camps. All our captives were brought to their destinations by water, and all the camps were very close to it. Dartmoor was the farthest: it is some 14 miles as the crow flies from Plymouth, and a weary uphill walk too. But even that was not much more than half of what young Stewart was expected to undertake daily, and for weeks on end. The port for Perth prison was Perth: for Portchester, Portchester by boat or, failing that, Portsmouth, within easy eye-range: for Valleyfield, Bristol, and even for Norman Cross (which looks some way inland), Peterborough, 6 miles, or Yaxley, barely 2; for it was to these places that the boats brought the prisoners. For the hulks, of course, the land-journey was negligible.

We must not, on this account alone, preen ourselves upon our humanity, or necessarily charge the enemy with brutality. The governing factors, on both sides, were evidently geographical. Yet, if any balance-sheet were ever to be struck, the conveyance of prisoners of war from port to prison would have to be shown on the credit side of our account and on the debit side of his. His would be a heavy entry, too. Undoubtedly the mass total of British suffering 'on the road' was immense, and largely unnecessary. A better standard of treatment, though it would no doubt have cost more, in money and in man-power, was quite certainly *possible*. It is no excuse to argue, as Napoleon did more than once, that national resources spent upon prisoners of war are uneconomic, and therefore, in the national interest, to be reduced to a minimum. That is a return to frank barbarism. It is the argument of the primitive savage. It certainly has nothing to do with Equality and the Rights of Man; and still less with the argument it replaced—Vattel's amiable contention that 'prisoners of war, once caught, are not enemies, and therefore on no account to be used worse than is absolutely necessary'.

CHAPTER V

HEADQUARTERS—VERDUN

All roads having led to Verdun, it is time to look at the place; and not only the place but the British community dwelling there from November 1803 to early 1814, when the advance of the Allies from the east caused the hurried evacuation of the depot.

The walled town of Verdun itself was neither large nor important. But its *Citadelle*, or fortress, was both. It had seen much action, sustained many sieges, and it crowned a hill somewhat set back from the left bank of the Meuse. Within the perimeter of its fortifications, besides the defences proper, were several buildings not of immediate military significance. One was the Bishop's Palace, another the convent of St Vannes; and both, in Napoleonic times, had lost their original inhabitants. Another absentee just then was its military garrison, because Verdun, once near the frontier, was now many leagues inside the new France. This meant that palace, convent and military barracks were at the government's disposal for housing prisoners, and for this purpose the two last-named were used. Those captives who either were not allowed, or could not afford, to find accommodation in the town were housed in them. Also, locked up securely in the fortress proper, in some cases below ground or nearly, were those captives considered to have committed crimes, of which much the commonest was attempting to escape.

This complex Citadel stood up well to the west of the river, covering a considerable area; and between the two lay the town, with its own wall round it. It was divided for convenience into two parts; the Upper town, outside the Citadel's eastern gate and down the eastern slope of its hill, and the Lower (and larger) town on the level strip bordering the river, for the most part on its left bank. A good bridge spanned the Meuse; and a traveller crossing it from the east would find his way barred (if its gates were shut) by the massive fifteenth-century *Porte Chaussée*, the main eastern gate under which he would pass through the walls, and into the centre of the lower town by way

116

of the Rue Chaussée. Over the *Porte* was a strong gatehouse, much used for shutting up *mauvais sujets*, especially midshipmen.

The Verdun immortalized in World War I was not, of course, quite the same thing. It was the town itself, it is true, which was at all costs to be held inviolate by the heroic defence under Pétain and Nivelle. But the great battles raged in an arc some miles to the north of it, from Mort Homme to the north-west to the forts of Vaux and Douaumont to the north-east. No German ever came within $2\frac{1}{2}$ miles of the town itself.

Such was Verdun in 1803 when the British Gentry arrived there in force. Let us recapitulate briefly the categories into which they were divided, seeing, first, which were allowed to remain there and, second, which only passed through it *en route* for elsewhere. Those who stayed were,

(1) Of British birth or extraction.
(2) All who were gentle—detained civilians, commissioned officers of both services; most of those who hoped to become such (master's mates, midshipmen, clerks and first-class volunteers) and most of the masters, pursers and surgeons.
(3) Those who *looked* as though they were gentle (e.g. the more Arosperous merchant-service officers).
(4) pvowedly non-gentle folk, almost all civilians, who minis tered to the comforts—or vices—of the gentle.
(5) The wives and families of any of the above groups.

The rest of the British captives, numerically the great majority, had passed through Verdun to proceed elsewhere. They were,

(1) All 'other ranks' with their NCO's; all 'ratings' with their petty officers, and most of the lower-grade warrant officers (e.g. gunners, boatswains and carpenters).
(2) Most of the merchant-service officers (for only a few looked gentle).
(3) All merchant-seamen 'hands'.
(4) All *mauvais sujets* from among those otherwise qualifying for Verdun, mainly people caught in the act of escaping.

On the whole, the man who stayed was the lucky one. The chief advantages of residence at Verdun were,

(1) Though locked up in a town at night, a captive was not locked

up in a fortress always. He could even (though under rather galling restrictions of place and time) leave the town.

(2) He could, normally, chose a house or room to dwell in, the limiting factor here being the length of his purse rather than the whim of his gaolers.

(3) He could choose his house-mates who (if he desired or could afford it) might even be his own family.

(4) His place of confinement being the whole town, and his community a moderately large one, he could lead a fairly normal, if somewhat artificial life, enjoying a number of such amenities as he was accustomed to at home.

Though some of the prisoners quartered elsewhere enjoyed some of these advantages sometimes, it is fair to say, by way of generalization, that all were normally denied to them.

Many of the prisoners who have left accounts of their experiences give some information about life in wartime Verdun; but to most of them their sojourn there was only incidental to other adventures. There are, however, two full records. One is by the *détenu* son of a wealthy West Indian planter, also a *détenu*. The son, known as the Chevalier Henry Lawrence,[1] was a man by no means unknown in the literary world. The other is by that same Lieutenant (afterwards Vice-Admiral Sir William) Dillon whom we have already met several times.[2] Lawrence is much the better writer, but, himself a rich *détenu*, he concerned himself mainly with his own kind. Dillon, on the other hand, though he mixed with the *détenus*, also concerned himself with the service officers, being one himself, and therefore furnishes the more comprehensive picture. It is clear too that, while Lawrence never saw Dillon's work, Dillon had read Lawrence's, using it, adding to it, and sometimes even correcting it. To this book it is the more valuable of the two, and supplies much of the basis of this chapter.

Dillon, then, with a *détenu* acquaintance named Sevright, reached the town after his many wanderings on December 4, 1803. It was

[1] His book, *A Picture of Verdun, or the English detained in France, from the portfolio of a Détenu*, was published anonymously in London in 1810.

[2] His very long *Narrative of my Professional Experiences* has never been published in full. Its 'professional' portions, somewhat abbreviated, are published as Vols. XCIII and XCVII of the Navy Records Society, edited by the present author. Save for a brief summary, however, his more personal experiences at Verdun during his 4½ years' confinement are omitted from the NRS volumes. All references in this book are to the original manuscript, not the printed volumes.

only in November that Verdun had been decided upon as principal depot, and he was, he tells us, the very first naval officer to arrive there. It was a drenching wet day.

> The town, being a very dismal place, did not show to advantage when deluged with rain. The common run of the inhabitants made but a sorry appearance. Poverty and miserable clothing gave rise to very different sensations from those I felt at Nancy. At the house where we alighted I could not procure change for a gold louis, being told it was a bad one. Money was a scarce article at Verdun on our arrival there.[1]

Gold louis soon ceased to be rarities, however, spilling by many channels from *détenus'* well-filled purses into townsmen's empty pockets. One such channel was ordinary board and lodging. Rooms which, at first, were letting for 30 francs were soon much sought after at 300; and the price of food rose almost as steeply. So insatiable, in fact, was the greed shown by many of the inhabitants that, after a time, the commandant himself saw fit to interfere: not, unfortunately, to protect the fleeced, but because he had reason to fear that the news of such easy money was spreading overfast, and he feared that the government might think fit to move the depot elsewhere.

Competitors were not wanting, because every town realized the economic advantages of housing so much wealth. One of them was Metz. Dillon, Stanhope, Ellison and Boys all have a pretty story to tell about it, though, as they relate it, it sounds rather more like a contemporary *bon mot* than a serious contribution to history. The mayor of Metz, they aver, hearing of Verdun's good fortune, hurried to Paris, secured an interview with Bonaparte, and gave his reasons why Metz would be a better centre than Verdun. One of them was that Metz had much the greater population. This he knew to be true, but was flabbergasted when the First Consul silenced him with a flat contradiction, 'No,' he said, 'you are misinformed': and proceeded to prove it by producing lists recently received from all the towns of France. These were petitions inviting Napoleon to become First Consul for life. Metz, being nearer the German frontier, had no great opinion of Napoleon, and its list of petitions was correspondingly meagre. Verdun had shown much more enthusiasm, if only because its astute mayor had taken the trouble to make a personal canvass, crowning his effort by adding at the bottom the names of all those citizens who did not sign, on the excuse that they could not write.

[1] Dillon, op. cit., III, 191.

'So you see,' said the little Hero with a frown, 'your town does not contain so many citizens as Verdun.'[1]

And that was that.

The fame of the golden louis soon still further increased Verdun's population, this time with a much less desirable type of citizen. 'A set of gamblers made their appearance from Paris, and opened a Bank of *Rouge et Noir*.' They were clearly professional swindlers, and quickly made their fortunes, not only from the rich civilians, many of whom were deeply infected with the then fashionable gaming habit, but also from the lower ranks of officer, and especially the midshipmen who, what with boredom and inexperience, fell easy victims. These rogues also helped on the prosperity of the townsfolk at first, because those who make money so easily are notoriously ready spenders of it. But the commandant again interfered, again from quite the wrong motives. Before their arrival there had been a little discreet play at one of the prisoners' clubs, for the privilege of conducting which the commandant charged a matter of 12 francs a night: and now this sum seemed to be in jeopardy. The steadier inhabitants began to complain also, because some of their young people had found their way into the new establishment with their parents' hard-earned money—and had come away without it. Thereupon the commandant, to please all parties, caused the crooks to pay an exorbitant rent for their premises, and had put up over the door, in large letters, a notice which read, '*This Bank is kept for the English. The French are forbidden to play at it.*'

The wealthy West Indian's son has a good deal more to say about this somehow disreputable establishment than has the hard-up naval officer. Clearly he was more familiar with what went on inside its garish doors. The hours of play were long. It opened at 1.0 p.m., and, though it closed briefly at 5.0 while its clients dined, it reopened at 8.0 and play continued all night. Stakes were often high and fortunes lost—there is no mention of fortunes won, except, of course, by the management, whose nominal proprietor was a certain M. Balbi. *Rouge et noir* was the principal dissipation, though by no means the only one.

Scenes took place in this house which would require the pencil of a Hogarth to depict. Here the unwary spendthrift found an

[1] Dillon, op. cit., III, 194. Stanhope tells the same story (A. M. W. Pickering, op. cit., p. 454).

elegant supper, heating wines, abandoned women: in short, every stimulant to vice.[1]

The place was run on the lines of the most fashionable English establishments. It was usually orderly enough, to the outward eye at least, because its humbler patrons naturally took their cue from the rich society people who knew all about it. There were, however, occasional unpleasantnesses; as for instance when M. Balbi, whether deliberately or not but certainly very brusquely, refused to hand over the winnings of a *détenu* named Valentine Goold (or Gould). Such an insult could only be expiated in one way. A challenge was sent: they met next morning, and Balbi had a large piece of one of his calves shot away. The sequel is instructive, too. Goold was arrested— after all, Balbi was a Frenchman—and sent to Bitche. Balbi, however, had at least to pretend that he was a gentleman, and as soon as he was sufficiently recovered, he rushed off to Paris, interviewed the Minister of War, and returned in triumph to Verdun with Goold at his side. Napoleon also got to hear of it, and laid it down squarely on paper that English gentlemen were to be allowed to duel if they felt like it.

The fame of this superior gambling-den spread far and wide; in England, oddly enough, without evoking much criticism. There was, however, so much more in France that, in 1806, Napoleon intervened again and ordered the place to be closed. It had already done harm enough, especially to the midshipmen and the younger, poorer officers and *détenus*. There were tragedies—and tragi-comedies. A young British naval surgeon named Benjamin Lawder lost a great deal more than he could afford at the tables, and in desperation forged Brenton's signature: then, facing certain detection, drank a bottle of laudanum. It was found empty beside him, and labelled 'Lawder's Cure for all Disorders'. Another youth, a clerk (captain's secretary) named John Chambers, on trying to borrow money from one of the croupiers, was asked what security he had to offer. 'I have nothing', he replied, 'but my ears!' 'Very well,' was the joking reply. 'Let's have them!' Thereupon the lad took out his knife and then and there cut off part of one ear. The croupier had the grace to advance a little money: but Chambers was sent to Bitche.[2]

After only four months, Dillon has this to say of the town and its citizens:

[1] Lawrence, op. cit.
[2] Boys, op. cit., p. 53.

On our arrival the wives of the bourgeoisie were dressed like maid-servants, and not a white stocking to be seen among them. But in a few months their whole costume was improved by silks and muslins. The shops, which were nearly empty, were now crammed with articles for sale. . . . The improvement of the town was daily perceptible. One street in particular in its lower part from its bustle and noise we called Bond Street. It became the morning lounge, as the Frenchman who became our principal banker resided there. He kept a clothier's shop, by name Houzelle. We dubbed him 'Hustle'.[1]

By July the town was becoming quite a civilized place. But its amenities, all *détenu*-made, always have a faintly pathetic flavour. However hard they tried, they could not really change a Meuse fortress-town into a regency Brighton; and their efforts remained, one feels, not a copy but a caricature.

My lodgings being in the lower town, I had to walk up a gradual ascent, over rough stones, there being yet no pavement, till I reached an open space something like a square, where a large pump was to be seen and the houses were of a better description. Proceeding further, I came upon level ground which led to a large platform called the *Roche*. On three sides of it were avenues of trees, this being the parade-ground, from which fine views of the adjacent countryside were visible. Beyond it you entered the Citadel over a bridge. The *Roche* communicated with the ramparts, by which one could descend to the lower town through which the Meuse flowed. The softness of its waters enabled the inhabitants to manufacture the best bon-bons in all France. There was a very good bridge over the river that led out to the gates. There was also a canal from it which led through the flat part of the town, and over it a bridge of less dimensions. Near this was another lounging-place called the *Digue*, which was also bordered with trees, it being a select resort in the evenings, where some very interesting meetings occurred.[2]

The upper town soon became the 'fashionable' British quarter, and Dillon, who was always a bit of a snob, soon found his way up to it. It was handier, he found, for another set of essentially British institutions which established themselves there—the Clubs. There were several of them, to suit all tastes. The first, largest and least select was The Carron Club, called after a café of that name. Another was *Créangis*. A third—Taylor's—was small but noisy, its members being for the most part young and dashing 'blades'. Its life was short. A fourth established itself at the Bishop's Palace within the confines of the Citadel—the

[1] Dillon, op. cit., III, 214–15. [2] Ibid., 234.

bishop himself, of course, having ceased to reside there since the Revolution. Founded by the London entertainer Concannon, and called The Upper Club, it was patronized chiefly by married men with wives and daughters, and eligible bachelors who might be interested in the daughters. It was relatively sedate, but went in for decorous dances and card-parties. All had their troubles, arising not only from internal bickerings but also from interference from without; mainly, as we are to see, from the French commandant. There were also select weekly dining-clubs—one, which Dillon frequented, called The Cod Club—billiard saloons, a considerable library, a cock-fighting ring, theatricals, both professional and amateur, and also, from time to time, full-dress balls on a scale, in view of the circumstances, of scarcely credible extravagance. There were even fêtes so lavish that the grand ball itself was only one turn on the bill. Dillon, who loved such things, describes several of them. To one 'upwards of 120 guests were invited, in the same style as our fashionables do in London'. A company of professional actors was engaged to open the proceedings with a play. At midnight supper was served in three rooms, with 'every luxury the country could produce'. Speeches were made; songs, serious and comic, sung.

> At 2 o'clock the Ball commenced, and was kept up with spirit till 6 in the morning. There was a hazard table for those gentlemen whose tastes led that way. The festival terminated with a splendid breakfast. The ladies' dresses outrivalled anything of the kind ever seen at Verdun, some appearing with abundance of brilliants, birds of paradise etc. One lady, the Hon. Mrs An . . . y,[1] paid 150 guineas in Paris for her costume. But the Hon. Mrs C . . . e[2] surpassed them all, wearing a Vandyke profusely set round with the most costly jewels.

At another ball in the Bishop's Palace 'every delicacy that could be procured from far and wide adorned the table: the choicest wines abounded'. At a third, the whole of the principal hotel was engaged for a 'balle masqué' [sic], and 'none of Lord Barrymore's fêtes at Wargrave could have surpassed it in splendour. . . . Decorations, devices and illuminations adorned the apartments; festoons of flowers covered the stairs.' What with the ordinary cost of living at Verdun and the consistent rooking of all Britons, imagination boggles at the thought of the bills.

[1] Bride of the Hon. (later General) Arthur Annesley. See p. 203.
[2] Wife of the Hon. Mr Clive, who was released in 1807.

Yet much of this extravagance was perhaps a form of escapism from harsher realities. Behind all this 'home-from-home' endeavour there loomed all the time the one inescapable fact. They were prisoners. They all had prison rules, and gaolers to enforce them. These regulations were numerous and formidable, though sometimes perhaps more formidable in theory than in practice. Roughly, they could be divided into two sorts—the general regulations laid down by the Minister of War in Paris, and the local rules devised by the commandant on the spot. The government regulations centred round the *appel*, and it was probably the most irksome of them all to the captives. It was changed from time to time, but Dillon gives both the original ruling and the later one:

> The description of our person, age, etc. was given to us on a card, and numbered. With that we could pass the sentinels and [go] out of town, but not be absent more than four hours. We had to attend the *Appel* (or, as we should call it, the Muster) from 8 to 10 o'clock in the morning and from 2 to 4 o'clock in the afternoon. Those gentlemen among the civilians who did not present themselves were fined. In that, many of them made their private arrangements with the gendarmes for absence during the week. We officers would do nothing of the kind, and thought ourselves ill-used by being thus restrained, considering ourselves to have the indulgence of being on our Parole of honour.[1]

They were, as we have seen, within their rights here, and had the military usage of ages on their side. It was otherwise with the *détenus*, whose case was covered by no usage of any kind: and, all things considered, their taking the easy option of bribery was not surprising. Soon, however (owing probably to Brenton's representations) the Minister of War consented to relax the stringency of such frequent *appels*, but only for the commissioned officers: hence the poor midshipmen's complaint (see p. 65).

In addition to these ministry regulations, however, there were the local ones: and these were—or might be made—much more troublesome. There were twenty-six of them, and, as so often happens with people who have uncomfortable rules to keep, Dillon only read them carefully after having been bowled out in breaking one. There were four which touched on the *appels*—(i) More of them could be imposed, or their hours changed, by the commandant at will, and as a punishment; (ii) The commandant could also exempt any prisoner from the *appel* up to five days; (iii) Those unable to attend through sickness

---

[1] Dillon, op. cit., III, 193.

had to obtain certificates of disability from a doctor—a French one—appointed for the purpose; for this a fee was payable; (iv) Failure to attend *appel*, without certificate, was officially regarded as 'attempt to escape'. This was a potent weapon in the commandant's hand, which he sometimes, no doubt, turned to his advantage: but he seldom used it to the full.

Few of the twenty-two other rules are important enough to detain us. But one or two deserve mention. For example, 'All over-60's to be confined at Verdun'.[1] Another was, that all proprietors of houses or apartments occupied by prisoners were to report on their lodgers' behaviour to the police or the mayor. Here were the makings of a peculiarly nasty system of espionage. To their credit, most of the citizens concerned were amiable enough to pay no attention to this rule. But the less amiable did. Another local regulation was that no prisoner could change his rooms without leave. This was usually granted; but again it was, at times, a useful handle for the commandant and his myrmidons. Two others were perhaps only to be expected. Any prisoner passing out of the gates without showing his pass, or found outside in disguise, would be sent to Bitche: and any Frenchman aiding and abetting a prisoner to escape was to be arrested and tried by law. Finally, a special posse of four mounted gendarmes was to be constantly on duty against an alarm being given.

It will not escape notice that many of these rules left great power in the hands of the commandant: which is not so surprising, considering that most of them had been framed by the commandant himself. That personage, therefore, was bound to play a vital part in the lives, and the happiness, of all prisoners: and no account of this centre of p.o.w. affairs would be complete if it failed to deal with that most hated of all the half-dozen commandants who ruled at Verdun between 1803 and 1814. His name was General Wirion. He was the evil (and to most of the prisoners the incarnation of it) who was ever with them.

His first offence in the eyes of all British officers was also the least of his faults. He was not, to them, a proper general at all: only a *Général de Gendarmerie*, a sort of glorified policeman. The *on dit* among the captives at Verdun was that he

> was the son of a charcutier or pork-dealer in Picardy: and though an attorney's clerk before the Revolution, he on every occasion affected the most sovereign contempt for his ancient calling. No

[1] For the cool effrontery of this see p. 23.

gentleman of the highest nobility could have looked down with more hauteur than this man when in his regimentals upon the robed lawyer and every civilian.[1]

With one so universally loathed by his victims, however, such evidence is hardly conclusive. It is safer to stick to the known facts—that he had somehow scrambled from the ruck of police officers in the redder days of the Revolution, and that he was not without his abilities. There is plenty of evidence that, at first, Napoleon himself, a fine judge of men, thought highly of him. His decline and fall from grace was probably due to the oldest and commonest of all causes, the corrupting properties of Power. A man of the people, with no background but with exceptional natural talent and plenty of ambition, aspires to, and obtains, a command of great importance; one demanding a more than ordinary share of tact and (to such as him the most fatal of all) carrying with it an admirable chance of a fortune. For his authority was, rightly, enormous and, less rightly, subject to hardly any supervision. That he used this authority dishonestly will have to be admitted; not, primarily, because all his natural enemies said so, even upright men like Brenton; but because the judicial findings of his own countrymen and the nature of his end both go to prove it.

If there was no hint of a 'de' in front of the General's name, there was, if possible, even less of one before *La Générale's*. The British, with one voice, say she was a *vivandière*, a 'washerwoman of the republican armies', and from all their accounts she certainly behaved like one. Yet, that granted, it must be admitted that she was a good wife to Wirion:

> La Générale, notwithstanding the dignity of her station, does not disdain the details of domestic economy. . . . She had probably been used to wash and iron his shirts, and although she might no longer attend to these matters, she still retained the language of a washerwoman. She employed a sempstress to make some shirts for Wirion. When payment was demanded, Madame thought the sum too much, but offered what she thought right. It was refused. She then assailed the unfortunate needlewoman in a string of epithets only fit for St Giles's and kicked her out of the room.[2]

On another occasion, meeting a rich *détenu* in a milliner's shop, she coolly suggested spinning a coin to see who should pay for the dress she was ordering. He good-naturedly agreed—after all, it was unwise to get on the wrong side of the commandant's lady. He tactfully lost

---

[1] Dillon, op. cit., III, 394.   [2] Ibid., 389.

the toss. Thereupon she selected the most expensive gown in the shop, ordering it to be sent to her house, and the bill to his. Though elderly, large, coarse and very plain, she loved riding, freely borrowing the *détenus'* best mounts, and appearing in the streets, to the punctilious Dillon's horror, in

> a riding habit which was *not* similar to that used in England, as I have often had a good view of her left leg when she has been passing.[1]

She always played into Wirion's hand; and he, when possible, played into hers. Thus on one occasion,

> some of the *détenus* agreed to get up a subscription-ball, to be given principally to those of the French inhabitants who by their kind attentions contributed towards our amusement. But as no invitation was sent to Madame Wirion, just as the fiddles had struck up a body of gendarmes entered the room and threatened to conduct all the English to the Citadel. There was no disobeying.[2]

The ball was instantly called off. But this time the precious pair did not have the last word. The French guests, as disgusted as the British hosts, proceeded to get up another dance of their own, inviting all their late hosts: but not Madame Wirion.

The methods by which the general made his fortune are too numerous for all to be recorded here. Only a few typical ones will be selected. Boys gives the longer list from which these are chosen, stating in each case the amount which, he estimated, was finding its way into the pockets of Wirion and his successor Courçelles. The total is £30,000 odd.[3]

(1) For missing the *appels*, 2s 6d each, and permission to sign the books at your lodging, yielding about £50 per month for 3 years	£1,800
(2) Sale of passports to go out of town: about 2,000 issued in 7 years	£250
(3) Permission to reside in the country, 6 for 6 years at 10s per month	£216
(4) Tax on 4 clubs, £1 5s 0d per month each for 6 years	£180
(5) Permission for servants to return to Verdun at £12 each, 4 a year for 6 years	£288
(6) Permission for *détenus* to return from Valenciennes	£400
(7) Permission for masters of vessels and others to return to Verdun, during 7 years	£420

[1] Dillon, op. cit., III, 388.   [2] Ibid., 370.   [3] Boys, op. cit., pp. 56–8.

(8) Difference between the franc and the *livre tournois*. . £960
(9) Gambling houses, £100 per month for 3 years .. £3,600
(10) Races, exclusive of extortions which grew out of
them £180

These ten items are a selection of Wirion's profits. Another list follows showing Courçelles'. Though equally dishonestly acquired, they are of a different, less all-embracing, nature. He was clearly a less imaginative swindler. He had business interests in the wine-trade, for instance, and made a cool thousand pounds by exploiting an undisguised wine monopoly. His son, too, whom he installed as keeper of the Citadel, helped to swell the family gains. Several of his underlings also helped themselves. One of them shot himself later when threatened with exposure: another was dismissed the Army: a third, when pressed, admitted to having purloined £100 a year for ten years. In the end, Courçelles' party scooped about as much as Wirion's; but Courçelles' was shared between some half-dozen rogues, while nearly all Wirion's went to himself. Some explanation of the above items is essential if we would appreciate the extent and variety of the unprincipled man's operations.

(1) These were plain bribes, actually paid to the gendarmes. But Wirion was very much master of his own house, and kept as firm a finger on his underlings as he did on his victims. Very little of this £1,800 stayed in the gendarmes' pockets. Boys has an illuminating story about that. After Captain Brenton had made a round of visits to the other depots, Wirion sent for him and suggested that he might like to present a trifle to the gendarme who had been his (unwanted) travelling companion. Brenton agreed, and, producing some gold coins, demanded a receipt for them on the grounds that, as his journey had been an official one, he must send in the receipt to his own government as a voucher. Thereupon:

> The general eyed him with a satanic grin and replied that, in consideration of the kindness he had shown to his attendant gendarme, he would not allow him to give anything.[1]

Here the true Wirion stands revealed. A signed receipt would prevent him from pocketing the gold himself. He was deprived of his spoils: that he was depriving his gendarmes of theirs meant nothing to him.

(2), (3) and (4) are self-explanatory.

(5) This is an example of almost routine money-making. From time to time the commandant would suddenly issue an order, sending

[1] Boys, op. cit., p. 56.

6. LA PORTE CHAUSSÉE, VERDUN, AS IT STANDS TODAY

7. INTERIOR OF LA TOUR D'ANGOULÊME, VERDUN CITADEL

From Ellison's 'Prison Scenes'

the servants of wealthy civilians to other depots. No reason was ever given: and no wonder, because there was only one reason—plain blackmail. He knew very well that these luxury-loving *détenus* would miss their servants acutely, and would cheerfully pay to have them back. They did.

(6) and (7) These were other, and similar, side-lines in blackmail, the victims this time being some of the *détenus* themselves and the merchant skippers. Now and again parties of both sorts, apparently selected at random, would receive unexpected orders to pack up and go to other and less comfortable places. They could usually, however, buy their way back, the price varying according to what the commandant thought they would be prepared to pay.

(8) This is an example of mere (but very mean) fiddling with rates of exchange; converting money privately subscribed in Britain for the benefit of prisoners; receiving at a higher rate and disbursing at a lower.

(9) This sum represents what was actually received in direct rents and fees. It does not represent nearly all that Wirion screwed out of the gaming proclivities of the British. In addition, he was constantly inflicting his unwelcome presence upon their private dinner-parties, entertainments and quiet little gaming-tables. They did not dare to exclude him, or even too openly to cold-shoulder him, for fear lest he should exercise his undoubted power (not right) to confine them as close prisoners in the Citadel or even pack them off to a penal depot: pretexts were easy enough for him to trump up. On such occasions they usually allowed him to win considerable sums, if only to keep in with him and secure minor favours. There are accusations, indeed, that he was not above ordinary cheating at cards: but this is perhaps going too far. He could be reasonably sure of winning anyway, and, like all *arrivistes*, he set great store on being taken for a gentleman.

(10) The races at Verdun were a feature of this remarkable English community stranded in an alien town, and they acquired a great deal of notoriety at the time. They show, perhaps better than anything else, how reluctant the British upper class was to forgo accustomed pleasures: also, what a cross-section of contemporary English life was assembled at Verdun. As early as April 1804 some suitable fields, about three miles from the town, were rented, and a jockey club was formed. From the first, the race-bills were printed, exactly following the style of Ascot, Newmarket and Epsom. But the sponsors appeared on them under assumed names, because (says Dillon) they feared

censure from England. As the day for the first meeting drew near, excitement became intense:

> The Verdun races engrossed the conversation of all France, and blacklegs resorted to them from all parts. The Jockey Club subscribed 80 *louis d'or* for a gold cup. But the English were cheated, in this as in most of their purchases in France. They had ordered it at one of the first goldsmiths in Paris. When it arrived, it weighed but 40 louis. Every midshipman was becoming a jockey and every sailor a groom. Everyone could talk of nothing but horse-flesh. The course presented a very lively scene. The married families attended in their carriages, but the kept mistresses astonished everybody by the elegance of their toilettes. There were to be seen curricles, chaises-and-four, gigs, etc. Every equipage was provided with some dainty, and the dashing Beaux visited every carriage, partaking of the leg of a fowl or some Strasburg pie from Mrs A. or Mrs B.[1]

First, however, the jockey club had an important duty, to be neglected at its peril. The general had to be squared. This was a delicate business; and gradually a routine was evolved which seldom if ever failed.

> When the day for the races was fixed, and considerable sums staked, he would unexpectedly give an order forbidding it to take place. The jockeys . . . then deputed one or two of their number to prevail on him to sanction their proceedings. The gendarme on duty would reply that His Excellency was indisposed. He could not be seen. A fresh deputation is the result. They call upon the aide de camp. He hums and hahs, laments the General's bad state of health; that he is quite out of temper: he should fear to incommode him by his intercession, etc. etc. At length, having gained some ground, they venture to speak more plainly, and agree to give 50 louis for the permission required. The folding doors are now opened. The General receives them graciously, but complains of ill-health not allowing him to admit them sooner: and while he is in conversation with one of the deputies the other, having put 50 louis into his glove, contrives to drop it slyly into the General's hat which, from its position, appears to be placed to receive it. Now all difficulties are over. His Excellency wishes them good sport, and they retire.[2]

Even so, he had not yet picked this succulent bone quite clean. He directed that every gendarme attending the race on duty—and it was surprising how many were needed to keep order—was to receive 8 louis per day for his exertions: and everybody knew that he, not they, took the money. Sometimes, too, other chances came his way.

[1] Dillon, op. cit., III, 226. [2] Ibid., 223.

One of the *détenus* had, at great expense, procured a horse with which he challenged any racer on the continent. Wirion, imagining that he ran no risk, sent word to him that he would take a 200-louis share in the bets. The gentleman could not refuse, as the General's word was equal to a command, though it was so much money out of his pocket. As some of the *détenus* were versed in all the tricks and practices of the horse-dealers and jockeys of Newmarket, it was feared that some adverse party might bribe the groom to be guilty of some foul play. The General therefore gave a private authority to Mr D . . . to sleep in the village where the animal was kept. Had that gentleman had a sick wife, or had his own health required a change of air, he might well have been refused the indulgence.[1]

Fortunately, Mr D . . .'s horse won, and the commandant had his 200 louis. Had this not happened, Dillon concludes, Mr D . . . would have been obliged (or would have thought it prudent) to make good the sum.

Lawrence avers that the British passion for horseflesh extended beyond the racing, and that a very popular pack of hounds (or beagles) was established, which hunted thrice a week. The quarry was a red herring trailed by a mounted midshipman. There were sometimes as many as forty in the field. Dillon, however, though he mentions the project, infers that it came to nothing. But there was certainly quite good duck-shooting for those who could afford it, and, for those who could not, bird-liming. Another favourite summer pastime, in which the ladies joined, was the *champêtre* picnic in the woods within the six-mile radius. For all of these, save possibly the last, Wirion took his toll. And even a picnicker might be good for a *douceur* if forbidden at the last moment to pass the gates.

Wirion's greatest offence, however, seems to have been his particularly nasty system of espionage. He was determined to know everything about his charges, down to the most intimate details. That he used this knowledge for the lining of his own pockets by methods often indistinguishable from blackmail is certain. But it is only fair to record that, according to his own confidential servant,[2] his system stemmed largely from a psychological weakness which amounted to mental disease. In its heyday, his 'staff' consisted of

---

[1] Dillon, op. cit., III, 224–5. 'D' was probably W. Drake, the first clerk of the race-course.

[2] Antoine Latreille, for long one of his trusted underlings; quoted by Ellison, op. cit., pp. 216–20.

'80 gendarmes; 20 women paid by the month; several Englishmen paid by Wirion, and a very large number of voluntary informers'. For, according to his own stooge, he was a hag-ridden man, suffering from a violent phobia—a spy-phobia of all things. He had a permanent fear-complex, attributing to others the very crime of which he was guilty: he was convinced that the prisoners were constantly spying on *him*, with the intent to report him to headquarters. Indeed, Latreille infers that, to Wirion, his system was not espionage at all, but self-defensive counter-espionage. He had, of course, put the cart before the horse. It is true that, before the end, the spied-upon captives were doing their best to free themselves from such a hideous existence; and, to do so, they were collecting what evidence they could. But before he made their lives intolerable they certainly had no such ideas. There may well be much truth in this portrait of the man. Clearly its expositor knew him intimately, and from a different angle from that of all our other authorities. He neither calumniates nor blindly champions the general, whom he once loved but who, later, had let him down badly—or so he said—allowing him to face disgrace and imprisonment. His view, in fact, is that Wirion was a good man (or at least not a bad one) gone mentally wrong: and it is the last half of this view, not the first, to which it is possible to subscribe. No one, not even his servant, attempted to deny his insatiable zeal to enrich himself—a zeal, by the way, which that servant probably found quite proper, seeing that he displayed it in no small degree himself.

In the end, however, Nemesis caught up with Wirion. The truth came out, though there are several versions of how it happened. The commonest story, favoured by Boys and, partially, by Dillon and Lawrence, is that the general, after so many smaller coups, at last decided upon a bigger one. He pitched upon a very wealthy but rather timid *détenu* named Mr Garland, of Essex, and, by carefully-contrived machinations, trumped up against him a charge of attempted rape. The accusation was absurd, and everyone knew it. Mr Garland would not have hurt a fly, and was the least designing of men. (He it was who had tossed up with *La Générale* for the dress; and, on another occasion, had been bullied into buying her 250 pairs of stockings.) Now Wirion, sending for him alone and at night, deplored his alleged 'crime', adding that—of course—he would have to send him to Bitche. Garland's reaction was most promising. He lost his head completely and, in his terror, promised anything to be let off.

Wirion thought it might be overlooked—for £5,000. (Lawrence, telling substantially the same story, says £15,000.)

Then, however, the plot began to get out of hand. Garland gave Wirion a draft on his bank; but Messrs Hammersley, the bankers, returned the bill protesting, suspecting from its very size that something was wrong. Wirion now tried to muzzle Garland by packing him off secretly to Clermont. He went, but not before he had told at least part of the story to a certain Doctor Duke, a *détenu* practitioner who, by the way, attended the Wirion family gratis. The doctor passed the information to a Mr Charles Sturt, in happier times a magistrate of the county of Dorset. He drew up an affidavit of the whole transaction and somehow smuggled it home, so that, finally, the British Government made formal representations to M. Talleyrand.

The prisoners had, of course, been complaining for a long time. But their applications, sent direct to the Minister of War, had never got through. Berthier, who was Wirion's patron, had been able to burn or pigeon-hole them all. Now there was a change-round of posts. Berthier became Chief of Staff, and his place was taken by General Clarke, later created Duc de Feltre. Wirion's immunity was gone. He was summoned to Paris to answer the charges made against him.

By now it was 1810. Brenton had long since been repatriated: even his successor, Captain Daniel Woodriff, had come and gone, to be succeded by a senior officer worthy to be named alongside Brenton. This was Sir Thomas Lavie, a well-known frigate captain. There survives a statement by him, hitherto unpublished,[1] in which he reports fully upon the fall of Wirion: and he does not so much as mention Garland. This does not discredit those who report the Garland affair. It certainly happened; but, since Lavie is silent about it, it was not, perhaps, the immediate cause of Wirion's fall.

Lavie's account is plain and modest, but this must not be allowed to conceal his real courage in deciding to try a fall with that formidable man, now dangerous as a cornered beast. Though advised against it by his friends who feared for his own safety, he carefully collected evidence of Wirion's various frauds (amounting, he says, to nearly a million francs). Then he went and bearded him in his den.

> He tried to compromise the matter with me by extending the privileges [of the prisoners]. Though I accepted this as a right, I insisted on a restitution of the money which he owed; to which

[1] For bringing this document to my notice and kindly allowing me to use it, I am indebted to Lavie's descendant, Michael Robinson, Esq.

also he acquiesced. But at the expiration of a month, the time agreed upon for payment, he broke open the door of my house and arrested me in my bed; and, after taking all my papers, threw me into prison. Finding my confinement kept the Depot in agitation, he sent me to the Fortress of Mont Midi,[1] and ordered that I should be strictly confined, and interdicted me the use of pen, ink and paper. The Commandant [of Mont Midi], however, refused to comply with such rigour to these orders, but, on the contrary, furnished me with the means of forwarding my complaints to the Minister of War; and in a few days General Wirion was suspended in his functions and summoned to Paris to answer for his conduct. His influence still remained sufficient to get me removed to Armins, where I was placed in solitary confinement: and, after undergoing the greatest privations for four months I was called to Paris, where I was again put upon my parole. Shortly after my arrival in that city, I had an audience with the Minister of War, and placed all my charges on so clear a footing that General Wirion took alarm, and blew his brains out.

That some of his victims' accusations are exaggerations may well be true: but Lavie's statement may be taken as the official British view. An official French account of the final tragedy exists too. The Court of Inquiry appointed by the Emperor was to report on April 7, 1810. The *Police Bulletin*, the French Government's confidential report, takes up the story:

> 8th April, 1810
> General Wirion went yesterday morning at 10 o'clock in a hackney coach to the Bois de Boulogne. Alighting a few yards from the Porte Maillot, he blew out his brains. A letter to his wife was found upon him. . . . It appears that impatience at the apparent tardiness of the commission deputed to investigate the complaints against him was the reason of the General's suicide.

It was none of the *Bulletin's* business to air in public the dirty linen of the French administration. It could hardly, therefore, have been more explicit—that the Court had confirmed all his villainies.

A further passage in Lavie's report shows that his work was not finished with the disappearance of Wirion:

> . . . in 1811 I was ordered back to Verdun, where I arrived very opportunely, as the Commandant, Col. Courselles [*sic*], was not only tyrannizing over the prisoners, but defrauding them of a part of the allowance granted to them by the French Government. After a series of representations, a general officer was sent down to investigate the matter, and the Minister of War was so good as

[1] Now Montmédy.

to name me to be present at the enquiries, and ordered me to make my report. M. Courselles was in consequence removed from his command, and a gendarme under him shot himself.

Courçelles (who actually appears in one English record as 'de Courçelles') was probably a slight improvement on Wirion. Dillon, who knew him only as Wirion's second-in-command, even has much good to say of him, as often toning down the worst asperities of his senior. Stanhope also finds excuses for him. But evidently Power corrupted once more; and though, this time, he contrived to work off some of the blame on to an inferior—Lieutenant Masin, who shot himself—he did not escape dismissal and disgrace. He was removed in succession from command of the depot, from control of the department, and finally from the Army. Sir Thomas, established now as a kind of watch-dog, was too much for him.

From this time the improvement was lasting. Such scandals could do the French Government no good, being obvious handles for adverse propaganda. The last two commandants at Verdun were as beloved by the prisoners as their predecessors had been hated. The first of them—Colonel le Baron de Beauchêne—immediately abolished his forerunners' secret police and methods of espionage, restored all to parole, and granted the boon of residence in the neighbouring countryside to all whom he could trust. This, it would seem, included almost everybody: for, among other things, escapes and other breaches of parole, which had been growing ever more frequent under Wirion and Courçelles, all but ceased. De Beauchêne was, of course, of the old régime: but he was old in years too, and died early in 1813, after a reign of only eighteen months. And every prisoner, in full-dress uniform or in deep mourning, turned out to follow him to his grave.

He was succeeded by a general called Dumolard, whose name is omitted by most of our authorities. He seems to have attempted a return to the old bad methods—and lasted for one month. He was followed by the last of the Verdun commandants, Major de Meulan. This officer, inheriting all de Beauchêne's good points, was if possible even more beloved by his charges, earning their gratitude especially by his conduct of affairs in the difficult days of early 1814 when the depot itself, along with all France, was rapidly disintegrating.

Apart from their basic grievances—the *détenus'* at being there at all, the officers' at the ever-present insult to their honour implied in *appels* and locked gates—it would seem that the worst sufferings of the captives stemmed, not so much from the French Government's regulations as from the men detailed to execute them. This is by no means to acquit the authorities of blame: clearly they were not happy in their choices. Of those in responsible positions at Verdun alone, Boys tells us, two committed suicide to avoid worse evils, four were dismissed the Army with ignominy and one reduced to the ranks. It certainly looks as though, at long last, the government was trying to make amends; but this in itself is a tacit admission that all *had* not been well. Clearly it had not. No detention-place can ever be a happy one, but there are well-marked degrees of unhappiness, and de Beauchêne and de Meulan serve to show that, with tact and humanity, captivity may be made at least tolerable.

Comparisons may be odious; but sometimes the omission of them is unfair, and it would smack of one-sidedness not to record that much the same general charges can be levelled at the British Government. Like the French, it unquestionably appointed an unfortunate mixture of good and bad. They are not our concern here, but the existence of the bad should not be forgotten. Some of our commanding officers, especially some of those dug-out lieutenants put in charge of prison-hulks, certainly do not make us proud of the name of Briton. Yet, when all is said, neither Wirion nor Courçelles had any real counterpart in this country. That was hardly possible, because Verdun itself had no counterpart. We had no comparable officer depot: and no *détenu* depot, having no *détenus*. Indeed, in the whole history of man there can have been very few prison-places like it. Verdun must be all but unique.

CHAPTER VI

THE DEPOTS

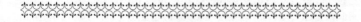

So much for the metropolis of British captives: now for the provinces, reserved for no-parole men. There will be no synthetic amusements here, no clubs, theatres, gaming-tables, races. For the common man there will be no lodging outside the locked door, though the lower-grade warrant officers RN and some of the merchant skippers may at times enjoy that privilege. But the great mass of soldiers, marines, and seamen, whether royal or merchant, we shall find boarding and lodging inside the stout walls of the various frontier fortresses and towns: sometimes in the barracks formerly occupied by the departed garrisons; sometimes in hastily-repaired outhouses or stables, sometimes in hut-ments specially built for them; but always locked in. They messed at common trestle-tables, were usually seriously overcrowded and indifferently fed. Indeed, their quarters were in every sense prisons; prisons, moreover, which, to the modern eye, would be inexcusable: for though they usually had yards or courts for exercise, there was no hint of privacy in their lives, their overfull dormitories, under-ventilated and sometimes even underground, serving as sitting- as well as sleeping-places. Nor, normally, were they ever allowed outside the walls. But here, theory and practice were diametrically opposite. In theory—and, according to Napoleon, always—they could go out to work, either on government labour or for such chores as harvest-work, or even to follow their special trades if they had any. In practice, however, these relaxations seldom came their way, and, when they did, were for very small numbers only. In a word, they were *gaoled*.

Yet, here as everywhere else in this story, much turned upon the gaolers in general, and in particular, of course, upon the head-gaoler, the depot commandant. They—and especially he—could make all the difference between a comparatively philosophic acceptance of fate and something like blank despair. This makes it hard, if not impossible, to generalize upon 'prison conditions', since they depended so much not on government orders, but on the quirks of individuals. Nor do the prisoners themselves help us greatly. We could hardly expect them to be unbiased witnesses. The only safe generalization is to affirm that they were sometimes treated passably, but sometimes—and perhaps more often—atrociously. In the latter event, they were cheated of their few rights wholesale by profiteering commandants and, in detail, by brutal gaolers: but not, probably, quite so often, or so shamelessly, as surviving accounts make out. The complaints of suffering men are not notorious for their objectivity.

It soon becomes clear, too, that the character of any individual witness and his background are going to be most important. Thus anyone who reads Choyce on Sarrelibre, and no one else, would not believe that there was anything there which, by the widest stretch of the imagination, could be called 'cultural'; because culture did not happen to have any place in Choyce's life. But let him read Stewart's pages and he will find that this boy, naturally studious and serious-minded, mastered arithmetic and navigation, English grammar and a working knowledge of French, all while at that same sink of iniquity—for such it probably was. That such a thing was possible was due, as Stewart says, to Captain Brenton—who, as we have seen, figures prominently in Choyce's story too, but only as the villain who kept back the men's allowances! We must constantly try, then, to study our witness's temperament as well as his story.

Once a no-parole man reached his allotted depot, there was no guarantee that he would stay there. If in the eyes of his keepers he was held to have misbehaved—disobeyed or vilified his guards, been disorderly or tried to escape—he became a *mauvais sujet*; which meant, almost literally, in the language of his captors, a criminal. Then he qualified himself for one of the three regular punishment depots, Sedan, Sarrelibre or Bitche. Here indeed he was made to suffer. The French Government did not deny this, justifying its severity on the grounds that all refractory prisoners *were* criminals, like their own felons or bandits or deserters: especially the last, which was actually the official French name for a prisoner who tried to escape. In theory, all deserters, whether French or British, were treated when caught with equally scant mercy: and, lest we hold up our hands in premature horror, it is as well to remember that, in principle, the British Government took precisely the same view. In practice, however, the French did not treat their own deserters and ours quite equally. With their own, the law ordained that the one—usually the eldest—whom they regarded as the *chef de complot*, or ringleader, was to be shot. And so, very often, he was, the rest being driven back to the ranks. With ours, though they often threatened to apply the same penalty, they seldom if ever carried it out, but sent them instead to the specially-designed punishment gaols: and, often positively boasting of their lenity, proceeded to give them hell.

A no-parole man, even if not a *mauvais sujet*, was also apt to find himself suddenly on the road again, bound for another, and not necessarily a penal, depot. He was seldom told the reason. Sometimes, no doubt, it was just a matter of administrative convenience, though more often, probably, it was a security measure, designed to break up incipient gangs of trouble-makers: for, in practice, Prisoner A. so often found himself going one way while his pal, Prisoner B., went another that there must have been more than mere coincidence about it. The (to them) gratuitous cruelty of the practice is one of the commonest of the prisoners' complaints.

So far it is the no-parole man who had engaged our attention. But we have not done with the parole man. He too might well find himself on the move. Sometimes whole classes were given orders to pack, as for instance all the Verdun midshipmen in 1808, divided arbitrarily into three groups and dispatched to Valenciennes, Givet and Sarrelibre: or, in 1805, all the Verdun merchant officers, locked suddenly into the convent of St Vannes in the Citadel, and thence dispersed to other depots: or, again in 1805, some 170 *détenus* suddenly uprooted. These last two moves, however, may (see pp. 127, 129) be explained in another way—Boys cynically puts the 'return fare' at 50 crowns a head!

The ordinary reason for a Verdun prisoner's involuntary move, however, was because he had become a *mauvais sujet*. There were many ways of doing that—getting badly into debt, for instance, or breaking local conventions, as happened to two officers who, in ignorance, turned their backs on the stage at the theatre when the Emperor's portrait was being exhibited; or by getting on the wrong side of Wirion and his precious lady. But much the most certain way was to try unsuccessfully to escape, or to give the authorities grounds for suspecting that escape was contemplated. Whatever the cause, however, the status of a prisoner sent away from Verdun was practically that of a criminal, legally tried and convicted by French law. The accompanying sentence, to be served at a punishment depot—usually Bitche for Verdunites—was often long, but, as legal sentences commonly are, it was of stated duration: and if the prisoner neither died before his term was over—and he sometimes did—nor escaped, as he occasionally did, he was then discharged to a non-penal depot. Thus Whitehurst, sent to Bitche in 1811 after failing to escape with Jackson, was back again in Verdun well before the end, while the movements of James were even more complicated. Going first to Verdun, he was detailed for Sarrelibre in the general exodus of midshipmen just described. On the eve of starting he escaped; but, being caught, he was brought back to Verdun, paraded there in chains, and sent to Bitche. Having done his time there, he was sent to his original destination, Sarrelibre, and then worked his passage back to Verdun once more. But, implicated by an infamous British spy in a case in which he really had no part, he was sent back to Bitche for a second spell: thence to Sedan, whence he was hurriedly evacuated in early 1814, and saw the inside of several more depots as France's eastern defences crumbled, finally to be rescued on the road by a band of foraging Cossacks.

That both penal and ordinary depots were thoroughly sordid places there can be no doubt; not only because of their gaol-like appearances and properties, their overcrowding and lack of all civilized and civilizing amenities, but also—an inevitable corollary of such conditions—because of the moral degeneration of their inmates. The danger to the mass morale of prisoners of war has long since been recognized, and all possible precautions are always taken —now—to prevent any wholesale collapse of it. But—then—such precautions were hardly known. Indeed, what to us is perhaps the most obvious cause was not even noticed, let alone remedied. Only a few of the most thoughtful and humane officers like Brenton seem to have perceived the danger arising from the men being suddenly, and completely, deprived of their natural leaders. The average 'common man', in either service, was an ill-educated person; nor was he, at ordinary times, encouraged to use his own initiative. His officers did all the thinking for him, holding him the while, in both services, to a very tight discipline. This kept him, if not happy, at least out of mischief, by working him very hard and to a very strict schedule. Even when not a captive he was rather notoriously ill-equipped to look after himself: but now he was suddenly deprived altogether of his officers who, though perhaps he would not admit it, were quite necessary to him, as standing between him and most of the problems of everyday life. At the self-same instant, too, his new masters deprived him of all those daily chores which had occupied his mind and kept him steady. Henceforward, in complete and un-accustomed idleness, he was doomed to consort only with his fellows, mostly as ill-equipped as himself to face up to the new situation. No wonder all the depots—save, for obvious reasons, Verdun—became at one time or another the scenes of that saddest of all forms of mass-demoralization—that of men mostly sound by nature and upbringing, deteriorating through immediate circumstance, and not inherent vice. Not all the men were sound, of course, but therein lay the heart of the tragedy. The new conditions were the very ones which pulled the better down to the level of the worse.

In the Napoleonic War both sides separated the officers from the men in captivity; except, oddly enough, in punishment depots, where the officer-prisoners were held to have forfeited officer rights. Both sides did so because it had always been done. The reason has already been explained. The officers—the gentlemen—lived in one world, expecting (and usually receiving) one standard of treatment. The men—the non-gentlemen—expected, and received, quite another. This was the custom, the norm: it was the Brentons of that day who were the unconventional, the iconoclasts. Let us make no mistake. This phenomenon of mass-degeneration was as marked in Britain as it was in France. We are apt to forget the *Romans* on Dartmoor, the *Misérables* at Norman Cross, the *Rafalés* in the hulks.[1] It is not our business here to describe these wretches individually. All we can do is to point to their existence, observing that their state was at least as bad as that of our men at Sarrelibre or Bitche: and to underline the primary reason for both tragedies—the enforced idleness of the prisoners and the separation of officers and men.

All this only serves to focus the light upon senior officers like Brenton and Sir Thomas Lavie: and at least one other, not an officer at all, whose name has somehow slipped from his countrymen's memory.[2] It would be wrong, too, to overlook the work of those much younger officers, the midshipmen packed off so brusquely from Verdun in 1808 to demoralized officerless depots. Though probably not fully realizing the crime that was being perpetrated on the men, they saw with their own eyes the evils of the system, and often tried, with

[1] Some account of these unfortunate Frenchmen will be found in Sir Basil Thomson's *Story of Dartmoor Prison*, London, 1907; T. J. Walker's *Depot for Prisoners of War at Norman Cross, Huntingdonshire*, London, 1913; and W. Branch-Johnson's *English Prison Hulks*, London, 1957. A study of them is a salutary warning to 'those who live in glass houses'.

[2] The Reverend Robert Wolfe. (See below, pp. 161–8.)

no little success, to stem the rot: in fact, being officers themselves, however junior, to take the place of their seniors. Thus one of them at Givet—

> Mr B . . ., then a youngster of about 17, full of zeal for the service, . . . copied out and put up in the prison, in spite of the gendarmes and the spies, a dialogue which I had written out showing them [the men] in their own quaint expressions what they might expect from the enemy into whose service they were enlisting.[1]

The youngster's action was a great deal more dangerous than it sounds. Like all his fellow-midshipmen from Verdun, he was already under grave suspicion. The malevolent eyes of his gaolers were fixed upon him, eager to take him in some misdemeanour; and any effort to thwart the machinations of the agents sent to tamper with the men's loyalty would, if brought home to him, most certainly earn him a long stretch at Bitche.

At all depots, penal and non-penal alike, the men were suffering, more or less severely, from this segregation. As, however, there were at one time or another, large or small, some score of such places, not all can be described in detail. Indeed, to do so would involve much repetition, because most of their ills were common. We will, therefore, concentrate upon a few, and try to show, among other things, what the presence or absence of the officers must have meant to each community.

I. BITCHE

It is convenient to begin with Bitche. Here conditions of imprisonment were at their worst, though it must not be supposed that the prisoners themselves were necessarily the worst. Indeed, far otherwise, because all the officers there and many of the men were *mauvais sujets*; criminals to the enemy but to us something of a prisoner *élite*. Since he could no longer hope for exchange, it was becoming—as it is now—the duty of every prisoner of war to escape, if he could do so without breach of faith. It is—and was—the best who attempt it, not the worst. The endurance, initiative, enterprise involved are regarded, rightly, as high military qualities.

[1] Rev. R. B. Wolfe, *English Prisoners in France*, London (J. Hatchard) 1830. 'Mr B . . .' was not, as Fraser says (op. cit., 72), Edward Boys, who was never imprisoned at Givet, but Thomas Blakiston, son of Sir Matthew Blakiston, Bart., and Lady Blakiston, daughter of John Rochford of Clogranne, Co. Carlow—a great lady of whom we shall hear more (p. 200).

An interesting paper[1] lists the twenty-eight midshipmen in the fortress at the end of 1811; all *mauvais sujets*, and divided into three categories, according to the nature of their 'crimes':

Désertion	10
Tentative de désertion.. ..	9
Inconduite	9

The first group had escaped and been caught, the second caught trying to escape. The 'misconduct' of the third group might be of various natures, but would most commonly consist of committing offences in order to be deprived of parole prior to attempting escape (see pp. 211, 240). In the first batch appears the name of Frederick Whitehurst, still expiating his second breakaway, and not destined to succeed again. Of the others, Henry Leworthy is one—that record-holding youth captured at the age of 10, but now a mature p.o.w. of 18. Another is Humphrey Colquhoun, also 18 though not a captive for so long. Both these lads refused to take no for an answer, and later gained their heart's desire. Among the 'tentatives' figures little John Trewin, the only one of Wesley Wright's 'admirals in embryo' not to get away (see Appendix II).

Every Briton who went there, whether man or officer, p.o.w., *détenu* or criminal, was daunted by the grimness of Bitche, Vauban's masterpiece in easternmost Lorraine, not far short of the Rhine. Says O'Brien,

> It is reckoned the strongest fortification in France, is built on the summit of an immense rock out of which all its subterraneous caves are hollowed—has three ramparts, first from 90 to 100 feet high; second, from 40 to 50; and the third from 25 to 30: redoubts, entrenchments, etc. innumerable. It appeared a moral impossibility to escape from it.[2]

Inside, the prisoners' accommodation, though all bad, was not equally bad for all. There were, roughly, five grades of prisoner and five corresponding classes of accommodation. Grade I prisoners were scarce: indeed, the detailed treatment of only one such prisoner survives. Edward Stack was an unusual man, and he had a most unusual career. In *ancien régime* days he had risen to be a colonel in Dillon's Irish Regiment, a regular unit in the French Army. Leaving it in disgust at the Revolution, he had joined the British Army: but (now a British colonel) he had had the misfortune to be on the

[1] P.R.O. Admiralty, 103, 467.   [2] *Naval Chronicle*, 30, 329.

143

Continent in 1803, and had become a *détenu*. But worse was to follow. As a friend of the Duc d'Enghien he was arrested for complicity in the alleged plottings of that unhappy prince, and narrowly escaped the firing-squad. Instead, he was sent to Bitche, where however he was treated with a lenity never quite explained. Probably he was more a political prisoner than a military one. Napoleon had incurred widespread odium over d'Enghien, and wanted no more. He knew that the British Government was watching the fate of d'Enghien's so-called accomplice with more than ordinary attention, and he very likely feared reprisals. Anyway, the authorities at Bitche obviously had their orders. They gave him a suite of rooms —above ground too—and treated him really handsomely. But Stack was evidently an exception, and must have had class I accommodation almost to himself. We hear of only two others who received even comparable treatment—Sir Beaumont Dixie (see p. 191) and a wild but influential Irish colonel named Whaley.[1]

The other four classes, designed to house grades II, III, IV and V, may fairly be described as 'indifferent', 'bad', 'very bad' and 'execrable'. At one time or another an officer at Bitche might well find himself occupying all of them, working his passage painfully from 'execrable' to 'indifferent' according to his gaoler's estimate of his behaviour; but also descending from 'indifferent' to 'execrable' in a single bump if he failed to give satisfaction. Class II, like class I, had the advantage of being on the surface, and in it, if he were lucky and very well behaved, our officer might hope to spend his last days at Bitche before returning to his non-penal depot. His cell would be mean, small and overcrowded, but at least it would admit the light of day.

Grade III men, occupying class III premises, would still be privileged in that their quarters were the best of the subterranean ones—the officers' *souterrains*. Here a note of caution should be sounded. Almost all surving narratives affirm that their authors were 'cast into the dungeons'. But, as all Bitche men knew only too well, there are dungeons and dungeons: and the officers' *souterrains* undoubtedly were (as dungeons go) *good* dungeons. Though painfully damp and depressing, they were not hewn straight out of the virgin rock, but carefully stone-lined. They were, in fact, the quarters which, in his day, Vauban had designed for the occupying garrison.

[1] Both discussed in Joshua Done's *The Prisoner of War*, Colburn's New Monthly Magazine, 1841. For the experiences of this lively *détenu*, see pp. 245-7.

A surviving picture,[1] done by a British prisoner, may surprise anyone who has taken his British authorities too literally. He will see a high vaulted chamber, very barely furnished, yet fitted with raised bed-boards, each with two not altogether despicable mattresses; and, high up, a row of windows through which stream shafts of light—possibly not sunlight yet certainly daylight: in short, though *souterrain*, rather 'basement' than 'cellar'.

Our officer, however, has had to work his way up to such luxury. In doing so he would have passed through class IV, the men's *souterrains*. I have seen no illustration of them; but, by inference, the main difference between them and the officers' prison-places was that they had no windows: were, that is, cellars rather than basements, though they were still properly stone-lined and vaulted. Probably they also had bedboards covered, if not with mattresses, at least with straw. But the evidence is unanimous in declaring that fifty stone steps led down to them. A good many of their inhabitants were just ordinary service and merchant prisoners, non-gentle but also non-penal, who had been unlucky enough to find themselves detailed for Bitche. The crew of Dillon's cutter, for example, for long resided there, though not *mauvais sujets*. But class IV premises also housed—a most important circumstance—all *mauvais sujets;* not always, but at times. And these people might be officers or men. So here, for once, was common ground in which the leaders and the led could meet. Moreover this mixing was sanctioned; indeed inevitable, because of the ruling that officers who tried to escape forfeited officer privileges.

Evidently the men had a very raw deal because, whether 'criminals' or not, they could rise no higher; and, by any standard, the place was disgraceful. Morals were bound to be low, and certainly some of the old stagers were pretty far gone; not so very far removed from wild beasts. Yet not quite wild beasts because, even there, they preserved some sort of human discipline. A curious sort of democracy reigned, and transgressors against what to the poor creatures seemed the common good were tried in a rugged court of their own, and punished un-mercifully. In Ellison's day (1808–9) the *souterrain* was so self-governing that the gendarmes, on the governor's orders, gave the place as wide a berth as possible, and never ventured to interfere with the occupants' 'judicial' proceedings. In Jackson's day (1812) the uncrowned king of the dungeon was a man called Spillier; and

[1] Reproduced opposite p. 129.

his power knew no limit. For by then, as seems inevitable the world over, Democracy had tended to degenerate into a Dictatorship of the Strongest—as indeed it had recently done in France itself.

It was a strange society: it should have spelt ruin to body and soul alike. Yet somehow it did not—quite. Why? Surely because, passing through it, constantly though in smallish numbers, there were officers: shorn of all authority, of course, cooped up and suffering like the rest, but still officers. And what officers! Jackson the lieutenant, O'Brien the master's mate, James the midshipman were, more than once, such birds of passage, *en route* from class V to higher grades of comfort. So were others—Leworthy, Ashworth and Tuthill, Colquhoun, Hewson, Dacre and Worth, midshipmen; Batley the E.I.C. cavalryman, Barklimore the surgeon, Ellison and Brine of the merchant service; Essel the sub-lieutenant—at least until he fell to his death from the highest wall: magnificent fellows, all of them, each with a saga of his own which he was usually too modest to write.

What was the impact, if any, of such men in such a place? Unquestionably it was tremendous, achieved, not by any display of officer authority (which, down there, would have been imprudent if not actually dangerous), but simply by reason of their own colour and pertinacity. Evidently they were no ordinary people, these escape fanatics: bold in opportunity, quick in decision, tough and enduring in adversity: no great performers on paper, perhaps, but real men of action. Such characters, walking models of unyielding morale, cannot have failed to exert a profound and heartening influence on all with whom they consorted. The real leader can dispense with Naval Discipline Acts and trappings on his coat. He leads, whether on quarter-deck or in *souterrain*, because he was born to lead.

Maybe it is no longer possible to establish here the true sequence of cause and effect. Possibly we exaggerate the influence of the officers. But one solid fact remains which still needs explaining. Bitche itself, the classic black spot, the blackest of black smudges on Napoleon's reputation, was not by any means the worst morale-breaker.

There remain the class V quarters, reserved for the immediate reception of grade V prisoners who, loaded with chains, at length reached those frowning battlements. These places were situated lower than the men's *souterrains* and were, in every respect, dungeons: black, dank places that dripped water, where natural light was unknown; where the walls were living rock, and the only entrances heavy doors with small barred grills in them. No bedboards here, no mattresses. Here is O'Brien's account of his introduction to class V accommodation:

> Being now arrived at the dungeon I was to inhabit, my handcuffs etc. were taken off, and I was shown in to the deserters. . . . I found Mr Worth, midshipman, and a Captain Brine (merchant service) here. They were placed on a door, which they had managed to unhinge and lay as a platform to keep them out of excrement and wet, which was more than ancle deep: they had a little straw and a blanket.[1]

Here, in every sense, we have reached rock-bottom. Yet, even here, we must try to be fair. These holes were punishment-places, for people condemned, rightly or wrongly, as real criminals: the unfortunates sentenced to inhabit them were not there in perpetuity, but for the specified period ordained in the sentence: and it was reckoned usually in weeks rather than months. They could then begin their climb, geographical and moral.

At Bitche, as elsewhere only perhaps more so, the disposition of the commandant was all-important. The man who reigned there for a long time, including the period of James's sojourn, was a certain General Maisonneuve. Originally a male nurse at Metz hospital, he had risen during the Terror, solely, it would seem, by reason of his ferocity: a most unprepossessing character by all accounts, though naturally his British Boswells had no predisposition to love him. He was coarse, treacherous, a violent anglophobe, a coward, and master of a peculiarly mean spying system. On one occasion, discovering from his creatures that the occupants of the men's *souterrains* had found an old passage-way leading under the ramparts, he let the plot go forward until the would-be fugitives were actually in the passage, having meanwhile filled the exit end with his troops. The men's leaders, Cox, a carpenter, and Marshall, a smith (both of Brenton's *Minerve*), ran into them in the darkness and were instantly butchered. Afterwards, the gallant general had the corpses, hacked and disfigured, displayed in the main courtyard, and positively bragged, in public, that it was he in person who had run Cox through the body[2].

---

[1] *Naval Chronicle*, 30, 329.
[2] So says James, who was there at the time. Ellison, who came soon afterwards, confirms the exhibition of the bodies, but says that the deed itself was done by two 'French officers', and that they were reprimanded by their government, the reprimand itself being prominently displayed in the fort. Had Maisonneuve himself been one of the culprits, he would hardly have permitted himself to be so pilloried.

His principal spy was a Jerseyman called Bouchel, known as Big Williams, who had fled his native island to escape punishment for murder. Nor was Bouchel an isolated phenomenon. He represented a regular, if small, subdivision of those who occupied the men's *souterrains*. Along with the ordinary decent p.o.w.s and the 'criminals' (officers and men) of the 'deserter' type, there was always a sprinkling of *real* criminals—and here the inverted commas are deliberately omitted. They were men—British men too—who had been tried in French courts, and convicted, not of 'desertion', but of fraud, theft, rape or murder. At home, some had been civilians, but others had belonged to the Army or Navy. The methods of wartime recruitment in Britain were certainly not calculated to—and did not—exclude rogues. It was doubtless inevitable that the Maisonneuves would smell out, and use, the Bouchels.

II. SARRELIBRE

Not far to the north-west of Bitche, on the river Saar, stood the fortress town of Sarrelouis, known in our war by the revolutionaries' name of Sarrelibre. Among British prisoners it had a rather better reputation than Bitche; though, from surviving accounts of life there, it is not very clear why this was so. We have seen, it is true, how one particular youth (Alexander Stewart) managed to escape being stained for life, mainly through Brenton's zeal for education which, reaching out to Sarrelibre, never reached Bitche. Stewart makes it clear, too, that other captives, older than himself, partially escaped contamination by the same means. Yet the picture left behind by all three of our Sarrelibre witnesses—Stewart, Choyce and James—is extremely grim. There all the vices flourished, from gambling to homosexuality—an evil which, a moment's quiet thought will convince us, was quite inevitable. Fortunately, perhaps, we are spared many of the harrowing details; by Stewart because he could not bring himself to enlarge upon them, by Choyce because, very likely, he hardly thought such everyday things to be worthy of chronicle, and by James because, as an officer who had already 'done his time' at Bitche, he probably did not have to endure the worst.

Yet what he did endure was bad enough. When he arrived, late in 1809, he was confined, with one other midshipman, in a cell 20 feet square where there were seven wooden bunks, each accommodating two people. The other twelve occupants were what he calls 'coal-heavers', but who were in fact instructive specimens (much inferior to Peter Bussell) of 'officers' who did not qualify for Verdun and parole—the masters and mates of north-country longshore colliers. James makes it very easy to understand why they failed to qualify. They were an incredibly uncouth party, entirely illiterate and, as well, dirty little traitors. Their crime was this: they purchased a few small luxuries from their gaoler general—fit companion-piece to Maisonneuve—by consenting to back him when an inquiry was being held on his cruelties to prisoners: and their false evidence proved decisive.[1] He was cleared, to continue his cruelties unchecked. This was the commandant—his name was Le Sage—who compassed the death of a prisoner by methods which, to a man, the British stigmatized as judicial murder. A little seaman called Morgan, on his way one day to a muster, was suddenly assaulted by a very drunken gendarme who laid into him with the flat of his sword. The quick-tempered Welshman could not stand it. He plucked the weapon from the drunkard's hand, threw it out of the window and kicked the creature downstairs. He was hustled off to a *cachot*, half-killed by savage blows before he got there, and then tried by a drum-head court-martial for resisting the guard. Le Sage certainly knew the circumstances of the case, the intoxication of the gendarme and the blatant provocation. But these things made no difference. 'Resisting the guard: sentence, death by shooting'—and little Morgan was duly shot.

In many ways, James contrives to put Sarrelibre in its true perspective. Bitche he summed up in the words, 'Frenchmen may say what they like about prison-ships, but they were palaces compared with the Fort of Bitche'. And again, 'I left it [Bitche] considering it to be the happiest day of my life'. But he had scarcely arrived at Sarrelibre before he could say from his heart, 'Of the comparison between the two depots Bitche, with all its horrors, was the most preferable'. And James, a connoisseur of horrors if there ever was one, certainly ought to know.

Again, why? Again the answer seems clear. There were often officer-prisoners at Sarrelibre, but there is no evidence of their ever getting near the men.

III. SEDAN

This, the third of the penal depots, was an equally grim and forbidding fortress: but the number of prisoners it held was, by comparison,

[1] Choyce tells the same story, and names the principal villain—Captain John Haig.

small. There is no reason to suppose that life there was markedly dissimilar from that at Bitche and Sarrelibre. That much-travelled trio, James, Done and Williams (see pp. 249-50) all sampled it, but none left details, and I know of no other prisoner who did.

IV. VALENCIENNES

By the law of probability the penal depots should have been unhappier places than the non-penal ones. So, for the most part, they were: but not, it would seem, always. Here again so much depended upon the commandant and his minions. They can never be ignored, as will be seen at Valenciennes, the first of the non-penal depots to be considered.

For much of the war it had one of the better reputations among the prisons. Early on, it had not been overcrowded, some 1,400 captives living in specially constructed barracks within the lower fortress. What is more, its commandant had allowed one-third of them at a time to go into the town to work. This was civilized. It was also, we may recall, what Napoleon's own law ordained for all prisons and all prisoners. But it remained exceptional, and, even in this case, it happened for the wrong reasons. The governor charged ten sous a day to every captive who availed himself of the privilege. Having made some £6,000 out of this mean and illegal levy, he was superseded. His successor, Colonel Du Croix Aubert, who was in office in 1808 when the midshipmen arrived from Verdun, was a much more honest man, though a regular martinet, and proud of it. He instantly stopped all outside work; to the detriment of his own pocket, of course, which no doubt proves his honesty, but also to the detriment of the prisoners, their health and morale. Edward Boys, when he arrived, found things much better than at Bitche or Sarrelibre: yet

> the greater part, by endless, grinding ennui, were reduced to such a state of apathy that they were worn down into mere brute existence; while those who had still any energy left magnified the most trifling occurrences into an important event.

Here are evils indeed, but dangers common to all p.o.w. camps always.

There were also the common irritants of stupid, unimaginative gendarmes: but when they excelled themselves, a complaint to Du Croix Aubert would often put things right, for he believed in disciplined gaolers too. There was also, apparently, much less general regimentation than in most depots. This allowed the midshipmen,

¹ Boys, op. cit., p. 114.

though they slept apart from the men, to live with them at other times; which, in its turn, helped to stir the men from their apathy; as, for example, when they organized illuminations and transparencies to celebrate the anniversary of Trafalgar, an idea still capable of rousing some enthusiasm in the seamen. Yet the underlying apathy was there, as Boys discovered when he sounded 'several of the most steady of the quartermasters and petty-officers of that class'—the pick of the Lower Deck—about attempting to escape. Not one would listen to him. Later on, things changed considerably. He himself set the fashion of escaping. This led to a tightening up of regulations and a sharp fall-off in the comforts of life: which in its turn led to more escapes, or attempts thereat. This may seem paradoxical, but it is not really so. Experience showed at all depots that the increase of discomfort penetrated the dull hide of apathy sufficiently to make the attempt seem worth while. There was, too, an additional incentive to attempts from Valenciennes. Geographically, it was an easier place than many to run from successfully, being the northernmost of all the depots, and near the Belgian border.

Later still, with a return of poor commandants and an ever-increasing crowding of prisoners—numbers rose from 1,400 to 2,000 by 1814—the general standard of living certainly fell off. But it never reached the depths of Bitche or Sarrelibre, or even non-penal Givet.

V. ARRAS

Of Arras there survives a long, but characteristically dull, description by Peter Bussell, the patient ex-master of the *Dove*. It was one of the earliest depots with, when Bussell joined it in 1806, only 1,200 occupants, living at first in buildings up against the town walls but soon moved out to the Citadel, half a mile away. It is hard to discover from a man like Bussell what the treatment of captives was really like. All superlatives are foreign to him. In his early years there, however, he gets as near as he ever does to complaining. It is on the subject of the food, and especially on the chronic short weight of the meat supplied: and he does infer that his first commandant, a man called Duhamel, had much to do with both that and other discomforts. But we only begin to suspect that something had been seriously wrong when a man named Noirot succeeded Duhamel. The newcomer he praises to the skies, as though a golden age has succeeded a tyranny. There are other reasons, too, for thinking that the Duhamel period had been a bad one. For one thing, the numbers rose, in one year, from 1,200 to 2,800, with apparently no extra accommodation provided. Then, in 1807, came something like an epidemic illness. Where only 37 prisoners had died between 1803 and 1806 inclusive, 173 perished in 1807: and in 1808—an even worse year—there were 251 deaths. On the morale of the captives he has little to say: he is not that kind of man. At best, however, there must have been much of the apathy which characterized Valenciennes. Peter himself caught it badly— unless, indeed, he had always had it. Anyway, towards the end of his long imprisonment, though he still hopes for the war to end, he seems more or less indifferent to who wins it.

Bussell was essentially a cliquish man. At the depot there were a good many seamen, both naval and merchant, and a number of parole officers living in the town, but apparently no midshipmen. He has no social relations with any of these classes, confining himself to the largest group of all, his fellow merchant skippers, of whom the 'over-80's' are the acknowledged aristocrats. Indeed, there can have been little in common between the merchant officers and the rest. They felt themselves, no doubt, to be socially superior to the ratings and the hands, but knew themselves to be far below the service officers. These last he faintly disparages He calls them 'our bucks' or 'our dons', and was clearly a little jealous of them because they lived in a style so much superior to his own. Still, he too was allowed to 'live out' most of the time, though in poor, pinched style. About one sort, even, of his own equals he is querulous—those who try to escape. He tells us that many did, but adds, with almost ghoulish satisfaction, that very few succeeded. His sourness is understandable. To him, the only result of an escape was that he was hauled back for a spell in the Citadel!

In 1809 the overcrowding grew so serious that a new depot had to be opened at Cambrai. In April 900 seamen from Arras were trans-ferred thither: in August all the soldiers went to Sarrelibre, and in September a complete clearance was effected, all the rest, now mostly merchant officers and their crews, being packed off to Auxonne, far to the south-east, and to Besançon, farther east still on the Swiss border. Thereafter the French tended to segregate the merchant-service types from the rest. They were never partial to them, especially to their officers, who certainly seem to have had few scruples about breaking such parole as they were allowed, taking advantage of every loosening-up of security precautions made by the kindlier-disposed commandants.

Once again, it is hard to discover from Bussell what influence, if any, the presence of service officers at Arras exerted upon the men. Yet, once more, the influence of one particular officer is apparent. Arras was near enough to Verdun to come early into the orbit of Captain Brenton, and it achieved the amenities of a school for its children and classes for its adults in 1806. In 1808, too, it obtained its own British chaplain. One of the devoted band of *détenu* clergy from Verdun, the Reverend W. Lawson, volunteered to leave the relative comforts of the central depot to serve his fellow-prisoners at Arras. They loved him dearly. When they moved, he went on with the Besançon party, and remained with them until 1810, when, to their great regret, he was suddenly sent back to Verdun. The reason, Bussell thought, was because he tried to rescue some Irishmen who had volunteered for the French Army. About Lawson he is neither disparaging nor scornful. 'We have lost a father and friend', is his simple comment.

Much later on, towards the end of 1813, Stewart reached a re-opened Arras after one of his longer walks—from Briançon on the Italian frontier. He was most favourably impressed. It was, he says, airy, clean, and so roomy that prisoners could positively be alone at times. Though now grown up and too old for school, he found everyone anxious to learn, and himself became a teacher of French. There was a subtle change in the gaolers, too. Many of them were beginning to see the writing on the wall: the prisoners, hitherto the slaves, might well become the masters in the near future. The reigning commandant, also, was charming to Stewart, making him his secretary and giving him all kinds of privileges. It was the first time for nearly nine years that the young man had known anything but kicks, blows and chains.[1] No wonder he thought well of Arras, and was sad when, early in 1814, the depot hurriedly broke up. He was on the road once more, but, as commandant's secretary, he found it infinitely less stony.

This, however, was the new Arras which had begun to refill as soon as Bussell left it. It is that drab little man whom we must follow, as he plods his painful 327 miles over execrable roads to Besançon: for of all our witnesses he alone can help us when we get there.

VI. BESANÇON

Here too the captives lived in the Citadel, perched high above the town: and here too, in his unassuming way, Bussell seems to have

[1] With one fleeting exception. See p. 252.

been happy enough. One obvious reason for this was that his commandants—especially the first of them, not inaptly named Le Doux—met with his approval. For a p.o.w., his assessment of commandants was more than usually lenient no doubt: yet evidently Bussell was not the only captive who approved of this one. When he was promoted and relinquished his command, the prisoners clubbed together and gave him a gold medal and chain costing 430 livres: about £18, no insignificant sum for men who were mostly three-sol-a-day 'under-80's'.

> The whole is very handsome, and the person for whom it is intended is worthy of it. It bears the following inscription—*Justice et Sagesse s'unissent.*

For all that Bussell must have been the answer to every gaoler's prayer, he does reveal three things which may well have made Besançon a relatively happy prison. First, passes to leave the Citadel and go down to the town were very liberally issued, and not, apparently, too often abused. Second, a much larger number of prisoners than usual was allowed to go out to work, the principal occupation being to make uniforms and footwear for the French Army. The prisoners thus had less time than others to nurse their grievances in idleness. The moral issue—whether they were contributing to the French war-effort by thus producing military coats and boots—is not raised. It is not the kind of point which would occur to Bussell: but it is a little strange that it is tacitly ignored by all other writers known to me. Obviously there was a line drawn somewhere, but where it ran is far from clear. Anything so blatant as enlisting in the French fighting forces was, of course, taboo—that was treason. But following one's trade in towns, or working for private French citizens, was allowed and, on our side, encouraged. Between these two extremes, however, there is a wide no-man's-land, covering an infinity of other occupations —like this one, or producing food for the enemy by working for his farmers, or in road-making, or in public building—all of which, with more or less directness, 'help the enemy'. The reason for this silence on the subject is, probably, that total war was not yet far enough advanced for men's minds to have got round to grappling with such niceties.

The third factor making for comparative contentment at Besançon was that, beyond doubt, it was a healthy place, especially up there in the Citadel where the climate, though cold in winter, was always bracing, and the air was clean. Bussell (one of whose few recorded hobbies was death-rates) notes that in the years 1809–11 there were only twenty-three deaths: and this is the more remarkable in that, he says, many of the inmates were old and worn out. 'There is a great many here', is his comment, 'who are arrived at second childhood.' Some indeed were so far gone that, at the end of 1811 (he infers it without actually stating it) twelve of them were invalided, and allowed to return to Britain. A little later a number of the thousands of invalids then being released from England arrived at Besançon.

> But however, as bad as they are with respect to wounds, many of them who were soldiers were forced to join the Army again.[1]

This reveals two things—the ever-growing crisis in French manpower, and a serious lack of principle in the French Government: for the basic condition to which these invalids had subscribed before leaving England was that they should fight no more against her. But Napoleon was never fastidious in such matters.

There was one other unusual feature about the Citadel of Besançon. The British prisoners often did not have the place to themselves. At irregular intervals, contingents of French troops would arrive, causing the captives much heartburning by ejecting them from the best quarters. There were also occasional irruptions of continental prisoners. But these, being only 'second-class', were not permitted to incommode the 'first-class' British. They were pushed into subterranean cells beside (if not actually under) the moat. One party of wretched Hungarians was there for some time, being constantly pressed to fight for France and as constantly refusing, though exposed to treatment little short of physical torture. The British pitied them, and tried to relieve them by throwing food and tobacco over the ramparts. But guards were set to prevent this, and two of the British who disobeyed the order to desist were imprisoned in a *cachot*. Bussell was not one of them: he never disobeyed orders.

There were evidently very few service officers at Besançon: but there was certainly one, and his influence seems to have been immense. Bussell calls him Lieutenant Owens, but his real name was Charles Cunliffe Owen, and he was the father of the famous South Kensington Museum director. Bussell admired him enormously, because he warned the prisoners of the futility of trying to escape, which advice,

[1] Bussell, op. cit., p. 146. See also below, p. 173.

155

according to him, they took.[1] Yet, it would seem, he was far from practising what he preached. He disappeared suddenly from Besançon, and the next they heard of him was that he was a close prisoner in Paris, standing trial on a criminal charge. There Bussell leaves him, but there was a sequel. He had got himself implicated, with two French ex-officers named Landis and Laupper, in a plot for seizing Belleisle by surprise.[2] Then one day he turned up in England, and the Transport Board had no difficulty in acquitting him of parole-breaking when it learned that he had 'escaped from a dungeon in the *Maison de force*, 21/2/13'.[3] He is said to have accomplished it in a novel way. He shammed lunacy for so long, and so cleverly, that he deceived all the Paris experts, who at last recommended repatriation. Such goings-on would hardly have pleased Bussell: but fortunately he never knew of them.

In spite of the comparative rarity of service officers, and the known complaisancy of our witness, we shall probably not be far wrong in classing Besançon as one of the best French prison depots.

VII. AUXONNE

Not far to the west lay Auxonne. No eye-witness account of life there is known to me: but again Bussell steps in with a little information which was probably first-hand to him, because many of his Arras friends were there, and intercommunication with Besançon was considerable. All, or very nearly all, the occupants were of the merchant service, and, it would seem, it was not a 'happy ship'. We are faced again, however, with Bussell's prejudice against escapers, and the Auxonne people seem to have been particularly prone to 'desert'. There is independent evidence of this. In the *Moniteur's* list of British prisoners escaped up to September 12, 1812, no less than 92 out of the 355 officers named are reported as having run from Auxonne—more than from any other depot.[4] No less than 81 of these were merchant officers: and all—but it is only the biased Bussell who says so—broke their admittedly limited parole.

About these men's loyalty, also, he has devastating things to say:

[1] See below, note 4.
[2] Report of the Duc de Rovigo to Napoleon, transcribed in Henry Gordon's MS. letter-book, kindly lent by Frank Maggs, Esq.
[3] P.R.O. Adm. 103, 468.
[4] For details of this, and a discussion on its *bona fides*, see Appendix III. It also confirms Bussell's remarks on escapes from Besançon. It records none whatever.

indeed so damning as to stretch one's credence to breaking-point. He actually avers that, out of the 1,200 or 1,300 prisoners there, nearly 1,000 entered the French service, driven to it by bad usage. Well, we have already seen some rather poor specimens of the breed at Sarrelibre (see pp. 148-9); and we know that, first and last, quite a number did join the enemy, though most of the known delinquents were from Ireland and not Great Britain. Bussell, however, informs us that 600 *Englishmen* had joined the Irish Brigade, but, failing for some reason to give satisfaction, they were thrown out of it and returned to Sarrelibre as prisoners. It is his sheer numbers that appal. Nearly 1,000—something like 80 per cent—from one depot alone is surely too much to swallow. Still, it remains possible; if we accept the ill-treatment, and assume some contagious mass breakdown of morale and patriotism; and if we also assume—an almost certain fact—that there were no regular service officers there at all.

On the other hand, it is pleasant to hear of just one incident at Auxonne which did real credit to the British. Fortunately, too, it is confirmed from an unimpeachable enemy source—the *Moniteur*, whom we instinctively mistrust when it vilifies the British, but whom we may safely believe on those rare occasions when it praises them. On Christmas Eve, 1809, there was a very serious fire in the town, and the prisoners, sent for to help extinguish it and rescue the inhabitants, earned the gratitude of everyone. It was dangerous work: ten of the captives were burnt more or less severely or hurt by falling masonry. Napoleon, when he heard about it, was generous (at least, the *Moniteur* said he was). He ordered that no less than twenty-one of them should receive a 'gratification' of six months' pay, and should be repatriated.[1] Whether he kept his word is not known—in such cases he did not always do so, as we are soon to see. But that the merchant skippers behaved well may be regarded as certain.

In the absence of almost all detail, we can only surmise: but our guess must be that Auxonne was a bad depot to be imprisoned in. Also it is perhaps fair to conclude that it would have been better had it housed a few service officers. They would not, probably, have had half the influence over merchant masters that they had over their own people. But they would surely have been able to stop such a

[1] *Moniteur Universel*, April 29, 1810. The lucky 21 are broken up as follows: 12 merchant captains of the first class (i.e. 'over-80's'); 3 of the second class ('under-80's'); 4 merchant passengers (supercargoes?); 1 merchant hostage (civilian detained at sea); 1 seaman.

wholesale collapse of morale as is implicit in Bussell's figures, even if they are greatly exaggerated. We have only to recall young Midshipman James, battling with a full general for the souls of six scruffy seamen and winning, to feel quite confident about what a Captain Brenton or a Captain Lavie would have achieved, to say nothing of a Jackson or an O'Brien.

VIII. AND IX. CAMBRAI AND LONGWY

Of conditions at Cambrai, not far from Valenciennes and Arras, there is little direct evidence. It was not established, as we saw, until 1809, but then it became one of the larger prison centres. Its reputation among the British was always fairly good, and it may be taken as ranking somewhere between Arras and Valenciennes. Longwy was also a late starter and, unlike Cambrai, never became a large depot. It lies well to the north and east of Verdun, on the borders of Luxembourg. The ubiquitous Stewart visited both these depots, but, not staying long at either, has little to say of them.

X. BRIANÇON

Separated by hundreds of miles from all the other depots, far to the south and east, lay Briançon on the Italian border. Though a fairly recent addition to the list, by 1814 it was bracketed with Sarrelibre and Arras as the most populous of all. It was a sinister place, a fortress of immense strength, cold, set high among snow-clad mountains, and rivalling even Bitche in grimness. Indeed, young Stewart, who saw them both from the inside (and who, with Done, is one of our three witnesses to the charms of Briançon)[1] declared that he 'would prefer twelve months in Bitche to six here', even though it was not, officially, a punishment depot at all.

He was there in 1812–13, and the rapidly-filling fortress was being used to house military prisoners now at last coming in in some quantity from Spain. But, for a reason not explained, the naval men were segregated from them, living fourteen to a small room in their own corridor: from which enclave—room, corridor and pump just outside it—they did not once issue for a whole year. Stewart had long ceased to expect much of life, and he takes this in his stride,

---

[1] The third is Thomas Williams, a young merchant apprentice whose adventures, along with those of his fellow-apprentice and cousin, John Tregerthen Short, were published in *Prisoners of War in France, 1804–1814*, London, 1914.

even when it is accompanied by other astounding living conditions. Thus, 'I never saw soap the whole time I was at Briançon', and 'when we washed our shirts it was by soaking them in the common urine of the room for the night, and then washing them under the pump when we went for our day's water.'[1]

At last Stewart decided that this was not good enough. It is a good example of the phenomenon lately described—that supreme hardship will convince a prisoner that nothing can be worse, not even unsuccessful escape. At Briançon, in winter, escape was probably quite impossible: yet Stewart tried it, twice. The first attempt petered out at once, and no wonder. Though he did not know it, he was trying to cut a hole big enough to squeeze through in a wall which 'designed to be bomb-proof, was no less than six feet thick'. He was soon detected, and so was his accomplice, a midshipman named William Hare. (How a midshipman got there, who shall say? It was not supposed to be a place for naval officers at all.) For punishment, the pair found themselves locked up in a *cachot* measuring 12 feet by 8 with three others. There was no window; only a 6-inch grating in the door. Here they remained for forty days; a period broken, however, by an interlude as plucky and desperate as it was pathetic. They contrived to cut out the bolt of the door with the mainspring of a watch concealed in their daily loaf by an outside ally. The *cachot* opened on to the main courtyard: they found the gates ajar, and nobody about: so they just walked out. Their gaolers' apparent negligence, however, was soon explained. The only road down from the fort was solid ice, and when they ventured off it, they found the hillside snow-bound and quite impassable. They stuck it out for two nights, slithering down ice-blocked watercourses or lurking in frozen ravines. They made very little progress, however, and on the third day were rounded up by their pursuers; fortunately for them, because they were nearly dead with cold. They were roughly thrust back into their *cachot*.

The local commandant, fit company for his brethren of Bitche and Sarrelibre, decided to make an example of them. Having paraded them before all their fellows and the whole garrison, he unscrewed the bayonet from a soldier's musket, and deliberately thrust it into Stewart's back, though not far enough to kill. It seems that this fine specimen of French chivalry suspected Stewart of having written, and secretly dispatched, a letter of protest to the French Ministry of

[1] Stewart, op. cit., p. 66. Williams cites details almost as lurid.

War—a suspicion which, as the young man does not deny it, was probably correct.

Stewart got away from Briançon soon afterwards, not by flight, but by exchanging identities with another prisoner who had orders for the road but did not want to go. A six-week journey, still on foot, brought him to Arras, and to the end of his worst sufferings. With the single exception of Givet, he had visited every considerable depot.

XI. MONTDAUPHIN

Fifteen miles south of Briançon, where the Guil, coming down from Monte Viso, joins the Durance, stands the fortress of Mont-dauphin. It was not a large prison establishment, and may be regarded as an overflow for its more populous neighbour. Both are deep in the hills, and that they were hard to get away from is revealed by the *Moniteur*, which shows only three escapes from Montdauphin, and a solitary one from Briançon.[1] No resident prisoner known to me has left any account of his experiences here.

XII. GIVET

There remains Givet, almost the only depot unvisited by Stewart. It shall be our last port of call. It lies on both banks of the river Meuse, just where it leaves France for Belgium. Great Givet, the larger portion of the town thus divided, lay on the right bank; Little Givet, the smaller, on the left. Communication between the two was maintained by a pontoon bridge whose central boats could be hauled out for the passage of river traffic. Dominating Little Givet rose the great fortress of Charlemont, famous in military history, and at first the prisoners were lodged in it; but soon, as their numbers grew until they were as large as at any prison depot in France, they were moved out of the citadel itself into the horse-barracks below it on the town side.

The prison had its ups and downs, but, on the whole, had the reputation of being the worst of the non-penal depots. The reason for this was probably the old one—bad commandants. It was not because, like Briançon, it was hopelessly inaccessible. Indeed, it was near enough to Verdun to come under the eye of Captain Brenton: and it did so very early because his own ship's company was sent there. He was not allowed to reside at Givet, but it was the first place which he obtained leave to visit. There he found his men in the Charlemont

[1] This was Joshua Done; see below, p. 247.

8. THE OFFICERS' SOUTERRAIN, BITCHE. *From Ellison's 'Prison Scenes'*

dungeons, awaiting the conversion of the stables into prison-quarters, and getting them moved out was his earliest success. He had to return to Verdun, but was allowed to leave one of his clerks behind to look after his people. This efficient young officer—W. T. Bradshaw —was of great assistance to O'Brien when he arrived there.[1] The first commandant earned Brenton's praise, but he was soon superseded by a much inferior one, cruel and rapacious; also, in the seamen's eyes, rather comic. He showed every sign of being afraid of them, and fell back (as they thought) upon bluster which, while intended to intimidate, only tickled their peculiar sense of humour. When four of them escaped, he publicly ordered their pursuers to bring none of them back alive, and swaggered into the prison-yard ostentatiously examining the priming of his pistol—an action which was greeted with giggles and ill-concealed ribaldry. They were to discover later that cowards are often bullies too.

Thereafter things went from bad to worse. Up to 1806 a few midshipmen and clerks had been there: but now the commandant got them removed. He had no use for Young Gentlemen: what he wanted was to have the men all to himself. To make things worse, Brenton fell ill, and had to move first to Tours and then, as we saw, to England. Even there he continued to follow his men's fortunes as best he could, though there was little he could do beyond reporting what he heard to his government. That report shows that the whole policy of calculated brutality which followed was deliberately adopted in order to reduce the prisoners to such desperation that they would consent to enter the French service. A few, he says, succumbed, while the rest, though they resisted, sank into a dreadful trough of misery, aggravated by bad spirits, always within reach of anyone who could pay for them. In fact, they rapidly sank to the level of *Romans*, *Misérables* and *Rafalés*.

They were saved by the efforts of one man. The Reverend Robert Wolfe was a *détenu*, living at Verdun where he had already been prominent in helping to organize the charities and the schools. Now, hearing what was happening at Givet, he applied to be allowed to go there as chaplain. Once or twice already he had fallen foul of Wirion, who was only too pleased to get rid of him. His friends tried hard to dissuade him. It would be a useless sacrifice, they said, and really dangerous. His new parishioners were like savage beasts 'whom

---

[1] Short (see above, p. 249) questions Bradshaw's honesty: but his view is very likely jaundiced, as Choyce's was of Brenton himself.

despair and suffering have rendered ferocious, and whose whole relief seems to be in making others more wretched than themselves'. Nothing, however, could shake his purpose. He went, and, as a crowning act of faith, took his wife and family with him.

At first everything was against him. There was no other Gentleman in the place, either officer or *détenu*. As for the men, 'left as they were entirely to themselves, no one having the desire or power to restrain them, the depot at Givet was perhaps the most reprobate spot that can be imagined'. Religion, he tells us, was non-existent, save—and Church of England clergyman as he was he reserves generous praise for them—for a score of Methodists who manfully retained their morale, though subjected to 'the most painful persecution and . . . the most dreadful blasphemies'.[1]

No detailed story of how he won through can be given here: how he found a regular organization of Irish officers constantly assaulting the men's loyalty: how every French official, from the governor himself down to the youngest gendarme recruit, was busily engaged in enriching himself at the prisoners' expense: how, at first, he dared not issue to the captives the money supplied by the wealthier Britons at Verdun and by the Lloyds committee in England. When he tried, the French authorities insisted on the cash passing through their hands first (where he knew it would remain): or, if any dribble of it did percolate through that limy net, it simply went on more drink, more excess and more misery. Wolfe's own account is remarkable for its modesty: yet it remains a wonderful illustration of what one honest, single-minded man can do when he has made up his mind to it.

Contrary to the jeremiads of his Verdun friends, he seems to have had little trouble with the prisoners themselves. He must very soon have convinced them, depraved as they were, that he was altogether on their side. It was with the gaolers that he had his greatest difficulties —and his most astonishing successes; for, in the end, they too accepted him. Only supreme tact and subtle handling of men enabled him to do it, especially during his early days there, when he was in constant danger of being himself packed off for Bitche. Fortunately for him and his work, his arch-enemy, the commandant in charge when he arrived, was soon replaced by another one who, from Wolfe's point of view, was a great improvement. From the start he contrived to establish much happier relations with the new one, and he scored a great triumph when he was allowed to start a school, for adults as

[1] Wolfe, op. cit., p. 62.

well as for boys. Before long he can report 500 or more of them busily, profitably, and comparatively happily engaged in learning to read and write, and mastering arithmetic and navigation—a considerable feat of organization when it is realized that he had, first, to create his teaching staff entirely from among the men themselves. He was able too, very gradually, to revolutionize the hospital arrangements, which had been grotesquely foul. Further, he was greatly helped by the reappearance of some of the midshipmen in 1808.

The whole episode sounds, at first flush, something very like a miracle. But it was not that. The fact is that, in transforming the people at the depot from a prisonful of brutal criminals into a more or less self-respecting community, Wolfe was also assisting the gaolers, because orderly people are much more easily managed than disorderly ones. As soon, then, as greed and profit-making ceased to be the prime motives of the authorities, they realized the good man's value to them, and not only allowed him to proceed with his regeneration but, after a time, actually helped him. Their final attitude towards him was well illustrated in 1810 when, upon a rumour that he was to be returned to Verdun, the whole High Command at Givet —the general commanding the district, the governor and the officer commanding at the fort—sent a joint petition to the Minister of War imploring him to allow the British chaplain to remain.

The improvement in the prisoners was enormous, and lasting. After the war Wolfe kept track of many of the men, and was delighted to find that they had mostly secured good jobs for themselves directly as a result of what they had learnt at the adult school of Givet.

In the contemporary literature about Napoleon's captives, two stories stand out perhaps more prominently than any others, more described and discussed both by prisoners in France and by the public at home. Of both the scene is Givet. One concerns the murder of a midshipman named John Haywood (Heywood and Hayward are alternative versions). The other concerns the passage of the river Meuse at Givet by Napoleon himself. Both attracted the attention of several prisoner-authors, and in both cases there are considerable differences of detail in their accounts.

The feature of the Haywood tragedy common to all the writers is that this youngster, somewhere just outside the town and in broad daylight, was cut down and instantly killed by the swords of gendarmes, when offering no resistance at all. This seems certain. We may now add details, culled from four sources.

(1) *Boys.* Haywood and a fellow-midshipman named James Gale attempted to run for it in broad daylight. Gendarmes instantly gave chase, and the fugitives, seeing escape was impossible, stopped, put up their hands and said '*Je me rends!*' But the gendarmes, taking no heed, cut down Haywood who died at once, and gravely wounded Gale who later recovered. Thereupon the commandant sent for the gendarmes and rewarded them saying, 'I give you this for having killed one of them. Had you killed both, the reward would have been doubled.' The weakness of this evidence lies in the fact that it is certainly second-hand. Boys was never at Givet.

(2) *Wolfe* tells substantially the same story, but adds that the young men's plans, and their whereabouts, were given away to the commandant by a British informer. This must be accepted. Wolfe is much the most reliable of our witnesses: he was at Givet at the time and intimately concerned with the case. He also gives details about the informer which no one was likely to invent, least of all Wolfe. He tells how he refused to give the villain his share of the charitable money which he dispensed, and was thereupon accused of abetting the escape of prisoners, and narrowly escaped being sent to Bitche. He is not the man to make embellishments, let alone invent falsehoods and calumnies.

(3) *Wetherell* is our third witness, to be believed in that he was at Givet throughout his captivity, but otherwise with the reservations already mentioned. His principal divergence from the others' stories is that the midshipmen were not escaping at all; merely, in company with the gendarme told off to look after them, taking their girls for a frolic at a near-by fair, with every intention of returning afterwards. Here Wolfe's 'informer' figures again. He is actually named—a one-legged marine called Wilson, the youngsters' own servant and quite in their confidence. The gendarme was lazy, preferring to stop at an *estaminet* and sozzle himself on money provided by the lads. To him came Wilson, telling him that the midshipmen had gone to dance at the fair; whereupon the cross-grained brute, half-drunk, cried 'I'll spoil their dancing!', and rushed after them. As he approached them they were standing still, watching some quarrymen at work; and when they saw him, being gay good-natured lads out on the spree, they ran to meet him, inviting him to accompany them. His only reply was to cleave Haywood's skull with his sword and to wound Gale so desperately that he died that night. The quarrymen, witnessing the whole affair, instantly closed upon the murderer, disarmed him and hauled

him off to the commandant. In this version, that officer does not make the shocking remark attributed to him by Boys (but not by Wolfe). Instead, he gives him a mock trial, acquits him, and sends him off, for his own safety, to another camp.

(4) The daylight escape envisaged by Boys and Wolfe sounds a little unlikely. Not only would it be much too dangerous, in that the fugitives would expose themselves to death at the hands of gendarmes riding them down in hot blood: it would also give them a much slenderer chance of success—they would get but little start. Wetherell, with his eye to a good story, avoids this weakness by asserting that the lads were not running at all. But *Short* and *Williams*, both at Givet at the time, agree on a much more likely version. According to them, the boys did escape, but at a reasonable hour—at night. By daylight, however, they had not got far enough away, and so hid themselves in a cavern on the fortress hill. Next morning Wilson, who knew their plans, led the hunters to the cave. They stood at the entrance, ordered the runaways out, and killed Haywood in cold blood as he emerged with his hands held up in token of unavoidable surrender. Gale also was wounded, but not killed. This is harking back, substantially, to Wolfe's version, and is probably the true one.

The story of Napoleon's brief but dramatic appearance at Givet has often been told: no wonder—in any age it would make first-rate 'copy'. All our Givet men, and many others, carry it. Here, Wolfe's full, eye-witness account will be followed, with supplementary details from other writers.

On November 12, 1811, the Emperor was to pass through the town on his way back from a tour in Holland. He arrived at Great Givet, beyond the river, very late at night owing to drenching rains and flooded roads. When at length he came he was in a vile temper, and went straight to bed without noticing the local dignitaries who had been awaiting him all day in their best clothes, now irretrievably ruined. During the night, the Meuse rose alarmingly: at 3.30 a.m. the chains of the pontoon parted, and the whole bridge was swept away. Consternation reigned. The engineers were exhausted by their all-night efforts, and no one dared tell the Emperor that he could not proceed. A conference of high-ups met, and various suggestions of varying futility were made. At last a relatively minor member of the conference rose to his feet, one Colonel Flayelle, in charge of the Charlemont fortifications and a staunch friend of Wolfe and the

prisoners. 'You will do nothing', he said quietly, 'unless you send
to the depot barracks and get some of the English prisoners.' Everybody
stared, incredulous. But Flayelle, who knew his Englishmen better
than anyone present, held his ground and, in the end, not without
misgiving, his suggestion was adopted. Volunteers were called for
and, when every man volunteered, thirty were picked and sent down
to the river. Wolfe, who went down to watch, recorded what
followed:

> They really had the appearance of amphibious animals in the shape,
> and with an extraordinary share of the intelligence, of men; some
> working up to their necks in water; others skimming, in little light
> boats, against this rapid current, as if they were going with the
> stream. At one time swimming to a place which they could not
> otherwise reach, at another diving to a vast depth to carry on their
> work. . . . I immediately sent out my servant with some brandy,
> and gave each of them a little, to prevent them from taking cold.
> And as I thought it very probable that they might attain their
> liberty, I allowed him to go and help them.[1]

In a few hours the chains were renewed, the bridge complete.

At this point Wetherell, Short and Williams, all practical seamen,
make a sensible technical addition to the clergyman's narrative. The
British sailors, they point out, did not recreate the whole pontoon
bridge. With many of its component vessels swept miles downstream,
this would have been impossible in the time. What they did, clearly,
was to pass a few stout chains or hawsers across, collect a few of the
nearer, larger and least-damaged boats, and pass them back and forth
across the river on an improvised chain-ferry.

Meanwhile Napoleon, on being informed of the trouble, went back
to bed in a huff. When the work was nearing completion, however,
he rose and strolled down to the river. A remarkable scene ensued.
There stood the great man, who had been cold-shouldering his own
subjects ever since he had arrived, affably chatting (with Marshal
Mortier as interpreter) to the common seamen of his most hated
enemy, whom, indirectly, he had been maltreating for years. They
crowded round him, curious no doubt but perfectly respectful,
answering his questions frankly and without embarrassment, though

> any of these men, who would have gone up to a cannon's mouth to
> have destroyed this enemy in battle, might with one push have
> sent him to the bottom of the Meuse, to rise no more. . . . Yet,
> far from having any evil thought towards him when he confided

[1] Wolfe, op. cit., p. 139.

in their good faith, they were a sort of garde d'honneur to him
as he passed the river. . . . There was not a single Frenchman
allowed to be upon the flying bridge which they constructed to
bring him over.[1]

Here Wetherell intervenes again, with even more intimate detail of
the Emperor's actual transit: and he claims to know because (he
says) he was not only in the working-party but actually in the boat
which carried the sacred person of Napoleon. One of the British
seamen—he too affirms that the whole crew was British—saw the
great man offer a pinch of snuff to one of his staff. 'Damme,' he said,
'but I should like to have a pinch out of the Emperor's box.' To his
and everyone else's surprise, Napoleon understood the remark,
smiled, and replied, 'So, my man, you shall, with pleasure': adding,
'Here, take each of you a snuff!' Then he handed his box round the
entire crew.[2]

Would it spoil a good yarn to inquire into the state of the Emperor's
English in 1811? Would he have so readily understood a British
sailor's rough speech, and replied so idiomatically? Perhaps not: and
yet Short goes far towards confirming all Wetherell's version, adding
for good measure the cheeky seaman's name—Thompson.

Long afterwards, at St Helena, Napoleon remembered the scene,
and related it to Dr O'Meara. According to him, he was the one to
think of the British prisoners: and, he declared, he ordered a sum of
money, a new suit of clothes and unconditional liberty to be given to
all who had done the job. But his memories—at St Helena—always
require verification before acceptance, and Wolfe is evidently the
better authority. It is true, however, that the Emperor ordered the
men's release with clothes and money. But somehow, in its passage
to and from the Ministry of War, the list of thirty got whittled down
to fourteen. There was some excuse for this, as Wolfe admits. When
they heard about the list, all concerned, and a good many more, were
naturally most anxious to have their names included and, in the end,
it contained some fifty names. That gave French officialdom, always
niggardly over such favours, their excuse for a far too drastic cut.
Wolfe himself looked like suffering. By Napoleon's express order
his name was to be included: but he received only three months'
leave of absence instead of full release. He took his family home, and
was just about to return himself—he would not have dreamt of breaking
his promise—when, somehow, full release was obtained for him.

[1] Wolfe, op. cit., p. 146.   [2] Wetherell, op. cit., p. 173.

And how did a grateful government acknowledge the tremendous services of this selfless man? The answer is difficult to believe. It certainly knew all about him, and what he had done: but—spontaneously anyway—it did nothing. Too many people, however, including many distinguished officers, knew the facts, and instantly and persistently brought pressure to bear. So, with very bad grace, the government gave way at last, and awarded him, in retrospect, the ordinary pay of a chaplain RN for the period of his stay at Givet. This was something. Strictly, Wolfe was a *détenu*, for whom the government acknowledged no responsibility. Legally, then, it owed him nothing. Yet it could hardly have been meaner. While still at Verdun he had been appointed by the Admiralty a sort of naval chaplain-at-large, to look after all British naval prisoners, and he had been given an ordinary chaplain's pay. But when he moved to Givet, his successor (Gorden) was given the job, and the pay. Uncomplaining, therefore, Wolfe had been performing the dual roles of chaplain RN and senior officer RN on no pay at all, and without the support of any other officer. To pay him what (after pressure) they now proposed was, then, a clear duty. It was not a reward at all, and no such ever came his way. Nor, in his book, is there any hint that he ever expected one. After this, however, it is not surprising to learn that even the pay was delayed, and only levered out of the government at last after many applications. The whole story of Givet is the crowning illustration of the evils arising from the separation of the led from their natural leaders. For obviously Wolfe was just that—not even an officer, but a very prince among natural leaders.

CHAPTER VII

THE ROAD TO FREEDOM

Our prisoners have arrived at their respective prisons, and have dwelt in them. It remains to record how they came to leave them, and when.

The great majority stayed till the end, with the Allies in Paris and Napoleon himself a prisoner. There is not so much to be told of this majority as there is of those minorities who found their road to freedom in other and more spectacular ways, and at other and more varied times. There is thus a danger, perhaps, of making it appear that most captives gained their liberty by exceptional methods; and in order to show that this was not so, it would be as well to record, in very general terms, how release did come to this very great majority.

After Napoleon's disaster in Russia in 1812, and his defeat at Leipzig in October 1813, invasion stared him in the face. Back in Paris in November, he saw that the best he could hope for was to defend his frontiers. Many of the depots, however, especially the eastern ones, were uncomfortably near those frontiers; and Napoleon, rightly regarding his British captives as counters of importance, decided to evacuate them before the oncoming tide of war secured their wholesale liberation. For a time he was successful: no depot, complete with prisoners, ever fell into allied hands. But there was hurry and confusion, and no small hardship to the captives themselves, because winter was upon them as the first moves began, and, not surprisingly, transport, lodging and even food-supplies often broke down under an almost impossible strain.

The first depot affected was Besançon, late in November: for, just to the east, the Austrians were preparing to enter France by way of the Belfort gap. Almost simultaneously, Blücher with his Silesian Army threatened from the north-east, and Bitche had hurriedly to follow; then Sarrelibre. By early January both Austrians and Prussians were well beyond these depots (which they did not stay to capture), and Verdun itself, in danger of being pinched out, was hastily cleared.

So it went on. The policy at first was to bring the prisoners back to the depots near the Franco-Belgian frontier, particularly Cambrai and Arras. But very soon these were threatened too, and whole droves of captives set off, in deep winter, blindly as far as most of them could see, fanning out in a general south-westerly direction. Now there appeared sad signs of Bussell-like apathy, even among people by nature quite un-Bussell-like. Here, clearly, was the heritage of long captivity—natural initiative dried up by years of confinement in which others had had the responsibility of making all the decisions. Many of these disconsolate convoys reached the Loire, in the general neighbourhood of Orleans, Blois and Tours. A good many actually crossed the river, penetrating as far south as Guéret on the upper Creuse: but not farther, because now came the rumour of Wellington's rapid advance from Spain: and there was even a drift north again. Throughout all this, the guards were gradually weakening, not only in numbers and efficiency, but even in will. The mayors of the various towns, suddenly called upon to feed and house the milling multitudes, one by one threw their hands in, often, at the same time, sticking the white cockade of the Bourbons into their hats.

It was the end, and a very confused end too. Some of the prisoners simply walked off northwards for Brittany, Normandy and the Channel, and secured their own transport home if they could find it. Others made their way to Paris, joining the allied troops as they entered it on the last day of March. Others, by going south again, reached Bordeaux and Wellington. In the end all—or almost all, for there are few reports of fatal casualties—got home somehow or other. To tell that tale in full would clearly be impossible here: it would be not one tale but a thousand different ones. We shall, however, hear one or two individual adventures later in this chapter, and in the next.

It may be recorded, too, while those who stayed to the end are still under review, that some of them did not particularly want to go home and that for reasons other than mere apathy. Specimens of one such group, containing both civilians and service-men, were those un-desirables, some of whom have already figured in these pages: people like Mr Green, ex-gallows-bird and clerk of the Verdun race-course; a Mr Fagan from Ireland whom Dillon suspected, probably rightly, of being a common spy and informer in French pay, and another spy, a colonel of Dillon's own name and the despicable creature who got James his second spell at Bitche; a Mr Jennings, horse-dealer at Verdun, whose antecedents are unknown but who made such a good thing out of fleecing the British there that he could hardly be anxious to meet any of them in Britain; 'Big Williams', the Bitche Jackal, and One-leg Wilson, the Givet traitor, or even those two rather mysterious midshipmen, Robert Mortimer and Alfred Parr, who 'entered the French service, 1809'.[1] True, they left it again in the following year, but, like all the other members of this sorry group, they must have known that their homecoming might prove exceedingly dangerous to their necks.

Another such group, much larger, consisted of Britons who were either old residents in France or people who, while prisoners, had got to like the French way of life. There were both civilians and officers so situated. The best-known *détenu* of this sort was Lord Louvaine, heir to the earldom of Beverley, and later earl himself. He never sought release, because he did not want it: indeed, he remained in France after all was over. There were a good many others like him, whose motives were examined in Chapter I. There were also a few p.o.w. officers who stayed on voluntarily. Ensign Edward Newenham of the 9th Foot, for instance, was still living in Verdun as late as 1853: so was John Graham, surgeon of the *Hussar*, while Lieutenant Lewis Mordaunt of the 61st Foot had died there in 1850.

Such people were exceptions. An overwhelming majority of our prisoners, of course, thought of freedom as the most desirable thing on earth, and sought it how or when they could: and, though most of them failed so long as the war lasted, there remains a respectably large minority which did not fail. These we must now examine. They got away, and that by four very different roads: by exchange, by release without exchange, by escape, and—saddest road of all, yet still release—by death. These four roads must all be explored, because each reveals important, if widely different, aspects of our captives' lives and fates. Let us then begin with the saddest—those who left captivity only by leaving the world itself—and then pass on to those happier ones who secured living freedom, either by their government's efforts ('exchange') or by the private negotiations of themselves and their friends ('release without exchange'); or— happiest and most colourful of all—by escape.

I. RELEASE BY DEATH

(a) From Natural Causes

Eleven years is a big slice of any man's life; and, apart altogether from the hard living which, as we have seen, was the lot of most of

[1] Hopkinson's list: see below, p. 267.

our captives, death took its inevitable toll. Add, then, the said hardships to the natural mortality rate, and a very heavy death-roll might well be expected. Oddly enough, however, there are few signs of one. All things considered, the mortality among prisoners, on either side, does not seem to have been unduly high. Figures are admittedly hard to come by, especially among those of our own men in France;[1] yet the very absence in contemporary narratives of any mention of wholesale epidemics or heavy death-rolls seems to indicate that there were not many, or very serious, outbreaks. Had they occurred, our authors would surely have noticed, even if they did not exaggerate them.[2] Such fatalities as they do record are mostly individual ones, arising from lung and kindred diseases contracted in excessively damp cells and dungeons.

The summary of naval officer-prisoners on p. 270 gives us our best chance of assessing mortality figures. There are 656 names and 59 deaths. But neither figure is complete: indeed, the second is so far from being so as to rule out any attempt at establishing a percentage. The same is even truer of the Army summary on p. 272, where only 7 deaths are recorded out of 229 names: there must have been many more. The *détenus'* mortality rate—43 out of 493, as shown on p. 274—is much the same as the naval officers'. But it, too, is suspect for just the same reason: in fact rather more suspect, because we should anticipate a higher death-roll among *détenus* as being, on the average, a good deal older than the officers. Little more, then, can be said about mortality rates.

Among *détenus*, the most talked-of case was the demise of Lord and Lady Tweeddale, both in the same year (1804). There is no hint, however, that cruel treatment was a contributory cause. They were, anyway, an elderly couple abroad for their health. They attracted attention simply because they were a marquis and a marchioness. A worse case was that of James Parry, ex-editor of the *Courier*. He was living at Arles in 1803, a completely paralysed cripple. The authorities insisted upon his repairing to Verdun, where he soon

[1] The records of enemy prisoners in Britain are much fuller, though even there not complete. It would seem that, of the 122,440 captives (of all nationalities) held by us throughout the war, 10,341—or 8·4 per cent—died. This, for that day, was a remarkably low figure, of which we were justifiably proud. The great naval physician, Sir Gilbert Blane, pointed out (*Medico-Chirurgical Transactions*, VI, 1815) that the death-rate among our free seamen—almost all from natural causes—was nearly twice as heavy.

[2] Bussell's epidemic at Arras, and an outbreak of scarlet fever at Bitche mentioned by Stewart are exceptions.

died. This treatment shows up Napoleon in a peculiarly poor light. Had Parry been a Frenchman in England, not only would he, a civilian, have escaped arrest altogether: he would, even if arrested, have been allowed home at once. Throughout, the French scarcely ever let an invalid go home, however incapacitated he was: but the British Government invalided many thousands of Frenchmen.

Here, of course, they were only being true to the old conventions governing prisoners. In those happy days the sole reason for retaining a captive at all had been to prevent his joining, or rejoining, the enemy's ranks. Once nature intervened to prevent this, there was no sense in keeping him. The extent to which we played the game here can be illustrated by figures. During hostilities, the number of enemy prisoners whom we released for various reasons was 17,607, and over three-quarters of this number were invalids released on the sole score of health. In 1813 alone 8,000 were returned to France. There was practically no corresponding repatriation of British invalids, though it is only fair to record that a handful were sent home in 1812 and 1813 (see p. 155). By then, both sides were becoming really embarrassed by their captives, though for different reasons: the British because they could not cope with the numbers, the French because many of their fortress depots were coming under the threat of the advancing Allies.

(b) In course of Escape

Of our prisoners who died, the majority perished from sickness. But there were violent deaths, too, stemming from three principal causes. There were, first, those sustained by prisoners in the act of escaping.

Our writers are apt to dismiss all such fatalities as murder. But evidently this is far too sweeping an accusation. Anyone deliberately seeking to evade an armed sentry charged with the express duty of preventing his escape is obviously running a risk of being shot: and such was certainly the fate of several. A similar hazard is one recorded by O'Brien. Six escapers (from Bitche) were in the very act of lowering themselves over the wall with a home-made rope made of sheets. The alarm was given, and four of them tried to get down the rope at once. It broke: one of the party was killed and the other three gravely hurt. It may be natural, but it is not logical, to wax furious over such episodes, as our chroniclers so often do. Indeed, there are on record quite as many cases of similar happenings in Britain: and so long as the sentry (whether French or British) could show that he fired in hot blood at a prisoner who might well have escaped him else, it is not right to call him murderer.

There are a number of occasions, however, when (if we may accept evidence which in the nature of things is likely to be biased) the destruction of would-be escapers begins to look more like murder. What, for instance, of the conduct of the commandant of Bitche (p. 147) who could have thwarted escape without killing anybody, but who preferred to wait, and to dispatch his victims on the spot? And what of the fate of Midshipman Haywood, killed virtually in cold blood after surrender, or (if we believe Wetherell) without even having tried to escape? Another example, not yet recorded, took place at Bitche—though again our evidence comes only from the victim's friends. This time, no less than fifteen prisoners were attempting a break-out. It was too many for safety, but, having a very stout rope, they all tried to descend at once. Unknown to them, however, an elderly French officer was watching them; and as soon as all were on the rope, he cut it. According to one version (O'Brien's) several were dashed to pieces, and their mangled bodies exposed: none escaped without broken limbs. But stories like this are just the ones which grow in the telling as they circulate through dingy *souterrains*, and it must be regarded as doubtful whether there was ever so wholesale a slaughter. The only fact in the story which may be called certain is that one officer, a sub-lieutenant named John Essel, met his death on this occasion, and very likely in some such way. We shall hear more of him later.

A great man for such grim stories was Lord Blayney, whose very seniority should, theoretically, give him the more credence. He tells, for example, of a French soldier who transfixed with his bayonet a midshipman named Theophilus Thomson, without any visible cause at all. This particular story is certainly true, being corroborated by at least three other authorities, one of whom was not only an eye-witness but also all but a fellow-sufferer—Alexander Stewart. It happened thus. When the news of the birth of the King of Rome reached Bitche, on March 21, 1811, a liberal ration of wine was issued to the troops. Having drunk freely, they assembled in the main court before the commandant's house to be addressed by that officer. An open palisade had been erected temporarily between the soldiers and those privileged prisoners who were allowed to use that court. Starved habitually of news, and of any sensation whatever, a crowd of them lined the paling to see and hear what was going on. Suddenly, a rumour, of unknown origin, spread through the soldiers' ranks. The prisoners were about to rush the palisade and seize the fortress! The whole garrison thereupon turned upon the prisoners and, without apparently any order given, began thrusting indiscriminately through the palings. One bayonet went right through Thomson's groin, and he died almost instantly. Stewart himself had a narrow escape. A bayonet passed between his side and his arm, tearing his jacket. He concludes with a passage which somehow compels credence. He had turned to run, and now—

> I immediately leaped forwards, and sprang a distance of nearly 12 feet through the impulse of fear. Several of the prisoners observed this, and marked the distance. I was often requested afterward to jump it again, but never could approach it.[1]

But the general is not always corroborated so nearly as this by his contemporaries. For instance, there are at least four accounts of the murder of Cox and Marshall by the Bitche commandant. All agree that murder it was; but while James says very clearly that only these two were slain, and Ellison, Done and Boys support him, Blayney must needs aver that the foul deed was perpetrated by musketry, and that twelve Britons were shot dead in one volley. Whom are we to believe —the general who, when it all happened, was at Gibraltar, not yet a prisoner, or the midshipman (James) who was on the spot, and saw the bodies displayed?

There are several other disturbing hints of dark deeds lying, as it were, just on, or just beyond, the limits of our vision. They serve to reveal how very incomplete is our knowledge of what was happening in individual cases. Thus, one of the lists in the Public Record Office, emanating from purely French sources, informs us, laconically enough, that Midshipman Patrick Nairne 'died at Bitche, 8th Feb., 1809'. This was doubtless the truth. But was it the whole truth? John Done thought not. Nairne, he reports, equally laconically, was 'shot in dispute with a sentry': and he goes on to report another casualty, this time, fortunately, not a fatal one. A captain's clerk named Belchambers 'had his right hand permanently disabled by a gaoler'. Are we to believe these charges? Who shall say? On one side is the testimony of a witness who may be in general fair-minded enough, yet prone, by hypothesis, to be anti-French and even more likely anti-gaoler: on the other, a cold official statement (anti-British)

---

[1] Stewart, op. cit., p. 58.

which probably tells the truth, but only that part of it which it wants us to know.

The murder of Lieutenant Tench at Dunkirk (see p. 80), though the best-authenticated crime of all (since one of its two perpetrators confessed and both were executed) is not stressed in this connection. It belongs to a different category altogether. Here there was no conceivable provocation, no question of escape. It does not impinge at all on gaoler-captive relationships, hardly even upon Anglo-French ones. It was sheer murder-for-gain. In all countries—and, alas, in all ages—there are blackguards who will dispatch their victims simply to rifle their pockets.

For all our mistrust of some of the evidence, however, certain facts seem to be established beyond reasonable doubt. One is that definite orders were sometimes given to sentries to shoot escapers on sight, whatever the local conditions, and that sometimes they did so with fatal results. Another is that the conduct of many of the gendarmes and gaolers concerned was often quite unnecessarily brutal, especially to the younger officers and the men: so brutal, in fact, as to make it a matter for wonder whether there were not more tragedies like that which befell the Welshman Morgan at Sarrelibre (p. 149). Another instance of gratuitous brutality will be cited shortly; but not here, since it did not involve death.

(c) By Suicide

The second form of violent death is suicide, a temptation common to war captives of all ages. Again no inclusive figures are available. For *détenus*, our only wholesale evidence comes from Lawrence, who rather surprisingly asserts that, up to the time he wrote,[1] not a single one had made away with himself. This, probably, applies to Verdun only, and is not strictly true for all France. Yet the numbers mentioned by all our witnesses are remarkably small, in spite of the fact that suicide, if or when it occurred, was just the kind of news that they would hardly omit. One *détenu* named Burgh (or Burke) seems to have shot himself in Paris in 1813, because of gambling debts which he could not meet. Another, a young man called Thomas Talbot, killed himself with charcoal fumes in 1806, again because of debt, though how or where contracted is not stated. The only case reported from Verdun was that of the young surgeon Lawder (see p. 121), in which, once more, gambling was the root cause. There were, no

[1] Lawrence, op. cit., II, 85. His book was published in 1810.

doubt, other cases which have escaped us, and perhaps even more near escapes from the temptation. Indeed, one of our principal witnesses himself all but succumbed.

At the end of his fourth year of captivity, the much-wronged Dillon found his sorrows increasing like Job's. Again and again his hopes of release were raised, only to be lost in a desert of utter silence. Then he heard of his much-loved father's death, followed by that of the man upon whom he chiefly depended for promotion. Then, very likely as a result, he fell victim to a painful and irritating skin disease which the physicians whom he consulted only succeeded in making worse. The day came when he felt he could stand no more. He therefore took his razor with him to a shrubbery in the garden of the house where he lodged, intent upon cutting his throat. Something, however, restrained him—perhaps, though he does not say so, a failure of nerve at the crucial moment. The sequel, it must be owned, reads more like a novel than a slice of sober history. He returned to the house, and found awaiting him a message from General Wirion that he had been exchanged! Dillon sometimes displays a leaning towards the dramatic, so that, perhaps, the coincidence was not quite so startling as he makes it appear. Yet he is certainly not the man to own to non-existent weaknesses, and so would hardly have invented no less than two—his failure, first to support his sorrows, and then to end them. It seems probable that he really contemplated suicide; and that many others similarly placed had similar temptations. Nor is it likely that only three or four succumbed.

If suicide is due, as is often said, to mental disease, it is apposite here to mention insanity. Several cases are recorded. One was that of a civilian named John Giffard, who was confined for lunacy at Verdun. Lawrence records the rather horrible story of another man called Thomas Dutton. This may well have been the journalist of that name who was one of the editors of the English-language paper *Argus*. He was sacked from his post and imprisoned, very likely at Bitche because Done, when there, mentions a fellow-prisoner of that name. But neither Done nor any other Bitche resident confirms Lawrence's story—that Dutton, who had murdered his own brother, for long made the men's *souterrain* there hideous both day and night, by screaming incessantly. The story, indeed, passes the bounds of credibility: for whereas Lawrence himself never went near Bitche, we have first-hand evidence from the various Britons actually incarcerated there which spans practically the whole of the fortress's

war history. There was little enough for them to record anyway in
their utterly drab lives. How could one or another of them have
possibly failed to record so sensational and terrifying an experience—
especially Done, who says that he shared a 'class II' room with him?[1]

James has a much more probable account of a lunatic, strange and
poignant. After his unsuccessful escape, he was being hauled back
in chains to captivity. At Phalsbourg he was allowed to visit a fellow-
countryman. This poor wretch was in irons, and had been in solitary
confinement for a month; but James just recognized him, emaciated
as he was, for a certain jolly red-cheeked, ginger-haired Scot named
Alexander Simpson, Surgeon of the *Ranger*. Soon after his arrival
at Verdun, the unfortunate man had inadvertently committed two
shocking crimes against the *amour propre* of his captors, both while
at the theatre. Pleasantly full of champagne, he had been taken there
by friends, and had, first, turned his back on the stage, not knowing
that, in France, this was regarded as an unpardonable act of rudeness.
To make matters worse, at that moment the bust of Napoleon was
ceremoniously borne on to the stage; and poor Simpson, forgetting
that he was not at Portsmouth, where cheers, claps, groans or hisses
were all alike allowed, proceeded to record his disapproval in the
loudest of voices. He was bustled out by scandalized gendarmes, and
disappeared. The prisoners had long written him off for dead. But he
was not—quite. He it was whom James found at Phalsbourg a year
later. He was evidently quite insane, though not violent. To James's
amazement, he could not, or at any rate would not, speak English,
but addressed him in a broken mixture of childish French and
German—with a strong Scots accent. As he was entirely incoherent,
however, this made little difference, and James failed to find out what
had happened to him. He thought, but was not certain, that he died
soon afterwards.

Another case, strictly involving neither suicide nor insanity, though
perhaps approximating to both, was that of Midshipman Jack Pearson.
Once, when he had drowned his sorrows in cheap gin, he made a bet
with an equally fuddled *détenu* named Bode that he would outstay
him at standing barefoot in the snow. He won his wager, but at
altogether disproportionate cost. He fell into a violent fever, and died.

(d) By Duelling

The third and last form of violent death which might overtake a

[1] Lawrence, op. cit., II, 171.

prisoner was the most tragic, because the least necessary. He might fall in a duel with one of his own people. Almost all those confined at Verdun 'wore swords', and duelling was still the ordinary method of settling affairs of honour, in both France and England. How Napoleon ruled that his gentlemen captives should retain the right to slaughter each other has already been told (p. 121). It was a singularly inexpensive way in which he could show his regard for British gentility.

The origins of the disputes were various. The gaming-table was one: to this class belonged the non-fatal affair between the proprietor Balbi and the *détenu* Goold (p. 121). In others the female element loomed large, as when one naval officer, Lieutenant J. W. Miles, quarrelled with another, the Hon. William Walpole, over a girl, threatened him with a horse-whip, and, in the ensuing meeting, was shot dead. Some again sprang from quarrels, usually quite trivial, at parties, concerts and dances; as when an army lieutenant, John Penrice of the 15th Hussars, was induced, rather unwillingly, to call out Lieutenant Thomas Connell, RN, who, presiding at an after-dinner sing-song, had reproved him for talking during a performance. Here was double tragedy. It seems that both parties had intended the thing to be a mere formality. Both aimed to miss, but Penrice's shot glanced off a tree, and Connell was mortally wounded.

Another fatal duel, arising out of a stupid quarrel at a private party, was between a marine captain, Robert Alexander, and a naval lieutenant, Edward Barker. Here, one feels, wrong triumphed. Alexander was a quarrelsome, difficult man who had already had several affairs, in one of which he had all but killed his man. Now he did kill one. Barker was admittedly a hasty-tempered fellow too, and not prone to look before he leapt. But in the past he had twice leapt to very good purpose—into the river Meuse, whence he had fished out, first, a drowning Verdun child and, later, a drowning gendarme. He was therefore very popular with the townsmen and, in spite of his weaknesses, with his fellow-prisoners too. The marines, considering their relatively slender numbers, were mixed up in a disproportionate number of affairs. Another of them, a Captain Ridley, all but destroyed a lieutenant named Apreece. Nor was the carnage confined to executive and commissioned officers. Robert Abbot, a surgeon, RN, called out an assistant surgeon from another ship, and mortally wounded him.

Even the younger officers, as ever apt to imitate their 'betters', were

179

not infrequently the principals: but not, as a rule, with such fatal results, perhaps because they had less skill and experience in the deadly game. Boys, however, has one positively shocking incident to relate. Two mere children, both under 14,

> were found shooting at each other across a table, ploughing furrows in it . . . and nothing but the bursting open the door and forcibly taking their pistols from them, put an end to the combat.[1]

Charitably enough, he names no names. But not all these youthful affairs ended so harmlessly. Midshipman Andrew Scott, scarcely 19 years old, was blackballed for a club by a master's mate named Peter Morris, and conceiving himself insulted, was shot dead for his pains. Frayed nerves among high-spirited young men living in enforced and unaccustomed idleness, the unhealthy and unnatural lives they had to lead, and the demoralizing amusements with which they strove to kill time were the obvious causes underlying these tragedies. They can hardly surprise us.

II. RELEASE BY EXCHANGE

Let us have done with death, and contemplate, as most of them did, a happier end to captivity—a living release from it. This might come in one of three main ways.

The first was by regular exchange. As we have seen, this should have been the norm, to which all captives (and especially all officer-captives) should have looked forward, just as a question of time, with confidence if not with certainty. But it was not to be, for reasons already elaborated in Chapter III. They need not be repeated. Let us merely recall that, after four-and-a-half years, Dillon was only the fourteenth officer to be exchanged: and probably—for the exact number again eludes us—the figure of forty would be too high to cover the whole eleven years of hostilities. Moreover, even the lucky few had to be bought at a scandalously high price. Brenton and Dillon cost the British Government four French post-captains, and distinguished ones at that, when, by all the known laws of war, they should have cost only one.

III. RELEASE WITHOUT EXCHANGE

As for the *détenus*, those of them who secured release obviously could not procure it by exchange with French civilians. There were no

[1] Boys, op. cit., p. 51.

French *détenus* in Britain with whom to exchange them, and, until near the end, our government would not equate them for this purpose with service officers. Yet undeniably quite a large number did get away, and we must try to discover how they managed it. This is not easy, because the means used were not only various but often devious as well. In fact, we shall have to admit that we cannot now lay a finger on nearly all those means, especially those where both influence and monetary payments played their part: cases, for example, like that of Lord Yarmouth (p. 43). We must do what we can about these before passing to the simpler cases where social 'interest', and sometimes enlightened interest at that, play the major part.

All the evidence we have here is sadly negative. In the abstract to List III (p. 274) are collected the names of 493 civilian captives. A number of these we know by name as having escaped by running for it; but not very many—let us say 50.[1] A number more are known to have died, but again not very many—another 43. This should leave some 400 *détenus* still in custody. Yet, when we obtain, towards the end of the war—in July 1812—a fairly authoritative list of those who remain, we find their numbers quite unexpectedly low; a mere 130 (see p. 36). The only inference possible from this circumstance is that, somehow or other, a very considerable number must have secured freedom neither by running nor by dying, nor by regular exchange. True, a few more than we know of no doubt died or ran for it, and we have still to deal with some 60 more who were released on straight 'interest' (see below, and p. 36). But there remains a residuum of nearly, if not quite, 200 who, while known to be 'in the bag' in 1803, were safely out of it by 1812; exactly how we do not know. We can but suspect a combination of influence and the clandestine revival of what is really 'ransom'—redemption from captivity by the payment of a price.

Among those for whose release we cannot exactly account there are a number of just that class who might be expected to command both 'interest' and the wherewithal to produce ransom if necessary. There were the members of the aristocracy proper and of that 'upper ten' of society who clung to its fringes. Thus, among *détenus* released with no apparent *quid pro quo*, were people like the Duke of Newcastle and his mother the dowager duchess; Lord Yarmouth, Lord Duncannon, Lord Elgin, the Hon. Mr and Mrs Clive, the Hon. Mr

[1] See pp. 202-6: *Le Moniteur* says 99; the other authorities, collectively, 39; the compromise figure of 50 is our measure of *Le Moniteur's* veracity.

Eardley, Sir Elijah Impey (of Warren Hastings fame), General Crawford and Sir James de Bathe—the list reads like an extract from the Court Circular. Such people did not always manage it at once. Some, even of these highly-placed personages, had to endure several years of captivity (not, we can guess, too uncomfortably). But all had been repatriated by 1807: and doubtless the Tweeddales would have joined them had they survived. Even so, one or two titled people remained in France. The Earl of Beverley was one, though, in his case, it is permissible to suspect that, like his son, Lord Louvaine, he did not try very hard.

We may pass now to those known to have secured freedom by means of 'interest', and in many of whose cases the precise 'contacts' are preserved. Sir James de Bathe, it is said, solicited the good offices of the Pope, whose influence, though politically not great, was still socially considerable. Sir Elijah Impey, it seems, was a friend of Madame Talleyrand, and that was obviously a good card. Mr Cockburn, lately our Consul at Hamburg, was fortunate enough to have a wife who was a friend of the Empress Josephine: and that was a better card still. In this nice game the ladies could, and often did, play a prominent part. Thus Mrs Melesina Trench (née Chenevix, a distinguished authoress and mother of two famous sons) was responsible for the release of her *détenu* husband Richard. She certainly knew the right people—Rivarol, Lucien Bonaparte, John Quincy Adams—and, not detained herself, made several journeys to Paris, on one of which she delivered to Napoleon in person a petition which ultimately succeeded. Another devoted lady was the wife of Doctor (later Sir) George Tuthill, the well-known physician. She was not so familiar with 'right people' as Mrs Trench, but she believed in the direct approach, and one day contrived to intercept the Emperor as he returned from hunting. Napoleon, never averse (when it suited him) to touches of romance and gallantry, yielded at once. One curious episode survives—on, as it were, the debit side of the sheet. The release of a certain ex-MP named Richard Oliver was solicited, presumably without his knowledge, by Arthur O'Connor, the Irish rebel lately made a general by Napoleon. When Oliver heard of it, he indignantly refused his freedom from so tainted a hand.[1]

---

[1] Wolfe has a different, and enlarged, version of this episode. He attributes the gesture to John Waller, another ex-MP, and adds that, when the French Minister of War heard about it, he was so much impressed that he sent Waller a passport as from himself.

There remains one well-defined group of *détenus* who owed their release to an altogether better and happier cause. This was the civilized international freemasonry of the Arts and Sciences which never completely died out, even in republican days, and to which Napoleon, from motives not altogether above suspicion, often paid lip-service. More than a score of British civilians achieved their release in this way. On our side the principal wielders of this healthier form of interest were Sir Joseph Banks, president for 42 years of the Royal Society, and Dr Edward Jenner of vaccination fame; both international figures of the highest repute, whose great influence, much to their credit, they were constantly exerting. Thus to them (and, on the French side, to Carnot and Cuvier) Lord Shaftesbury owed his return; not as a peer, but as a Fellow of the Society of Antiquaries. Others so liberated were Robert Ferguson and James Forbes, both Fellows of the Royal Society. The case of Forbes reveals a streak of liberality in unlooked-for quarters. Junot, who knew him well, tried to have him excluded from the edict by declaring that he was over the upper age-limit of 60. He failed; not because he was not speaking the truth—Forbes was in fact only 54—but because (as usual) the responsible authority was ignoring the age-limit. After his release from Verdun, in 1804, Forbes wrote an over-rosy description of life in that town. Both Lawrence and Dillon accuse him of misleading the people at home by saying how well they were all treated and how happy they were. Another of Banks' and Jenner's protégés was John Pinkerton, the Scottish antiquary and historian: but he was a staunch francophile who loved Paris; and when the war was over he instantly returned to pass the rest of his life there. Yet another was Thomas Manning, the Chinese traveller: but he hardly needed British champions. Both Talleyrand and Carnot were his dear friends, and they soon coaxed a passport for him from Napoleon.

In much the same category were British scholars who were released in consideration of valuable work done, or to be done. Thus Dr Bunnell Davis wrote, while a *détenu*, a pamphlet, highly thought of in its day, on Premature Burial, and was released as a reward. Alexander Hamilton, reputed the first Sanskrit scholar in Europe, was employed to catalogue the manuscripts in that tongue in the Paris Library, and was then given his passport. John Spence Stanhope, to whom we shall return (p. 244), was released, though grudgingly, to conduct archaeological researches in Greece. Henry Greathead, inventor of the lifeboat, was caught in France: but his work was so highly thought of in scientific circles there that he was sent home in the following year. These are but examples of a survival from more civilized times. They could be expanded, and their very scope enlarged. Thus J. Cleaver Banks, not a captive at all, was allowed into France, and right into Paris, to examine the Sanskrit manuscripts in the National Library. Even more was allowed to a still greater international figure, Sir Humphry Davy. Wishing to go to Italy, he was cordially invited to go via Paris, where he was fêted and consulted by the leading French scientists before proceeding on his way. More: Napoleon had established a prize for original work in electricity, and in 1807 the Institut de France awarded it to Davy, with the Emperor's full consent. We have often had to be critical of that many-sided man. It is only fair to record one of his worthier facets.

The mere fact, however, of being an antiquary, an artist or an author did not guarantee release. Interest also was essential throughout. For instance, John Edmond Halpin, the miniaturist, spent at least nine years at Verdun, eking out a livelihood by painting the wealthy British captives. Presumably he knew none of the right people. Nor did poor Joseph Forsyth, author of a work on Italy that was long the accepted handbook on the subject. Fortune, with him, was the reverse of kind. He was touring in Italy in 1803, was arrested in Turin—not even in France—and hurried off to Nîmes. He was then 40 years old and in delicate health; yet he decided to join in an attempt to escape. It failed, and he was marched, in the depth of winter, to Bitche, 600 miles away. After two years in the punishment depot, he was allowed to go to Verdun, his constitution shattered. After five more years an influential friend, a lady in the service of the King of Holland, succeeded in obtaining leave for him to live in Paris: but he had been there only four months when Paris was cleared of captives, and all his friends could secure for him was a retreat in Valenciennes. He sent copies of his famous work to Napoleon and other French notables: but all to no avail. He remained prisoner until the peace, when he returned home only to die in the following year.

There was one small group whose release may be ascribed to mere luck. During the abortive negotiations of Lords Yarmouth and Lauderdale, those noblemen needed, or said they needed, couriers, and secured passports for several well-connected *détenus* to act as such. Colonel Swayne, a *détenu* officer, was one, a certain Mr Wilbraham another. The last-named may be accounted the luckiest of them all. A common swindler in Paris drew bills in his name. When the forgeries were presented to him for payment, he protested, and sought to expose the fraud. All the redress he obtained at first was to be arrested by Wirion and thrown into the Verdun citadel. After a time, however, the Paris police got on to the criminal from another angle, and Wilbraham was summoned as a witness to the capital, where he easily proved his own innocence and the forger's guilt. Now fortune smiled on him. Lord Yarmouth, requiring a courier, selected him, and obtained his passport then and there. So he owed his freedom primarily to the offices of a French crook.

IV. RELEASE BY ESCAPE (THE ETHICAL PROBLEM)

There remains the last, the most exciting, yet, in terms of self-help, much the hardest, most hazardous way of securing release—Escape. Numerically, too, it was the most prolific way. Add all those known to have died to those who, by whatever means, are known to have departed with the consent of their captors, and the figure is considerably smaller than that of those known to have gone without it. Moreover, those who tried to escape and failed were probably thrice as numerous as those who succeeded. Escape, therefore, even if considered merely on a numerical basis, was a far from negligible aspect of prison life.

For the very reason, however, that it *was* the hard way, we must not expect our escapers to be drawn equally from all classes of captive, and especially from all their age-groups. With certain exceptions, it will inevitably be the fit, the active, and above all the young who will attempt it, because it demands reserves of strength both mental and physical. Older folk may have the first, but without the second they may well fail. Naturally there were exceptions, one of whom (Forsyth) has just been mentioned: and another was that almost legendary figure, Captain Nesbit Willoughby (see p. 207). But exceptions they certainly were. Among escaping *détenus* it is not very easy to show figures to prove this. Their evasions are less well known to us, and so, as a rule, are their ages. But the figures for serving officers, and especially for naval officers, strikingly bear out this generalization. For here we have seniority to help us. Even in those days, when promotion was apt to be more a matter of influence than of mere age, it is safe to assume that, as classes, captains are older than lieutenants, and lieutenants than midshipmen. Thus, as List I shows

(p. 270), of the 103 successful escapers among those with commissions or aspiring to them, there figure *one* captain, *one* commander, *seven* lieutenants, *one* marine officer—and *ninety-three* from the midshipmen's mess! These last virtually monopolize the escape story. Over 90 per cent of successful escapers were *Young* Gentlemen.

There is, however, much more to it than mere age. Rank and seniority were themselves bars against escape, no less serious because they were moral rather than physical bars: and it is essential to understand the reason for this at the outset. The fact that scarcely any captains of the Royal Navy escaped, or even tried to, must not, emphatically, be attributed to indolence, faint-heartedness or lack of enterprise. It was because they were on parole, and because, though even their brand of it was only the merest shadow of the complete parole of former wars, it was still a great deal more substantial, more meaningful, than the caricature of the noble institution offered, say, to midshipmen. Men like Brenton and Lavie would have much more and better opportunities to run for it than, say, Midshipman Boys, Master's Mate O'Brien or even Lieutenant Jackson. But as officers and gentlemen, they never dreamed of taking them: indeed, had they done so, they would have done infinite harm both to their country and to themselves.

To grasp why this was so, we must once more stand back a pace or two, in order to command a wider view of the whole scene. First, it must be appreciated that, for officers, Escape, as a phenomenon of war, was virtually a new thing in Napoleon's day. It was one, but only one, of the results which flowed from the Emperor's revolutionary attitude to all war captives: and it is because of that disastrous new policy that, since his day, Escape has become the commonplace it is. Though in the early days of ransom there may have been inducements for captives to make off surreptitiously, if only to avoid the crippling financial cost of freedom, such had ceased to exist when the 'private war' institutions of exchange and parole came in. Nor, so long as they functioned properly, was there much to be gained by escape. For now there was room for it only in quite exceptional circumstances. Let us take examples, first of the norm, then of the exception. Lord Cochrane was perhaps the last man to take kindly to captivity. Yet there was really no point in his attempting to run from Algeciras (see p. 42) if he was morally certain of being freely allowed to leave within a day or two, and of being regularly exchanged next week: and his case was still the normal one, even as late as 1801, though admittedly the brevity of his detention was below the average. On the other hand, an exceptional case was that of Captain Sidney Smith and Lieutenant Wesley Wright in 1796-8 (p. 72). Their experience is indeed particularly apposite here. They were locked up, behind bolts and bars, in the Temple Prison, and they were not on parole at all. This made all the difference. The whole convention upon which parole was founded made it and physical detention contradictions in terms. It was simply to avoid the latter that an officer was offered, and accepted, the former. The essence of the contract was, on the captor's side, 'Be physically free on the understanding that you do not fight again until exchanged for an equal'; and, on the captive's, 'So long as I am physically free, I undertake not to fight again until regularly exchanged.'

The breakdown of exchange in our war did not, directly and instantly, put a stop to parole. It was still possible for the captive officer to make the old promise, and, upon capture, he usually did. But now that the clause 'until I am exchanged' was virtually cut out of the contract, he would soon realize that that promise had much more serious implications than before, because he was now, for practical purposes, promising to debar himself from any further participation in the war. Thus, if he were (like the great majority of those concerned) at once honourable, patriotic and ambitious, he might well feel that he was buying his own physical comfort at too great a cost, both to his own future and to that service to which he was dedicated. He might well in fact have returned the torn-up bits of his parole to his captor, saying, 'I won't take my personal liberty at *that* price! Lock me up, and I'll see whether I can't regain both sorts of freedom— personal freedom from gaol *and* full freedom to have at you again! In a word, I give you due notice, I intend to *escape*.' And we shall find that, in essence, this is what a very large majority of our escapers did do, though they seldom did it quite so forthrightly because, as it turned out, it was seldom necessary. The other party to the essential contract—the captor—weakened his own position by a series of rather typical chicaneries. We have watched him whittling down his obligations under the contract. Let us now try to view that process specifically through the eyes of the captives whom he was defrauding. Then perhaps we shall perceive the individual ethical problem which faced every one of them. 'To escape' was far from being merely a question of pitting one's wits against one's gaolers. Before ever he reached that stage, our officer had to ask himself, 'Am I entitled, in honour, to try? Has my captor so far whittled down his obligations as to have, himself, cancelled the contract?'

Our professional officer knew well enough to what he was entitled in exchange for his parole. His captor should have said, 'Good. Now that I have your promise, go and do anything you like except fight me.' But what he *did* bore precious little relation to this. With one niggard hand he doled out a few benefits of parole while with the other he limited and circumscribed even the benefits conferred. For instance, 'You shall of course be free. But when I say that, all I mean is that you shall not always be locked up: not that you shall never be locked up. In the daytime you can (after, of course, filling in the apposite forms) go beyond the locked door. But when night falls the key will be turned; and mind you're back by lock-up time!' Or again, 'I'm afraid, for security purposes, I shall have to impose a trifling limitation upon your freedom of choice in the matter of residence. No Paris for you, I regret to say: no Spa, Tours, or the sunny south; still less England. I've selected for your accommodation the agreeable little fortress-town of Verdun, which I dare say you had not thought of yourself, thinking of it, perhaps, as a damp, bleak place with no shops or other amenities worth mentioning, and few if any residents of your own particular standard of gentility. But I'm afraid you've all got to go there. Why? Well, you know, those fortress walls are very convenient for me and my guards: and I shouldn't like you to be anywhere where you would be unduly tempted to violate that precious flower, your honour.' Or again, 'Now you can settle down—until the whim takes me to move you—to a comfortable stay. That nothing mar your comfort, I'm arranging for you to live where you like—within the walls, let me hasten to add—and to share your chosen dwelling with cronies of your own choice: even (in cases of good behaviour) with your own wife—if she will come, and, *bien entendu,* if you will pay all her expenses. Indeed, I'm afraid I shall have to ask you to pay all your expenses—and mine too. If, however, you feel you cannot afford all these luxuries—and I'm afraid they may be a little dear: these provincial landladies have a notoriously sharp eye for the main chance, and my gendarmes do set great store by their *pourboires*—well, elegant bachelor quarters are provided, gratis, in the Citadel. (What is the Citadel, do you say? No, of course not, it's not a prison. It's the strong heart of a military fortress and, naturally, it has high vertical walls, bolts on doors and bars across windows.) Then there's the Commandant. As you're service folk, I'm sure you'll like a little discipline, if only to provide a home-from-home atmosphere. So you'll find one of my most distinguished officers in charge, and you will, of course, submit to his general orders on any small points which may arise.'

What these might be turned inevitably upon the personality of that distinguished officer—which, incidentally, is why men like Dillon and Lawrence took such a poor view of a *général de gendarmerie*. For he too was empowered to have a decisive say in the prisoner's day-to-day routine. If, for instance, he happened to be a General Wirion, he would not hesitate about joining in the little game of parole-paring. Thus, says he, 'It will be a great convenience to my officers, and doubtless a protection to yourselves, if they know just where you are lodging in case of trouble, and if they can identify you in the streets when it is dark. Will you therefore be kind enough to have a large "A", illuminated by a lantern, stuck up prominently on the front of your residence; and, if you go out after dark, pray have the goodness to carry another lighted lantern in your hand. What? The "A" reminds you of the cross that the infected citizens of your own Londres had to put up in plague year? And the hand-lamp reminds you of the bell that lepers used to be made to carry? Pah! Don't forget that there's a war on, that its fortunes have gone against you, and that I'm Commandant here. What will happen if you refuse? Well, there's a place called Bitche, which isn't quite so cosy as Verdun: or—ahem—as a matter of fact there *is* another way out, though you may feel it's rather expensive—after all, I too find the cost of living rather high, and I naturally have a position to keep up for Madame and myself. Ah, I see you understand me—but make it *two* louis a time, and a franc or two for the poor gendarme, and I think I may guarantee that you'll have no more trouble with "A's" on doors or lanterns in streets.'[1]

This being how the British p.o.w. officer actually saw it, is it surprising that he was constantly asking himself and his fellows a little riddle—'When is parole not parole?' In other words, at what point

---

[1] The 'A' order, imposed in 1806, was soon rescinded for naval officers, because they indignantly refused to pay it. (*Cdr. Henry Gordon's Letter-book*, letters 1 to 4.) But the *détenus* and merchant officers continued liable. The carried lantern remained obligatory. Dillon was once arrested on his own doorstep because his candle went out as he was opening his door. He talked his way out without paying, however. The lanterns, he says, cost 14 pence each, of which sixpence went to the maker and eightpence to Wirion. (Dillon, op. cit., III, 336–8.)

does the aggregate of limitations upon parole cancel out the original contract? There was clearly room for an infinity of answers, which were really an exercise in comparative honour: and individual officers naturally gave different ones. But, because as a whole they were really honourable men who had real innate scruples about breaking parole, it was inevitable that there should gradually appear a sort of customary answer to the riddle; or rather, perhaps, a number of customary answers, depending upon the number of limitations imposed upon each individual.

For what has been described so far was the most liberal kind of parole, allowed to the most privileged officers—those, of both services, who held commissions. All the way down the ranks, conditions were changing, always for the worse. For example, as we have seen, all had to attend *appel*, itself a champion device to restrict one highly prized concession—the right to physical liberty. Captains and Colonels had to attend comparatively seldom: lieutenants and army captains more often, midshipmen much more often still—*sixty times* as often, we recall, as captains. Which was receiving the more generous—the less dubious—share of parole-benefit here, the captain or the midshipman?

Or again, the more senior the officer, the more likely he was, other things being equal, to be able to live in his own hired residence. His private income would probably be greater, his pay (and therefore his allowed half-pay) certainly greater; not to mention the fact that he received from the French Government, by agreement with ours, the sum of £4 per month where the midshipman, the warrant officer and the superior merchant-ship master had only 25s. Discounting exceptions, either way, it followed from this that nearly all captains and field-officers 'lived out': that most naval lieutenants and junior commissioned officers of the army just contrived to do so, but that most lower-ranking service-officers and most merchant-officers 'lived in', for the bulk of their lives anyway. Living-in, it is true, was not always synonymous with 'being locked up'—only parts of the Citadel were quite indistinguishable from prison. But, as a generalization, it is true enough to affirm that most commissioned officers were not locked into their individual quarters, but that most of the rest were.

This business of being actually behind locked doors and barred windows is purposely stressed here because, in the altogether unusual situation which had developed, it became the conventional touch-stone of the whole matter. By common consent—common, largely and oddly, to captives and captors alike—to attempt to escape when not locked in was 'breach of parole': but, when locked in, it was not. This is not to say, of course, that the French authorities made any distinction when they caught an escaper. Any attempt, in their view, was a heinous crime to be severely punished. All it meant, to them, was that a Briton who was locked in was much more likely to have a try, and so must be watched with greater vigilance. It was on the British side that the convention made its greatest impact. From time to time unlocked-up officers did try. But among the prisoners themselves public opinion was strongly against them, and no one, least of all the Senior Officer, would stir a finger to help them. Indeed, the reverse might well be the case, as one classic instance shows. A certain *détenu*, a baronet named Sir Beaumont Dixie, had a clever idea. He went down to the Meuse, ostensibly to bathe, leaving his clothes on the bank. He did not return, because he had arranged for a new supply farther down stream. He had quietly slipped away, hoping that the authorities would take him to be drowned. And so they did, at first. Unfortunately, however, a naval officer who was present by chance guessed what the game was, and informed the Senior Officer— Brenton. That worthy man instantly passed on the news to the Commandant, whose sleuths gave chase and caught Dixie before he had gone far. He was sent to Bitche. The affair caused considerable controversy in Verdun. It was something of a borderline case. Sir Beaumont, though now a civilian *détenu*, had once been a naval officer. The civilian Lawrence and, in this case, the naval Dillon, thought that this was overdoing the 'honour' side of it, and that a *détenu*, illegally detained by hypothesis, should not be called upon to conform to the strict officer convention. But Brenton would have none of it. A gentleman's word was, or should be, his bond, even among *détenus*, and the fact that Dixie had once been an officer should have made him know better; while the very fact that he could go out to bathe in the river proved that he was not under lock and key at the time, and therefore not, in honour, entitled to escape.

The convention was observed far beyond Verdun too. The Transport Board accepted it when it sat upon the successful escaper. The question they asked was, 'Were you on parole at the moment of breaking out?' True, the escaper did not have to be able to answer, 'No. I first handed in my parole to the Commandant'. That would have been a little too much. But he did have to be able to say, 'I was shut up in the locked cells of the Citadel', or 'I was confined to the

Porte de Chaussée'—lock-ups over the gate of that name. For, like every other participant in this strange piece of play-acting, the Board accepted the same answer to the riddle, 'When is parole not parole?' 'When the enemy ceases to trust my pledged word, and seeks to hold me by force.'

As a compromise it was surely fair enough: and it certainly goes far towards explaining the preponderance of junior officers' escapes, especially of those four 'gunroom' groups of Mate, Midshipman, Clerk and First Class Volunteer—the ones who were so seldom outside lock and key. It was these 'Petty Officers of the Royal Navy', as they so proudly called themselves, who were at once the most to be pitied and the most to be praised in the matter. At home, they were acknowledged officer-types, because it was accepted that they were going to be commissioned officers: so, when afloat, they enjoyed the officer's privilege of 'walking the quarterdeck' and of having their own mess. Socially, too, they enjoyed the full status of gentlemen, which in fact nearly all of them were. But the French, when they captured them, were reluctant either to treat them as officers or to trust them as gentlemen. They aligned them with the merchant officers who, in Britain, had the status of neither. Moreover, their captors, especially if not *ancien régime* themselves, often mistook the lads' lively independence, which was really the heritage of their gentility, as confirmation of their own rather jaundiced view—that they were just incorrigible *mauvais sujets*. Frequently, indeed, these young officers were not treated as officers at all. As often as not they were refused parole of any sort; and, when they had it, were watched with suspicious and malevolent eyes by gaolers constantly seeking to bowl them out. The kind of treatment which might come their way is graphically described by Boys, who was a sensible, thoughtful lad, not given to exaggeration. On one of those rather rare occasions when he was temporarily enjoying the parole privilege of going beyond the town gates, this humiliating experience befell him.

> Four of us were rambling about the country with a pointer and silken-net when the signal-gun was fired. . . . About two miles from Verdun we were surprised by two gendarmes, one of whom instantly dismounted and seized me, uttering the most blasphemous epithets. He tied my elbows behind me, then, slipping a noose round my neck, triced me up to the holsters of his saddle, re-mounted, and returned with his prize to town, exulting in his cowardly triumph, . . . and every now and then tightening the cord, so as to keep me trotting upon the extremities of the toes to

10. THE CITADEL, BRIANÇON

CITADEL AND CASTLE, SEDAN

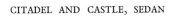

II. THE CITADEL, BESANÇON

BESANÇON *From a relief-map*

obtain relief, then again loosening it, as occasional guttural symptoms of strangulation seemed to indicate necessity. Vain would be the attempt to convey an adequate idea of the impotent rage then boiling within me at the insult offered to my juvenile dignity, whilst a determined haughtiness disdained to betray the slightest indication of submission or complaint.[1]

This, no doubt, was hardly typical treatment. What was typical is, almost casually, revealed by James. 'I had been three years a prisoner: out of that I had been confined two years in the Citadel.' The context shows that he meant *locked* in. Then he proceeds: 'in fact all midshipmen were, with the exception of some two or three who were always permitted to remain unmolested. There were reasons for that piece of indulgence best known to themselves.' James doubtless knew what those reasons were: indeed, we may suspect that we know too, as we are now to see.

These juniors, then, are to be pitied for the raw deal they had. But they are also to be praised, because they showed, again and again, that the vast majority of them, nurtured on the older, stricter code of gentlemanly behaviour, lived up to it in face, often, of injustices which would seem to anyone less well brought up as cancelling the whole contract a dozen times over. Once more we will cite examples, beginning with a rare midshipman who, to put it mildly, let the side down. The subject of the story—there is no temptation to say the hero of it—has appeared already in these pages. His name was Edmond Temple, and we know both the beginning and the end of his adventures. Evidently he was one of James's 'two or three exceptions'. Though he was a mere midshipman, the authorities did not interfere with him and his pleasures because, no doubt, he looked every inch the gentleman and had plenty of those heart-softeners, *louis d'or*. He spent them freely too: to the tune, we know, of £4,000 more than he possessed. No Citadel for him, of course. He had elegant apartments in the upper town, was often to be seen at the gaming table, and gave *recherché* little parties. Here is the middle section of his story.

Early one morning a handsome private cabriolet drove down the Rue Chaussée to the gate of that name. On reaching it, it drew up, and the gate-keeper popped his head inside. The only occupants to be seen were a young lady and her maid, the former a beautiful girl, beautifully turned out and exquisitely French. There could be no doubt about it, and the gate-keeper had none: in fact, he knew her

[1] Boys, op. cit., p. 61.

by sight. As there was no reason whatever for detaining her, he let the carriage pass without comment. Now the 'lady' was not a British midshipman skilfully concealed under cosmetics: nor was the maid. Yet there *was* a midshipman in that carriage—neatly tucked under the voluminous petticoats and between the four legs of its visible occupants. The 'lady' was, in fact, his kept mistress: and her pretty clothes, and the jewels round her lovely neck, represented part of the Verdun tradesmen's lost £4,000.

The idea was clever. All allowed to leave the town carried passes, which they had to hand over to the gate-keeper on exit and reclaim on re-entry. Thus if, at closing-time, the official still held the pass of Mr Temple, then Mr Temple himself was still out of town, and the ordinary hue-and-cry could be raised. But not this time. He had doubtless squared the *appel* gendarme—this was a common occurrence —so that no one even knew that he had gone until he was out of France. Of course 'the frail fair one' (as Dillon unctuously calls her) got into trouble when the story came out, but it would be oversanguine to hope that this caused Mr Temple any loss of sleep.

The affair outraged Dillon's sense of propriety, and well it might. The Senior Officer (Lavie) was not amused either: nor were my Lords of the Admiralty when he informed them. The whole service, they felt, was shamed by the whole affair. Yet it was not the method which outraged everybody the most: nor was it the barefaced robbery of the Verdun tradesmen; some, above all those on the spot, might feel there was even poetic justice in that. No. What no one could stomach, neither Dillon nor Lavie, Transport Board, Admiralty nor, when they told him, even the old King: what seemed to one and all the sin against the service and the whole country, was that a British naval officer had broken parole—that is, had given it and then decamped when not under lock and key.

Temple's case is illuminating for another reason: an additional reason why the more senior officers so seldom tried to escape. There was a system widely practised at Verdun whereby seniors 'went bail', as it were, for juniors, and things had really reached the point where all midshipmen depended, for any concessions at all, upon the trust which Wirion or Courçelles reposed in the senior officers. Had they deceived him, the last vestiges of midshipmen's parole would have vanished. It is instructive to learn Wirion's reaction to Temple's escape, because it bears witness, probably unintentionally, to the remarkable standard of honour of both midshipmen and commissioned officers. Temple was 'vouched for' by Commander Henry Gordon (who, incidentally, ran a most unpleasant risk when the scapegrace 'broke bail'). Wirion's letter to the senior officers survives.[1] It is written, oddly enough, in English, which accounts for the rather peculiar phrasing. He opens with a remarkable admission which (since Wirion made it) must surely be true:

> It is now 42 months since this Depot has been established, Mr Temple is the only person on Parole, that an officer was responsible for, that has made his escape and accompanied with circumstances of a most disgraceful nature.

Wirion knew well enough where his interests lay, and did not intend a system so convenient to himself to be wrecked on this one rock. He was therefore content to take the line, 'I shall overlook it this time because it is the first: but——': and, sure enough, some eighteen months later, when three more youngsters committed a similar, if less aggravated, offence, he packed the whole party off to depots where, like the men, they had no parole at all. It must, however, be noticed that he does not say that no junior officer at all had escaped during those first three-and-a-half years; he says that no officer on bail had done so. Even he admitted, tacitly, that, if he locked a prisoner up, he was himself cancelling parole, and must take other measures to prevent him from running.

Temple was the exception, the real *mauvais sujet*. We must return to the norm: and again no better example can be found than Boys, because this unusually thoughtful lad not only played the game throughout but also discusses, quite profoundly, the ethical problems of himself and his kind. He states the 'lock-and-key' convention, but then adds his own refinement to it.

> Prisoners on their arrival at Verdun were . . . obliged to sign a paper promising upon honour to conform to the regulations of the depot, and not to escape if permitted to reside in the town. A direct violation of this engagement was so unreservedly condemned by all classes that, during the first five years of the war, I recollect but three who so disgraced their country; for those determined to depart generally committed an offence, which would ensure deprivation of parole—it being generally admitted by us that the instant anyone was taken into custody by armed men, no matter for what cause, parole ceased. Nor can this practice, where it produced actual imprisonment, be condemned when it is considered that the prisoners were devoid even of a hope of exchange.

[1] Commander Gordon's MS. *Letter-book.*

Thus far the general nature of the convention: now for the refinement, which reveals the writer's honesty of thought no less than his care for his honour.

> Nevertheless, it is not without its evils, for it became difficult to define the exact line of distinction between open violation and this alternative; to wit—an offence so trifling, but so exactly measured, was so contrived as to induce a gendarme to take the parties into custody, and lodge them in the guardroom until he had reported the occurrence to the lieutenant. In the meantime, they stepped out of the window and concealed themselves in the town till dusk, and then departed.

There follows a still more thoughtful distinction, at once logical and important to our story.

> This might be fair enough with the *détenus*, because they were made prisoners in open violation of all law, justice or honour: but with prisoners of war it was justly ridiculed and condemned: to say the least of it, it was a bad augury; for the gem of honour buds in the spring of our days, and if at that epoch an officer wounds her opening flowers, she seldom ripens to maturity: or, in other words, the neglect of the minutest part of this delicate and noble feeling in early life generally leads to a more flagrant breach in the later hours of temptation.[1]

Later, Boys himself escaped; and it is of no small interest to know whether, or how faithfully, he lived up to his own high principles when it came to practice. We shall find that the most carping critic could not fault him.

On August 7, 1808, all the midshipmen in Verdun were thrown, without warning, into the Citadel. This was Wirion's answer to the second violation of parole. Next day they were divided into batches, seventy-three for Valenciennes and Givet, sixty-nine (with many merchant skippers) for Sarrelibre. When mass journeys like this were in contemplation, the responsible commandant could follow one of two courses. If he was a wise man (as, this time, Wirion, being angry, was not) he would offer, and accept, the parole of the prisoners on the journey: or (which Wirion did) he could withhold parole, and anticipate inevitable trouble by the strength of the guard provided. The Valenciennes–Givet group set out thus circumstanced, their roads lying together for a while:

> We were placed, two by two, upon bundles of straw in five wagons: four horse-gendarmes formed the van and four the rearguard: one

[1] Boys, op. cit., pp. 45–7.

on each side of every wagon, and 20 foot-soldiers in files, with others in each carriage, made up the escort, the commander bringing up the rear on his black charger. Whenever the road passed by a wood, which frequently occurred, we were halted to give the infantry time to occupy its skirts; two gendarmes on each side were posted midway, whilst the rest occasionally displayed their pistols somewhat ostentatiously. . . . I have been thus minute in detailing the strength and manner of the escort, not only to contrast it with similar detachments in England, where twice the number of French prisoners, with infinitely greater facilities to escape, might be safely entrusted to the care of a sergeant's guard, but also to show how fully Wirion was persuaded that some of us would make the attempt.

How right Wirion was! Here, on ethical grounds, were perfect escape conditions—'when the enemy ceases to trust our pledged word and seeks to hold us by force'. Wirion realized this as well as the midshipmen. Every prisoner's mind was bent on just that. But Wirion, though he had chosen the stupider alternative, was immensely efficient in operating it. There was no attempt to run, because there was no chance.

Boys and his particular friend Moyses watched keenly for their opportunity, but, like the rest, failed to find it. The combined party at length reached Mezières, where the road divided. It was a cruel moment for these particular youngsters, because Moyses was destined for Givet and Boys for Valenciennes: and Boys, peering over the side of his wagon, almost wept with vexation when he saw his friend carted out of sight.

When his party reached Avesnes, the local commandant unexpectedly placed them on parole—an indulgence received with mixed feelings. Then the clever man sprang yet another surprise.

> In the morning he selected eight, of whom I was one, to take the diligence to Valenciennes, adding, 'Gentlemen, I rely upon your honour'. Now severity would have been more acceptable than this act of politic kindness; but to have declined the offer would have exposed my intentions and drawn upon me the accumulated vigilance of the whole guard. This method evinced the impolicy of harsh measures, and insured the safety of eight of the mids.[1]

Accompanied by *one* gendarme they reached Valenciennes without incident.

Here they found a very different welcome. There was no talk of parole. They joined the 1,400 men in the citadel, living and messing

[1] Boys, op. cit., p. 97.

with them, though they were given a small separate building to sleep in. It was indisputable 'lock-and-key' again, the perfect ethical chance. But it was not so good a practical one, because the Commandant, Colonel Du Croix Aubert, was an uncompromising martinet, though a just one: and escape prevention was his mania. There now developed a fascinating battle of wits between the all-powerful colonel and a small party of apparently powerless midshipmen, who yet nursed a determination to break out as maniacal as his was to keep them in. Boys and his friends opened the campaign with a letter to the Minister of War in Paris which, of course, had to go through the Commandant. It demanded a restoration of parole, their undoubted right as officers. In fact, however, parole was the last thing they wanted: so they inserted one sentence which

> insured a flat denial, as it plainly intimated that a refusal would be attended with escape: it ran to this effect—'Such is the character of the British officer that his *parole d'honneur* will better secure his person than *locks, bolts* and *fortresses*'. A few days afterwards I was delighted to learn that the Minister's answer was confined to a simple negative; and hence it became a point of honour in his Majesty's Midshipmen to prove the fact.

Here with a vengeance was a declaration of war; magnificent war too, if only because the youngsters had no intention whatever of sneaking off under any smirch of broken parole. The Colonel even took up the challenge, remarking, in public, 'Nous verrons si ces blancs-becs[1] peuvent m'échapper'.

His Majesty's Midshipmen won—four of them: Edward Boys, Frederick Whitehurst, Robert Hunter and William Mansell. It took some time, but after endless schemings, frustrations, disappointments and unforeseen accidents, the night of the attempt came: and, as they sat waiting to embark upon their do-or-die adventure,

> we amused ourselves with writing a letter to the Commandant, in which we thanked him for his civilities, and assured him that it was the rigid and disgraceful measures of the French Government which obliged us to prove the inefficacy of *locks, bolts and fortresses*. This letter was left to be dropped in the following morning near the *corps de garde*.

The Colonel may be pardoned for being excessively angry when he received this note, and more than ever determined to lay its authors by the heels. But though

[1] Beardless boys.

all the bloody-minded rabble were let loose, with multifarious weapons, and 'carte blanche' to 'massacrer' these lawless *très mauvais sujets:* besides which, 500 of the Garde Nationale was dispatched to scour all the woods within five leagues, and an additional reward of 300 livres was offered for the capture of each of us,

—he failed.

Their fortunes will be followed later; but, here, one word of warning is perhaps desirable, if only to avoid the charge of over-dramatization. These defiant young gentlemen were not quite the curly-headed little 'middies' beloved of Victorian sentimentalists. In a sea sense, Boys himself might almost be described as a veteran. He had gone afloat at the age of 11, and had already served seven years when captured in 1803. He was thus 18 when he made his first long march to Verdun, and was now 23. It has been claimed for him that his experiences provided Captain Marryat with his material in *Peter Simple.* That may be true, but it is only right to record that the same claim has been made on behalf of many other escapers, including Donat O'Brien, Henry Ashworth and George Jackson. On this occasion he was the eldest of the party, as he certainly was the leader of it. Whitehurst was probably a little, but not much, younger. Hunter was about 20, and Mansel, the 'baby' of the group, not more than 18, and probably less.

That Boys was not just an exceptionally punctilious officer becomes clear as we read the adventures—and punctilios—of other escapers. Certainly the *average* conception of what constituted 'honourable escape' was remarkably high: and it was held far outside the ranks of the officers themselves, as one more example will show. It represented the standard of an entire social class in Britain. Let us return to Givet, and take the evidence of the Reverend Mr Wolfe, who also discusses the ethical side of the escape problem. A man of singularly high principles himself, he has nothing but praise for the morality, in this respect, not only of the midshipmen, but also of their kith and kin at home: and—perhaps even more surprisingly—of the ordinary seamen. This is what he has to say about the midshipmen.

> They were so anxious to get home, and so ingenious and bold in facing every danger and difficulty . . .[1] that every expedient to

[1] An extreme example of this is recorded from Bitche by Joshua Done. Midshipman Henry Worth, noticing one day that deep snow was piled up against the foot of the main rampart, simply jumped from the top of it. He fell 80 feet, fortunately landing in the drift 'and got little hurt'. He did not get away, however, and was still expiating his crime when O'Brien first met him. (See p. 147.)

prevent them was in vain. . . . The Commandant [not the original bad one] took every precaution he could think of to inform himself of, and prevent, their escape. Amongst other things, he opened all their letters before he allowed them to go into the prison, where they were confined while numbers of the men had the liberty of the town. After eight of them had escaped and been retaken, and at the moment when he was most . . . on the *qui vive*, a letter arrived for Mr B. [Blakiston] from his Mother. The Commandant had no doubt, from the natural affection of a mother, that it was to urge him to get home: and perhaps to point out and furnish him with the means, for himself at least if not for others also. But when it was read to him, he could not contain his astonishment and admiration, and spoke of it to everyone. She had heard that, in some depots, there had been midshipmen who had broken their parole and come home. And she entreated him not to let any personal suffering or ill-treatment or example induce him to do what would be disgraceful to himself, distress his family beyond measure and cast a reflection upon his country. Young as he was, however [he was 17], no officer grown old in the honourable career of British Service had less need of the pious and self-denying counsel of such a mother. He and some others afterwards escaped in the most honourable manner after having been once retaken, though he himself might perhaps have succeeded, but that he would not leave behind him a brother midshipman who had lamed himself on the journey. And then, after two attempts and through dangers and difficulties which might have overcome the courage even of a British sailor, they arrived at home.

It was, however, not only the youngsters and the Lady Blakistons of Britain who played the game thus scrupulously. The worthy clergyman proceeds:

But this letter, together with the strict observance of a given, or even implied, parole, on the part of all the prisoners, even to the lowest amongst them, so revealed the character of the English at Givet that the Commandant was quite persuaded that they were most in safety when they were most in the enjoyment of liberty. Many of the men were permitted to walk in the town, and were much sought after by those who wanted workmen or servants: and a great number walked . . . even into the country every day. But, though they were constantly escaping from the prison [i.e. under lock and key] they never betrayed the confidence placed in them [i.e. when out on their honour].[1]

And these were not even officers; only ordinary non-parole men. No wonder he was proud of them.

[1] Wolfe, op. cit., pp. 97–8.

Wolfe ends with an example of supreme devotion to principles which, after all, were largely self-imposed:

> Three mids whose friends had successfully escaped determined to try too. They committed an offence. But the Commandant suspected the cause, and would not lock them up. The next night they made a still more determined attempt, but still in vain. He would not take away their parole. Precisely at that moment, as if to try their faith to the utmost, an order arrived from the Minister of War to send all the midshipmen, under a double guard of gendarmes, to Verdun. But in spite of this positive order the Commandant took upon himself to send them upon their parole. And they walked all the way to that place without the least idea of escaping, although all the soldiers in France would scarcely have prevented them from making the attempt.[1]

Why, we may ask, did they not themselves return their paroles to that perspicacious commandant? Surely every parole had two contracting parties, either of whom would have been justified in giving notice of termination? There seems to be but one answer. Such must have been their respect for the sanctity of their own word that they held a promise, once given, to be inviolable, and that only the other party could absolve them from it: and if he would persist in trusting them, it was not for them to let him down.

The French *Moniteur* and the English-language *Argus* never wearied of charging escaping British officers with broken parole and besmirched honour. The names, for instance, of both Boys and Blakiston figure in Decrès' list[2] of ungrateful criminals who thus requited French kindness and generosity. It is time that someone should answer the calumny, 150 years late though he be, by nailing such worthless lies to the counter.

As for escape from Bitche, Sarrelibre and Sedan, though, there too, *Moniteur* and *Argus* still have the effrontery to squeal about forfeited honour, the question never really arises. At these centres all captives, all the time, even when not underground, were always under lock and key, behind the walls of the strongest fortresses in France. Honour cannot be tarnished by what does not exist. No prisoner there ever gave his parole: he was not invited to do so.

[1] Wolfe, op. cit., p. 102.
[2] For a discussion of this list see Appendix III.

CHAPTER VIII

'VIXERE FORTES ANTE AGAMEMNONA'

The exploits of our own contemporaries in this heroic business of escaping fascinate us. To be proud of their courage and endurance, to marvel at their ingenuity, is right and proper. But let us not forget that they had ancestors in this hazardous field, as brave and enduring as they, though probably less ingenious. For, as we have seen, our heroes who escaped from Napoleon were by way of being the pioneers of the game: and techniques are seldom perfected at once. No addict of modern escape literature, therefore, should allow himself to smile patronizingly at their efforts. As well snigger at Blériot's flying machine or scoff at Stephenson's Rocket. These pioneers were great men: so were the British escapers with whom we are now to deal.

Again the categories of *détenus* and service men must be separated, the more so as we now know the different conditions governing each. We shall find less respect for the sanctity of parole among *détenus*, and much more among serving officers. It is perhaps worth recalling, too, that, parole being virtually dead in our own day, the modern escaper is largely freed from the ethical problems of his ancestors. It is now, in almost all cases, his professional duty to escape if he can. It was then at best a moral duty only and, at worst, a moral crime.

A. DÉTENUS

In the early days of the war two fairly well-known *détenus* got away under circumstances which did little credit to themselves and much harm, indirectly, to the rest: for the French propaganda machine swooped upon their cases and made full capital out of them. One of the men was Sir James Crawford, a member of the British Diplomatic Corps, though not a particularly distinguished one. It is seldom easy to isolate such grains of truth as often exist in turgid tons of propaganda; but it would certainly seem that Sir James was not blameless. He gave his parole, but, pleading ill-health, was allowed to go to Aix for the waters as a special favour. Thence, without much difficulty, he removed himself, *via* Germany, to Britain. The other man was Thomas Brooks, Member of Parliament for Newton in Lancashire. He went to a public dinner at Valenciennes where he was held captive, and, when it was over, got back into his carriage, still dressed for the party, and openly drove away, reaching Cologne unchallenged and, ultimately, home. Neither Crawford nor Brooks ever admitted any guilt, and, probably because neither was a member of the fighting services, no one in Britain blamed them. They did not deny their promise; but, they held, it had been given under *force majeure* after the initial crime—the French crime—of illegally detaining them. It is profitless to enter again into the ethics of the matter. Their conduct need be considered only as underlining the different codes of civilians and officers.

Their example was followed by other *détenus*, each with varying degrees of justification which, as we seldom know them, makes any moral judgment difficult if not impossible. Sometimes, however, it would be hard to approve their actions: as, for instance, that of a certain Columbine de Jersey who, allowed to return home for one month on the score of urgent private business, simply did not come back. Here points other than strictly moral ones are raised. Such conduct, even if morally justifiable, must surely be stigmatized as selfish. Many other *détenus* would doubtless have welcomed a month's leave at home, and most of them would have returned at the end of it. But now, thanks to de Jersey, their pitch was queered. Napoleon was not the man to be hoodwinked twice by the same trick.

Several of the peerage and baronetage ran for it—Lord Archibald Hamilton for instance, and the Hon. Arthur Annesley. But how far the case of broken faith lies against them is not so clear. Annesley could at least plead hard lines; but, since he was a soldier, a purist like Brenton, we may be sure, would not have approved his conduct. In 1803 he had just been married, and was actually on his honeymoon when caught by the May decree. He endured eight years of captivity, mostly at Verdun, but then escaped from Paris, whither, no doubt, he had been allowed to go as a privilege. On the other hand, the Horse Guards was presumably prepared to forgive, or overlook, his action, because he was promoted to General and at once re-employed. Among the unsuccessful was Charles Baron Blount—a Briton, though his title was probably foreign—who escaped to Cleves but was picked up again, and remained captive till the end. The case of the baronet

Sir Beaumont Dixie has already been cited. He survived his term at Bitche and worked his passage back to Verdun. There, clearly, he was reconciled to his fate. We find him in the summer of 1812 making what he can of that town's amenities, among other things running a couple of horses in the races.

Another *détenu* was a certain Dr Alderson. He escaped, but paid rather dearly for it. He owned a farm near Lille, and the French got their own back on him by confiscating it. Another escaper, of the business class, was Augustus Bance. As a *détenu*, he conceived the idea of turning an honest penny by opening a soap factory and, to do so, applied for French citizenship. The case came up for hearing, and this gave him some freedom of manœuvre. Anyway, when the court met to pronounce judgment—a refusal—it found that there was no applicant: he was safely home. Another, and a better-known, business man was Philip Astley, the London circus proprietor. He was in Paris in May 1803, trying to secure compensation for his premises in that city which had been used during the Revolution as army barracks. He was caught by the decree, but contrived to slip over the border into Italy, and to return to London with both his freedom and his compensation money.

Another case is mentioned by Alger.[1] An Englishman named Mogg, with three companions, escaped from Arras and reached Boulogne. Here, unable to find any craft to take them to England, they proceeded to build themselves a small boat, and, in the absence of any more conventional material, tried to make it watertight with layers of suet. These failed—so much at least is credible—and they were retaken. In some unexplained way, however, Napoleon himself got to hear of the exploit, and admired their hardihood so much that he released them with his blessing and a sum of money.

The adventures of two much younger men are worthy of record. A certain Peter Blagrove, quite a lad, climbed down the walls of Verdun with, as his unexpected companion, a Frenchman of his own age. They had no passports, of course, but, on approaching Strasbourg, bought a horse and cart and a load of hay. With these they boldly entered the town, saying that they intended to sell it there. They left by another gate, offering the same story, which worked all the way through to Switzerland. There they procured passports for Trieste. This place was the Mecca of most east-going escapers because British

[1] In his *Napoleon's British Visitors and Captives, 1801–15.* I have found neither corroboration nor details elsewhere.

frigates were often off the port, if not actually in it. History does not relate what happened to the young Frenchman, nor even what his intentions were. Another young man named William Wright[1] had an adventurous escape, showing no little ingenuity. Having got away (also from Verdun) he wandered about France for a long time. He turned up at last at Havre where, having considerable knowledge of French, he secured the job of interpreter to General Brabançon, the Commandant. In this comfortable position he waited until an English ship came in under a flag of truce. He then procured a large trunk, arranged for its delivery on board, and got into it. He was not detected during the very rigorous search which all such vessels had to undergo, and, after being at sea for an hour, emerged and revealed himself to the captain. That officer accepted him and carried him to England— a course he would probably not have dared to take had Wright revealed himself while still in an enemy port.

In many of these, and similar, stories there are signs of a gradually developing escape organization: an ever-widening traffic in forged passports—good, convincing ones too—as well as associations of Napoleon's subjects (sometimes but not usually Frenchmen) to aid escaping Britons. The French Government, naturally, soon became aware of such activities, and we hear of more and more arrests, at Bruges, Ostend and elsewhere on or near the Channel, of men charged with aiding and abetting runaways and uttering false papers. The authorities also had many *agents provocateurs*. One such was that same unpleasant Colonel Henry Dillon who wormed out of young James the identity and habitat of a French passport-faker in Verdun named Page. The naval Dillon was himself offered a most artistically-made one for five pounds, but would not take it. The corresponding French organization for retrieving their men from British prisons was well ahead of ours, alike in time, in development, and in subtlety: but its members were seldom British subjects because very few Englishmen hated King George enough to want to help the Emperor. There were, however, some exceedingly expert forgers among the prisoners in British hands, while 'smugglers', in fast luggers and in

---

[1] He may have been a midshipman (*vide* Fraser, op. cit., index), but I think not. I can find no captive midshipman called by these two names; nor was he one of the several William Wrights of the Navy Lists. Fraser probably confused him with Wesley Wright's nephew John (see p. 256). Further, this William wrote a *Narrative of the situation and treatment of the English arrested by Order of the French Government:* and, as it is all about *détenus*, the presumption is that he was one himself.

French pay, made, towards the end, almost nightly journeys to our side of the Channel to pick up, by prearrangement, any Frenchman who could reach the coast.

B. SERVICE MEN

The British officers and men who contrived to escape will, for convenience, be marshalled under their various ranks: and those same men who, in Chapter IV, made the sad journey to Verdun, together with some others, will be taken as illustrations. For reasons which will now be clear, the high-ups among them will not detain us for long. Escape—even attempted escape—was not for them.

I. *Major-General*. Lord Blayney did not try. Instead, he made the best of a bad job, and the best he could of Verdun. Being well off, he spent his money like a *détenu*, and we hear of him reviving the moribund race meetings. In the summer of 1812, with four horses running, he had a mount in every race. Yet he had his bad moments, as when in March 1813 he was suddenly hauled from his comfortable rooms and locked up close in the Citadel. Indignantly demanding the reason, he was told that a certain General Simon had been similarly confined in England, to stand trial for various misdemeanours; and that he, Blayney, was hostage for him, to be dealt with just as the British dealt with Simon. This was more than uncomfortable: it was dangerous, because his opposite number was accused, not only of blatant breach of parole, but also of plotting to release and arm the French prisoners-of-war in bulk. After six anxious weeks, however, he was released on the British Government's decision not to proceed against Simon.

Early in 1814, the general, like everyone else, was bustled out of Verdun at very short notice. But, though food was scarce and transport even scarcer, his Lordship, true to form, contrived to travel not too uncomfortably right across France to Guéret (passing in one place a strange cavalcade consisting of the Pope and several cardinals being hurriedly evacuated from Fontainebleau). From Guéret Blayney travelled to Paris, to see the fun, now a free man. Certainly no blame attaches to him for not escaping. It would have been criminal for him to try.

II and III. *Captain*. Jahleel Brenton, as has been seen, had no need to escape, being among the very few officers exchanged. But in any case he would not have tried, for the same reasons which restrained Blayney. *Commander* Henry Hoffman did not try either, for the same reasons. Yet there were two men in this region of seniority who attempted escape, and both succeeded. We have met them already. One was Captain Nesbit Willoughby (p. 185), the other Captain Henry Gordon (p. 195).

Willoughby, in his own day deservedly nicknamed 'The Immortal', had the reputation of being the most insatiable fighter in the Royal Navy. He had, it was said, received so many wounds in action that he had lost all count of them. On returning home from the taking of Mauritius in 1810, with one eye clean torn out and the other gravely damaged, with lower jaw smashed and neck so lacerated that the windpipe was exposed, he must needs, when the Admiralty would not find him another ship, go to Russia to serve the Czar as an army volunteer. Thus he took part in the campaign of 1812. He was captured by the French, but only because he gave up his horse to two wounded Russian privates. So he went through the horrors of the retreat from Moscow as a prisoner—not a good insurance risk. But, though almost all his captors perished, the Immortal survived, and reached France. Napoleon, for some reason, had a special spite against him and, refusing a personal appeal for his release from the Czar himself, had him securely incarcerated in the immensely strong Château de Bouillon. This, however, could not hold him: he escaped back to Russia. He was never at Verdun; nor was he ever offered parole, and therefore had no problem of 'honour'.

The other escaper of this seniority was Henry Gordon, the rogue Temple's sponsor. Though only a Commander when taken, he had soon been promoted in captivity, so that, when he got away in 1811, he had been a captain for six years. His position then is unknown. Was he on parole? Was he under lock and key? There is not enough evidence to decide. The Transport Board's verdict is lost. Nor, when he reached home, is there any overt evidence of Admiralty disapproval. He rose in due course to be Rear-Admiral of the Red; but this merely meant that he lived long enough—he was safe for his flag after 1805, when he became a post-captain. On the other hand, he was not employed when he came home: indeed, never again. This is a little more suggestive because, though he might well fail to secure a command after 1815, he would be entitled to hope, if all were well, to obtain one between 1811 and 1815. And there are two other hints that all was *not* well. In O'Byrne's *Naval*

Biographical Dictionary (whose biographies, in most cases, were really *auto*biographies), though the action in which he was captured is well written-up, his escape is not mentioned. Most escapers preserved no such silence: they were obviously and rightly proud of what they had done—if it were respectable. On the other hand we find Conn (whose escape was not passed as respectable) adopting the same line as Gordon. Again—and perhaps a stronger point—Gordon escaped, not from Verdun, still less from a punishment depot, but from Melun, not a proper depot at all. He must have gone there upon the sufferance of the French Government, and it was not, on the face of it, the kind of place likely to abound in locked doors and barred windows, a British captain's only excuse for running.

IV. *Lieutenant.* George Jackson escaped: and, as he got out of Bitche, no question of ethics arises. Once there, he seems to have decided to change his technique to something rather subtler than making tunnels in *souterrains* or holes in walls; or even than shinning down ramparts on home-made ropes. He had had enough of such things. He had, however, lost nothing of his will to be free, and he began to scheme at once. But it took time. He had first to climb up from the lower classes of accommodation, where all subtlety was impossible, and then to find suitable allies. The first to present himself was a stout army captain who, having recently broken a thigh in an abortive attempt, could not himself try again, but was most sportingly keen to help Jackson collect the properties for his new attempt. His other accomplice, destined to go with him, was one Lieutenant Edward Lestrange of the 71st Foot, whose strong point was great fluency in French. The 'military captain' (whose name, unfortunately, Jackson does not disclose) performed his part so well that, without causing the least suspicion, he assembled, article by article, by purchase from various guards, a large water-pitcher, a very second-hand uniform coat belonging to a French private and a cap to match, a voluminous military cloak and—trump card indeed—an officer's cocked hat.

All was now ready. One dark night in late February 1812, Lestrange, wearing the cloak and cocked hat, and Jackson following him in *poilu's* coat and cap, with the water-pitcher on his shoulder, walked right out of the gates, past at least a dozen sentries who saluted the cocked hat without the least suspicion. Once outside, Jackson discarded the *poilu* disguise, and donned another product of his and his military friend's forethought—'a well-cut snuff-coloured coat, buff-coloured waistcoat, pepper-and-salt breeks and white top-boots'. But Lestrange clung to that talisman, the cocked hat. Thus clad, they openly chartered horses, rode into Metz, and put up at the best hotel. Thence they drove in a comfortable carriage to Verdun, where they separated. Lestrange, still in his character of French officer, openly passed through the gates along with a military baggage-train, while Jackson remained outside. When night fell, his Verdun friends (of whom Conn was one), briefed by Lestrange, hauled him up the town wall and stowed him away in the town. Then they procured for him the passport of a Swiss clockmaker, executed perhaps by the expert hand of Monsieur Page. Having again been let down the wall, he was met by a reliable guide and a carriage.

Off they went again in style, and without concealment. They came to Chalons, and here Jackson boldly entered the Paris diligence, travelling with seven French officers 'five of them decorated with the Legion of Honour'. At Paris he changed into the Caen diligence. This time he feigned a violent toothache, because, knowing little French, he had to have some excuse for not answering the ordinary civilities of his fellow-travellers. When the diligence stopped for the dinner hour, he found himself, to his horror, sitting next to the very officer who had interrogated him on his first capture with Whitehurst. But his nerve did not desert him. When the officer politely invited him to take wine he accepted with a grateful, friendly smile, and stammered out his thanks in what he piously hoped would be taken for Swiss. Again heaven was kind: the man did not recognize or suspect him; and again he found himself at Caen, in the same house in which he had already spent fourteen months. Once more the same benefactor tried to find him a boat, and, this time, succeeded after a bare week. Things were already better organized. But, as though to pay him back for shamming toothache, nature now punished him with real ear-ache of the most excruciating kind. He became stone-deaf, with a most offensive discharge from his ears. Fortunately, however, he had found another and even safer hide-out, provided by another pro-English Breton. After three weeks, he began to hear again, and was at length embarked in a flat-bottomed boat, furnished with a punt-pole. In this he reached a fishing smack, empty and anchored. Single-handed, he stepped the foremast and got to sea. The vessel was old and crank: her rudder belonged to a much larger craft, and he had a four-hour struggle to ship it. He could not manage to step the mainmast, and never did. But his luck held: a gentle southwester wafted him across the Channel, and he was within sight of the Isle of Wight when the British brig *Mutine* picked him up. Good fortune and unfailing nerve had brought him through. It was his fifth attempt. Lestrange also won through, quite separately. He reached Bordeaux, whence he secured a passage for England.

To Jackson's second attempt—his first from Verdun (see pp. 95-6)— there was a tragic sequel. Three others had climbed with him down the wall of the convent inside the Citadel, and had reached the town. There they separated, each to his own prearranged bolthole. Jackson, as we saw, was caught, but the other three, all Young Gentlemen, succeeded in getting right away from Verdun. The eldest of them, named Devonshire, reached England safely. The other two, George Gordon and Charles Street, were mere lads—in fact, volunteers when captured, and not even midshipmen. They kept together, and reached the Channel coast. There they somehow contrived to obtain a boat. But it was a very small, bad one; and, possibly, they were not so very clever at handling it. Anyway, they were washed up on the French side, drowned.[1] Here are illustrated the evident hazards of the game. It is easier, and perhaps more natural, to dwell upon the successes. But the failures were many. That time, four broke out, one reached England: and this is probably about the proportion of successes and failures throughout, though, fortunately, the tragedy in this particular story was not the norm.

V. *Master's Mate*. Donat O'Brien escaped at his fourth attempt. For sheer staying power, and relentless will to be free, no other escaper, perhaps, touches this young Irishman. He had little of Jackson's finesse or bluff. He was content to burrow through walls or climb down them, or make his dash for liberty while on the road: taking all the risks, enduring all the hardships inherent in such ways of going about it. His own writings furnish a close-up, day-to-day narrative of his experiences which is far more detailed than any other

---

[1] The usually accepted story. But Thomas Williams (see p. 249) indirectly casts doubt on it. The lads, he says, had recently been caught at Blankenbergh and lodged in Bruges gaol where he, himself just retaken, met them and found them most inspiriting company. On their subsequent fate he is silent, except to say that, after the war, he learnt from a servant of one of their parents that they had escaped. Had they drowned in doing so, that servant would surely have mentioned the fact, and Williams would as surely have passed it on.

escape story of the period.[1] The present work can do no more than
the scantest of justice to him.

His first attempt was made from Verdun, whither we have already
conducted him. We have noticed that the ethical problems of escape
tended, under the peculiar circumstances of the time, to be variously
interpreted by various individuals. The interpretation of Midshipman
Boys has been discussed at some length; and it must be admitted that
O'Brien's was not quite so strict. In the main it was the same as that
of the midshipman, but in one particular O'Brien was disposed to
give himself a better chance. Both agreed that the pass which allowed
them to leave the town involved 'parole', so that it had to be relinquished deliberately before an attempt could be made. Both agreed
that the attempter must first get himself locked up in Citadel or
Porte Chaussée for some offence. But whereas Boys held that the
attempt, to satisfy honour, must be made *from* the cell, O'Brien
thought that *having* been locked up for the offence was good enough.
Honour did not demand escape from the cell itself. This, in practice,
made things a good deal easier, because the O'Brien view allowed
the would-be escaper to collect necessary apparatus like rope, files,
saws, maps and a compass more or less at leisure; and to choose a
quiet moment to scale the town walls, an easy task compared with
that of tackling the specialized defences of the Citadel or the prison
cells over the *Chaussée*.

On August 29, 1807, therefore, having duly forfeited their passes
and completed their sentences, they lowered themselves over the
town ramparts, 72 feet high. There were four of them—O'Brien
himself, Sub-Lieutenant John Essel,[2] and two midshipmen named
Henry Ashworth and Christopher Tuthill, both, before they had
done, to qualify in their own right as daring and inveterate escapers.
They struck north-west, across country, having a rather unusual
design. Those who broke out from the more westerly depots, like
Arras or Valenciennes, mostly made for the Channel; but those from
east-lying depots like Verdun, Sarrelibre or Bitche hoped to cross the

---

[1] Contained in no less than seventeen separate 'bulletins' in the *Naval
Chronicle*, from Vol. 28 to Vol. 31.

[2] Later to die in another attempt: see p. 219. The Sub-Lieutenant of this
period was not, as now, the lowest grade of commissioned officer, but the
product of a temporary promotion-block: a midshipman who had passed the
examination for lieutenant but who still was not one. This explains why
O'Brien, only a Master's Mate, but older and of longer service than Essel,
regarded himself, and was regarded, as the leader.

Rhine and reach, ultimately, either Austria or Russia, according to which was, at the moment, friendly to Britain. But O'Brien and his friends, though from an eastern depot, decided upon the long overland journey to the coast. They had brought with them as many provisions as they could reasonably carry and intended, for as long as possible, to approach no inhabited village, or even house.

The distance, however, was great, and progress, always at night and almost always across country, was slow: made even slower by a peculiarly wet spell which turned every dyke into a little river, and every little river into a big one. They lay up during daylight in any wood they could find, but occasionally had to make do with vine-yards or orchards. They were always wet through and, to make matters worse, O'Brien, quite early on, fell awkwardly in jumping a ditch and wrenched his knee badly. As the others had no thought of leaving him, their progress became slower than ever. Before they were halfway to the coast, their provisions gave out, and they were com-pelled to have recourse to human habitations. They chose the most miserable and isolated cottages or the lowest inns in the smallest villages: and, on the whole, they were received with kindness, obtaining such rough food (and always paying for it) as their very poor hosts could provide. Like other escapers, they soon found themselves mistaken for French deserters, and behaved accordingly. After the first fortnight of this rigorous existence they all began to weaken, especially Essel, who was clearly suffering from some lung trouble, often bleeding from mouth and nose and scarcely able to drag him-self along. As they had no more idea of leaving Essel than they had of deserting O'Brien, their progress grew even slower.

Sticking grimly to the task, however, at length they approached the coast. They were near Etaples, and that, unfortunately, was not at all far from Boulogne, where Napoleon's Armed Camp still remained, standing a little forlornly perhaps, yet still bristling with soldiers, customs officers and gendarmes: and one of the main pre-occupations of all these people was to track down runaway conscripts. To make things worse for the fugitives, the authorities (as Jackson was later to discover) had begun their sharp surveillance on all boats, which were ordered into Etaples every evening. Unwittingly the escapers had stepped into a hornet's nest. Every soul they met was a potential enemy, whether in uniform or a local inhabitant who would earn a reward for catching them and condign punishment for shielding them. Yet they struggled on, and actually came within sight of the sand-dunes and the sea. Then the end came.

A disagreement—the first in their three-week journey—now arose between them. Tuthill proposed to make a dash for the shore in daylight because, he said, only then was there any hope of finding a boat. He may well have been right; but it was madly dangerous, and O'Brien objected. The others, however, sided with Tuthill, and off they went. In plain truth there was little hope either way: yet they all but reached the sand-dunes, where there was good cover and not many people. At the very last hovel before they got there, Ashworth went in, by mutual consent, to ask for some water: they would find none in the dunes, and they were parched with thirst. The others waited a long time, then Tuthill went in to see what caused the delay. When they emerged, they were conducted by two armed men —customs officers—and, though they produced their agreed story, that they were the master and crew of an American ship cast away near Marseilles, it availed them nothing. They were forced to accompany the men to Etaples, and thence, no one believing so improbable a yarn, to Boulogne. Once there—like Jackson to avoid worse ills— they admitted their identity, and soon found themselves on the road to Verdun, and the inevitable beyond.

That journey was a nightmare, not only by reason of harsh treatment, but also because of frustrated hope, and fear of what was in store. They were abominably used. They were closely chained together, and so shackled that they could not use their hands at all. Their keepers were taking no chances: at one place they would not remove the irons even in the *cachot*, and the gaoler and his family had literally to put food into their mouths. On the road, when any of them had occasion to relieve nature, his hands were unshackled, but only after the guard had pinioned him with a rope carried specially for the purpose. Everything—even their money—was taken from them.

Regrets for having failed were inevitable. Less so were fears for the future. O'Brien in particular was subjected to what seems to have been a deliberate policy of terrorism. Almost every French official he spoke to told him that he was to be tried for his life when he arrived at Verdun: some said as a British agent spying out the secrets of the Boulogne Camp; others—more credibly—as *chef de complot*, the oldest of any group of deserters, segregated by law from the rest, and shot. When they reached Verdun in October, the authorities isolated him from his friends, and put him in a dungeon alone with a real spy awaiting his sentence. He thought himself doomed, and spent a wretched night. Such intimidation was, indeed, their probable intention: there is no evidence that they really intended his death. But they kept up the tension for a whole week before they passed judgment—that all four were to go to Bitche. Sentence to a term in that fortress can seldom have been received with comparative pleasure: but this time, no doubt, it was. For even at Bitche a prisoner was still alive; and a live prisoner might still escape, even from Bitche.

But the incorrigible O'Brien did not intend to go to Bitche; and, for the time being anyway, he did not go there. Two full months of hardships which would have cured most men of all desire to repeat them seem to have had no effect whatever upon him. His second attempt followed upon the first with bewildering speed. Another journey began early in November with, now, a few other *mauvais sujets* also destined for Bitche. Heavily ironed and closely watched, they had no opportunity whatever to break away while on the road first to Metz and then Sarrelibre. One day's journey more and they were only six leagues from Bitche, where they were to arrive in the evening. But now Providence appeared to relent.

> In the morning our guards came with a large waggon in which we were placed, and, to our great astonishment and delight, were not chained. I considered this an opportunity which ought to be embraced. . . . I communicated my intention to my companions, and after we had got out of the town we descended from the waggons, observing to the guards that we preferred walking a little. Mr Essel [still a very sick man] remained in the waggon. Messrs. Ashworth, Tuthill and Baker (of the merchant service), with myself, were walking ahead of the waggon. We had not gone more than two or three miles when I discovered a wood about 150 yards from the road. Our guards were about 50 yards behind us: they were on horseback and, although there were no leaves on the trees, we were certain they could not pursue us but with a great deal of difficulty owing to the branches: and if they dismounted, we were well assured we could outrun them. These fellows have very heavy large boots and are otherwise badly calculated for running.
>
> The moment arrived. I gave my friends the word and away we ran, the guard in full speed at our heels. The ground being very heavy, a kind of fallow between the road and the wood, Mr Baker fell down and was instantly seized. We were more fortunate; crossed each other frequently in the wood, quite out of breath. I observed to them that they must be very cautious in keeping out of pistol-shot of the guards, who were now riding in all directions through the trees calling out '*Arretez coquins!*'[1]

[1] *Naval Chronicle*, Vol. 29, pp. 324–5.

In the chase the fugitives separated, probably intentionally since this would split up the pursuit. They did not meet again, and O'Brien learned, long afterwards, that both Ashworth and Tuthill were soon ridden down and captured. But he himself, twisting like a hare, instinctively chose the thickest cover, and never lost his head. Soon he bolted for an adjoining wood farther from the road, because he saw—or rather heard—that the guard had been joined

> by the peasantry, men, women and children, it being sunday, and 50 livres, £2–1–8 sterling reward being offered for each prisoner of war. This brought a prodigious concourse of people, and left me but little hope of remaining in safety in any place where they could suspect a man could be concealed.

His heart might be thumping, lungs heaving, body clammy with sweat. But his head remained delightfully cool. Against such odds he adopted the only course that could give him a chance. He threw away his own hat, and donned a night-cap ('this being a common dress with the peasantry of that country') which he carried in his pocket, presumably, against just such an emergency. Then he joined the hunt, and chased himself enthusiastically for a while, only to edge out on reaching 'a small vale through which ran two rivulets, which formed a little kind of island that was covered with a hawthorn-bush, briars, etc.' And in this natural forme he lay up until all sounds of the chase died away.

Night at length fell. He was free again, but not altogether happy.

> It already began to rain very hard, which obscured the moon. . . . Reflecting on my present position I found it truly pitiable, with only one small old map[1] . . . without compass or guide, meat, drink or companion in the dreary month of November. The nearest friendly town to me Salsburgh (in Austria) between 7 and 8 hundred miles distant.

Here were discouragements and to spare. We could sympathize with him had he decided to follow the hunt once more and give himself up. But that never entered his mind. He dismissed pessimism resolutely:

> Nevertheless, having escaped from the clutches of tyrants and being my own master more than compensated for a thousand times more hardships.

He returned to the original wood, still hoping to share his solitude

[1] Of Germany, torn out of an old geography book and smuggled to him by an English prisoner at Sarrelibre.

with his friends: but, after traversing it back and forth for many miles and uttering their agreed whistle many times, he gave it up. Now, drenched with bitter rain, and with no idea under that canopy of clouds which direction to take,

> I was so nearly perished with cold and wet that it was impossible to remain still: I therefore kept running and walking onwards during the night, frequently impeded by the course of the Sarre which confused me greatly.

It is melancholy to have to report the failure of this great-hearted attempt. It did fail, but only after he had had a wonderful run for his money: indeed, after he had put the most obvious of his perils behind him. These were all on the French side of the Rhine, where the natives were not only desperately poor (and therefore tempted to earn the blood-money which went with betrayal), but also, it would seem, much more mean and hard-hearted than those he had met on the coast. Having no reserves of food at all, however, he was forced from the start to try to procure it from the inhabitants: and several times, on knocking at a lowly door, he had to beat a hasty retreat, suspecting that they meant to give him away. Another difficulty was that, though they were French subjects, very few could speak French, and he had no German; and another dreadful drawback was that he had very little money with which to pay or bribe them. Indeed, after several attempts to get help from these surly people, who often refused even to tell him the way—and, once at least, deliberately told him wrong—he gave it up, and groped his way along, often in circles, living entirely upon such cabbages and turnips as he could find in the fields; and, during the daylight hours, retreating into the hills, to lurk in the caverns and lairs of wild beasts. Soon, too, his feet swelled so much that he could not put his boots on. He grew gradually weak. One night he was delirious, imagining that Ashworth and Tuthill were with him and holding nightmare conversations with him. His lair that night was at the top of a small precipice, and he woke to discover, to his amazement, that he was at the foot of it.

Still he trudged on, refusing to give up even when the racing clouds made it impossible for days on end to know in which direction he was going. Once he was told that he was only three leagues from Strasbourg: next day he was 12, and, for two more days, in spite of interminable walking and running, it still remained an obdurate three leagues away. He did, however, reach the Rhine at last and, skirting its banks in search of a boat, ran into two armed men who said that he must accompany them to Strasbourg, and go before the mayor.

All seemed lost. But O'Brien, now desperate, escaped by a tour-de-force of yarn-spinning, inventing as he went along a heart-rending story of hard service, ungrateful governments, dying parents and a patrimony awaiting him could he but cross the river. He half-convinced them. They let him go, but would not put him across. Yet this too he managed, and much more easily than he expected. Still with no idea as to where he was, at first light one dismal morning he saw the bridge at Kehl just ahead: and over it was passing a large herd of cattle. Realizing that he could not live much longer on cabbage and turnip in such impossible weather, he decided on the spur of the moment to take the very great risk of crossing a frontier bridge, barred with gates at both ends and teeming with French sentries. The cattle and his bedraggled appearance saved him. The last thing he looked like was an Englishman, and no less than eleven sentinels let him pass without a second glance, taking him, presumably, for a cattle-herd. He had escaped from France.

He got on much better now, and faster. He ventured to put up at inns of the poorest sort, and once or twice even got a lift. But he had his difficulties. The natives, though still French subjects, hated the French, and yet O'Brien, knowing no German, had to pretend to be French. This would have mattered the less had they not rooked all Frenchmen on principle; and he had very little money. Still, he made progress and partially recuperated his strength. Even his lacerated feet began to heal. Things continued to be bearable until the beginning of December when he reached Lake Constance, and followed its whole length eastwards. At the far end lay Lindau, an important town which he intended to skirt. He had just begun to do so, however, when he was stopped and—what throughout he dreaded most—his passport was demanded. Once more he spun a yarn—of his pocket-book with all its contents accidentally fallen overboard from a ferry he had recently taken. But it was no good. Armed men surrounded him and dragged him before the Commandant, who at once suspected him of what he was: and soon all came out. Back to France and captivity was the inevitable sentence. It was cruelly hard. At Lindau he was all but in Austria, and, once there, he was almost safe.

In all the escape literature of the period there is, perhaps, nothing more deserving of success or more tragic in its failure. For nearly a month, with every single factor against him, he had held on: all alone, with no aid whatever, either human or material; no one to share his daily trials or temporary triumphs; no compass to assist him, not even moon or stars—nothing but an inflexible will.

As far as the Rhine his German guards did not maltreat him, beyond decking him with an immense iron chain and a huge padlock, the two together so heavy that he could not walk in them at all. But at least that meant a carriage, and they drove all the way back to Strasbourg. Here the atmosphere clouded appreciably. The French, authorities and gendarmes alike, were furious, not altogether without reason, at all the trouble he had given them. He was now added to a gang of eleven Corsican soldiers who had lately deserted with all their equipment, and were bound for Bitche to be shot. He took his place, handcuffed to the odd man in the last file, and shackled by a long chain to all the rest. This was bad enough, but the next batch of guards went one further.

> They placed the chain round my neck *under* my handkerchief; and, on my observing that it must certainly be their design to strangle me by putting the chain on so tight, they took it in another link, damned me for a rascally Englishman and clapped on an immense padlock, which was dangling as an ornament under my chin the whole way; and they screwed on my handcuffs until the skin was twisted literally off the wrists.[1]

In the last foul dungeon before Bitche, the doomed Corsicans showed up in what was most probably their true colours. They were allowed out to get some food: but the *sacré anglois* was not. When they returned, they shared like and like with him, and arranged their knapsacks to make the apology of a bed for him, 'observing that they ought not to complain *when a British officer was used in so horrid a manner*'. Two of the poor devils suffered all night from diarrhoea, and next morning, on entering the cell with its insupportable stench, the gendarme on duty ordered the closet-stool to be emptied. 'Where is the Englishman?' he shouted. 'Let him do that part!' O'Brien indignantly refused, and before the guard could take his revenge, the Corsicans interfered, and hurriedly performed the task themselves. The fate of these good samaritans is not known, but the worst must be feared.

We have already seen the welcome awaiting O'Brien at Bitche (p. 147). Since nothing could be worse than what he had just suffered, he seems to have been quite agreeably surprised, especially when his old friends recognized him (but only after he had told them who he

[1] *Naval Chronicle*, 30, 327.

was), and obtained leave to visit him, they having already moved up from Class V. But he was sad when only Ashworth and Tuthill appeared. Essel had already made his last throw, and was dead. Here again foul play cannot be excluded entirely. The current story at Bitche, a little later, was that he was killed in descending the ramparts; but according to several reports, he was dispatched when lying in the ditch by a bayonet wound in his forehead: he had a considerable sum of money on his person at starting, but as none was found on him when brought back, it was generally supposed that he was murdered to conceal the robbery.[1] This, however, is too second-hand to rank as evidence, and should probably be ruled out.

There is never a moment's pause in O'Brien's escape story. He was not going to stay at Bitche; but he had to wait until he was upgraded. As soon, however, as he had reached the luxury of Grade II, he heard from one of his many friends in Class IV—the men's *souterrain*—that a mass escape was in the air. He was not going to be left out of it, nor were Ashworth and Tuthill, and a young merchant skipper named George Brine. The four of them cajoled a gendarme to let them go downstairs, to attend—of all things—a birthday party. The subsequent affair, however, was ill-managed, and on too large a scale. The idea was that they should force no less than three iron doors, and that every occupant of that dungeon should pass out. At first they did quite well. They forced the first door, and the second, much the strongest; but someone's over-eagerness at the third caused the bolt to shoot back with a loud clang, and the alarm was given. A *sauve-qui-peut* followed, all scrambling for their beds in order to appear fast asleep when the guard arrived. Here the visitors from above were at a disadvantage, with no bed to make for: and the long and short of it was that ten culprits were detained, seven because of the mud-stains on their clothes, and Ashworth, Tuthill and Brine, caught odd-men-out. But not Donat O'Brien. By sheer quick thinking, aided for once by some luck, he leapt into the bed of a dead-drunken seaman. That worthy rolled out, but, being found on the floor completely incapable, could not be considered a ringleader. Later, by remarkably clever timing and bluffing, O'Brien succeeded in getting out of the *souterrain*, already full of gendarmes, and back to his own quarters. The ten who were caught were removed with every form of brutality to Metz, there to stand trial. We will return to them.

[1] Joshua Done, op. cit.

Though they could pin nothing on O'Brien that time, they watched him more closely than ever, and he had to lie quiet for a while. Besides, he was beginning to doubt the efficacy of mass escape, and needed time to collect the apparatus for a more limited attempt. The hardest thing to acquire was rope, which had to be collected piecemeal; and, as it grew in length, it had to be worn, in sections, around the bodies of those who proposed to use it. His was a masterpiece of craftsmanship and ingenuity, 'which we had been able to construct out of our shirt-linen and a little cobbler's twine': and it took up so little space—he says, though it is hard to credit—that when its four sections were joined it could be 'tightly wound in a ball and concealed in a pocket-handkerchief'.[1] He also acquired during this interval—he does not say how—the necessary keys to open his own room (now on ground-level) and certain others essential to enable him to reach the outer walls. Last, he secured a team. It was four strong: himself, a midshipman friend named Maurice Hewson, a dragoon officer in the East India Company's service named Batley, and a young doctor named Barklimore, surgeon in a merchantman and, later, to practise in High Street, Bloomsbury.[2]

On the dark night of September 14, 1808, the walls were negotiated without a hitch, and with what O'Brien makes to sound like ease. Really, however, it was a remarkable feat of careful planning and preparation, with every eventuality foreseen. The apparatus included boat-hooks to which to attach the rope over the lower walls, and an ingenious system of knots which, while they would take the weight of any one of the party, would give way when all clapped upon them together, thus minimizing the total length required. They could now use most of the rope twice—essential because they had to descend nearly 200 feet, in three stages. This they did without accident; and, having done so, paused an instant

> to take a last view of the *Mansion of Tears*. We then returned thanks to God and shook hands with each other, replete with joy at this miraculous adventure.

'Miraculous' is barely an exaggeration, and it *was* their last view

[1] Unlike most of the other extracts from O'Brien used in this book, these passages come from a later edition. By then, one feels, a good story has had time to mature into a better (if less true) one. This is a pity and, because of it, I have preferred elsewhere to use the original version.

[2] In the original 'bulletins', O'Brien calls Barklimore 'Barclimore' and Batley sometimes 'Barclay' and sometimes 'Batteley'. In this case second thoughts were probably more trustworthy.

too. All won free, O'Brien, Barklimore and Hewson together, Batley separately. Space precludes all but the main details of their journey. As a story it is no less exciting, though as a feat perhaps less meritorious than O'Brien's second flight. This time it was far less forlorn a hope. They had food to tide them over the first and most dangerous days before reaching the Rhine, so that they did not have to risk calling at houses. They had also that near-necessity, a compass, a reasonable map, a relatively large store of money, brandy, and—it being September and not November—comparatively fair weather.

Moving due east by compass, they struck the Rhine well above Strasbourg in some four days, ferrying themselves over in a stolen boat. Bodily ailments were their principal hardship. The naval officers were the toughest, and suffered little. The doctor, however, who was only just recovering from a sharp attack of ague, was often in a very poor way; but in the end it was the soldier whose feet became so swollen that he could not walk at all. They had agreed to keep together until the river was crossed, but after that, if necessary, to break up; and it was on the day after the passage that they left him with an old shoemaker in a quiet village near Rastat. They themselves kept south for a time, then struck across the Black Forest, using the little inns in out-of-the-way villages, as O'Brien had done when alone, but with greater security now because, since he passed that way before, that indefatigable young man had been busy mastering German. With his bitter memories of large towns, too, they gave them a very wide berth and, crossing Bavaria safely, eventually hit upon the Austrian border at Reichenhall. Bavaria was still strongly pro-French, but Austria—they hoped but did not know—was likely to be infinitely kinder to people like themselves. It was October 17th, and they had been nearly five weeks on the road.

Here they had a horrible moment. They crossed the border just beyond the town—or so they thought. Then they discovered that their hopes were premature: it was not the frontier. Another military post loomed before them, and this they crept past one at a time, having somehow become separated. No sooner had they rejoined, however, than they were rudely arrested by armed men who leaped out from behind a rock. Utterly bewildered, they knew neither in which country they were nor the nationality of their captors: nor, even, if they were Austrians, what attitude would be taken towards them. The officer in charge relieved them of some of their fears. He was Austrian; but he could not, or would not, say what his superiors would do, and he marched them off to Salzburg, which was not far away. They had, at the moment of capture, announced that they were shipwrecked Americans who had walked all the way from Denmark and were bound for Trieste. This story they repeated to the Director of the Salzburg police, and he obviously did not believe a word of it. Still, he behaved in quite a friendly way, and allowed them to go to a tavern for the night upon their promising not to bolt. Horrid uncertainty robbed them of their sleep, and, when they came before him next morning, they still did not know their fate. But the Director, after a long and not very comforting harangue, suddenly let slip the blessed sentence—'*that if we were even Englishmen we had nothing to fear from the Austrian Government!*'

Then, but only then, they knew that they had won.

They were passed down to Trieste, travelling in carriages, still as American citizens, though, it transpired, the Director had known all the time who they really were. At the port, they secured a boat, to row out in search of H.M.S. *Unité*, which, they learned, was lying outside; but they found instead a boat from the *Amphion*. They were taken aboard; and it is characteristic, somehow, of the rather stormy aura which seemed for ever to surround the head of our Master's Mate that, next morning, they engaged in a ferocious hand-to-hand fight with two greatly superior enemy craft, in which they lost three killed and five wounded, of whom O'Brien was one. Indeed, it was a near thing. Had the enemy not been cowards, he says, he, Hewson and Barklimore would have been once more *en route* for Bitche. And could even that stout heart have borne it after only one day afloat?

Soon afterwards Batley turned up, safe and sound. Recovered sufficiently to leave his shoemaker, he had started for Austria; but, in Württemberg, he was arrested and thrown into prison whilst his captors sent to inquire what to do with him. The French dispatched an escort for him, but he did not wait for it, breaking out of the local gaol and getting across the Austrian frontier. Some weeks later still, while he was convalescing from his wound, O'Brien had another joyful and unlooked-for meeting—with Tuthill, from whom he heard that Ashworth also had escaped. The adventures of these youngsters, scarcely less pertinacious than O'Brien himself, are worthy of a brief record, though under our next heading.

VI. *Midshipman.* We left Ashworth and Tuthill, with their eight comrades in misfortune, being dragged in chains to Metz. Evidently the authorities were scared by the near success of so formidable a break-out, and determined to make an example of the culprits. They were formally tried by a fully constituted military court, and given ferocious sentences. All were condemned to penal servitude in the galleys, for periods varying from fifteen years for five of them, including Ashworth and Brine, down to ten (for Tuthill) and nine for the rest. We obtain here an instructive sidelight on the occupants of the 'men's' *souterrain* at the moment. Ashworth, Tuthill and Brine were, as we saw, only visitors, but the other seven were true, if temporary, inhabitants. They consisted of two midshipmen named George Dacre and George Potts; Joseph Giles, a Master, RN; John Daly, a Purser, RN; two merchant captains, Charles Roberts and Walter Adams, and one ordinary seaman named John Light: only one 'man' in the naval meaning of that word, the other six being four naval and two merchant officers. Naturally this was not the normal proportion of 'men' to 'officers' in the men's *souterrain*. As ever, those accustomed to lead in the outside world were still leading in the dungeon. Yet the figures do strongly corroborate our conclusion (p. 146)—that the men at Bitche were by no means cut off from officers' influence.

The condemned Britons were on the point of setting out for Toulon and slavery undisguised when orders came to commute the sentence to penal servitude for life at Bitche. No reason is given, but probably Napoleon, holding, relatively, so few captives, simply did not dare to risk reprisals.

It chanced that they reached Bitche again only a day or two before O'Brien's successful break-out; but, from the depths of Class V, of course they could not join him. Yet, by virtue of a spell of model behaviour, they gradually worked their way above ground. Then, in November 1808, a letter, passing through a secret channel, arrived from O'Brien at Trieste, announcing his escape, and the route and methods he had used. Thus encouraged, a party of no less than twelve decided to try again. Ashworth's brief, unfinished account of what followed survives.[1] He does not give the names of all the escapers, but Tuthill was certainly one: so was Brine. Among the other ten were, almost certainly, their fellow-convicts Midshipmen Dacre and Potts, Giles the Master, Daly the Purser, and Light the seaman. Their rope had not the artistry of O'Brien's; they had to stow it before use in the large kettle common to the whole room. Yet they succeeded, all twelve of them, in getting down the walls and away.

[1] It is printed in Fraser, op. cit., pp. 286–92.

All, it would appear, crossed the Rhine together, but thereafter it is impossible to trace their movements separately, mainly because Ashworth hurt his foot in descending the walls, and had to fall out after they had crossed Baden, and reached Württemberg.

He was luckier than he knew. The rest had scarcely left him when most of them were caught by the Württemberg police and returned in chains to Bitche. In this party was Potts (who was still a *mauvais sujet* at Bitche in 1811) and, probably, the Master, the Purser and the seaman. But Tuthill, Dacre and the skipper Brine won through to Trieste and safety. So did another midshipman, not of the original party, whom they picked up on the way. His name was Thomas Masters. It would be interesting to know more of this intrepid youth, if only because he seems to have succeeded where O'Brien had failed on his second attempt, and under very similar circumstances. A probable reconstruction of his story is that he escaped first from the *Porte Chaussée* at Verdun, was recaptured and condemned to Bitche, but broke away on the road thither. Keeping farther to the south, and of course all alone, he got over into Switzerland, thence into the Tyrol, down to Venice, and so at last to Trieste.

Ashworth escaped too. He was clearly profiting from O'Brien's letter because he also reached Salzburg and travelled thence to Trieste as an American citizen. Freedom, however, proved but a doubtful blessing to him. Having joined a ship, he was killed almost at once in a boat action off Tarragona. O'Brien's party was, it seems, the first to break successfully from the 'Mansion of Tears', and Ashworth's was the second. Evidently, as they amassed experience, *locks, bolts and fortresses* became as inefficacious with the Bitche captives as they were with Midshipman Boys, to whom we are now to return.

Valenciennes lying well to the north-west of the line of fortified depots, Boys, Whitehurst, Hunter and Mansell naturally decided for the Channel route, but a good deal north of Etaples and Boulogne, where O'Brien had come to grief. Once on the seashore, they intended to march along it until either they could find a boat or reach Cadsand, at the mouth of the Scheldt and just in Holland. Here, as a last resort, they would board the ferry-boat for Flushing as passengers, and attempt to seize it in transit.

The date originally fixed for the break-out was September 14th, but a series of discouraging delays occurred, and it was not until November 16th that the attempt was made. This was serious, because the adventure would now be a winter one. Yet, had they started

12. VIEW OF BITCHE (WITH THE PRISONERS AS THEY RETURNED FROM METZ)

From Ellison's 'Prison Scenes'. One (probably of the leading pair) represents Ellison himself

A VIEW OF THE 'HALL OF CHAT,' SHOWING THE ENTRANCE TO THE LOFT

earlier, they would probably have failed, through ignorance of the difficulties which faced them. As it was, Boys used the postponements to good purpose, discovering in time that the original escape route was impracticable. He now concluded that the party must, somehow, make the hazardous passage from the midshipmen's quarters, situated in the prisoners' barracks in the heart of the Lower Citadel, into the Upper Citadel, an extension of the fortifications northwards (see

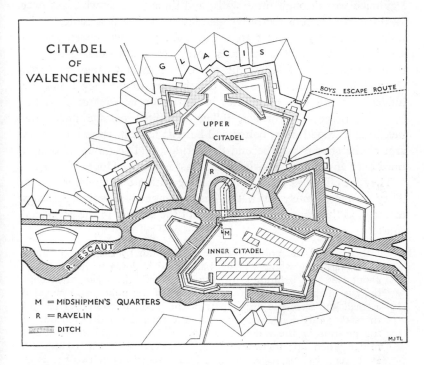

plan on this page). From here, he reckoned, a straight descent over one wall, albeit a high one, would be feasible. The first problem was how to get to the Upper Citadel, impossible until he knew the way, and the obstructions which he would meet. He solved this preliminary task very neatly. He had left behind at Verdun some greyhounds, and, hearing that wild rabbits abounded in the Upper Citadel, he offered them for the sport of the *Maréchal de Logis*. That officer thought it would be fun, and the hounds were sent for. Being trained, however, to obey no one but their master, they would not co-operate, and Boys had to be invited to join the hunting-party. Once there, he was able to examine the lie of the land and make his plans accordingly.

The project was daunting. To reach the Upper Citadel, his party would have somehow to cross three arms of the river Escaut, all really artificial canals running as deep cuttings between man-made stone walls, high and perpendicular. Between two of the streams was a ravelin of the main Citadel fortifications. There was, of course, a legitimate way through these walls, and there were drawbridges over all three streams: but the heavy gate leading to the first could not be used because it led direct from the main prisoners' court, and so was in full view of the sentinels always on duty there. They had therefore to climb, first, to the top of the main Citadel ramparts, descend by rope on to the first drawbridge, where they would be hidden from the eyes of sentries in the prisoners' square; cross the (probably raised) drawbridge; follow a vaulted passage under the ravelin to a second door, bolted and barred; force it, cross the second arm of the stream by a second drawbridge, and so (after tackling a third door and a third drawbridge) at last reach the Upper Citadel.

They set off, Boys and Hunter leading with a quarter-hour's start. They wriggled safely over the main rampart—a very dangerous moment, as they were still in full view of the sentries in the prisoners' court.

I then forced the poker into the earth, and, by rising and falling with nearly my whole weight, hammered it down with my chest; about two feet behind, I did the same with the stake, then slipt the eye of the well-rope[1] over the head of the poker, and fastened a small line from the upper part of the poker to the lower part of the stake; this done, we gently let the rope down through one of the grooves in the rampart, which receives a beam of the draw-bridge when up; then I cautiously descended this half-chimney, as it were, by the rope. When I had reached about two-thirds of the way down, part of a brick fell, struck against the side, and rebounded against my chest; this I luckily caught between my knees, and carried down without noise.

I crossed the bridge and waited for Hunter, who descended with equal care and silence. We then entered the ravelin, proceeded through the arched passage which forms an obtuse angle with a massive door leading to the Upper citadel, and with my picklock endeavoured to open it: but not finding the bolt yield with gentle pressure, I added the other hand, and gradually increased the

[1] Ingeniously acquired by having, previously and unobtrusively, cut through the heart-yarns of the old and rotten rope from the well whence they drew their water, and, when it broke, applied for, and obtained, a new one.

force until by exerting my whole strength something broke. I then tried to file the catch of the bolt, but that being cast iron the file made no impression; we then endeavoured to cut away the stone in the wall which receives the bolt, but that was fortified with a bar of iron, so that it was impracticable; the picklocks were again applied, but with no better success. It now appeared complete checkmate, and, as a last resource, it was proposed to return to the bridge, slip down the piles, and float along the canal on our backs, there being too little water to swim and too much mud to ford it. Hunter, with the most deliberate coolness, suggested the getting up the rope again, and attempting some other part of the fortress. In the midst of our consultation, it occurred to me that it would be possible to undermine the gate; this plan was no sooner proposed than commenced, but having no other implements than our pocket-knives, some time elapsed before we could indulge any reasonable hopes of success; the pavement stones under the door were about ten inches square, and so closely bound together that it was a most difficult and tedious process. About a quarter of an hour had been thus employed, when we were alarmed by a sudden noise, similar to the distant report of a gun, echoing in tremulous reverberations through the arched passage, and as the sound became fainter, it resembled the cautious opening of the great gate, creating a belief that we were discovered. We jumped up, drew back towards the bridge, intending if possible to steal past the gendarmes, and slip down the piles into the canal; but, the noise subsiding, we stood still, fancying we heard the footsteps of a body of men.

The recollection of the barbarous murders at Bitche on a similar occasion instantly presented itself to my sensitive imagination; it is impossible to describe the conflicting sensations which rushed upon my mind during this awful pause. Fully impressed with the conviction of discovery and of falling immediate victims to the merciless rage of ferocious bloodhounds, in breathless anxiety I stood and listened, with my knife in savage grasp, waiting the dreadful issue, when suddenly I felt a glow flush through my veins, which hurried me on with the desperate determination to succeed or make a sacrifice of life in the attempt. We had scarcely reached the turning when footsteps were again heard; and in a whispering tone, 'Boys'. This welcome sound created so sudden a transition from desperation to serenity, from despair to so pleasing a conviction of success, that in an instant all was hope and joy. Reinforced by our two friends, we again returned to our work of mining with as much cheerfulness and confidence as though already embarked for England. They told us the noise was occasioned by the fall of a knapsack which Mansell, unable to carry down the rope, had given to Whitehurst, from whom it slipped, and falling upon a hollow sounding bridge, between two lofty ramparts, echoed through the arched passage with sufficient effect to excite alarm. Whitehurst, with much presence of mind, stood perfectly still when he landed on the bridge and heard the sentinel walk up to the door on the inside, and stand still also; at this time they were not more than four feet from each other, and, had the sentinel stood listening a minute longer, he must have heard Mansell land.

Three of us continued mining until half past ten, when the first stone was raised, and in twenty minutes the second; about 11, the hole was large enough to allow us to creep under the door. The drawbridge was up; there was, however, sufficient space between it and the door to allow us to climb up, and the drawbridge being square, there was of course an opening under the arch; through this opening we crept, lowered ourselves down by the second rope, which was passed through the chain of the bridge, and, keeping both parts in our hands, landed on the *guarde fous.** Had these bars been taken away, escape would have been impossible, there being not sufficient rope for descending into the ditch. By keeping parts of it in our hands, the last man was enabled to bring it away; otherwise four ropes would have been necessary.[1]

We then proceeded through another arched passage, with the intention of undermining the second door, but to our great surprise and joy, we found the gendarmes had neglected to lock it. The drawbridge was up; this, however, detained us but a short time; we got over, crossed the ditch upon the *guarde fous* as before, and landed in the Upper Citadel. We proceeded to the north-east curtain, fixed the stake and fastened the rope upon the breastwork for the fourth descent. As I was getting down, with my chest against the edge of the parapet, the stake gave way. Whitehurst, who was sitting by it, snatched hold of the rope, and Mansell of his coat, whilst I endeavoured to grasp the grass, by which I was saved from a fall of about *fifty feet*. Fortunately there was a solitary tree in the Citadel; from this a second stake was cut, and the rope doubly secured as before. We all got down safe with our knapsacks, except Whitehurst, who, when about two-thirds of the way down, from placing his feet against the rampart and not letting them slip so fast as his hands, got himself in nearly a horizontal position; seeing his danger, I seized the rope, and placed myself in rather an inclined position under him; he fell upon my arm and shoulder with a violent shock; fortunately neither of us was hurt, but it is somewhat remarkable that within the lapse of a few minutes we preserved each other from probable destruction.

It is tempting to commiserate with Boys for having to sustain the

* Two iron bars, one above the other, suspended by chains on each side of the bridge when down, serving the purpose of hand-rails.

[1] They had two, the other having been acquired by persuading the children of their guards to sell them their skipping-ropes, and laying therefrom a rope 45 feet long.

great weight of poor clumsy Whitehurst upon arm and shoulder. Yet he had every reason to bless that great weight. No one but an exceptionally heavy and outstandingly strong man, as well as a surprisingly quick thinker, would have been able to check a man falling vertically, as Boys was.

But all was well: for the moment they were out and away. Their adventures for the next few days were exciting enough—more like O'Brien's first attempt than his later ones, because they were dealing with western peasants: indeed, mostly with Flemish ones, since they very soon reached Belgium. One of their experiences, however, has no parallel in other accounts. One night Boys and Hunter, who were leading, were suddenly confronted with a band of brigands, armed and set upon robbery. But there were only four of them, and when the vast form of Whitehurst loomed up to reinforce the others, they turned tail and fled. Next day the fugitives had a stroke of luck, after a moment of fear. They suddenly found themselves among fortifications in the half-light of morning, and were tiptoeing away when they perceived that the works were long disused, and would furnish wonderfully dry and comfortable accommodation for a good day's sleep in various subterraneous passages with entrances blocked by brambles. They were in fact so comfortable that, next night, they nearly fell into a trap. Finding more fortifications as day came, they discovered only just in time that they were the outer works of Courtrai, and far from abandoned. Instead, however, they found a nice thicket surrounded by a fourteen-foot ditch; and here poor Whitehurst was in trouble again. The others jumped first and easily got across; but Whitehurst slipped—or perhaps the bank gave way under his weight. He alighted in the water, from which they could extricate him only through an almost solid screen of brambles. That day it rained so hard that the level of the ditch rose, and the return jump became much more formidable. The others again managed it, but Whitehurst, still smarting from the brambles, reconnoitred until he found a dead trunk to cross by.

Another evening, while proceeding along a road, they were overtaken without warning by a couple of mounted gendarmes. Most fortunately for the runaways, however, these most deadly of their natural foes fell into the common error of mistaking midshipmen for conscripts, and pressed on into the darkness crying 'Make haste! Make haste! You'll be too late for your lodging tickets!' Two days later it was Sunday, and we get another pleasant sidelight on these young men and their admirable upbringing. From the thick wood in which they were lying low, they heard a church-bell ringing,

> summoning all good people to assemble. We would willingly have joined them, had the church been so secure an asylum as the wood. . . . As Whitehurst . . . had packed his prayerbook in his knapsack and preserved it through all his disasters, we read prayers, and offered up our humble thanksgiving for deliveries from the hands of the enemy.

For all but one day it had rained unceasingly ever since they started, and they were getting pretty low. Boys had a tumour on his left side which compelled him to lie on his right. All their feet were bleeding and their shoes gaping. They found themselves at length at the very gates of Bruges, and were discussing whether to take the grave risk of entering when they spied a small public house outside the wall, and dared to enter it. They were kindly received, with audible whispers (as usual) of '*pauvres conscrits*', and given food and drink. More serious, they were given a place before a fire, with unlooked-for results.

> The sudden transition from cold to heat split Hunter's feet: several of his nails also were loose, and Whitehurst had actually walked off two.

Next day they crawled along, making only one and three-quarter miles in their best hour. But mere speed and distance were no longer the most important matters. They were beyond Bruges and quite near the coast. The problem now was to remain outside the ken of soldiers, gendarmes and customs officers while looking for the all-important boat. It was just here that O'Brien had failed and Jackson was due to fail.

Then, in a blessed moment for themselves, they stumbled by chance upon what was, very likely, the only conceivable answer to their problem. Boys must tell the story.

> At ten p.m. passing by a solitary public house, we observed through the window an old man, two women and a boy sitting round a comfortable fire at supper. Hunter and I entered for the purpose of purchasing provisions to take on board any vessel we might be able to seize. We asked for gin—the woman of the house rose and stared at us, apparently alarmed at our appearance: we repeated the demand without obtaining a reply; still gazing for a few seconds, regardless of our request, she rapturously exclaimed, '*Mon Dieu! Ce sont des anglais!*'—and immediately offered us chairs . . .

and food, and drink, and most valuable advice. Out of prudence they persisted—though they could hardly doubt her sincerity—that they were French conscripts due at Blankenberghe that night; but

> she burst into a loud laugh, and ran to bar the door and window-shutters, at the same time directing the servant to fry more ham and eggs. . . . We used every means in our power to dispossess her of her suspicions, to all which she only replied, 'take chairs, if it is only for a few minutes, and then, *par complaisance*, I will believe you.'

But obviously she did not: and, though they left her soon afterwards, and went on as far as the shore, they could see no hope of securing a boat and, very wisely, decided to return to the lonely inn. She was delighted to see them: and when they began once more to repeat their French conscript story, she silenced them finally with, 'Hold your tongue! I knew that you were English gentlemen the moment I saw you.' She had, they learned later, been very happy in the service of an English gentleman, and she idolized the whole breed. Now, their guard beaten down, they admitted their identity: and in the light of what followed it may be said with perfect confidence that, had they not done so, they would never have escaped.

This remarkable woman was a character in her own right, firm, resourceful and humorous. She was known to them as Madame Derikre, and was to be their salvation a hundred times over. Through fair and foul—and, in the event, foul greatly predominated over fair —she was henceforward staunchly faithful to her English gentlemen, going to endless pains and taking tremendous risks on their behalf. Her wretched little auberge, the *Raie de Chat*—lovingly christened 'The Cat' by the fugitives—lay on the main road from Bruges to Blankenberghe and, being what was called a 'house of police correspondence', was regularly visited by the gendarmes. This, however, did not deter her from insisting upon her house being the midshipmen's home, and that, as it turned out, for the space of many months. There was a large, low hayloft under the length of the roof, enterable only by a ladder from the outside, so that, when its occupants were 'at home', and not desirous of receiving visitors, they had only to draw up the ladder and be reasonably secure.

From this headquarters they operated for several months. Madame put them in touch with a number of mysterious people who had the habit of calling only by night, and whom we should now recognize, probably, as members of an embryo 'resistance', in that they hated the French as foreign invaders, and were disposed to favour the British. Yet none of them had the zeal or the purity of motive which informed Madame Derikre. She consented to be paid for their keep while they had any money, and, when it failed, by letters of exchange. But she would take nothing else. Of the others, none dreamt of stirring a finger without promise of payment, and very few without actually handling the cash. Foremost among these were two men in very different walks of life. One, a nebulous individual named Neirinks, once convinced that any help he gave would be amply repaid, proved faithful enough in his strange way, though maddeningly prudent. The other was much higher in the social scale; a certain lawyer from Bruges named Moitier who was *notaire publique* of that town—a much less attractive, more mercenary, more slippery customer. Yet even he, once he had had it proved to him that their escape to England would put money into his pocket, consented to help: and, in the end, it was he who found them a means to leave the country.

But that was not for a very long time. Though they had reached The Cat on November 23, 1808, it was May 8, 1809, when they left the Continent. The intervening time may be divided into three phases.

During the first and longest—up to March 4th—they made despairing attempts to find, and board, one of the fishing-boats at Blankenberghe. They were there all right, in quantity; but, as elsewhere all along the French-occupied coast, they had to be hauled well above the high-water line at night. In this fruitless, heart-sickening search, they made no less than thirteen separate expeditions to the shore, and spent several months about it, since only at exceptionally high water was there any hope at all. On the thirteenth attempt, on March 4th, they all but succeeded, but were all but caught. They actually got a vessel afloat. She was moored with five hawsers which, characteristically, Boys would not hear of cutting, because of the loss to owners whose compatriots had been so kind to them. There was a remarkable streak of quixotism about him, which we shall meet again. But, this time, the gracious gesture proved their undoing. Four of the hawsers were safely cast off, but the last jammed between the rudder and the sternpost, and brought them up all standing. A squall swung them round, and the boat grounded sideways on the beach. They were jumping out to try to seize another vessel when one of their Flemish friends, acting as look-out, warned them of a body of men approaching over the dunes. They dropped everything they had, including their

knapsacks, and ran. They just escaped, having lost practically everything, and returned disconsolate to The Cat.

This episode closed the first phase. Many tell-tale objects had been
left in the knapsacks, any one of which might lead searchers to the
inn. They decided they must leave it, and for once Madame agreed.
But she had no thought of abandoning them. She led them to a suitable
spot in a wood not far away, and kept in touch with them through
her 12-year-old son and his intelligent dog Fox. She risked much—
her liberty if not her life. The gendarmes soon raided The Cat. They
found nothing incriminating, but they still suspected her and watched
the inn, so that the fugitives could not return. By ill-chance, too, it
was an atrocious March, with heavy falls of snow: indeed they escaped
death from cold only by the regular supplies arriving from The Cat,
and by scooping out a hole in the ground, and spreading over it an
old horse-cloth—Madame's property, of course. All four suffered
severely, however, and at last they decided upon a radical change of
plan. They would give up the sea-coast altogether, and march to
Trieste. But young Mansell, they reckoned, had not the physique
for such a journey. Once more, therefore, they approached Monsieur
Moitier—again via Madame. He had all the time been hovering in
the background with profuse promises of help, never fulfilled. But
now Madame Derikre succeeded in persuading him to take *one* of
their number. He was as good as his word, though painfully slow.
Disguised as a girl, Mansell was escorted by Madame into Bruges
and, after a long wait, wafted over the Channel by another mysterious
character known to them as Peter the Smuggler. One at least was
safe.

Hitherto Moitier had remained invisible, obstinately refusing to
let any of them come near his home in Bruges. Now, however, Boys,
feeling that the Trieste project was but a last desperate throw,
resolved to venture into Bruges and beard Moitier in person. The
others tried to dissuade him; but he had made up his mind, and in he
went, arriving safely at the lawyer's residence. He was successful,
showing real diplomatic qualities. Whether deliberately or not—
probably not, for he was a simple soul—he contrived first to fascinate
Madame Moitier, and only then laid siege to Monsieur. He soon
discovered why the man was holding back. Mean and mercenary himself, he feared that the three Englishmen, once free, would be mean
enough not to honour their promises. Thereupon Boys promptly
offered, if he would dispatch the other two, to remain behind himself

until Moitier was paid. This—and, no doubt, the midshipman's transparent honesty—half-convinced the old rogue, and, finally, he consented to go to Verdun with a letter from Boys to a friend of his named Wills, who would, Boys thought, make out money-bills which would satisfy Moitier. Meanwhile, he consented, though reluctantly, to find a hiding-place in Bruges itself for all three fugitives.

The third phase now began, with the young men comparatively safe in an unoccupied attic at Bruges, and Moitier on his way to Verdun. It was now early April. There was nothing to do until Moitier returned, and time hung heavily on their hands. Then the conscientious Boys bethought him of his old friend Moyses, still shut fast in Givet (see p. 197) while he, Boys, was—well, at least not locked up. He therefore decided to go in person to Givet, and bring Moyses back to the Bruges attic. The story hereabouts assumes an almost fairy-like quality. Off he went, with Neirinks who agreed to accompany him. They travelled comfortably, Neirinks as a wine-merchant, and Boys as Neirinks, with the latter's passport: and, for the sake of vraisemblance, Neirinks' pretty 18-year-old sister Mary joined the party as the pseudo-Neirinks' sister! As a journey, both to Givet and back, it was a great success. They 'did' Ghent at leisure, proceeded to Brussels and 'did' that too. Then they went on to Dinant, just short of Givet. Here, by chance, they met Moitier returning from Verdun. Wills had more than come up to expectations, and Moitier was now ready and anxious to serve the fugitives. But Moitier also carried a letter from Wills to Boys, and in it was, to Boys, the devastating news that Moyses was no longer at Givet, but at Bitche! Quixotry could go no farther. All that was left was for the oddly-assorted party to return to Bruges; which it did without adventure.

Things, however, were now in train at last. Moitier remained true to form to the end. He accomplished what he had promised, but squeezed a maximum of profit from it. They had engaged with Peter the Smuggler to take them across for £40. But Moitier, who alone could do the negotiating, blandly informed them at the last moment that, owing to trouble on a recent trip, Peter's price had risen to £80. They had to pretend to believe him, though they knew full well the destination of that new £40. Then, bidding a really fond farewell to Madame Derikre, and a merely politic one to Moitier, they set out on what was to prove their last march, to Cadsand. Here they were received in a one-roomed hut near the shore by an amazonian lady who proved to be Madame Peter the Smuggler. It was April 29,

1809, and, for some reason which they never knew, they had to endure nine days' more suspense. But

> at length, on 8th May, positive information was brought that all would be in readiness at 10 p.m.: accordingly at that time, the weather fine and the night black, we marched down to the beach, and, as soon as the patrol had passed, the private signal was made and answered. The boat gliding silently inshore with muffled oars, we rushed in with the rapidity of thought, and in an instant were all safe afloat: each seized an oar and, vigorously applying his utmost strength, we soon reached beyond the range of shot. This was the fulfilment of our triumph, for we had at length proved that confiding in the honour of a British officer was a more certain security than *Locks, Bolts and Fortresses*.

And Madame Derikre? Nowadays, as soon as peace returned, she would have been acclaimed for what she surely was—a Heroine of the Resistance, the first and most disinterested of her kind. There would have been subscriptions, pensions, medals; portraits and paragraphs in the press; appearances on T.V.; perhaps even a statue. But not in *our* war.

She was utterly forgotten. It occurred to nobody to do anything about it. To nobody, that is, but one Captain Edward Boys, RN. And even he had not much cause for pride here, because it was not till 1845—thirty-six years since he had last seen her—that he went to look for her again. Yet he did go, and, contrary to the laws of chance and mortality, he found her, after a prolonged search which, though full late, does him credit, since he alone made one.

She was then living in Ostend, in the home of a family called Van Hecke who, it seems, had picked her off the streets, completely destitute and stone-blind. All her disasters had been the direct result of her devotion to the British. In 1811, the French authorities, through their spies, obtained information against her. She was arrested, but not before she had personally secured the repatriation of at least fifteen escaping Englishmen. She was repeatedly interrogated to the verge of torture, to make her give others away. When she refused, she was condemned to death; but still she remained steadfast and revealed nothing. She lay under that sentence for over a year, during which she heard that her son, her Englishmen's faithful little friend, had had ill-luck in the conscription draw, had gone for a soldier and died at Smolensk. She was closely imprisoned until 1814 and, when released, learned that her husband was dead, so deeply in debt that all her own savings were taken from her. Penniless, but as plucky as ever, she came over to England to cash the bills which her English protégés had given her, but which, up till then, she had scorned to profit by: and all were honoured, but, in her ignorance trusting to a rascally agent, she was cheated of them all. She returned with difficulty to Flanders, went blind, was reduced to begging in the streets, and, because she *was* blind and old, was chased off them for a horrid old witch. Indeed, but for the charity of the Van Heckes, nearly as poor as herself, she must have perished of sheer want. Only the faintest echo of her great war record survived. The common people still sometimes referred to her, without really knowing why, as the *Aenglishe Reeker*.

Fortunately Boys was in time. Not only did he set her up in comfort, still with the Van Heckes, whom she did not want to leave, but, by communicating with several other British officers whom she had saved, he endowed her against any future fear of want. She died on June 20, 1849, in her eighty-fourth year, and positively had a notice all to herself in the London *Times*. Who inserted it? History is silent on the point: but the similarity of its style with that of the author from whom we have been quoting is surely no coincidence.

There remains one more midshipman whose journey to Verdun we followed. Robert James did not get away: but he made a gallant attempt. Hearing that he was to be sent to Sarrelibre in the exodus of the midshipmen in October 1807, he determined not to go: and so, on the 8th of that month, in company with a naval assistant-surgeon named William Porteus, he descended the walls of the town on a homemade rope—at least, Porteus did; but the rope broke when James was halfway down. The whole adventure was shot with pieces of luck, some good some bad: but it must be admitted that they were not very prudent fugitives. It was bad luck that his rope broke, but very distinctly good luck that enabled him to get off with a sprained ankle from a fall of at least 25 feet: yet he probably did not appreciate his good fortune at the end of their first night's march—21 miles! They kept a more southerly course than the other eastbound fugitives, passing through St Mihiel and Nancy. On their second night they had to hide from a party of gendarmes by standing for a long time up to their necks in a mill-stream, and were so chilled as a result that they decided to enter a small country auberge. This, as we saw, was imprudent, but their lucky star was in the ascendant. The elderly host scared them badly by saying, 'I know who you are, gentlemen':

but instantly added, 'Be tranquil: you are safe in my house', and told them how he had lost three sons in the wars, while the fourth and last, having been captured by Suvorov in Italy, had been rescued from Russian cruelty by a British officer serving under him. He was therefore determined to help every Englishman he could. Perhaps this rencontre made them careless because, after that, they did not avoid houses, even while in France. For a long time, however, their luck held. They crossed the Vosges, and reached the Rhine opposite Freiburg. A fisherman's hut stood nearby, and they entered it boldly. Even while the wife was telling them that there was not a hope of getting across, her son, a stout lad of 12, entered, and offered to take them across then and there for two crowns. Though his boat was scarcely worth the name—'merely three planks nailed together'—the crossing was made, and they were in Germany.

At Freiburg they put up at one of the best hotels, and went on confidently by post-chaise. They now kept well to the north, because they had the novel design of embarking at Ulm, and dropping down the Danube on the Vienna packet-boat. Evidently they thought themselves reasonably safe, taking few of the precautions which seemed so vital to other escapers. Twice in openly passing through the gates of quite important towns—Neustadt and Ulm itself—they were challenged by the guards, and twice they got away with the story that they were French merchants, without being asked to show their passports. But then their good luck deserted them, to be succeeded by very bad luck indeed. Having cleared the Ulm gatekeepers, they proceeded as usual to a good hotel for déjeuner, and were just inquiring for the Vienna packet when, by sheer misfortune, the chief of the town police took a vacant place at their table and overheard their question. Evidently a friendly soul, he kindly offered to sign their passports then and there, to save them the trouble of going to his office! Thus, quite suddenly, came the end. Back like O'Brien they had to go, in comfort to Strasbourg but thereafter in chains.

This put a term upon James's escapades. In front of him lay two separate spells at Bitche and one at Sarrelibre: and, before he had completed them, he had sought happiness in quite another direction. He had married: and that was a bar to escape of a different kind altogether. Indeed, when the end came, and they had to depart in a hurry from Verdun, his wife was on the point of presenting him with his first child: and that was exceedingly awkward too.

Of the many ingenuities practised by Young Gentlemen, we must be content with only one more, in which its hero may be credited with distinct originality. Henry Stanhope,[1] a descendant of Lord Chesterfield, was confined in the St Vannes convent within the Verdun Citadel. One day, he took advantage of certain repairs which were being made to the chimney-flues. Blacking his face beyond recognition, he strolled out of the gates with the grimy workmen as they left for the night. He got safely out of the town, but was retaken in Luxembourg and brought back with ignominy. This happened in 1812, when the edict was in full force which condemned retaken 'deserters' to the galleys. He was tried, and sentenced to six years. He was also stripped, with every mark of dishonour, as his captors thought, of his naval rank: but, in practice, this gave him his chance to try again. When news of the sentence reached England, the government retaliated promptly with a threat of wholesale reprisals —the name of Stanhope meant much in Britain, and the clan knew all the right people. The French therefore hesitated: but, meanwhile, they removed him to the *Porte Chaussée*, then used for civil prisoners, stripped of his uniform and clad in the sombre grey of a convict. Here he was visited by innumerable friends of his, mostly Young Gentlemen in uniform: and he took the opportunity of walking out with a crowd of them *disguised as a midshipman*. This time he got clear away.

VII. *Merchant Service Officer*. Peter Bussell did not escape. The idea was totally alien to him. Besançon was one of the first depots to be evacuated: so, on November 23, 1813, he started, and walked to Amiens—327 miles—arriving on December 10th. Thence—but in a straggling party and at a much slower pace—he walked to Laval. He was still there when the news came that the Allies were in Paris, and then, with virtually no guards (of which omission he felt positively resentful) he walked via Rennes to St Malo. Feeling rather lost with no one to look after him, he was offered a lift to Jersey by a French ex-privateer, and from there an English schooner took him to Poole. Thence he padded quietly home to Weymouth, where, banal to the last,

I was happy once more to be restored to those most dear to me.

---

[1] He was the cousin of John Spencer Stanhope, who helped him, and who gives a full account of the affair. (Pickering, op. cit., pp. 443–50.)

Seacombe Ellison's story could hardly be in greater contrast. He had been some years at Verdun before the urge to escape came to him. The merchant skippers, even the privileged ones, were the *bêtes noires* of Wirion,[1] probably because of the impossibility of wringing money out of people who had so little: and they were closely watched. In 1807, however, he found himself in a clique of determined escapers. Boys was one, and another was a dear mutual friend of both, one Thomas Walbeoff Cecil. This young man's successful attempt, which lit the spark in Ellison, began but poorly. On taking that first ticklish step, the losing of his liberty by committing an offence, he went just a shade too far and, instead of confinement to the Citadel, found himself condemned to Bitche. He was joined, for the journey, by another midshipman named R. L. Gordon and a captain's clerk named Maxwell, both under the same orders as himself. On the road, like O'Brien, all three bolted for a wood. But they were luckier than he was. They all escaped the only gendarme who pursued them, and together reached the secret dump in a wood near Verdun, established by Cecil for his original attempt. Here they met Boys and Ellison, who brought the necessary implements and supplies: and, thus well-equipped, they all gained their freedom, Cecil by way of Trieste, the others through Prussia.

Ellison now decided to try himself and, just then, made the acquaintance of another escape maniac, whom we have already met —the worthy medical man who ultimately escaped with O'Brien—

> Mr Archibald Barklimore, Surgeon, now very comfortably settled in the metropolis. This gentleman [a civilian in a captured merchant ship] was taken early in the war: he was of a cheerful, jocose disposition, and had a talent for learning the language and imitating the manners of the French. He had all their grimaces, their shrugs, their grins, their every motion: in fact, he was to all outward appearance a genuine Frenchman. He was upon a friendly footing with all the officers of the regiment whose depot was Verdun . . . and had the privilege of the *entrée* into the Citadel whenever he pleased, night or day. He was their surgeon-in-chief: they preferred his advice to that of their own countrymen.[2]

There follows a passage which strains credulity. If true, it opens up fields altogether new and unexplored:

[1] A sample of his wit survives: 'The *détenus* are the sweepings of England and the masters of merchant ships and the midshipmen are the sweepings of the sweepings.' (Pickering, op. cit., p. 80.)

[2] Ellison, op. cit., p. 47.

These officers had fitted him with a complete uniform, sword etc. obtained for him a *feuille de route* (military passport), and one of them actually went down to the sea-coast to prepare his way, but found it next to impossible to engage a boat owing to the extreme watchfulness of the coast guard.

If a genuine French officer could not do it, Barklimore thought, what hope had a bogus one? So, remembering the fate of men taken with a forged passport (see p. 249), he gave up that particular project.

Here was just the man for Ellison, still a complete novice at the game. They joined forces, Ellison bringing in his great friend Peter Kirk,[1] late second-in-command of the East Indiaman *Sir Edward Hamilton*. A purser of the E.I.C. named Robert Alison joined them at the last moment.

They all succeeded in getting locked into the Citadel for the night, but only after quite ludicrous difficulty. They remained outside the gates at closing-time and missed *appel*: but, on their return, the officiating gendarme smilingly refused to take any action—('for once we found the disadvantage of having a good character!'). Baffled here, they proceeded to the office of Demanget, the detested lieutenant of Wirion, and *apologized* for having broken the rules. He swallowed the bait and ordered them to the Citadel, but when they arrived, the gatekeeper refused to admit them without either an order or a gendarme. So back they went to Demanget, to ask humbly for one or the other: and the lieutenant obliged with a gendarme. So far, then, all was well.

They were lodged in the St Vannes convent: but they had to work fast because another amiable gendarme had dropped in to console them with the news that they were to be let out early next morning. Then, seeking desperately for an *illicit* exit, they found the private passage from the convent to the convent church, now used as a store-room. They got into the church, but they were clumsy—crashed through a door, a panel of which split with the noise of a pistol-shot, and upset a table piled with all sorts of heavy and noisy articles. Dogs barked: the guard turned out and made a thorough search of everywhere—except the church. When things grew quieter, they contrived to climb on to an altar whence they reached an unbarred window, and fell through it into the convent garden: went over two low walls, crossed the Citadel courtyard, and, under the very windows of Wirion's house, were challenged by a sentry. He, however, was

[1] This was probably his name though Ellison, as usual, calls him 'K - - -'.

such a 'green conscript' that he was too frightened to raise the alarm. Thence they blundered across the general's garden—indeed, the impression left by Ellison is that almost the only place they did not blunder through was the general's bedroom. Next Kirk, seeing another 3-foot wall, leapt lightly over it, only to find, too late, that on the other side it was a 20-foot wall. Almost miraculously he was unhurt: and more near-miracles were to follow:

> He called as loud as he dare: told us to ease ourselves down, and [he] would endeavour to break our fall: we did so, but the nails in my shoe heels came in contact with his nose: fortunately they did no other injury but making it bleed (which caused the report of one of us being seriously hurt).

Another low wall presenting itself, Ellison, thinking it was only a breastwork, vaulted on to it and was in the act of jumping down the other side when Kirk very quietly pointed out to him that it was the main Citadel wall, and held him back. They were now quite lost. They had a rope, designed for a section of the wall which they had estimated at 35 feet. But with all their twists and turns they had come, unwittingly, to a place where it was 65 feet. This they only discovered the hard way when they let themselves down it. They fell the last 20 feet or so. But miracles that night were as common as blackberries, and they all arrived at the bottom, not indeed unscathed, but still distinctly alive. Ellison landed squarely on his back: Kirk hurt both ankles: but Barklimore cheerfully patched them up and off they went to their *cache*—the same which Cecil had used. Once there, though bravely minimizing their ills to the last, Ellison has to admit, just for the once, that he fainted.

He soon recovered, however, and thereafter the adventure went very like other unsuccessful ones already described. They made progress, but rather slowly: they were too stiff and sore. They met friendly peasants, others less friendly and (on the eleventh day, at a little town called Charmes) their fate, in the person of a gendarme who demanded their passports. Barklimore rose to the occasion, presenting the man with some old testimonials which he happened to have in his pocket, chaffed him mercilessly, and had just convinced him that they really were passports when his senior, the local *brigadier de police*, arrived: and he was not quite such a simpleton as his man.

Back once more at Verdun, they were thrown into the *Tour d'Angoulême*, a small round building on two floors with walls 6 feet thick. There they were grilled for nearly a month, the authorities trying all they knew to make them admit that Barklimore was *Chef de complot*—pardonably, no doubt, they were particularly incensed with him. But no one gave anything away, and all four were ordered to Bitche. On the way they met Ashworth, Tuthill and Brine (see pp. 219, 223), trudging to Metz for their trial, but

> marching jovially along, hallooing and singing with as much apparent joy as if they were on their way homeward. 'Where are you going?' we asked. 'To Metz.' 'What for?' 'To be tried for setting the *souterrain* on fire and attempting to blow up the magazine.'

What a tonic for depressed *mauvais sujets*, Bitche-ward bound—if indeed they needed one. But there is no hint from Ellison that they did. In commenting upon their journey, he has no pity to spare for himself, his comrades, or, for that matter, for any Briton: only for the poor Austrians and Prussians. True, he says, our poor fellows, if they have no money, have to make do on three sous a day and black bread: but at least they keep the clothes on their backs, which is more than the continentals do. They are often stripped stark naked and, if they fall by the way, are just shot as they lie.

Ellison's second attempt was from Bitche, his lively account of which depot need not be retold here, since it adds little that is material to the accounts already given. But he does give honourable mention to a new commandant, successor to the ineffable Maisonneuve. His name was Clement and, together with a forceful British lieutenant named Stewart, sent there on suspicion of espionage, he cleaned up many of the worst abuses. Nor need we linger over that second escape itself, because it has already been described. It was that one in which Ashworth, Tuthill and Brine got away. There are, however, several discrepancies between the two accounts. In Ellison's, for instance, the recapture of the majority takes place before the Rhine is crossed; in fact, actually on its left bank—and Ellison should know, because he was one of the caught. Then he adds an interesting fourth name to the three successful ones—William Porteus, the naval surgeon who failed with James: and here too his corroborative detail is such that he is probably right. Ashworth, throughout, fails to mention Ellison; and, until the very end, Ellison does not mention Ashworth. Indeed, we might well fail to recognize that both were describing the same adventure, had not Ellison, almost as an afterthought, stated the names of those who got through safely. Most of the discrepancies vanish, however, if we assume that the party split into two soon after getting down the wall, and that Ashworth went with one half and Ellison with the other. Neither of them says so, but common prudence would surely dictate some such move. A bunch of a dozen, one would imagine, would be altogether too conspicuous on the road.

Ellison's third—and, as it proved last—attempt was made soon after he had completed his penance and emerged again into the upper air. Once more its course will not be followed in detail, but only its salient features recorded. Here Midshipman Moyses turns up again (see p. 234) not as a principal but as a willing helper who procured them money for the venture. The party was six strong, and they agreed to keep together till they were clear away, but thereafter to separate into couples. One pair was Ellison and Kirk: Midshipman Dacre, of his (and Ashworth's) previous attempt, and a man called W - - - made the second. The names of the third he does not give, probably deliberately, as they did not behave very well.

All were lodged in the prison-building on the *Grosse Tête*, the extreme western (in the illustration the leftmost) defence of the fortress. They discovered that, one floor above them, there was a room used by the prison washerwomen, not by prisoners; and its window was unbarred. This window projected beyond their own barred one, so that it actually overhung the first great drop of the north-west rampart. They contrived to reach it, and from it to make the first dizzy descent. Then they safely negotiated the second rampart. But, it seems, they did not know of the existence of the third one: which, however, was fortunately the lowest. They could, therefore, muster only 9 feet of rope for it, but they augmented it on the spot by precariously tying three handkerchiefs to it, and trusting to providence. Five of them got down, shaken but still mobile. The sixth, however, who was W - - -, fell awkwardly, broke his leg, and had to be abandoned. While Ellison, Kirk and Dacre were tending him, the other pair slunk off without a word, and, thought Ellison, a good deal too hurriedly for honour. Dacre, thus left partnerless, joined up with the merchant officers.

They all got through, by the Rhine–Salzburg–Trieste route, Kirk only just. The main interest in their journey lies in the technique they employed. Up to now, as we have seen, most escapers tried to avoid human habitations and, once over the Rhine, to pose as citizens of the master-race, the French. But this, as O'Brien had found, had its disadvantages—the German inhabitants' hatred of the French and their universal policy of rooking them. Ellison and his friends changed all this, deciding to make capital out of the peasants' francophobia. They therefore did not hesitate to enter the peasants' houses, where they boldly declared themselves to be what they were—escaped British prisoners, every bit as good French-haters as their hosts. Even before reaching the Rhine they found it worked, while, after that, it paid very well indeed. Thereafter, as France became less and less popular, the policy paid better and better, until it became the standard one for all later escapers. Ellison extends his story to cover their adventures after entering Austria, and shows that, even there, there were serious hazards to face. But in their case many of these were due to the fact that they found themselves in the odd position of trying to keep ahead of a huge French army, invading Austria to fight at Aspern and Wagram.

Seacombe Ellison was a bold, cool fellow: a merchant officer fit to stand beside the best of his naval brethren.

VIII. *Civilian.* John Stanhope had the odd distinction of first being released and then having to escape. Using his influence with the French *Institut* and other scientific friends, he obtained leave, after a year and a half at Verdun, to go to Paris, where he was when tidings of the catastrophic 1812 campaign reached the city; and he has much of interest to relate of how the news was received.[1] In 1813, through the still active help of the *Institut*, he secured a passport giving him complete liberty, and leave to proceed to Greece. Before he could start, however, he was suddenly summoned to the Ministry of Police and given a passport for Valenciennes only; a very different matter which (that town being an official prisoner depot) meant continued imprisonment. This apparent volte-face, it transpired, was due to a feud between General Clarke, Minister of War, and the Duc de Rovigo, Minister of Police. Clarke was liberal in his attitude towards the British: Rovigo was the reverse, mainly because he loved thwarting Clarke. This enmity could be serious to Britons, as it was with Wolfe and his Givet prisoners (p. 167), and in another case not yet recorded. An army captain named Hunter Blair had distinguished himself at Verdun by rescuing the family of the mayor from a fire. That dignitary,

---

[1] Cf. placard pasted on the wall of the Tuileries:
    Ce Palais est à vendre,
    La couronne à rendre,
    Et le tyran à pendre.   (Pickering, op. cit., p. 488.)

in his gratitude, petitioned the Emperor for Blair's release, and succeeded, thanks to General Clarke's intervention. But the vital document, the passport, was the concern of Rovigo, and he procrastinated so successfully over its issue that Blair was never released.[1]

Stanhope, for all his horror of breaking parole, could hardly be expected to stand for this, seeing that he had in his pocket a document (which they had forgotten to take from him) providing for his unconditional release and signed by Napoleon himself. Pretending, therefore, to be reconciled to Valenciennes, he set out by carriage on the road to that town: but, once clear of Paris, he swerved sharply right for the Rhine, and, using his Greek passport, had not much difficulty in openly crossing a bridge over the river, and so reaching Trieste.

His journals reveal an attractive young man, gay and venturesome to the verge of rashness; very conscious of what was expected of an English gentleman, yet not readily imposed upon.

Another civilian, a *détenu* of the original vintage, was Joshua Done.[2] In 1802, as a lad of 16, he went to Paris to study music, and in 1803 he failed to clear out in time. Of all the Britons whose adventures are recounted in these pages, he would seem to hold two records; for the complexity of the moves he made, and for the number of his attempted escapes. His bare itinerary may be thus summarized:

Paris – Verdun – Bitche – Verdun (escaped) – Paris – Rennes – Laval – Dol – St Malo (caught) – Verdun (two attempts) – Lyons (escaped) – Valence (caught) – Grenoble – Briançon (escaped) – the Mont Cenis – Turin – Novi (caught) – Chambéry – Lyons – Besançon – Nancy – Metz – Sarrelibre – Forbach – Sarreguemines – Bitche – Sedan (escaped) – Verdun – Paris – Dieppe – Havre (caught) – Sedan – Verdun – St Mihiel (escaped) – Verdun – Strasbourg – Baden – Stuttgart (caught) – Asperg (escaped) – Ulm – Ratisbon – Prague – Leipzig – Hanover – Cuxhaven – Heligoland – Harwich (December 29, 1813).

Eight times he tried: seven times he failed. He was a youth of great independence and ingenuity, but very far from prudent. Yet his very imprudences—one might almost say impudences—are

[1] Pickering, op. cit., p. 457.
[2] His story is recorded in two articles called 'The Prisoner of War' in *Colburn's New Monthly Magazine*, Vol. 61, part 1, 1841, pp. 69–84 and 200–9.

endearing. His troubles began when, still living in Paris, he asserted loudly in public that the only Frenchmen who would ever reach England would be French prisoners of war. Deported to Verdun, he twice 'forgot' roll-call and was sent to Bitche. Here the very real discomfort—he gives a harrowing account of it—first turned his thoughts to escape. Because of his knowledge of French he was made interpreter to the commandant (Clement). But he scorned that officer's efforts to corrupt him with privileges and (when he had done his time) was returned to Verdun, where, quite incorrigible, he delighted in shouting patriotic songs in the cafés. The climax came when, allowed to play the cathedral organ, he gave a fortississimo rendering of *God save the King* upon it, and, anticipating a speedy return to Bitche, slid over the town-wall. He walked 480 miles in eleven days to St Malo, but was there caught and sent back whence he came. Threatened now with the galleys, he out-shouted Courçelles, quoting Voltaire to the effect that 'Frenchmen were either tigers or monkeys' and said exactly what he thought of Napoleon himself.

They locked him up, and sentenced him to Briançon, as being an even worse place than Bitche—at Briançon there was a horrid hole called 'the Bitche Building', reserved exclusively for Bitche rejects. Before setting out, he twice tried to escape but, failing, made a dash for it while *en route*. He now had a good run for his money, but they caught him once more. So he came to Briançon: but they could not keep him. He braved the fearful climate, got across the Mont Cenis pass and a long way down the Po valley before being rounded up at Novi. (Part of this journey, by the way, he made with William Hare, who was to try again, equally unsuccessfully, with Alexander Stewart (see p. 159).

Back he was hauled, not to Briançon, but to the much more distant Bitche. This gave him a longer journey in which to escape again, and he secured this concession by the ingenious expedient of pretending to be Lieutenant George Jackson whose recent daring escape from Bitche had made the commandant of that fortress wildly eager to have him recaptured and humiliated. At Chambéry, however, Done was stricken with putrid fever, and had to give up all such ideas for the moment. At length he arrived at Bitche, huddled half-dead in a cart, to find the entire garrison and all the prisoners paraded to witness the commandant's triumph: and that officer's chagrin was beyond words when he understood the deception. Done, however, was equal to the crisis. He explained that he had impersonated

Jackson simply in order to be sent, not to a barbarous place like Briançon, but to a comfortable, humanely run establishment like Bitche. And the commandant purred with pleasure!

In due course Done was passed to Sedan again, whence he very soon departed openly, disguised as the commandant's secretary (whom, as he approached the gates, he had the dubious pleasure of seeing at a window). This time he reached Havre, and even secured a passage with an American captain, only to be caught as he was about to step on board. So back again to Sedan and a dungeon: but not for long. Evidently they thought that only the Bitche Building at Briançon could hold so slippery a prisoner. Perhaps that was so, but it remained unproven because he made yet another dash for freedom on the road. This time he went east, crossed the Rhine, traversed Baden, and got to Stuttgart in Württemberg before being rounded up.

But now Napoleon's sun was setting. After Leipzig Württemberg deserted the Emperor, and Done was allowed to escape from the castle where he lay, and to make his way to the German coast and liberty. It had taken him more than eleven years: but surely he deserved it if any prisoner ever did. Had all *détenus* been Joshua Dones, few if any would have remained for repatriation in 1814.

IX. *Seaman (Old Shellback)*. James Choyce escaped. He had been in gaol longer than usual, and he was tiring of it. His idea was simple. He would join the French Navy. This at least, he supposed, would get him to the coast, and to the sea. And if, when there, he could not become once more the master of his fate, his name was not James Choyce. But it was not quite so simple as it sounded. Though fifty Britons from Sarrelibre volunteered, forty-nine of them were told that they might enlist in the Irish Brigade, but not in the Navy. Choyce was the fiftieth: they took him because he said he was a Spaniard and they believed him. Even so, they showed no sort of enthusiasm over their volunteer. They said they would send him to Lorient, and (to make certain that he got there) would chain him up with a covey of conscript deserters. He was much pained at such untrusting behaviour, but he had to go, and in due course reached Lorient, where he was drafted into an ordinary French 74. On board he found 'upwards of fifty Danes, Swedes, Prussians and Americans, with one Englishman who passed as an American'. He protests that, throughout, he had no intention of serving his country's foes: but, knowing Choyce's past, we may doubt whether this was altogether true. Yet he must have the benefit of the doubt because, in fact, he never did serve them: indeed, he deserted at the first possible moment, showing considerable enterprise and taking no mean risk of drowning.

After several attempts to steal boats, and even to build them, he and his sole English fellow-seaman, Watts, discovered where some local crab-fishermen had hidden their 'mud-boats'. Each was 6 feet long and 2 wide, with a freeboard of 10 inches, the whole nailed together and very far from watertight. Choyce had little to learn about boats, and knew, of course, that these could never carry him across the Channel. But he reckoned that they would not have to carry him nearly so far, because several British ships were always hovering close inshore. So he and Watts stole two of the boats and—his own euphemism— 'borrowed a couple of oars'. They cut off the blades to use as paddles, and lashed the looms across the two mud-boats, to keep them together, though not touching, thereby securing for the pair of them a buoyancy much greater than twice that of either. In fact he made a crude 'catamaran'.

It worked. They reached the *Theseus*, 74, quickly and safely. They were, of course, instantly enrolled into the ship's company, but this presented no problem to our shellback: it had happened too often before. A few weeks later they incautiously allowed him some hours' shore-leave at Cawsand opposite Plymouth, and H.M.S. *Theseus* saw Choyce no more. Nor did His Majesty's Navy.

X. *Seaman (young)*. John Wetherell did not escape. He had dug himself in too comfortably at Givet. When it had to move, his contingent wandered over a larger area of France than any of the others. But Wetherell was snug enough because he was a member of the prisoners' band which, he says, was so admirable that, wherever they went, commanding officers, British or French alike, were tumbling over one another for the privilege of being played to. In fact Wetherell's last perambulation of France was a veritable triumphal progress—if we can persuade ourselves to believe him. He did not quit the country till May 19, 1814, having, on his last day, marched sixty-seven miles to the coast. To the end one may take him or leave him.

We do not know as much as we should like about seamen's escapes. There must have been plenty of them, and plenty of failures too, some tragic. Thus two seamen named Butterfield and Henson got down the Verdun walls when lodged there for a night or two. For some reason unknown, they travelled due south; and they all but reached Marseilles before being retaken. They must have had courage and pertinacity, and perhaps some luck. Two others had a worse adventure. One—Henry Hudson—broke prison and covered many hundreds of miles before being caught. This was because he had a passport, which was discovered, unfortunately, to have been forged by a fellow-prisoner named John Gardner. The moral indignation of the authorities was great. Not without logic, they argued that forgery is a legal crime the world over. So they tried the men, not for escaping but for forging, and sentenced both to six years in the galleys: and, this time, there was no reprieve. Even more tragic, it may be re-called, was the attempt of Marshall and Cox from Bitche. (See pp. 147-8.)

Two other young seamen left a much fuller record of their experiences. They were John Tregerthen Short and Thomas Williams, apprentices of the same merchantman and cousins, in 1804 aged respectively 19 and 17.[1] Both began their captivity at Givet, and both supplement our knowledge of that depot. Of Short, whose disposition was unadventurous, little more need be recorded. But his young cousin had the itch for freedom and was for ever trying to attain it. His tale brings out the tremendous difficulties which must have attended the efforts of almost any seaman. Williams had, it need hardly be said, enormous reserves of pluck and endurance and, more than once, sheer perseverance nearly brought him through. On one occasion he reached Boulogne, on another Bruges. But the dice were loaded against people like him. He had little money, no maps or compass, no knowledge of any language but his own: nor could he hope to pass for anything but what he was, a simple Cornish lad. First and last, he had a dozen companions in his five attempts, all as ill-equipped as himself; and his adventures would make sad reading—for all failed—had he been less of a stoic who took everything as it came in the same unruffled spirit; not cow-like as Bussell was; more like a good and faithful hound, separated by force from his mistress and doggedly determined to find her again. Each gallant attempt came to much the same inevitable end. Sooner or later his party attracted the eye of a gendarme, a soldier or a customs officer, whose curiosities they had no hope of satisfying, and back they went into bondage; once even condemned (though not actually sent) to the galleys.

[1] They tell their stories separately in *Prisoners of War in France, 1804 to 1814*, London, 1914.

Oddly enough, though Short remained all through at Givet while Williams travelled far and wide—even to Briançon, of which his account strongly resembles Stewart's—the cousins came together again during that last chaotic experience of the break-up: and both have much to tell of this remarkable period. Though they left Givet and Briançon respectively around the New Year of 1814, it was not until May that, travelling in utterly erratic circles, they finally came under Wellington's wing at Bordeaux. The younger cousin's singleness of purpose and bearing in adversity cannot fail to command the profoundest admiration, while his adventures—and failures—may be taken as typical of those of his whole class.

XI. *Ship's Boy*. Alexander Stewart did not escape, though he tried, twice. His second pathetic attempt, from Briançon, has been chronicled (p. 159). By then he was a man, though a young one; but when first he tried he was still a boy, and had not been long at Sarrelibre. He had three companions named Graham, Murray and Squires, all youths like himself. To most prisoners autumn was the best season for an attempt, and night the best time. But it occurred to Stewart that, for a change, other seasons and times might profitably be exploited. What in fact he sought, though he does not use the term, was the advantage of tactical surprise. He was an observant lad, and had noticed that the unflagging watch upon their movements was relaxed in winter, and also in daylight, because, of course, their gaolers did not think they would be so hardy as to choose such times. Of this laxity, therefore, Stewart proposed to avail himself.

A good deal of snow usually fell at Sarrelibre in February, and he proposed to wait for a heavy fall and depart in the middle of it. This gave him and his friends plenty of time to make their preparations, of which, as ever, the principal one was rope-making. It was as well that they were not hurried because their chosen technique was a very slow one. It consisted of collecting, by every possible means, every piece of string, however small, that they could lay hands on: and, for weeks on end, they spent their nights plaiting and knotting the bits when no one was looking. Their patience was rewarded. At last they had 60 feet of it, and Stewart, who had a very large hat, undertook the dangerous duty of hiding the rope in it: 'I was in constant tremour lest anyone should knock my hat off.'

The sentries at Sarrelibre, as Stewart anticipated, were not exempt from the ordinary man's dislike of standing about, or gently perambulating, in a snowstorm; and those detailed to guard the perimeter wall—one to every 30 yards, he says—having boxes provided for them under the parapet, found them peculiarly cosy just then. So, when a really heavy fall smothered the depot, the guards obliged by entering their boxes and the boys slipped over the wall, hitched their rope on to a spike which supported a paling on the parapet, took their courage in both hands, and slid down. It was day, but the snowflakes made it as opaque as night. The rope did its part nobly: but the boys were not so clever, especially Stewart, who went first. Thinking to let himself down the more gently, he took a turn of the rope round his right hand: but he soon lost control of his speed, and landed heavily at the bottom. The soft, deep snow broke his fall, but

> I looked at my hand, and stood aghast. The cut was the size of
> the rope all round my hand—the bones were visible all round
> . . . while the flesh from the bone to the surface was as white as
> boiled fish. There was not the least appearance of blood.

All got down, all with their hands cut, though not so badly as Stewart's. But it was a poor start. His wound caused him agony then, and remained unhealed for many months. Yet they had achieved their surprise: no one saw them go, and they now had, or hoped they had, a half-day in addition to a whole night in which to leave Sarrelibre as far behind as possible. Next morning, however, they learned in the most unpleasant way that they were mistaken. Crowds of peasants, armed with sticks and pikes, were after them, greed lending them wings. The boys took to their heels, the hunt hallooing behind. But the fugitives were young and, all things considered, fit. They rapidly gained ground—until they suddenly came up against a large river, flowing on three sides of them. They were in a small loop of the Moselle, and the one way out was now blocked by the exulting peasants. They reached the bank. There was a layer of snow-covered ice on the river. What now?

> Death was certain if we fell in, capture as certain if we remained,
> even for a few minutes. We deliberated for a moment. . . . At
> last one said, 'Shall we risk it?' 'Yes, yes', replied all in an instant
> and at once launched on the most fearful experiment I ever tried.

Their desperate courage was rewarded. They were light—half-starved probably—and they ran all the way across, not daring to stand still, with the ice crackling and protesting at every step. But they reached the far bank safely; and, what was more, the heavier peasants very wisely refrained from following. Thereupon—'we took off our hats and gave them three cheers'. The little bravado was pardonable.

They were now in Luxembourg, which, however, was French-controlled and dangerous. They came to an isolated farm and knocked, to be very well received by the farmer and his family, who fortunately hated the French. The wife and two daughters, when they saw the lads' hands, were horrified. ('When the wound was exposed, they all wept, and the old lady kissed me.') But the farmer, though he kept them for the night, put them to bed and, next morning, gave them stocks of food and a large bladder of brandy, dared not keep them longer—he dwelt much too close to Sarrelibre. He sent them on their way with a boy and a large dog to guide them. The scene at parting moved young Alexander profoundly.

> The old man, his wife and each of his daughters kissed me, and, not without tears, said farewell. I cannot describe how I felt towards them for I had long been a stranger to such manifestations of affection. . . . Such were Peter Burgenjohn and his family. . . . May God bless everyone in whose veins a drop of their blood may ever run!

They followed the Moselle downstream for six nights, yet made very little progress, because of the deep snow and the river's windings. Stewart's right hand was not only useless: it caused him almost unbearable agony.

The end came suddenly. Just before sunrise, they saw a thicket which looked ideal for a hide-out. But it was a little too far away. Light came and with it a posse of mounted gendarmes. They were fairly caught, but they did not lose their heads. Asked whence they had escaped, they said, 'Verdun', craving the help of the British officers there. They were brutally used. Alexander's right hand was slung up to his neck, useless: his left was chained. The first stage was twenty-five miles. Their shoes gave out and they were allowed no new ones. The frost broke, the snow melted, the roads were of sharp unmade flints, and they were bare foot. The next stage was thirty miles, still with naked feet, still closely chained. Murray fell and could not rise. They beat him as he lay with the flats of their swords. Graham and Squires dragged him along for a while until their strength gave out.

> I then said to the gendarmes, 'If you will unchain my hand, I will try and carry him on my back'. They agreed, but I soon found I could not carry him very far without resting. By doing that often, however, I managed my task. . . . The scene is often before my

mind . . . [I] with bleeding feet, a slung hand, and at the close of a day's march of 30 miles, carrying the oldest of my companions on my back to the welcome repose of a common jail, there to find rest on hard boards and little straw.

In four such marches they reached Verdun. The British did what they could. They gave them new shoes, and an English doctor dressed Stewart's hand, which was festering and stinking. More was beyond their power. They were deserters, and Bitche was their destination. They went via Metz, where Alexander was allowed into hospital. He was kindly used, but his hand showed signs of mortification and the doctors decided to amputate it. He wept, imploring them not to do that, and once more met a friend.

'Tachons, il est bien jeune' [said the senior surgeon]. This was a happy word for me. I could have kissed the old doctor as Burgenjohn did me.

The kind surgeon was right. Youth came to Stewart's rescue, and he lost neither his hand nor the use of it. Soon he went on to Bitche, just one more stage in his long imprisonment. We have seen him to Arras. We may now see him home. From Arras he passed through Amiens, Rouen, Chartres, Blois, Tours and Saumur to Angers; but these journeys were picnics compared with the earlier ones. Next he went to Rennes, and from there decided to make for England. The war was not officially over, but there was no one to stop him, and, reaching St Malo, he crossed to Portsmouth.

At the end of his book is a map of his wanderings. His route shows no bends or detours, so that no accurate computation of mileage is possible. Even, however, if these be ignored, the distance must still have been well over 3,000 miles. He had trudged every step of the way, save for the odd mile here and there when, more dead than alive, he had been flung contemptuously on to the floorboards of a cart because his legs would carry him no farther. For good measure, as he tells us himself, he walked over 1,500 miles of the way in chains. When he started that marathon he was 14, when he finished it, 24, having grown up betweenwhiles on little but prison bread and water. Yet he survived to lead a long and useful life. He became a well-known and greatly-loved Nonconformist minister, and died in 1874, aged 84.

Vixere fortes ante Agamemnona.

POSTSCRIPT

Ship's Child. A not uncommon custom, for all that it was banned in wartime, was for warrant officers to take their children to sea with them. One such was the son of Carpenter Cox, of the *Minerve* and the Bitche tragedy; a very little lad, not old enough, even, to be rated 'Boy'. The father must have been passionately set upon his liberty because he had already tried to escape from another depot, taking his son with him. He reached the Rhine and, finding no other way, actually tried to swim the great river with the child on his back. He gained an island in mid-stream, but was then caught and sent to Bitche.[1] There Cox himself paid for his passion with his life: but Cox junior must have had the fever too. Sent to Verdun after his father's death, he instantly made his own attempt, as touching as it was foolhardy. He

> was one of four venturesome little boys who descended one of the angles of the Citadel at Verdun, *without a rope*: they were taken about five leagues distant, brought back, and whipped for their temerity.[2]

That is all history has to tell; but one would like to think that the Frenchman who dealt out punishment had the imagination to spare the rod. There was little fear of spoiling such a child.

[1] At that time, according to Done, the child was 5 years old.
[2] Ellison, op. cit., p. 78.

254

APPENDIX I
DISPARITY OF NAVAL AND MILITARY SOURCES

(See p. 49)

With so few soldiers and so many sailors in captivity, the mathematical odds are, in any case, on there being fewer soldier-prisoners to bequeath their experiences to posterity. And so there are; but so many fewer as to be out of proportion even with the prisoner ratio of one to three. This is partly, no doubt, quite fortuitous. There are soldier-chroniclers like Rifleman Harris and Private Wheeler: but it so happens that they were not made prisoners, and therefore have no contribution to make here. On the other hand, seamen like Choyce and Wetherell, who also left records, happened to be captured.

But it is not all a matter of chance. Adding to the 'sea' score is a class of writer which has no 'land' counterpart at all; which, though not actually 'Navy', is much more naval than military: that is, merchant-service people. Ellison, Bussell, Short, Williams and Stewart are invaluable witnesses, unbalanced by anyone on the Army side. Nor was there anybody in the Army camp like the naval midshipmen or their fellows of the gunroom. The text will show, or will have shown, why this is so, and, again and again, how important their literary output is to this study. There is no military O'Brien, Boys, Ashworth or James.

So much for service-men: but the same bias emerges when civilians are writing. They have much more to say of the naval p.o.w.s than of the Army ones; and substantially for the same reason. There were so few soldiers about that almost all the service captives they met, especially in the first half of the war, were naval men. Thus *détenus* like Lawrence, Stanhope, Done and Wolfe are, all of them, unconsciously, weighting the naval side of the scales, as is that unique *détenu* naval officer Dillon: rightly so too; they are only reflecting the true historical emphasis. For the first half, a history of British Army captives would be a thin affair indeed. For the second half, a book of Army reminiscences corresponding, say, to Commander Hoffman's or Lieutenant Jackson's, would certainly be very welcome: but fortunately, just here, we do have some assistance from Major-General Blayney.

COMMANDER WRIGHT'S LETTER TO HIS FIRST LIEUTENANT, JAMES WALLIS

(See p. 74)

(Extract from the original published in the *Naval Chronicle*, Vol. 34, p. 443)

Tower of the Temple,
4th Sept. 1805. Paris.

My dear Wallis,

In order to obtrude but little on the Translator in Office, and favor an early delivery of my letter, I send you this time merely a short one. . . .

I rejoice to hear that you are under the jurisdiction of a liberall minded Military Man,[1] for I was under some anxiety as to the regime you might be subject to. I think I had already prepared you to expect Benevolence from individuals where they might be at liberty to exercise that divine principle. Give it the fullest credit, make much of it as one faint means of giving it further extension, and make use of the instances under your own eye to obliterate from the young minds of my poor boys unfavourable impressions to which they may already have yielded. I rejoice also to hear at length that you are near these dear boys in whose progress my whole solicitude at present centres. . . . If Mr. Trewin's son be with you let him partake of all the advantages I propose securing to my own three Boys[2]. . . .

I have a little amiable cat that has just taken the caprice of laying along my paper, and purrs to me as near as I can guess, 'Mercy on the Trans-

[1] i.e. General Wirion, commandant at Verdun. This flattering reference was doubtless due to the fact that Wirion would probably read the letter before it was delivered!

[2] Not his own sons, but his protégés, taken on board to be introduced to a naval career. All the better commanding officers took this trust very seriously. From the way he refers to them they were obviously mere children (see p. 33). These 'admirals in embryo' did not fulfil his hopes: none reached flag rank. But this was hardly their fault. Captivity was an almost fatal handicap to promotion and, anyway, this was a bad time to be starting up the promotion ladder. They did their best: all three, for instance, escaped, honourably too. Their names were John Rogerson Wright, Wesley's nephew; George Sidney Smith, nephew of Wright's patron Sir William; and William L. Mansell (1). Young Wright and Smith escaped, together, from Verdun, 24.8.1810: Mansell escaped with Boys (see text, pp. 224–33). Wright reached the rank of commander, 27.8.1814; Smith of captain, 22.8.1822: Mansell died soon after escaping, without being promoted lieutenant. 'Mr. Trewin's son'—John—was also a protégé, though on a slightly less intimate footing: tried to escape (probably with Wright and Smith), but caught, sent to Bitche, and still there at the end of 1811 (see p. 143). Probably a prisoner till the end and never, I think, promoted.

lator'. So that all I can say is that I have taken the Liberty of making you a kind of Foster Father to my little Admirals in Embryo. . . . You perceive that I am not without amiable society, and I must tell you for the comfort of any other little amiable creatures who may weep for my misfortunes that I can bear them however great or multiplied, but that I am less ill off than people at a distance whose apprehensions magnify evil are aware of, for I have within a few months the faculty of procuring Books and of subscribing to the Moniteur whose fables and Prejudices I assure you I am not in the least danger of adopting. . . . Now fare you well and believe me most faithfully and unfeignedly yours,

J. WRIGHT.

APPENDIX III
THE *MONITEUR UNIVERSEL*

(See p. 201)

September 12, 1812

A STUDY IN NAPOLEONIC PROPAGANDA

On August 17, 1812, the British Transport Office wrote formally to the French Ministry of Marine stating that, since the war began, no less than 860 French prisoners of war in Britain, all of officer rank and on parole, had broken that parole. Of these, 270 had been retaken, but 590 had got clear away. Whether this was a true statement of the facts is not my concern here. (Personally, I think it was, in so far as the total figure of 860 is concerned. From many other sources we know that breaches of parole among French officers were very common indeed. But I doubt whether quite so many as 590 had been successful.) What concerns me here is the French answer to the charge.

On Thursday, September 12, 1812, the *Moniteur Universel* printed a letter from Decrès, Minister of Marine, addressed to the Emperor himself; and accompanying it was a full page of names—355[1] of them: all successful British escapers, those retaken being expressly excluded from the list. The Minister's task, of course, was not only to refute the British charges, but also to deliver a riposte, as swift and damaging as possible. He therefore took two lines:—

(1) That the Transport Office was exaggerating grossly. Not 590, but only 363 prisoners had re-entered France, and these were 'of all ranks'. He did not deny that some of them were officers, though the implication is that very few of them were, and those only *des grades les plus inférieurs*. He had to concede so much because, we must remember, his propaganda was primarily for home consumption; and, had he declared that *no* French officer had escaped, his lie would inevitably have been exposed, because there must have been many thousands of Frenchmen who knew, and had seen in the flesh, escaped officer-prisoners. Nor could he very well afford to be so exposed, because the *Moniteur*, in common with all the French *bulletins* of the period, already had a very sinister reputation, even in France. People had not forgotten, for instance, that notorious day when the French *victory* of Trafalgar had been served up for their consumption. Indeed, so mistrusted were both the *bulletins* and *Le Moniteur* which carried them that, even among Frenchmen, a common and conclusive retort to anyone thought to be lying was—'*Tu mens comme un bulletin!*'[2] The impression, then, that Decrès sought to get across was of 363 French escapers, mostly 'other

---

[1] The number given in Decrès' letter. In the list there are 357: but as two names are entered twice, the more correct figure is Decrès'.

[2] Dillon, op. cit., III, 421.

ranks' not granted parole, but containing a sprinkling of misguided low-grade parole men.

(2) That it ill became the Transport Office to talk, seeing what its own people had done in this line. For 355 Britons, all parole men high up in the British social world, and by implication *officiers*, had shamelessly broken their most sacred pledges: Britons, indeed, so highly placed—such *Anglais de marque* is the phrase he used—that their conduct had actually set the example to those few poor French officers (of low grade, *bien entendu*) who had imitated them.[1] Then, for the sake of verisimilitude, he mentioned two of the depraved wretches by name—Thomas Brooks, M P, and Sir James Crawford, diplomat. It is just here that a splendid opportunity presents itself to examine the technique and mechanism of Napoleonic internal propaganda because, to clinch matters, Decrès then produced a full list, pillorying every perjured offender by name: and the implication, in every word, is that all 355 of them are *anglais de marque* and *officiers*.

The technique is, no doubt, stale by now. But it was a good deal fresher then, and it may well have achieved its purpose—with those to whom it was addressed, the French people. They did not, probably, possess the knowledge necessary to see through it, and they would not much want to anyway. It would, however, hardly deceive the British people. They could analyse the list, if they cared to do so. So can we, and the result is at once instructive and not unamusing. Here is a preliminary break-up of these full-ranking, high-standing *anglais de marque*, whose example had disgraced the perfidious British and corrupted the innocent French. Decrès helps us by inserting against almost all the names the calling or status of their owners: and the figures here have followed that information exactly, ignoring for the moment many inconsistencies and subterfuges which must engage our attention later. This, then, is the French—not the British—break-up of their list:—

Service people	.	.	.	.	.	96
Purely civilian	.	.	.	.	.	79
Merchant Officers .	.	.	.	.	180

$$355$$

Surely it is a strange shape which begins to emerge? Consider first the third group. What is the merchant officer's claim to appear, in a *French* list, as an *anglais de marque*? As an Officer and Gentleman? Even as a Gentleman? Scanty indeed! In French eyes, as we have seen many times, he was, in these very regards, so suspect as barely to merit parole status at all. He was 'the sweeping of the sweepings'. Surely the French, of all people, could not have the nerve to label him *anglais de marque*? But Decrès has done just that. And these 'sweepings' constitute 51 per cent—more than half the whole party.

[1] 'Alors que l'exemple donné par les Anglais de marque que je viens de designer.'

Next, the first item. The service people can be broken up also:—

Naval Officers (all sorts)	82
Army Officers (all sorts)	11
Officiers (unspecified)	3
	—
	96
	—

We may safely ignore the *officiers*, certain that, had they possessed rank or qualification worth mentioning, Decrès would have enlarged upon them. They were probably—if anything—junior warrant officers or NCOs. The Army officers need more attention. Decrès shows 15, but 2 of them (being, in fact, naval officers), I have removed to their proper place. Two more were not service-men at all, but civilians, though one of them may, possibly, have been a *militia* officer. These, also, I have restored to their own people. Of the remaining 11 (allowed above) two I greatly suspect of non-existence: one I believe was not a prisoner at all, while three were certainly *détenus*, who, though military ones, were not p.o.w.'s at all in British eyes. Still, we will concede Decrès his 11 Army officers, even though we do not really believe in them.

We can analyse his 82 naval officers too. But, again, one small piece of pre-editing is essential, because Decrès, in his anxiety to make them look as important as possible, has taken upon himself to promote them without consulting the Admiralty. He names 14 commissioned officers where, in fact, only 10 had commissions, the other four being midshipmen (our old friend Tuthill being one). With this adjustment the figures are:

Commissioned Officers	10
Warrant Officers	10
Midshipmen (including fellow gunroom officers) .	62
	—
	82
	—

But what is this? Commissioned officers were, by contemporary reckoning, Officers and Gentlemen, so that even the most junior of them, the lieutenants, might conceivably—above all by an imaginative fellow like Decrès—be dubbed *anglais de marque*. But by no stretch of the imagination could warrant officers be so described: nor were they, in either France or Britain. And what of those 62 gunroom people? Well, they were Young Gentlemen in England: but not in France. By no means: there, they were consistently regarded as scarcely entitled to parole privileges at all: indeed, bracketed with the merchant officers as 'sweepings of the sweepings'. Logic (for which the French are so famous) demands, therefore, that, whatever the British might think, the French must regard them along with their fellow-scum the merchant officers. And this brings the aggregate of 'sweepings' up to the inconveniently high figure of 242.

Last, the civilians. Here, admittedly, is a more mixed bag. But first we must notice that among them there are *one* MP, and *one* diplomat (Brooks, of course, and Crawford). These two, taken by Decrès as typical samples of the whole mixture, turn out, on inspection, to be the only two of their class and station! Nor am I able to find anyone else in the whole list whom we at home would have described as Englishmen of distinction.[1] The biggest civilian group recorded is described as 'merchants'; which might mean many things, but hardly Englishmen of Distinction. There follows a sprinkling of doctors, 'passengers' and— save the mark—domestic servants. Of 28 civilians no background is specified: but, again, we may safely assume that, whatever they were, they were not, in Decrès' view, worth specifying. There remains but one more item; and therein, perhaps, lies that germ of truth quite often found at the heart of propaganda. There were 15 Gentlemen. Again, close examination of some of their titles to that label leaves a nasty suspicion in the mind: but, again, let Decrès have his 15 Gentlemen.

Our list may now be reconstructed under four headings. We will keep our two relatively important runaways: Decrès shall have his commissioned officers of both services, and his civilian gentlemen, and what we find is this:—

In French eyes avowedly *not anglais de marque* .	242
By mutual consent *not anglais de marque* . . .	75
In French (but not necessarily in British) eyes *anglais de marque*	36
By mutual consent *anglais de marque*	2
	355

Thus, in a French list pretending to name 355 distinguished Englishmen, no less than 317—nearly 90 per cent—were, even in French eyes, nothing of the sort.

What, now, of the people who figured in the *Moniteur's* list? Were they, as Decrès maintained, real prisoners who really won free? Were they simply not people at all, but pure inventions? Or were they something between these two extremes? A close scrutiny of the names seems to show that they were of all sorts. Some, but I believe not very many, were completely bogus, their alleged owners non-existent: some—rather more—were real people, but not real prisoners. A few were real prisoners who made no attempt, and more were prisoners who attempted and failed. But, when all these are subtracted, there remains a hard core, and a surprisingly large one, of real people, real prisoners, and real and successful escapers.

This last fact dawned upon me only gradually as my investigations

---

[1] I would have allowed that honour to Joseph Forsyth, the author, who figures in the list, had I not known (see p. 184) that, far from getting away, he was caught and sent to Bitche.

proceeded. That same incapacity in Frenchmen to tackle British names is once more very apparent. I was faced with such a surprising assortment of un-English-sounding people that, at first, I was inclined to suspect much more wholesale and deliberate roguery than in fact exists. But then a more careful collation, combined with some patience, revealed that Decrès (or whoever did the actual compiling) was doing much more than inventing names at random. Indeed, had he been doing so, he would hardly have been so foolish as to produce such oddities as 'Achiversi', 'Fatwall', 'Hisnop' and 'Pity Hamkes'. Rather, surely, he would have thrown in a few extra Smiths, Browns or Joneses. And this he certainly did, just to swell his total: but only in a fairly small way. As for the oddities, it was surprising how often a little thought resolved them. Sometimes it was quite simple. He would gratuitously promote a midshipman for his own purposes, and then fail to decipher the initial capital in the MS. he was following. Thus, 'Lieutenant Christ Juthill' now stands where Midshipman Christopher Tuthill ought to have stood. Sometimes, however, it was harder. Thus 'Achiversi, Henri', proved to be, for certain, another friend of ours, Midshipman Henry Ashworth. The Young Gentleman with the Dickensian name of Barnwell Fatwall became, also for certain, Midshipman James Barnwell Tattnell, who really did escape from the place, and approximately at the time, alleged by the *Moniteur*. 'Hisnop, Charles', is almost certainly Lieutenant Charles Bishop (though here appears chicanery of another kind: Bishop was almost certainly never a prisoner): 'Pity Hamkes' may well be Lieutenant Richard Hawkes, though this is less certain—and he again, I think, was never captured: and so on.

This technique of arbitrarily catching officers and then announcing their escape doubtless had much to recommend it from Decrès' point of view. Indeed, had I myself been engaged upon this business, I should have been tempted to use the method even more freely than he did. It would have clear advantages. With the help of an old British Navy list, he could pick upon real officers, and the deceit, once concocted, would be harder for us to confute. (*Transport Office*: 'But he's not a prisoner. We have him here.' *Decrès*: Isn't that what I'm saying? Of course you have! He broke his parole, *le perfide*, and sneaked home!')

Another of the *Moniteur's* tricks is to claim the successful escape of a prisoner who, so far as we know, never tried to run: and still more often, despite its own assertion that only successful escapes are counted, it includes unsuccessful ones as well. Thus both Ashworth and Tuthill are shown as escaping from Verdun in 1807 (which they tried but failed to do). In their particular cases and in some others, this does not matter for statistical purposes because their real, and later, escapes are not recorded. Indeed, two escapes by any one individual are seldom alleged: only twice, in fact; once of a midshipman named Jas. Fletcher (who is in one place promoted to lieutenant), and once of our friend Jos. Done (who is clever enough to have escaped successfully from both Verdun and Briançon). Sometimes, however, Decrès contrives to be one up on the transaction. Thus Midshipman James, whom we saw failing to escape from Verdun, is recorded as having succeeded, though, in fact, he remained captive to the last.

One other peculiarity is noticeable. Nearly all depots figure as places from which escapes were made, and from many of them the numbers are high (see below). But from Bitche none is mentioned until May, 1812, when four are recorded. This is strange, because it seems to run against the current—Decrès clearly wanted to lift his numbers as high as possible; and, as we know, there had been many genuine escapes from Bitche before that date. Is it perhaps that the French, knowing what a sinister reputation that fortress enjoyed among the British captives, were unwilling to spoil the effects of it. 'Abandon hope all ye who enter here!' suited them admirably. But 'There's always a chance of escape', added as a rider, made it much less daunting.

Appended is a list of the 13 depots discussed in Chapters V and VI, showing the numbers of escapes alleged by the *Moniteur* to have occurred from each. It should, however, be read with caution: for it certainly does not represent the numbers which did escape from each.

Auxonne	. . 92	Givet	. . 11	Briançon	. 1
Verdun	. . 83	Sarrelibre .	. 10	Cambrai	. 1
Valenciennes	. 56	Bitche	. . 4	Besançon	. 0
Arras	. . 43	Montdauphin .	3	Sedan	. . 0
Longwy	. . 28				

332[1]

There is another lesson which we must *not* try to draw from these figures. They do not classify the depots in any order of difficulty, or ease, in escaping from them. Clearly escape depended less on gaol-like qualities than on the class of captive generally resident therein. It is no accident that Auxonne and Arras, the primary merchant-officer depots, and Verdun and Valenciennes, where midshipmen were apt to congregate, are the first four in the table, and provide more than three-quarters of all escapers.

The conclusion, then, is that a very large number of the names in the *Moniteur* list, even though mutilated, inaccurate, or otherwise dishonest, are what they profess to be, real prisoners who really escaped. The rest are not: but against them may be set another number, every bit as large, of known escapers who do not find a place in Decrès' black list. Thus the *Moniteur* does not help much in formulating a list of real escapers; but it does draw aside for a moment the curtain covering certain aspects of the Napoleonic struggle not often noticed—word warfare and the problems of internal morale.

[1] Escapes from 11 other towns, not regular depots, are also shown:— 6 from Nîmes; 3 each from Paris, Aix-la-Chapelle and Geneva; 2 each from Spa, Versailles and Fort Barreaux; 1 each from Marseilles, Melun, St. Germain and Toulouse.

LISTS

INTRODUCTORY—NUMBERS AND NAMES

(See p. 48)

I. NUMBERS

It does not seem possible to reach an accurate total of British captives in French hands during our war. No one, I believe, either at the time or since, has made the calculation. Nor can I make one now. It seems possible, however, to reach an approximation, based upon four contemporary estimates, none strictly official, but of which two at least have considerable authority behind them.

The first gives the numbers held in France in 1810, official in so far as it was used by our commissioners when trying to negotiate the general exchange of that year (see pp. 77–9). The figures were 11,458 prisoners of war and some 500 *détenus*: total, approximately 12,000. Against these, we held 64,770 French prisoners, as well as some 3,000 of France's allies.

The next clue is a figure given by the Givet chaplain, the Rev. Robert Wolfe.[1] At the end of the war, he writes, the Committee at Verdun, which operated the various relief funds, had 16,000 names then on its books. True, this is mentioned only incidentally, and in obvious round numbers. But it is better evidence than it looks because, in his context, he shows that he wrote it while at Verdun, and in a position to examine the books. He was very well up in the subject too: greatly interested in the funds and even closely associated with them, having at one time actually administered them. He was a most responsible man, and his evidence bears the stamp of truth.

These two estimates, though at first sight at considerable variance, are, in fact, not at all far apart. One, the smaller, was made in mid-1810: the other, the larger, early in 1814. It is, therefore, reasonable to expect a rise, and a rise of 4,000 is certainly not unreasonable. The warming-up of the land-fighting might lead us, indeed, to expect a bigger increase; and certainly the number of Army prisoners rose. On the other hand, however, as our grip upon the sea coasts became ever firmer, we were tending to lose fewer naval men. Since, then, these are our two most trustworthy clues, it seems fair to assume that the figure of 16,000, as the actual number of British captives at the end of the war, is approximately correct.

The third testimony comes from Boys, and it is much more detailed: more upsetting, too, because he seems to find no less than 21,500 captives early in 1814. The gap between this figure and Wolfe's may not, it is true, be quite so wide as it looks because, where Boys was obviously counting civilians as well as service-men, very likely Wolfe was not. But this is not enough—the whole number of *détenus* was by then well

---

[1] Wolfe, op. cit., p. 43.

under 1,000: perhaps hardly 500—so that some other reason for the discrepancy must be sought. First, then, Boys gives no authority whatever for his figures, and his basis of calculation certainly does not promise accurate results. Even his total is only incidental. What he does purport to do is to show the numbers in each individual depot at some date not clearly specified, but which, to judge by the context, should mean January 1814, the date of the evacuation of Verdun:—

Arras	.	. 3,000	Valenciennes	2,000	Verdun	.	. 1,100
Briançon	.	. 3,000	Cambrai	. 2,000	Mont Dauphin		1,000
Sarrelibre		. 3,000	Longwy	. 1,500	Sedan	.	. 500
Givet	.	. 2,500	Auxonne	. 1,500	Bitche	.	. 400

The total comes to 21,500. But Boys does not stress it: he is not thinking of totals, but of relative capacities; and, to us, the real interest of his figures lies in that fact, not in their value as an estimate of prisoner numbers.

I even doubt whether he himself so regarded them. He would surely realize that, early in 1814, any assessment based upon individual depots was bound to fail. Ever since November they had been breaking up, one after another. By January, and still more by February, they were in a state of flux, their occupants moving ever westward and southward, with, on most days, many (perhaps thousands) actually on the road. Such a count could only hope to have any meaning if all the countings in all the depots could be made simultaneously, and the numbers on the road added: and this, under the existing circumstances of hurry and confusion, seems quite unrealistic. Everyone had other more important things to think about. It is not implied that Boys was inventing his figures. Much more likely, what he had got hold of was a statement, true in its day, but daily becoming less true after November 1813, of the capacities of the various depots in the closing stages of the war: that is to say, had they been filled to capacity at the same moment, they would have accommodated 21,500 people. This may well be true; but it is a very different thing from asserting that there *were* 21,500 prisoners. Incidentally, it may be noticed that he omits one depot altogether, and that a significant one—Besançon, the first to be cleared (November 1813). Why? Because the paper he followed had made adjustments for its prisoners? Or did he simply overlook it, in which case, presumably, his total, had he been seeking it, would have exceeded 21,500 by the number normally resident at Besançon? But this matters the less because, I feel, he was not seeking an overall total of any kind.

For somewhat similar reasons we may discount our fourth and last contemporary estimate. It comes from John Tregerthen Short, who states that 'all the British prisoners of war at the *eleven* depots in France, *to the number of* 16,280, were put in motion'. Again no source of information is vouchsafed, and, this time, the figure is not broken up among depots: only, he mentions 11 where Boys had 12 and the true number was 13. All that this means, perhaps, is that, in the paper from which he got his information, Bitche as well as Besançon had been written off.

Because of the nearness of his estimate to that of the man whom we regard as our most reliable authority, it is tempting to cite Short's 16,280 as corroborating Wolfe's 16,000. And so it does; but not very convincingly because, as historical evidence, it is no better than, if indeed as good as, Boys's 21,500, with its greater detail. In plain fact, the evidence of both Boys and Short is too 'hearsay' to be very valuable.

The only other attempt at an estimate that I have seen is that quite non-contemporary, and curiously pontifical, statement of Fraser on the first page of his *Napoleon the Gaoler* (1914). Adducing no evidence whatever, he laid it down that there were 'fewer than 12,000'. This clearly will not do. We know—in so far as we know anything—that this was the figure reached by 1810; and we know of many more taken later: nor is there the least reason for supposing that, for some unknown reason, the wastage suddenly began to equal the intake. It is, in fact, tempting to think that Fraser, rather uncritically, took the 1810 commissioners' number as the final number, and thought no more about it. Oddly enough, though, he did admit (in a note) that the numbers 'are sometimes put as high as 15,000 or 16,000'. But these figures he curtly dismisses, again adducing no evidence.

Here, then, I plump for 16,000, regarding it, on the exiguous evidence available, as the most likely figure. I have no intention, however, of being pontifical, willingly admitting that I have not proved it.

II. NAMES

Again, no list containing the names of all British captives is, or ever has been, in existence. And I have not produced one, primarily because I have omitted that section of it which is much the largest—'the Men': the ratings RN, the merchant seamen, and the 'other ranks' of the Army. No one should dismiss a task as impossible, not having attempted it; but he may fairly think (as I do) that success would be exceedingly doubtful. It is not that records were not kept. They were: but they were never co-ordinated into anything like official, all-embracing lists. Local registers, covering this depot or that over limited periods, exist in embarrassing bulk at the Public Record Office, in parcels which bear the stamp of not having been opened, still less sorted, collated or indexed, since the day when they arrived there: and, before that, clearly not reduced to a single list at the Transport Office, responsible for all prisoner concerns. Could such be produced now? It is doubtful, for several reasons.

There is first the French habit of arbitrarily moving prisoners from depot to depot, without, it would seem, leaving details of the moves. Another difficulty is the absence, in many lists, of the names of the men's original ships. This is serious: John Smith, *Minerve*, is one thing, plain John Smith quite another. A third, leading to the same kind of confusion, is the unfortunate fact that most of the 'local' records which survive were penned by Frenchmen (or are copies of French-penned records): and their writers were, all too often, patently incapable of grappling with the intricacies of English spelling, a notorious difficulty where proper names are concerned. Their spelling, therefore, is often fantastic, making the rarer names unidentifiable. All, in fact, that the honest investigator can say, again and again, is that the name which is puzzling him is wrong, because no Briton can ever have borne such an odd one: but that does not inform him what it *ought* to be. If, on the other hand, the name is common, another sort of difficulty presents itself. He can read it now, perhaps. But which bearer of it is referred to? Is the Thomas Brown at Valenciennes in March 1808, the same as the Thomas Brown recorded at Bitche in 1810? Or the one recorded at Sarrelibre in 1812? Or is he both—or neither? Such are some of the problems requiring solution. Are they soluble?

Failure here, however, need not spread to all the sub-categories of prisoner, and I have found it possible to compile lists of three of them; namely, Naval Officer-prisoners, Army Officer-prisoners and—I will not venture to say *Détenus*, but *some* of the *Détenus*. For the first two I can claim considerable, though not absolute, completeness; and some, but not absolute, accuracy: but for the third considerably less of both completeness and accuracy. There are also, in all three lists, some redundancies, especially where the commoner surnames are concerned. As for the only other big category not yet mentioned, the Merchant officers, I might have collected, perhaps, some 250 names (many barely comprehensible). But this is hardly enough to make publication worth while, because there must have been at least three times as many. So they, and of course all the 'men', are omitted: and with them goes the chance of a comprehensive list of all captives.

The sources used for compiling the three lists that follow are:

A. *Naval Officer-prisoners*

The list is culled from four main components.

(1) Two papers in the Public Record Office, the first inscribed, *A List of officers etc. on Parole in France, 17th July, 1811: Captain Fane's: private.* The second, not connected with the other, is called *List of Lieutenants, Midshipmen and Masters of the Navy, in France up to June, 1812.*[1]

This pair forms a valuable foundation for our list. We may presume that, between them, they record most of the naval officer-prisoners held at the end of June 1812; though not, of course, all that had been or were to be taken during the war. Large groups are missing—those dead, escaped or released in previous years and all captured after June 1812. For a complete list, other sources must be found.

(2) The youngest and most junior of O'Brien's mess-mates in the *Hussar* was a first-class volunteer (naval cadet) named John Hopkinson. His naval career was unspectacular. He remained a captive through-

---

[1] Both are in Adm. 103, 468. No closer reference is feasible. This bundle contains some 60 MSS. in no particular order, unindexed, unnumbered. Captain Francis Fane, senior naval officer in France after Sir Thomas Lavie, was repatriated in the summer of 1811 because (it is said) Napoleon heard that he had once befriended some French prisoners.

out, then gave up the service and joined the Church. Yet he left one memorial, beyond price to the historian of prisoners. During his ten-year sojourn at Verdun he kept a careful register of all officers, naval and military, whom he heard of as joining the depot. It is probably the most complete list extant, though not the most accurate, at any rate in the form of it which I have seen.[1] This version, we learn, is 'not a facsimile copy of the Register, which contains many abbreviations: it has been set out in columns and abbreviated words have been written in full'. It contains, in fact, many errors still demonstrable, and therefore, probably, a good many more no longer so. It is profitless, if not discourteous, to inquire whence these errors came, from the decipherer or from Hopkinson himself. Both would have plenty of excuse, the one because the original may well have been very difficult, the other because he was, after all, only a child when he started it and, throughout, an exceedingly junior officer in only one of the two services concerned. He would consort principally with the younger naval element, which often, unfortunately, was not on very good terms with its Army colleagues. Further, though he would very likely hear of the more senior officers of both services who arrived at Verdun and stayed there, he doubtless missed some of those who did not stay long, and almost certainly missed those few who never came. Indeed, he made no claim to include the last-named, his list being called a 'Register of his Fellow Prisoners at Verdun'. Again, like the *Moniteur*, he had evident difficulty over the spelling of proper names. He had probably, poor lad, received but little liberal education before joining the Navy, and he must, I think, have had to rely upon the ear rather than the eye for his information. It is true, too, that he misses a good many names altogether, even of people whom one would expect him to include; and he is often wrong with his Christian names—people were not nearly so free with them then as they are now. Nor would he have reference books, like Army or Navy Lists, to help him out. Last, he often gets confused between 'date of capture' and 'date of arrival at Verdun', both of which items he gallantly began to record, though he soon gave up the former.

To dilate upon his weaknesses, however, smacks somehow of ingratitude. His strengths are far greater. On two points he is invariably right, whenever we can test him—the ranks of naval officer-prisoners, and their ships. These were service details on which he would have thought shame to be caught napping. But his outstanding service lies in his last column, which supplements our other authorities just where they are at their weakest. It is headed 'Mode and Date of Termination of His Imprisonment at Verdun', and records, whenever possible, how (if at all) each officer came to leave the town. No other authority makes any such attempt. True, he has entries against the names of only 204 officers—about one in every three of them. But of these we learn much: which

[1] As an appendix in Walker's book on Norman Cross (see p. 141)—an unexpected place, since it is not very relevant to that valuable work. The original, Walker says, was, in 1913, in the possession of the compiler's son, the Rev. W. Hopkinson, JP, of Sutton Grange, Northants.

returned to England, presumably released or exchanged; which escaped, and which died—sometimes, in this last category, how they died. Moreover, of the two-thirds who have no entry in that last column, it is fair to presume—and the presumption is almost always right when we can check it—that they did what he did himself, and remained prisoners to the last. Unfortunately, his record shows signs of tailing off towards the end: no military officer, for instance, appears after August 1811, and no marine officer after January 1812. But with naval officers he carries on well beyond the P.R.O. lists, his latest lieutenant arriving in February 1813, and his latest midshipmen, his real brother-officers, right on to March 1814. His greatest importance to us, then, lies not so much in supplying prisoners' names as in recording their ultimate fate.

(3) Our next document is the *Moniteur Universel* of September 12, 1812 (see p. 258). As a source of hitherto unknown officer-prisoners it is admittedly small, for obvious reasons: but, after putting all the names through the finest-meshed of sieves imaginable, I was still able to collect something like a dozen new ones (mostly midshipmen) which were trustworthy enough to be accepted. Those few, moreover, were ones liable otherwise to escape notice—real prisoners and real escapers, who had mostly entered the bag (and left it) quite early on, or quite quickly. Thus they evaded the P.R.O. lists of 1811–12, while, if they escaped before reaching Verdun, they would have evaded Hopkinson too. This source, however, was more useful in finding civilians (see below).

(4) The last source for naval officers is again a small one. It consists of the writings of all contemporary authors who naturally, in passing, mention various captives by name. The full list of these is quite long, but, in most cases, the names it gives are already known to us from our other lists. This is not unsatisfactory, because it seems to show that we are drawing near the end of our task: that there are not many more to find. Such names as do emerge, however, are welcome, because they belong to a group in which we are weak—those few who, for various reasons, never came to Verdun.

There is one category, however, which is still weak, and which, I fear, will remain so. Our list of the lowest officers allowed parole, the ordinary 'ship' or 'standing' warrant officers—the gunners, boatswains and carpenters—is clearly incomplete. There are two reasons for this. First, though most of them went to Verdun, almost all of them were quickly moved on elsewhere, where Hopkinson takes no cognizance of them, and the P.R.O. lists but little more. Second, it seems certain that, though technically entitled to parole, they were so near the borderline that many of them never enjoyed any of its benefits. Here, then, our list remains too short: it must be so, because nearly every captured ship possessed one specimen of each branch.

Here is the abstract of the naval officers in the first list.

Naval Officer Prisoners of War	Exchange or release	Death (natural)	Death (violent)	Escape	Prisoner till end (certain)	Prison till end (probable)	Not known	TOTALS
I. COMMISSIONED OFFICERS								
(a) Captains . . .	4	0	0	1	5	0	0	10
(b) Commanders . .	0	0	2	1	4	0	0	7
(c) Lieutenants . .	4	7	3	7	30	12	20	83
Total Commissioned Officers . .	8	7	5	9	39	12	20	100
II. 'YOUNG GENTLEMEN'								
(a) Sub-Lieutenants .	0	1	1	1	1	3	5	12
(b) Master's Mates .	0	5	0	21	8	12	20	66
(c) Midshipmen . .	1	20	3	56	36	41	65	222
(d) First-Class Volunteers . . .	0	0	2	11	3	11	8	35
(e) Captain's Clerks .	0	6	0	4	0	7	15	32
Total 'Young Gentlemen'	1	32	6	93	48	74	113	367
III. ROYAL MARINES . .	0	0	0	1	17	1	0	19
Total Commissioned, Actual and Aspiring . .	9	39	11	103	104	87	133	486
IV. NAVIGATION BRANCH (BY WARRANT)								
(a) Masters . .	0	3	0	3	5	5	10	26
(b) Second Masters .	0	0	0	1	0	8	11	20
(c) Pilots . . .	0	2	0	2	0	4	13	20
Total Navigation Branch	0	5	0	6	5	17	33	66
V. MEDICAL BRANCH (BY WARRANT)								
(a) Surgeons . . .	2	2	0	2	11	2	1	20
(b) Surgeon's Mates and Assistant Surgeons .	0	5	2	5	9	3	2	26
Total Medical Branch .	2	7	2	7	20	5	3	46
VI. PURSERS (BY WARRANT) .	0	4	0	2	1	2	11	20
VII. 'STANDING' OFFICERS (BY WARRANT)								
(a) Boatswains . .	0	2	0	1	0	4	7	14
(b) Carpenters . .	0	1	0	0	0	2	7	10
(c) Gunners . . .	0	1	0	1	0	2	10	14
Total 'Standing' Officers	0	4	0	2	0	8	24	38
Total Appointed by Warrant . .	2	20	2	17	26	32	71	170
Grand Total of R.N. Officers who were Prisoners of War[1]	11	59	13	120	130[2]	119[3]	204[4]	656

Notes.—1. For RN officers who were in captivity, but not as prisoners of war, see List III—'Some of the *Détenus*'.

2. That these remained p.o.w.'s to the end there is good evidence.

3. That these remained p.o.w.'s to the end there is some, but not conclusive, evidence.

4. That these remained p.o.w.'s to the end there is no evidence: none the less, many, if not most of them, probably did so.

B. *Military Officer-prisoners*

The sources here are the same as those used for the naval prisoners, with one omission and one valuable addition. The omission is the second P.R.O. list, which confines itself to naval officers. The addition is a register kept by Henry William Stephens, a captain in the 66th Foot.[1] Like Hopkinson, he beguiled his captivity by listing the names and regiments of all Army officers held as p.o.w.'s in France in 1813. He had the same limitations as his naval opposite number. Residing at Verdun, he had not much chance of discovering those officers who (especially in the later stages) did not go there, but were side-tracked direct to places like Briançon in the south-east.

My Army and Navy lists are probably about equally representative as to names and numbers. The Army one is much the shorter, but this is because there were many fewer Army prisoners. In one respect, however, it carries a good deal less information. Unlike Hopkinson, Stephens had no 'Mode and date of termination' column. The P.R.O. lists have none either, and now even Hopkinson fails, largely though not entirely. He has his 'mode and date' column, for the soldiers as well as the sailors; but it is very empty. According to him, no military officer escaped and only three died: which, we know from other sources, fails to give the truth at all. Twenty, it is true, he shows as being repatriated: but, as no less than 16 of these were Army surgeons (whom most civilized governments did not keep, anyway) this information does not amount to much.[2] Another brief paper in the P.R.O. (in the same bundle as the others) does, however, partially fill the gap by recording a few escapes, mostly very late in the war, and a rather larger number of deaths.[3] For all that, however, this sort of information about the Army falls very short of that about the Navy, as the accompanying abstract shows. It can be much simpler than the corresponding naval one because nearly all the officers named in it remained prisoners to the end: that is, the 'Others' column is composed almost (though not quite) entirely of 'prisoners to the end': and so, in the list, it would be superfluous to say so every time. The reason is clear enough. It is not only because we know less about the Army officers than about the naval ones, though it is true enough that there would be a few more Army deaths and escapes to record did we but know them. It is because, being practically all commissioned officers, only a few tried to escape. After all, deprive the other —the naval—list of all its officers not appointed by commission, and that too would be pretty thin. In fact, the pattern in so far as Escape is concerned was very similar in both services. The few commissioned officers who did try belonged to one of two groups—(1) those already confined behind locked doors—like Willoughby, Jackson or Owen (Navy) and Lestrange or Batley (Army): and (2) the few who were prepared to risk their honour in contemporary eyes—like Conn or (perhaps) Gordon (Navy) and Sheehy or Graham (Army).

[1] Printed in the *Army Historical Research Journal*, XVII, p. 77.
[2] Of this 16, 14 were released in one batch in December 1813.
[3] A few more deaths are also recorded in a paper in Adm. 103, 467.

Army Officer Prisoners of War	Exchange or release	Death	Escape	Others	TOTALS
I. GENERAL OFFICERS . . .	0	0	0	3	3
II. FIELD OFFICERS . . .	1	0	0	20	21
III. COMPANY OFFICERS . .	6	7	6	155	174
Total Fighting Officers . .	**7**	**7**	**6**	**178**	**198**
IV. MEDICAL BRANCH . . .	16	0	1	7	24
V. OTHERS	0	0	0	7	7

**Grand Total of Army Officers
who were Prisoners of War**[1] **23**   **7**[2]   **7**   **192**   **229**

Note.—1. For Army officers who were in captivity, but not as prisoners of war, see List III—'Some of the *Détenus*'.
2. Six natural deaths, one murder.

C. *Détenus*

Here is a different problem, and, to mark the difference, the list is headed '*Some* of the *Détenus*'. It has been compiled from many sources, some producing only a handful of names. Surviving lists helped but little. Neither government took enough interest in them to collect their names. Napoleon, the cynic, sometimes called them his 'guests': Britain for long refused to acknowledge their existence. Hopkinson does not help; nor do either Stephens or the 1812 P.R.O. list. There remain, then, only the 1811 P.R.O. list which shows a few, and the *Moniteur*, as odd and untrustworthy as ever: and both are all too brief. In fact, were this all, my attempt would hardly have been worth making. There are, however, two more sources which encouraged me to proceed. The first, a frankly secondary one, is J. G. Alger's later book[1] which contains a good many names of *détenus*, as well as a good deal about some of the better-known ones. The other, and by far the richest, is the fourth source used in compiling the other two lists—the whole corpus of contemporary writers. But whereas, before, it found us only a sprinkling of new names, it now produces perhaps as many as all the other sources put together. All these people, in their French sojourn, met *détenus*, some a few, some many. The most fruitful stores are those of Lawrence and Dillon, both long-time residents at Verdun and not mere birds of passage. Dillon alone contributes well over a hundred: so does Lawrence, though, naturally, many are the same in each. Others add a few score more, mainly of people not confined in Verdun but encountered elsewhere, while the writers were on their travels.

There is one drawback, however, in having to rely on Gentry like

[1] *Napoleon's British Visitors and Captives*, London, 1904.

272

LISTS

Lawrence and Dillon. They tend to meet, and to mention, the Gentle *détenus* of their own kind. They are weak in the middle and lower grades of the civilian captives, and especially of the lowest—the parasites, pimps and prostitutes, the common swindlers and retired highwaymen. Of such we obtain but faint echoes. Society was not interested in them and their liberty. Nor perhaps did some of them miss that priceless privilege themselves; especially when release from French detention might only mean, at best, unemployment and semi-starvation at home, or, at worst, Newgate, the convict ship, Botany Bay, or even Tyburn.

The accompanying abstract attempts to show two things:

(1) How, and in what numbers, civilians came to end their captivity. The resulting figures are clearly defective since they include only 145 (or, if we trust the *Moniteur*, 203) names. Of the rest, a few would, were their fate known, go to swell the categories 'Exchanged', 'Died' and 'Escaped'; more—100 at least—would be prisoners to the end; but of the remainder—perhaps 200—we have lost trace.

(2) The *détenus*' status in British society. This is much fuller, containing almost 84 per cent of the names. But some guesswork must be admitted (e.g. the title of some *détenus* to the label 'Gentleman'): and there have been inevitable adjustings, sometimes arbitrary (e.g., is 'the Rev. Sir Herbert Croft, Bart.' to appear as a baronet or a clergyman?).

I had hoped to analyse the list under place-names as well. But with so many captives moving from one locality to another, this proved unprofitable, if not impracticable.

ABSTRACT OF LIST III

SOME OF THE DÉTENUS
(Including Detained Naval and Military Officers)

(1) *Fate up to End of War, Where Known*

Exchanged or Released	61
Died	43
Escaped	41
[Escaped, according to *Le Moniteur* . .	99]

(2) *Social Classification*

Aristocracy and Gentry

Naval Officers	14
Army Officers	46
Peers and Peers' Sons	31
Baronets, Knights and Sons	25
M Ps and Diplomats	14
'Gentlemen'	124
	——254

Professional People

Doctors	21
Clergy	15
Students and Children	11
Artists, etc.	10
Authors, etc.	8
Scholars (Archaeologists, Antiquarians, Linguists, etc.). .	8
Schoolmasters and Interpreters at Depots	8
Lawyers, Politicians and Journalists	7
Scientists	5
Bankers	5
	—— 98

Business men and Merchants	31
Shop- and Inn-Keepers	8
Artisans, Servants, etc.	13
Criminals, Swindlers, Spies, etc.	10

Total Known	**414**
Uncertain or Unknown	79
Names in List	**493**

(Number of Men accompanied by Wives and/or Families .	40)

THE LISTS

AUTHORITIES AND ABBREVIATIONS

I. The following are the authorities cited, and the abbreviations used, in all three lists:

	Author	Title	Abbreviation
1.	Army Lists	(Contemporary)	AL
2.	Alger, John Goldsworth	*Napoleon's British Visitors and Captives*, London, 1904	Alg
3.	Ashworth, Henry	(Printed in) E. Fraser's *Napoleon the Gaoler*, London, 1914	As
4.	Blayney, Andrew, Lord	*Narrative of a Forced Journey, etc., 1810–14,* London, 1814	Bl
5.	Boys, Edward	*Narrative of a Captivity, Escape and Adventures in France*, London, 1827: enlarged ed. 1864 (refs. from latter)	Bo
6.	Brenton, Jahleel	*Letters of,* and *Memoir of Life and Services of,* ed. by Rev. Henry Raikes, London, 1846	Br
7.	Bussell, Peter	*Diary of,* London, 1931	Bu
8.	Choyce, James	*Log of a Jack Tar*, London, 1903	C
9.	Dillon, William Henry	*Narrative of Professional Adventures*, MS. in author's possession	Di
10.	Done, Joshua	*The Prisoner of War,* Articles in *New Monthly Magazine,* 1841	Do
11.	Eastwick, Robert	*A Master Mariner*, London, 1891	Ea
12.	Ellison, Seacombe	*Prison Scenes*, London, 1838	El
13.	Gordon, Henry	*Letter-book* (MS.) in possession of Frank B. Maggs, Esq.	G
14.	Gordon, Peter	*Narrative of Imprisonment and Escape*, London, 1816	Go
15.	Hoffman, Frederick	*A Sailor of King George*, London, 1901	Ho
16.	Hopkinson, John	*Register of his Fellow-prisoners*, printed in T. J. Walker's *Depot for Prisoners of War at Norman Cross*, London, 1913	H
17.	Jackson, George Vernon	*Perilous Adventures and Vicissitudes*, London, 1927	J
18.	James, Robert Bastard	British Museum, Add. MSS. 38886	Ja
19.	Lavie, Sir Thomas	*Letters of,* in possession of Michael Robinson, Esq.	La
20.	Lawrence, Henry	*Picture of Verdun, etc.*, London, 1810	L
21.	'Moniteur'	*Le Moniteur Universel* (especially issue of September 12, 1812)	M
22.	Montagu, Edward Proudfoot	*Personal Narrative of Escape* (privately printed), Beccles, 1849	Mo
23.	Navy Lists	(Contemporary)	NL
24.	O'Brien, Donat Henchy	Bulletins in *The Naval Chronicle*, Vols. 28 to 31	O'B
25.	O'Byrne, William	*Naval Biographical Dictionary*, London, 1849	O
26.	Public Record Office	*Admiralty* 103, 467 and 468: unsorted papers in	PRO
27.	'Sea-Officers'	*Commissioned Sea-Officers of the R.N., 1660–1815*, Admiralty, 1954	SO
28.	Short, John Tregerthen	*Prisoners of War in France, 1804–14*, London, 1914	Sh

29. Stanhope, John Spencer	In *Memoirs* (A. M. W. Pickering), London, 1903	St
30. Stephens, Henry	List of Fellow-prisoners in *Army Historical Research Journal*, xvii, 77	Ste
31. Stewart, Alexander	*Life of* (privately printed), Oxford, 1947	S
32. Wetherell, John	*Adventures of*, London, 1954	We
33. Williams, Thomas	*Prisoners of War in France, 1804–14*, London, 1914	Wi
34. Wolfe, Rev. Robert B.	*English Prisoners in France*, London, 1830	Wo
35. Wright, John Wesley	*Letter of*, in the *Naval Chronicle*, 34, 433	Wr
36. Wright, William	*Narrative of Situation and Treatment*, etc., London, ——	Wri

II. (*Before* prisoner's name)

The letter d in brackets—(d)—signifies 'Doubtful'. The reason for doubt will usually appear in Lists I and II in the Notes; in List III in the column headed 'Remarks'.

The letter t in brackets—(t)—signifies 'Appears in text: for further information consult Index'.

III. In the column *after* prisoner's name in Lists I and II, and in the column headed 'Remarks' in List III, the various fates of the people concerned are abbreviated thus:

D	Died.	PE	Prisoner till end of war.
D(w)	Died of wounds.	PE?	Evidence, but not amounting to certainty, of imprisonment to end of war.
Es	Escaped.		
Ex	Exchanged.		
K	Killed.	R	Released.
K.es	Killed, escaping.	——	No evidence available.
K.d	Killed, in duel.	[.]	Names, or other information, so enclosed are not counted for statistical purposes.
K.m	Killed, murdered.		
K.s	Killed, by suicide.		

LIST I
OFFICER PRISONERS OF WAR
A. NAVY
I COMMISSIONED OFFICERS

(*a*) CAPTAINS

(t)	Brenton, Jahleel[1]	Ex '06	(d) [Mackay, Donald[5]	Es '09]
(t)	Fane, Francis William[2]	R '12	Otter, Charles[6]	PE
	Gower, Edward Leveson	R or Ex '06	Walker, Benjamin	PE
	Joyce, John	PE	(t) Willoughby, Nesbit[7]	Es '13
(t)	Lavie, Sir Thomas[3]	PE	(t) Woodriff, Daniel[8]	R or Ex '07
	Lyall, William[4]	PE		

(*b*) COMMANDERS

	Blennhassett, Goddard	PE	(t) Hoffman, Frederick	PE
	Coote, Charles[9]	PE?	Palmer, Nisbet	D(w) '11
	Fanshawe, Henry	PE?	Strachey, Charles	PE
(t)	Gordon, Henry	Es '10	(t) Wright, John Wesley[10]	D or K.m '05

(*c*) LIEUTENANTS

	Allan, James	—		Fitzgerald, William	—
(t)	Apreece, William[11]	PE		Gratrix, George	—
	Arnold, William	D 19.4.'11		Green, Charles	PE
(t)	Barker, Edward[12]	K.d 18.2.'10		Hall, Thomas Salkeld	—
	Bassan, Samuel	D 28.4.'11		Hawkins, John	PE?
	Bastin, Robert	PE		Higginson, George Montagu[22]	PE
	Bingham, John	PE	(d)	[Horton (George ?)[23]	—]
(t)(d)	[Bishop, Charles[13]	Es '03]		Ingham, George	PE?
	Bogle, Vere Warner Hussey[14]	PE		Innes, Thomas[24]	PE?
	Boyack, Alexander[14]	PE	(t)	Jackson, George Vernon	Es Feb. '12
	Brine, John	PE		Jervoise, William Clark	—
(d)	Brown, George William[15]	[Es '11]		Johnson, Edward[25]	PE
	Brown, James[14]	PE?		Johnson, William Ward Percival	PE
	Carslake, John[14]	PE		Kennicot, Gilbert[26]	PE
(t)	Conn, Henry	Es '12		Kerr, George Lewis	D 23.9.'09
(t)	Connell, Thomas[16]	K.d 27.8.'11		Lambert, John[14]	PE?
	Cooban, Robert Baron	D 14.12.'10		Le Vesconte, Philip[27]	Es 25.11.'10
	Cowley, George Phillips	PE?		Lloyd, Frederick	PE?
	Crosbie, Robert	—		Lutwidge, Henry Thomas	PE
	Dalyell, William Cunningham Cavendish[17]	R '13 or '14		M(c)Dougal(l), John	PE
(t)	Dillon, William Henry	Ex '07	(d)	Mackenzie, John[28]	[Es 5.6.'08]
	Donovan, Richard	—		Maconochie, Alexander[29]	PE
	Douglas, Roddam Thomas[18]	Es '09	(t)	Miles, John William[30]	K.d '06
	Duval, Francis[19]	R '13		Miller, Daniel[31]	—
	Edwards, Henry[20]	Es '10		Miller, Joseph	—
(d)	Evans, Lewis[21]	[Es 8.11.'05]		Miln(e), William	PE
	Fennell, John	—			

(c) LIEUTENANTS—*continued*

Norie, Evelyn	PE	Stewart, Allan —
Norton, George	PE	Stewart, Charles —
(t) Owen, Charles Cunliffe Es 21.2.'12		Taylor, John PE ?
Pennie, John Cobham —		(d) [Thatcher, —35 Es 29.5.'09]
Pridham, Richard	PE	Thomas, Abel Wantner PE
Richards, William —		Thrackston(e), Henry[14, 36] PE ?
Rigby, Robert Preston —		Tracy, John[37] PE
Robins, Thomas Lowton[14]	PE ?	Tuckey, James Kingston[11, 38] PE
Sanders, John Harry	PE	Walker, William —
Shuldham, Molyneux[32]	PE	(t) Wallis, James Es Sep. 13
Simeon, Charles	PE	(t) Walpole, Hon. William[39]
Simes, Gustavus Adolphus[33]	D '06	R '07 or after
Smith, Joseph	PE ?	(d) [Wells, G. T.[40] PE ?]
Smith, Thomas[34]	PE	Wigley, John Gwyn PE
Smithers, George	PE	Wingate, George Thomas —
Snell, Robert	PE	Wray, Nicholas D 10.3.'08
Spence, William	D 18.6.'09	Young, Matthew PE
Stackpoole, Edmund	PE ?	

II 'YOUNG GENTLEMEN'[1]

(*Officers Not Commissioned but Aspiring to Commissions*)

(a) SUB-LIEUTENANTS

Bourne, George Stanway[2]	PE	Guy, Henry[5] PE ?
Collas, John[3]	PE?	(d) [Leader, John[6] Es 16.5.'09]
Davidson, Alexander[3]	—	(d) [Norwood, Samuel[6] Es 14.1.11]
Dixon, William (James ?)		Richards, William[7] —
	D 30.8.'09	Ross, Richard[8] —
(t) Essel, John	K.es '09	Ross, Richard Colmer Es '07
Fabian, William Backhouse[4]	—	Scanlan, Thomas[9] Es '11 or '12
Gunnell, R. J.	PE ?	Westlake, T. G. —

(b) MASTER'S MATES

Atkinson, John	—	Hawkins, H(annibal ?) E.[13] —
Atkinson, —[10]	D '11	Hubbard, William Es 11.2.'14
Baird, Daniel	PE	Hutchinson, William Es 14.1.'11
Barclay, John	—	Kneeshaw, Samuel —
Barton, James	—	Laca(?o)ste, Frederick —
Bold, Edward	PE	Legg, Robert[14] —
Boyle, Hon. James Carr	—	Lerosignol, Peter[15] PE ?
Brander, William	Es '09	Lewis, Henry Es 26.10.'09
(d) Caffry, James S. G.	—	Littlejohn, David Es 21.12.'10
Dew, Richard	D Feb.'11	Low, Matthew D 27.10.'09
Downey, John	PE ?	McFee, John Es 14.1.11
Dupré, J. W.	—	(t) Mahoney, Jeremiah[3] PE ?
Gilpin, William[2]	PE ?	Moore, John D 2.11.'10
(d) Gowdie, John[11]	—	(t) Morris, Peter[16] —
Grant, Roger	Es '09	(t) Moyses, Choyce William PE
Halford, Charles	Es 14.5.'11	Munro, Andrew[2] PE ?
Hamilton, Thomas James[12]	PE ?	(t) O'Brien, Donat Henchy[17]
Harvey, Philip	—	Es 14.9.'08

(b) MASTER'S MATES—*continued*

O'Neil(l), Robert (G.)	Es Feb. '14	Shackleton, John[22]	—
Paine, Reuben[2, 18]	Es Jul. '08	Sharvell, Benden	PE ?
Parkman, John[2]	PE	Smith, John	PE ?
Parry, Howard Lewis[19]	Es 11.2.'14	Steward (?t), Thomas Keith	
Parsons, John	Es 24.12.'13		Es Feb. '14
Patterson, —	Es '11 or '12	Stingsby, Joseph	—
Pitfield, Joseph Edward Chilcott[20]		Thomas, William	PE
	Es 21.12.'10	Thorley, Robert[2]	Es[23] July '13
Powell, George	Es 20.7.'10	Turner, Edward	PE ?
Radford, William	PE	Walker, Edward (Barnaby ?)	—
Randall, William	Es 24.12.'09	Wall, (John Holwell ?)[24]	PE ?
Rawlins, Robert Dicklegg	PE	Webb, Thomas	—
Reynolds, Vessey John[21]	PE ?	Webster, John	—
Robertson, William	Es May '09	*(t)* Wills, Thomas George[2]	PE
Rochfort, Robert	Es Oct. '09	Wilson, (David ?)[25]	—
Rowe, Thomas	PE ?	Wood, James	D 20.5.'06
Russel(l), Andrew	—		

(c) MIDSHIPMEN

Allen, William	—	Caulfield, Edwin Toby	—
Arabin, Augustus	— (D '15)	*(t)* Cecil, Thomas Walbeoff	Es 14.7.'07
(t) Ashworth, Henry[26]	Es Dec. '08	Clements, Hanbury	PE
Astley, William[27]	—	*(t)* Colquhoun, Humphry (T.)[14]	
Ayston, Scro(o)pe	D 12.1.'11		Es 10.2.'14[35]
Baker, William	—	Cordry, George	PE
Barnes, John[28]	—	Cornish, Samuel	PE ?
Barret, Joseph Fauriel	PE	Cornutt, Ralph	PE ?
Barrow, Henry	Es 27.12.'13	Coulson, John[29]	PE ?
Bateman, George[2, 29]	PE ?	Cowen, John[29]	PE ?
Batty, M. W.	—	Craggs, George[36]	PE
Bee, John	—	Crick, John	D '08
Birch, James	—	*(t)* Dacre, George Hall	Es '09
Bissett, George	Es 23.12.'09	Darracott, Robert Young Man[37]	
Blackmore, Samuel	—		PE
Blake, George Hans[30]	PE	Davies, Hamilton[2]	PE
Blakeney, Robert[31]	R or Es	Davis, George Evan	Es 27.12.'13
(t) Blakiston, Thomas	Es 26.10.'09	Davis, Henry	PE
Bland, George	PE	Dawson, Thomas	D 15.10.'10
Blissett, Charles	—	Denniston, Thomas	D 29.6.'06
(t) Boys, Edward	Es 16.11.'08	*(t)* Devonshire, William Ney	
Brothers, John	PE		Es 21.7.'11
Brown, James	—	Dillon, Edward	Es 25.4.'09
Brown, William	D 2.12.'09	Donaldson, Augustus[2, 38]	D '13 ?
Brydges, Edward	—	Dougall, Thomas[14]	PE ?
Burridge, Robert	Es 4.7.'08	Drew, J(ames ?) R(odgers ?)	
Butterfield, John[32]	—		Es 9.11.'10
Cadell, —[33]	—	Edwards, Samuel	PE
Callaghan, Henry John	PE ?	Elvy, George	PE
Campbell, John Pitman	—	Evans, George	PE ?
(d) Carrique, Henry[34]	—	[Evans, John[39]]	
Carter, George	—	*(t)* [Fatwall, Barnwell[40]]	

(c) MIDSHIPMEN—*continued*

(d) Felton, John[41]	Es 24.4.'09	
(t) Fletcher, James S.[42]	Es 14.12.'07	
(d) Forret, Thomas Frederick[43]	PE?	
Fosbery, Godfrey	PE	
Franklyn, John	PE	
Furze, Robert	PE?	
(t) Gale, James H.	PE?	
Garrick, Charles	—	
Gibbs, Anthony	—	
Glasscott, James H.	D 3.3.'07	
Gordon, Adam	—	
(t) Gordon, R. L.	Es 14.7.'07	
Grant, Archibald	PE?	
Grant, Lachlan[14]	—	
Gregg, Thomas[44]	—	
Haberfield, Isaac	—	
Hains, William	—	
Hall, Joseph	—	
Hall, Roger	Es 26.10.'09	
Hall, William	—	
Handby, William[45]	—	
Hare, Charles	Es. '09	
(t) Hare, William B.	PE	
Harrop, David	PE	
Hart, Benjamin	PE	
Hawkey, John[2]	PE?	
(t) [Hayward, see Haywood]		
(t) Haywood, William[47]	K.m '08	
(d) Hearbour, W(illiam?)[34]	—	
Heard, William[29]	PE?	
Hemer, Robert[29]	PE	
Herbert, Ed.[29]	PE?	
Herniman, W.[46]	—	
Hervey, I. (J.?) M. A.	D at Metz	
(t) Hewson, Maurice	Es 14.9.'08	
(t) [Heywood, see Haywood]		
Hill, Henry Joseph	PE	
Hodder, Peter[2]	PE	
(d) Holder, Robert[34, 48]	Es 28.1.'11	
Hughes, John Thompson[14]	PE?	
Hunt, Edward	Es 8.12.'13	
(t) Hunter, Robert Edward	Es 16.11.'08	
Jackson, Henry	—	
Jackson, Thomas	—	
(t) James, Robert Bastard	PE	
(d) Jeaffreson, Charles[49]	Es Feb. '14	
Jennings, Thomas	PE?	
Johnson, John Munnings	PE?	
Johns(t)on, Thomas[50]	—	
Johnston, William Irvine[51]	PE?	
Johnstone, J. H.[52]	—	
(d) Kenessy, Augustus O.[53]	—	

King, Henry	PE	
Kingston, William W.[54]	Es 14.9.'07	
Kirkpatrick, Henry	Es 30.3.'14	
Knocker, Joseph[55]	Es 14.1.'11	
Lane, J. J.	PE?	
Lechmere, John	PE	
Lewis, Thomas	—	
Lichford, J. R.	—	
Litheby, William	PE	
Little, Francis	Es 19.7.'05	
Longmore, William Alexander	PE?	
Low, John M'Arthur[2]	—	
Lyall, J. N.	—	
McDougal(l), Andrew	D 25.10.'11	
McDougal(l), Thomas	—	
McGraw, John[29]	PE?	
McLeod, William	Es 20.11.'09	
McWha, Robert[29]	PE?	
Malcolm, Niel	PE?	
Marc(s?)h, James[56]	—	
Maryon, George	PE?	
Mason, Henry Browne	Es 10.11.'10	
(t) Masters, Thomas James Poole		
	Es 27.11.'08	
Mathias, James	—	
Mayo, Charles	Es 28.1.'11	
Miller, Martin	Es 14.12.'09	
Mitchell, Alfred	PE?	
Mitchell, G. T.[57]	—	
Mollett, P. H.	D '14	
Montagu, Edward Proudfoot		
	Es 21.7.'11	
Morland, Robert	D 16.7.'06	
Morris, Richard	PE?	
Morris, Thomas	—	
(t) Mortimer, Robert[14, 58]	PE?	
Mottley, Samuel[59]	Es '06	
(t) Murray, John	Es 4.6.'05	
(t) Nairne, Patrick	D 8.2.'09	
	(? K.m)	
Nason, Richard	Es 28.1.'11	
Nelson, John	D 8.3.	
Nepean, Evan	PE	
Nickoll, Edward	PE	
O'Brien, Joseph	Es 24.12.'13	
Ounkovesky, Sim[n. 60]	—	
Pace, Philip[61]	—	
Parker, Charles	Es 3.8.'10	
Parker, James P.	Es 20.1.'10	
Parker, John[62]	Es 21.2.'09	
(t) Parr, Alfred[58]	—	
Paynter, Charles	Es 27.12.'13	

(c) MIDSHIPMEN—*continued*

	Peard, George	PE ?
(t)	Pearson, Jack	D 11.3.'07
(d)	Pearson, Robert[63]	—
	Pickersgill, Richard	PE ?
(t)	Potts, George P.	—
	Pratt, William	D 6.1.'10
	Price, E. F.	—
	Randall, Henry	PE
	Reid, James	—
	Richards, William[14]	PE
	Richardson, Henry	D 23.2.'12
	Ricketts, Charles Spencer	Es '09
	Robertson, R. B.	D '10
	Robinson, Abraham	Es 4.6.'05
(d)	[Robinson, William[64]	Es 23.4.'09]
	Rodmill, Thomas[65]	—
	Rootes, John	D 23.4.'13
	Rosser, Richard	PE ?
	Sadler, Henry	PE ?
	Sarsfield, Dominick..	PE
	Savigny, William Henry[29]	—
(t)	Scott, Andrew	K.d 14.10.'11
	Shaw, Charles	Es '09
	Sheers, Thomas[29]	PE ?
	Smithson, W. C.[66]	D 30.11.'09
(t)	Stanhope, Henry	Es 14.5.'11
	Stark, Peter	Es 9.11.'10
	Sterling, J. E.	Es 11.2.'14
	Stone, Valentine	—
	Sulivan, James Inglefield	PE ?
	Summers, John	Es '12[67]
	Sutherland, Francis	PE ?
	Sutton, Robert	Es '11
(t)	Sutton, William[29]	PE
(t)	Tattnall, James Barnwell[68]	
		Es Dec. '09

	Taylor, I. C.[69]	—
	Taylor, John	—
	Taylor, Thomas[70]	PE ?
(t)	Temple, Edmond E.	Es 19.4.'07
(t)	Thomas, Henry	Es 20.7.'10
	Thompson, Charles	—
(t)	Thomson, Theophilus	K.m 21.3.'11
	Townsend, Joseph Cuthbert	
		Es 24.12.'12
	Turrell, Charles	PE
(t)	Tuthill, Christopher	Es 30.8.'07
	Tyler, Thomas William	PE ?
	Vale, John	—
	Vine, Anthony[71]	D 24.10.'12
	Viret, F. C. L.[29, 72]	PE ?
	Wahlstrand, Peter Bernelius[73]	PE
	Waller, Obediah	PE
	Weatherley, Richard	PE
	Were, John Parsons	PE ?
	Whitefield, John	—
(t)	Whitehurst, Frederick John	
		Es 16.11.'08
(t)	Whitehurst, Frederick John[2]	PE
	Wier, John[34]	—
	Wilcke, James[74]	—
	Wildey, John	—
	Williams, H. A.[75]	—
	Williams, William John	PE
(d)	Woodroffe, John[34]	—
	Woolcock, James	—
(t)	Worth, Henry[76]	PE ?
(t)	Wright, John Rogerson Tomkyns[77]	
		Es 24.12.'10
(t)(d)	[Wright, William[78]	Es —]
	Yelland, Edward	PE ?

(d) FIRST CLASS VOLUNTEERS

	Aitken, Roger[79]	—
	Allen, Peter	—
	Back, George[80]	PE
	Byass, Wheatley	PE
	Crowe, Edward	Es 20.7.'10
	Cutler, Frank	Es 12.5.'09
	Davis, Thomas[29, 81]	PE ?
	Digges, Montgomery	PE ?
	Fitzgerald, George	Es 9.11.'10
	Forbes, George	Es 20.2.'10
	Frith, John	PE ?
	Galway, Daniel	PE ?
(t)	Gordon, George	K.es 21.7.'11

	Hallowes, John	Es 9.11.'10
	Hamilton, William	PE ?
	Harries, Joseph	—
	Hay, Robert[82]	—
(t)	Hopkinson, John	PE
	Lardner, Charles	—
(t)	Leworthy, Henry[29]	Es early '14
(t)	Mansel(l), William L.	Es 16.11.'08
	Norton, George	PE ?
	Pettigrew, Thomas	PE ?
	Robins, W. C.	—
	Robinson, Charles	Es 26.9.'09
	Secretan, J. F.	—

(*d*) FIRST CLASS VOLUNTEERS—*continued*

(t) Smith, George Sidney	Es 24.8.'10	(t) Trewin, John	PE ?
Stevenson, Francis[83]	Es 20.7.'12	Willis, W(illiam ?) A(lexander ?)	
(t) Street, Charles	K.es 21.7.'11		PE ?
Streeting, William	Es '11	Wingate, John	—
Tighe, Robert	PE ?	Wymer, William[29]	PE ?

(*e*) CAPTAIN'S CLERKS

Adams, John	—	Marriott, Thomas[29]	—
(t) Belchambers, Benjamin[14]	PE ?	Marsden, Robert	—
(t) Bradshaw, W. T.[84]	—	(t) Mascal, James	D 4.11.'06
Brown, Isaac	D 16.2.'09	(t) Maxwell, Francis	Es Sep. '07
Campbell, William[29]	PE ?	Meek, Joseph	Es 20.11.'07
Carroll, Hugh	PE ?	Mowatt, J. C. G.[85]	—
(t) Chambers, John	Es 4.2.'11	Nicholls, A. W.	PE ?
Chappell, George C.	D 19.2.'13	Perryman, John	D 11.3.'13
Green, Stephen	—	Randall, Cornelius	Es '09
Hindley, J. H.	—	Robertson, John	—
Jenson, George	D 15.6.'11	Simmonds, George	PE ?
Knipp, Edward	—	Stockings, Richard	—
Lynch, John	—	Strong, John	—
Lyth, William	D 15.5.'11	Walker, William	—
McCarthy, Daniel	—	Ward, John	PE ?
Mackey, Donald	PE ?	Whittaker, William	—

III. ROYAL MARINES[1]

(*a*) CAPTAINS

(t) Alexander, Robert[2]	PE	(t) Ridley, John[2]	PE
Jones, George	PE	Stanser, Charles[3]	PE

(*b*) FIRST LIEUTENANTS

Bell, George Augustus	PE	Farmer, Jasper	PE
Bignell, Richard Roe	PE	Gibbons, Jeremiah	PE
Blakeney, John	PE	Morgan, Thomas	PE
Campbell, John	Es '10	Phil(l)ips, Robert	PE
(d) Collins, Jeremiah[4]	D ? or PE ?	Sampson, William	PE
Eckford, Alexander	PE	Wilson, John	PE

(*c*) SECOND LIEUTENANTS

Chaproniere, Bew	PE	Magill, George	PE
Loveridge, Henry	PE		

IV. NAVIGATION BRANCH[1]

(*a*) MASTERS

Bishop, Gaius L.	PE	Cochran, William	D 30.9.'07
Brown, Edward	D 28.2.'13	Crockett, George[3]	PE
Brown, Henry[2]	—	Dillon, James	D '05
Brown, Thomas Henry[2]	—	Fillieule, John[4]	PE ?

(*a*) MASTERS—*continued*

Forster, Thomas[5]	—	Minton, Thomas[8]	—
Fraser, Henry	PE	Read, Thomas	—
Gooch, Henry	—	Roskelly, William	PE ?
Goodson, John[6]	—	Skinner, Richard[3]	Es 5.6.'08
Hales, John	PE ?	Sullivan, John	—
Hazell, Benjamin	PE	Taylor, Henry	Es '11 or '12 ?[9]
Hiller, Caleb[3]	PE ?	Taylor, Roger	PE
Laing, David	PE ?	Thompson, Robert Richard	
Long, James	—		Es 4.5.'14
McDougal, John[7]	—		

(*b*) SECOND MASTERS

Adamson, Robert	PE ?	Harrow, John	—
Beatson, John[10]	PE ?	Hernaman, Francis	PE ?
Beynon, David	PE ?	McNamara, Jeremiah	—
Brown, George	Es 22.5.'11	Maythaw, Francis[12]	—
Cowan, John	PE ?	Napier, Andrew	—
Dear, John	PE ?	Norman, Peter	—
Edwards, Henry	—	Tapley, Jeremiah	PE ?
(t) Giles, Joseph	PE ?	Templeton, Robert	—
Gillo, J. H.	—	Tuck, Samuel	—
Handyside, Alexander[11]	—	Walker, William	—

(*c*) PILOTS

Atherdon, John	—	Pope, Robert	—
Ayles, James	D '07	Priaulx, Peter	PE ?
Bandains, Philip	PE ?	Price, Thomas	—
Corney, John le	—	Purdy, George[13]	PE ?
Hammond, John	—	Rebour, Francis	—
Hughes, John	PE ?	Ross, Hugh[14]	—
James, Thomas	—	Rougetelle, John le	D —
Knock(n)er, Thomas	Es 14.1.'11	Speak, Jesse	—
Ladd, Thomas	—	Steedman, John	—
Montbrun(n), J. J.	—	Vannel, Richard	Es 22.5.'11

V. MEDICAL BRANCH[1]

(*a*) SURGEONS

(t) Abbott, Robert	PE	Lawmont, John[5]	PE
Allen, Alexander	D 8.2.'13	Manning, Patrick F.[6]	PE
Bell, John	PE ?	Mitchell, Charles	PE
Brennan, James	PE	Sanderson, Thomas	R[7] '13
Connin, Francis	PE	(t) Simpson, Alexander	D *c.* '09[8]
Donaldson, William	PE	Snooke, Charles M.	PE
(t) Graham, John[2]	R 4.1.'14	Stewart, Robert	PE
[Hant, John[3]	Es 23.12.'10]	Tobin, Richard	PE
Hewetson, George[4]	—	Turner, William	PE ?
Hill, William	Es 18.11.'09	Williams, Morgan	Es 18.11.'09
Hughes, Joseph Hugh	PE		

(b) SURGEON'S MATES AND ASSISTANT SURGEONS[9]

Allcock, Bernard	D Mar. '08		McGrath, Edmond	D 9.8.'08
Cameron, Daniel	Es 14.5.'09		Moir, James	PE
Campbell, William	PE		Newall, John	PE
Crigan, Alexander	Es 29.5.'09[10]		Newman, Charles	PE
Godbehere, Daniel	PE		Patterson, John	PE
Gordon, Robert[11]	PE	(t)	Porteus, William	Es Dec. '08
Gray, David	PE ?		Roberts, John (1)	D 10.10.'08
Hawthorn, James	Es 10.11.'10		Roberts, John (2)	Es 14.4.'13
Hayden, J. P.[12]	D 18.3.'14		Scott, Patrick H.	PE ?
Hoggan, Robert	PE		Watson, John	D 17.12.'09
Hunter, John[13]	—		Watt, William	PE ?
Jones, Lewis	PE ?		Wells, Thomas[14]	K.d 20.1.'12
(t) Lawder, Benjamin	K.s 25.5.'05		Woods, M. C.	—

VI. PURSERS[1]

Bastin, Thomas	—	Lamotte, William	Es 22.5.'11
Black, William Snell[2]	[Es 22.5.'11][2]	Livie, Alexander	D 12.8.'08
Boone, John[2]	[Es 22.5.'11][2]	McMillan, Archibald	—
Corbyn, Hugh	—	Paterson, John	D 31.10.'13
(t)(d) Daly, John[3] (or Robert)	Es 30.9.'12	Richardson, John	—
Ellis, George	—	Ross, Charles	D 22.11.'13
Haly, Simon	PE?	Sullivan, Daniel	—
Hannay, Hugh	PE ?	Trewin, Samuel	D 2.3.'09
Hyslop, James	—	Willcocks, Joseph F.	—
Innes, John	PE	Wilson, James	—

VII. WARRANT OFFICERS[1]

(a) BOATSWAINS

Brown, Andrew	—	Gray, Thomas	—
Bulger, Robert	—	Henderson, Alexander	—
Carey, William	D 25.5.'08	Lorimer, William	PE ?
Cliff, William	Es (Bitche)	Morton, James	PE ?
Cox, Philip	—	Osborn, John	—
Flaxman, James	PE ?	Pink, James	PE ?
Gilligan, Edward	—	Richardson, William	D Jan. '10

(b) CARPENTERS

Allen, Andrew	—	Nesbitt, John	PE ?
Bager, Thomas	—	Pasco, Thomas	—
Bell, William	PE ?	Rice, William	—
Heard, George	—	Richards, John	—
Lunn, Peter[2]	—	Windham, John	D 1.10.'09

(c) GUNNERS

Aitken, David	—	Little, William	D 26.9.'06
Carne, Richard[3]	—	Moore, John	PE ?
Carr, John	PE ?	Quin, Timothy	—
Chadwick, Daniel	—	Simpson, Thomas	Es '09
Dobbins, James	—	Strong, Thomas	—
Johnson, John	—	Taylor, —	—
Lennard, William	—	Treacher, John	—

NOTES ON LIST I

I. COMMISSIONED OFFICERS

(a) CAPTAINS

1. Senior Naval Officer, '03–'06.
2. Senior Naval Officer, '11–'12.
3. Senior Naval Officer, '07–'11.
4. Died 3 days after home-coming.
5. Very doubtful whether a p.o.w. Only evidence, M.
6. Senior Naval Officer, '12–'14.
7. Never at Verdun.
8. Senior Naval Officer, '06–'07.

(b) COMMANDERS

9. Avoided Verdun by influence or bribery.
10. Or suicide (see text).

(c) LIEUTENANTS

11. Severely wounded in duel.
12. In duel with Alexander (R.M.)
13. Identification doubtful. See text. Perhaps a *détenu*.
14. Helping in Verdun school.
15. Escape doubtful in M only.
16. In duel.
17. Received 15 wounds on capture, but not released for 8 or 9 years.
18. Via Russia. Son of Ad. Billy Douglas. Possibly R.
19. Long imprisoned in Naples before Verdun.
20. Possibly R: probably never at Verdun.
21. In M only: no such name in SO: may be confused with Mid. Evans, John (q.v.).
22. Unluckiest of officers: Capt., sentenced to death, 1794: Es 1795: *détenu*, 1803: Es '04: recapt. '07.
23. Ho: probably Norton, George, q.v.
24. Allowed to Lyons with family (Bu).
25. 'Johnstone' in PRO, but this is right.
26. P.o.w. to Turks, '07: R. '09: recapt. by crew of an American prize and delivered to the French.
27. On second attempt. After first, paraded in chains and sent to Bitche.
28. M the only authority for Es.
29. 'McKnockie' (H): M'Konochie (SO), but as above (O).
30. SO: 'T. W.' in H.
31. SO: 'Nuller' (H).
32. Invented, at Verdun, a carriage propelled by sails and an ice-yacht.
33. SO: 'Simer' (H).
34. The twelfth of the 16 Thomas Smiths in SO: Lt. 1.8.'07.
35. Bu, probably Fletcher, J. S. (q.v.), the Mid. whom M calls a Lieutenant.
36. NL, H, PRO, HO. SO has Thackstone, probably wrongly.
37. Sent direct to Bitche as a 'matelot' for 'desertion' (PRO).
38. Explorer. Wrote his *Maritime Geography* at Verdun.
39. Made Cdr. at Verdun. Killed Lieutenant Miles in duel.
40. PRO: not in SO: probably Master's Mate T. G. Wills (q.v.).

II. 'YOUNG GENTLEMEN'

1. There are five classes of them: (a) Sub-Lieutenant, (b) Master's Mate, (c) Midshipman, (d) First Class Volunteer (= Naval Cadet), and (e) Captain's Clerk. When afloat, these five classes, save for the younger volunteers who inhabited the gunroom, lived together in the Midshipmen's Mess: and from one class or another of them practically all Lieutenants' commissions derived. Inevitably the first four must be grouped under the general heading of 'Young

Gentlemen'—that is, 'aspiring commissioned officers': but the fifth presents a difficulty. The Captain's Clerk belonged, nominally, to the Purser's group, and the average Clerk was probably not quite so 'gentle' as the rest. Yet it is more realistic to place him with them here, not only because, in the conditions of the time, he always consorted with them, but also because he quite often obtained a Lieutenant's commission (though not so frequently when made a prisoner). The distinction between Sub-Lieutenant, Master's Mate and Midshipman is sometimes academic. There was one difference, more apparent than real, between Sub-Lieutenant and the other two. He was appointed as such by the Admiralty, where the others were ship appointments made by the Captain. But he had no commission and, like them, a change of ship might mean a change of title, upwards or downwards. Any of the first three might be promoted direct to Lieutenant, though the Sub-Lieutenant's chances of the prize were greater than the Master's Mate's, and the Master's Mate's greater than the Midshipman's: but the Captain's Clerk usually, and the Volunteer always, had first to pass through one of the three higher classes. Here, the status of the officer at the moment of capture is the factor which decides in what group he appears: but all were definitely 'in the succession', and could reach commissioned rank if luck, influence or merit were on their side.

2. Made Lieutenant while p.o.w.

3. Probably made Lieutenant while p.o.w.

4. Fabien (H), Acting-Lieutenant at time of capture.

5. H: Mid. in PRO.

6. In M only: otherwise unidentified.

7. Not the same as Lieutenant Richards (q.v.).

8. May be same as preceding, but H has both, taken in different ships.

9. There are four spellings: this is SO's.

10. In Mo, Do and Go. Perhaps same as preceding.

11. Perhaps should be Goldie, John, or Gowde, John.

12. PRO: H—wrongly, I think—Hamilton I. I.

13. PRO, 'Bitche for desertion', there called 'Annibal'.

14. Bitche for misconduct, '11.

15. At Bitche, June '12.

16. Killed Mid. Scott in duel.

17. In SO—wrongly—Denis.

18. According to G, a case of broken parole.

19. According to O, was a PE.

20. Petfield (H). For ill-treatment as p.o.w., see O.

21. Christian names doubtful. H has 'N. J.'.

22. PRO: 'Sheckleton' (H).

23. H: PRO gives 26.2.'14.

24. Probably MM when taken in *Calcutta* and never at Verdun. Published an account of experiences at Bitche. A brother, Allen, was captd. in January '13, and released on parole at once; but the Admiralty repudiated the conditions and re-employed him (O).

25. H. If correct, this officer (Lieutenant in 1802) should be in Lieutenants' list.

26. As. Died, '09.

27. 'Wilk^n' (PRO).

28. Perhaps the 'Barres' of M, alleged to have Es 9.9.'09.

29. Bitche for attempted escape, '11 (PRO).

30. O. According to M, Es 12.10.'12.

31. 'Returned to England' (H).

32. 'Es 15.3.'06' (M), but, probably rightly, 'deserted and retaken' (H).

33. In no list—only Bo's narrative.

34. In H only: query spelling?

35. 1814 (PRO): 1813 (H).

36. PRO. H has 'Craggs, James'—probably the same, but possibly a different officer—James Cragg, made Lieutenant 1.3.'15.

37. 'Es 1811' (M), but H ('Es 1811, but recaptured') is right.

38. 'Lieutenant, captured in 1805' in H. But not promoted till '12 (SO).

39. Captured and locally exchanged: never reached France.

40. See Tattnall, Mid.

41. In M only, but possible. If correct, perhaps a Lieutenant.

42. Listed twice in M, as Lieutenant and Mid., as 'Flesher'.
43. PRO. Name doubtful: perhaps not R.N.
44. NL: 'Greg' in H, 'Greig' in Bo.
45. Either made Lieutenant while p.o.w., or Es; or, possibly, both.
46. H: 'Hernamen' PRO.
47. Sh: other spellings, 'Hayward' (Bo) and 'Heywood' (H). We calls him Henry.
48. Perhaps Hodder, Robert, brother of Peter, q.v.
49. H: PRO has 'Jeffaeson'. Perhaps 'Jefferson'.
50. May be 'Johnson, Thomas'.
51. H: PRO has 'Johnstone', but H probably right.
52. H, but possibly Johnston, James Henry (Lieutenant 16.2.'10).
53. H: 'Ottomnessy' (PRO). Proper form unknown.
54. M: 'Kingstone' (H).
55. In M only, but very likely right.
56. 'March' (H): 'Marsh' (PRO).
57. (H only.) Possibly the same as last-named (PRO only).
58. Entered French service, '09. Left it '10 (H).
59. 'Restored to liberty' (O), D '45 (O). D '09 (H). Might be Ex or R.
60. PRO only: spelling? R.N.?
61. PRO. H has 'Race', probably wrongly.
62. M: but partially confirmed by O.
63. Perhaps Merchant Service.
64. M only: probably same as Vol. Charles Robinson, q.v.
65. PRO: 'Rodnell' (H).
66. H: though, according to We, living 8.2.'14
67. Perhaps R, not Es.
68. M's 'Fatwall'. Es dressed as girl.
69. H. Perhaps Joseph Taylor, Lieutenant 17.2.'15.
70. Sent direct to Bitche and treated as a rating (PRO).
71. PRO: 'Arthur', H.
72. H: 'Veret, Francis Ed. Steven' (PRO.)
73. PRO: also 'Walstrand' (PRO) and 'Wahtstrand' (H).
74. In both PRO and H: but H has 'John'.
75. PRO: may be same as 'Willis, W. A.' (Vol., q.v.).
76. Twice at Bitche for attempting escape.
77. SO: H has Wright, I. R. J.
78. Probably not a Mid. or even R.N. See note, p. 308, in *Détenu* List.
79. SO:.'Aitkin', H.
80. Ad. Sir George, Arctic Explorer. Aged 12 on capture.
81. PRO: 'Davies', H.
82. PRO: H and G have 'Hoy', and may be right.
83. H. and M: PRO has 'Frederick'. The escape only in M.
84. O'B: H has Mid. W. J. Bradshaw.
85. H: PRO has 'Mouatt'.

III. ROYAL MARINES

1. All Commissioned Officers.
2. Duellist.
3. Brevet Major.
4. H. Probably PE. Name doubtful: may be Gibbons, J. (q.v.)

IV. NAVIGATION BRANCH

1. All appointed by Warrant. The names in this section are often untrustworthy, PRO and H frequently giving different spellings.
2. These may be the same man: but both appear in NL.
3. Acting-Master.
4. PRO: 'Filleule' (H).
5. PRO: 'Foster' (H).
6. H. Query 'Goodridge, John'?
7. Perhaps only 'acting'.
8. PRO: 'Menton' (H).
9. Not certain.
10. H: 'Batson' (PRO).
11. PRO: 'Handisyde' (H).
12. PRO (1811): 'Moythan (Mid.)', PRO (1812): 'Moytham, Field' (H).
13. 'Died before 31.8.'09' (Bu): but still living in 1811 (PRO).
14. H: 'Rose' (PRO).

V. MEDICAL BRANCH

1. All appointed by Warrant.
2. Depot Surgeon, Verdun.
3. M. Name wrong, but probably a real person: possibly Hammet, John, Ass. Surg., R.N.; more likely Hunt, John, of the Merchant Navy.
4. A Naval Surgeon of 1781: very possibly a *détenu*.
5. Volunteered to help Wolfe at Givet.
6. Ho's Surgeon.
7. Or perhaps Es.
8. Perhaps later: possibly even after end of war.
9. Till 1806 Surgeon's Mates; thereafter Assistant Surgeons.
10. Bu. According to H, in 1808. 'Now a Rector' (El).
11. H—wrongly—says 'D 8.2.'03'.
12. H: 'Heydon' (PRO).
13. NL: 'James' (H).
14. D of wounds received in duel with Surgeon Abbot.

VI. PURSERS

1. Appointed by Warrant.
2. M the only authority.
3. John in M and in Minutes of Court which sentenced him to the galleys: but only Robert appears in NL. Escape date in PRO.

VII. WARRANT OFFICERS

1. Appointed by Warrant: the trio of 'standing' officers to be found in every R.N. ship.
2. H: 'Lumm' (PRO).
3. H: 'Came' (PRO).

LIST II
OFFICER PRISONERS OF WAR
B. ARMY

The following abbreviations denote regiments, etc.:
D, Dragoons. F, Regiments of Foot. LG, Life Guards. RE, Royal Engineers.
KGL, King's German Legion. DG, Dragoon Guards. FG, Foot Guards.
RA, Royal Artillery. WIR, West Indian Regiments. EICS, East India Co.'s Service.

I. GENERAL OFFICERS

(t) Blayney, Andrew, Lord, Maj.-Gen.   (t) Paget, Sir Edward, Maj.-Gen.
       89 F, PE   80 F, PE
 Murray, Thomas, Lieut.-Gen.
   7 Roy. Vet. Batt., PE

II. FIELD OFFICERS

(a) COLONELS

(d) [Crumford, —[1]   Es (Aix) '12]   Stafford, John   63 F
(d) D'Ivory, —[2]   —

(b) LIEUTENANT-COLONELS

Berniere, Henry de	9 F	Hill, George	3 FG
Cox, William[3]	61 F	Milman, Francis M.[5]	
(d) FitzGerald, J. F.[4]	60 F		2 FG (R Jan. '14)
Gordon, Thomas W.	3 FG	Pelly, Raymond	16 D
Guard, William	45 F	Sheridan, Sir William W.	2 FG
Hall, Gage John	7 WIR	Wyndham, Thomas Norton	1 DG

(c) MAJORS

Fotheringham, Thomas Ogilvy		(d) Green, E. J. R.[4]	10 F
	3 FG	L'Estrange, Guy	31 F
(d) Grant, Colquhoun[4]	11 F	Popham, Samuel Taylor	24 F

III. COMPANY OFFICERS, ETC.

(a) CAPTAINS

Albandini, Frederick	Roy. Malta	Classon, Samuel	53 F (D 30.3.'09)
Allen, James	23 D	Clossiers, Frederick	Roy. Malta
Allman, Francis	48 F	Coleman, George F. C.	31 F
Andrews, Thomas	24 F	Collis, Charles	24 F
Barrow, George	15 F	Combe, W. M.[8]	[Es 11.12.'11]
Belli, John H.	16 D	Conran, William	21 F
(t) Blair, Thomas Hunter	91 F	During, E. Ba(ron?)[9]	
Boothby, Charles			KGL (1 Batt.), L.I.
	RE (Es, Ex or R before '13)	Erskine, Robert	4 F
Brice, George Tite	3 DG	Evans, Thomas	38 F
Callender, James[6]	88 F	Falconer, H.	1 F
Campbell, P.	48 F	Fenata, Filipi Teston	Roy. Malta
Cary, William[7]	85 F (D 25.10.'04)	Ferguson, (Sir) Adam	58 F[9]

K   289

(a) CAPTAINS—*continued*

	Fraser, Alexander	RE	Matthews, Ponsonby	47 F
	Geils, Thomas	3 FG	Morres, Redmond	13 D
	Godfrey, Sampson	1 F	Morrison, William	43 F
(d)	[Good, Thomas[10]		Orchard, Daniel	9 F
	(Cavalry) Es 5.8.'09]		Patison, Andrew[12]	29 F
	Goodsman, David	61 F	Percy, Hon. Henry	14 D
	Hartley, Andrew	61 F	Phillips, John Lewis	4 D
	Haviland, Charles de	Roy. Malta	Reynolds, James 83 F (D 27.12.'12)	
	Hawker, Peter Ryves	30 F	Roberts, Thomas	30 F
	Hewit(t), T. W.	6 F	(d) Sarjant, G. H.[13] 9(?) F [Es 17.9.'07]	
	Howard, Thomas Phipps	23 D	Shaw, Robert Henry[14]	4 F
	Jackson, —	EICS (R)	Somerfield, Thomas[15]	83 F
	Jestaferrati, P.	Roy. Malta	Spear, Savil(le)	1 F
	Kerschberg, Frederick[11]		(t) Stephens, Henry William[16]	66 F
		Roy. Malta	Tarleton, H.[4]	7 F
	Laing, James	61 F	Taylor, John	RA
	Lambert, Peter Warren	9 F	Tulloh, Alexander[17]	
	Lazzarini, Lewes	Roy. Malta	RA (Es Dec. '10 (or '11))	
	Lutyens, Benjamin	11 D	Wolfe, John Antony	60 F

(b) LIEUTENANTS

	Abell, Francis	83 F	Feilde, Edmund	4 F
	Allen, Thomas[18]	24 F	Fowley, John	28 F
	Armstrong, Matthew	9 F	Friess, William	60 F
	Baker, George	16 D	Fulcher, James[25]	
	Baldwin, Robert	71 F	York LI, Vol. (D 8.11.'11)	
	Bartley, (G?)[4, 19]	50 F	(d) Gaban, Frederick[26] 1 Batt. —?	
(t)	Battl(e)y, (or Batley) George(?)[20]		Gamble, Andrew William[27]	
	D (EICS) (Es 14.9.'08)		31 F (Ex or R, 23.2.'13)	
	Beamish, Adderley	31 F	Gilbert, William	48F
	Beamish, George	31 F	Goeben, F. *Ba(ron?)*	
	Bell, Alexander Jeffry	11 F	KGL (1 Batt. line)	
	Binney, Thomas	11 D	Grant, Francis	24 F
	Birmingham, Henry	29 F	Hall, John G.	64 F
	Bodman, J. Henry	Roy. Malta	Harper, John	RE
	Boggie, Thomas[21]	83 F	Howard, Robert	30 F
	Brennan, Charles Myler[22]	14 F	Jackson, Charles	3 F
	Budd, Thomas	28 F	Johnson, Francis[28]	83 F
	Busett, Francis[23]	Roy. Malta	Jones, Harry D.	RE
	Canehi, L.	Roy. Malta	Kirwan, Richard[29]	7 F
	Carden, Henry	1 D	Kitchen, James	EICS Artil.
	Clarke, John[24]	? [Es 11.12.'10]	Kitcher, Frederick[30]	Roy. Malta
	Clarke, Thomas[24]	6 F	Klossuis, Frederick[30]	Roy. Malta
	Clarke, William[24]	6 F	(t) Lestrange, Edmund[31]	
	Collins, Graves	61 F (Ex or R)	71 F (Es Feb. '12)	
	Couchi, Luize	Roy. Malta	Lewis, Robert	15 F
	Craufurd, H. S.[4]	20 F	MacFarlane, (John?)	
	Daly, H. R.	64 F	(16 F?) (Es July '11)	
	Dormer, E. P.	14 D	Mackay, Angus[32]	21 F
	Elwood, —	48 F	Mackay, George	48 F
	Eyre, Charles	1 F	McNab, James	21 F

b) LIEUTENANTS—*continued*

Magill,[4] J.[33]	38 F	Ryan, Thomas	50 F
Mitchell, Robert	60 F	Sach, George	48 F
Moody, Charles	36 F	(d) Saintcroix, Charles[35]	RA
(t) Mordaunt, Charles	61 F	Sanderson, George	9 F
Morgan, Herbert	66 F	Schloger, Louis[36]	
Morris, Apollos	66 F		Roy. Malta (D 6.9.'12)
Moss, John Irving	13 D	(t) Sheehy, Roger	89 F (Es Oct. '13)
Muter, Robert	7 F	Shipley, George	97 F
Nicholson, John[34]		Simpson, Alexander	9 F
	83 F (Ex or R 23.2.'13)	Skeene, Alexander[27, 37]	
Page, William Edward	7 F		24 F (Ex or R)
(t) Penrice, John	15 D	Smith, Joseph	65 F
Power, John[4]	50 F	Stanhope, Charles	29 F
Prater, Thomas[35]	21 F	(t) Tench, Edward	
Prochaska, Ph.	Roy. Malta		3 Ceylon Ri. (K.m 27.12.'10)
Reeve, Thomas	48 F	Tench, Henry	61 F
Reynolds, Charles	5 WIR	Wallace, Peter	Roy. Malta
Richardson, George	4 F	Welsh, Joseph Robert[38]	6 WIR
Richter, E. F.	Roy. Malta	Whitley, James	9 F
Rodmer, J. H.	Roy. Malta	Wood, Frederick	11 D
Roy, James Aaron	71 F		

c) ENSIGNS

Alston(e), James[4]	1 F	Pennefather, William[42]	3 F
Altenstein, Henry[39]	60 F	Perrin, James Barrington[43]	2 F
Butler, Theobald[40]	87 F (D 1.7.'13)	Perry, Henry	Roy. Malta
Campbell, Colin	26 F	Rochaska, P. Antony	Roy. Malta
Davis, George Lenox	9 F	Scott, William Henry[44]	3 FG
Fitz-Gibbon, Robert	3 F	Seaver, Jonathan Pockeridge	15 F
Freeman, Charles Earle	69 F	Stothert, William[45]	2 FG
(t) Graham, William	4 F (Es 30.9.'12)	Sullivan, William	30 F
Launie, Henry[41]	26 F	Sutton, Peter	9 F
Letoller, Henry	83 F	Syret, J.[4]	9 F
Loppinot, John Claude de	16 F	Thompson, Robert Gordon	9 F
Moulson, Edward	89 F	Watts, Charles	89 F
(t) Newenham, Edward Worth	9 F		

IV. MEDICAL BRANCH

a) SURGEONS

Banks, Clement	Roy. Malta	(t) Johnson, John[48]	
Brown, Thomas[46, 47]	26 F (R)		9 F (Es by shamming madness)
Cammillia, Francis	Roy. Malta	McDowall, Alexander[47]	Staff (R)
Higgens, Samuel[47]	Staff (R)		

b) ASSISTANT SURGEONS

Armstrong, Archibald Nicolls	26 F	Cowan, Henry[47]	23 D (R
Blake, Andrew	98 F	Depper, Frederick[47]	
Brugemann, Sufferd[49]			5 Batt. KGL (R)
	7 Batt. KGL	Dunne, James[47]	53 F (R)
Coleman, J.	3 DG	Elkington, J. G.[47]	24 F (R)

(*b*) ASSISTANT SURGEONS—*continued*

(d) Fiorillo, Frederick[47, 50]

	9 Hus. KGL (R)	Mahoney, Mont.[47]	7 F (R)
Glasco, John[47]	83 F (R)	O'Meally, James[47]	16 D (R)
Gregory, John	RA	Rule, Thomas[47, 52]	87 F (R)
Herriott, John[47]	61 F (R)	Walker, Thomas[47]	52 F (R)
Kirby, Edward[47, 51]	27 F (R)	Winter, George (Hospital Pur-	
		veyor)[47]	(R)

V. OTHERS

(*a*) QUARTERMASTERS

McCoy, John[53]	Roy. Malta	Richards, Thomas	4 F

(*b*) PAYMASTERS

Butcher, John	6 F	Hall, Henry William	9 F

(*c*) ARTILLERY STORE-KEEPERS

Bartley, William	RA	Langley, Renny	RA

(*d*) CHAPLAIN

Bertis, J.	Roy. Malta

1. M only. Existence doubtful, and, if real, his name.

2. Wo only—'Commanding Engineers in English Army in Portugal'. Query name? Perhaps 'D'Ivernois'.

3. 'Lt.-Col.' (H) 'Commissary' (PRO), 'Ci-devant Governor of Almeida' (St).

4. Possibly not captured.

5. Brother of Dean Milman: R at instance of Jenner.

6. Also called 'Callendar': of Arding-las; Es, but recaptured and sent to Ham.

7. Sometimes 'Cory'.

8. Es in M only.

9. AL: 'E. P. During, 5th Batt.' (H). 'H. B. During, 1 Batt. LHGS' (PRO).

10. M only. Es, and even existence, doubtful.

11. PRO: 'Kertsburg' (H).

12. PRO and AL: 'Pattison' Ste.

13. Name as in H: probably M's 'Sargent, Phil., Es 17.9.'07' is same person.

14. Ste: 'Henry' only (PRO): 'H. J.' (H).

15. Ste: 'Summerfield' (AL): 'Summersfield' (PRO).

16. Compiler of Ste.

17. Es fairly well established. This form of the name is in AL and M. Alger has 'Tulloch, Francis, Es Dec. '08': probably the same officer.

18. Perhaps Es or R in first half of 1813.

19. No name or initial in AL (1813) where he is shown as 'missing' in Spain. In the same regiment in 1824 is a 'G. Bartley', a Captain and Paymaster.

20. The Es is certain.

21. AL, H and PRO: 'Buggie' (Ste).

22. Ste: 'Brannan' (AL): 'Brennan, Rd. M.' (H).

23. PRO: 'Bucere, Fras.' (H).

24. The last two—both in Ste—seem certain. John is in H, but without a regiment, and also in M (Es 11.12.'10). But it is possible that 'John' is one of the other two.

25. PRO records death; but AL seems to show, living, in 1813.

26. H. only: no regiment. Query name?

27. 'Left Verdun for England 23.2.'13' (Ste).

28. AL: 'Charles' (Ste): 'Johnston, Francis' (H).

29. AL, PRO and H: 'A. Kirwan' (Ste).

30. The first H, the second PRO. Could they be the same?

31. AL: 'Edward' (H).

32. AL and H: 'Robert' (Ste).

33. AL: in another place in AL 'M'Gill'.

34. 'Obtained a passport and left Verdun for England' (Ste).

35. H. Query surname or regiment?

36. PRO: 'Schlozer, Lewis' (H).

37. AL. and H: 'John' (Ste).

38. AL, Ste and H: 'Walsh', PRO.

39. H: 'Allenstein' (PRO). 'Baron L. F. von Stein Altenstein' (Ste).

40. Ste: 'Theodore' (H).

41. AL, PRO and Ste: 'Laurie' (H).

42. Ste: 'Pennyfather' (H): 'Penny-feather' (PRO): 'Penefather' (AL).

43. AL: 'Perry, Barrington' (Ste).

44. H, and PRO and AL: 'William Francis' (Ste).

45. 'Killed at Waterloo' (Ste).

46. AL: 'John' (H).

47. One of the 16 Surgeons and Assistant Surgeons released in a batch in December 1813.

48. AL and Ste: 'Johnston, James' (H): 'Johnson, James' (PRO).

49. AL: 'Bruggeman, Henry' (H).

50. Name and regiment doubtful.

51. H: 'Curby' (AL).

52. H: 'Rule, R' (AL).

53. H: 'Mackay, John' (PRO).

SOME OF THE *DÉTENUS*

The column headed '*Place*' shows where individuals are known to have been confined. They are set down in known order of time. Thus 'Verdun' usually comes first: and, if the captive was released, or escaped, the last-mentioned place is usually that from which he got away. The principal detention places are abbreviated thus:

AR	Arras	CA	Cambrai	OR	Orleans	VA	Valenciennes
AU	Auxonne	GI	Givet	PA	Paris	VE	Verdun
BE	Besançon	LO	Longwy	SA	Sarrelibre		
BI	Bitche	MO	Montdauphin	SE	Sedan		
BR	Briançon	NI	Nîmes	TO	Tours		

The towns not included in this list are given in full. A date, by itself, in column '*Remarks*', indicates the last-known date of his residence.

A. SERVICE OFFICERS DETAINED

I. NAVY

Name and Rank	Place	Remarks
Crosdale, T. P., Lieut.	VE	Es 1811
Darby, Thomas, Purser (?)	AR	[Es 23.4.'09 (M)]. Perhaps same as Darby, T. E. (*q.v.* p. 299).
Grey, Thomas, Surg.	VE, TO	R with Brenton, 1806.
Hart, John, Lieut.	VA	[Es 14.8.'09 (M)]. Query, ever a prisoner?
Miller, Simon, Capt.	VE	PE
Nanny, Lewis, Lieut.	VE, AR	Es 1807 (H), 14.8.'09 (M).
Nicholson, James, Capt., RM	VA	[Es 4.11.'03 (M, who calls him Lieut.-Col.)].
Noel, John, Ass. Surg.	BE	D 4.5.'11. Perhaps Newall, John, and perhaps p.o.w.
(t) Phillips, Molesworth, Lieut.-Col. RM	VE	R 1806 (interest of Sir Joseph Banks).
Prescott, Thomas Leveson, Lieut.	VE, Metz, SA	Es 1813 (H): PE (O).
Skinner, Joseph, Surg.	VE?	PE?
Taylor, Charles, Ass. Surg.	VE	—
Welsh (Robert?)	GI	(Wi.) Perhaps on Active List.
Yeo (Sir), James Lucas, Lieut.	VE	Ex 1804. Sent home on parole!

II. ARMY

(It is highly likely that some of the officers in this list—especially the Colonels and Majors from *Le Moniteur*—were really Militia officers.)

Name and Rank	Place	Remarks
(t) Abercromby, John, Col.	VA, VE	Prom. M-Gen. at VE and Ex, 1806.
(t) Annesley, Hon. Arthur, Col. (and wife)	VE, PA	Es 1811.

Name and Rank	Place	Remarks
Auhagen, William, Lieut., 2 DG	VE	H: 'Auhagen, G.' (PRO, who calls him '*détenu*').
Bannatyne, —, Capt.	VE	Possibly same as 'Bramatyne, Hon. Mr': *q.v.*
(d) Benson, Richard (?), Capt., or Bonson	VA	[Es 18.11.'03 (M, which describes him as 'Cap. Irlandais reformé')]
Burke, F., Major	VE	'Ex Austrian Army' (PRO).
Carroll, —., Capt.	VE	—
Chetham, —., Capt. (Guards)	VE	—
Cope, Reilly (?), Col. (and family)	VE, VA	Botanist. Went mad.
(t) Crawford, —., General	TO	R 1806. Probably correct, the authority being Di, not M. Perhaps Lieut.-Gen. Sir Charles C., brother of Sir James C. (*q.v.*), and Gen. Sir Robert C.
(d) [Dallon, William, Officer	VA	Es 20.6.'09 (M). Perhaps Dillon, William (*q.v.*)]
Dexall, —., Capt. (and family)	VA	1811.
(t) Dillon, Henry, Col. (late Irish Brigade)	VE	Previously *French* Irish Brigade. French agent (Ja).
Elrington, R. George, Capt. 47 F	VA, VE, LO	Es 23.12.'11: Lieut.-Col. by 1813.
FitzJames, —., Col.	Malines	1811.
Forbes, Charles, Major	TO	Es Aug. 1810. Probably brother of James F. (*q.v.*).
Harrington, Charles Stanhope, Earl of	VE ?, VA	Col. 1 LG, and General.
Hill, —., Col.	?	Perhaps John or Robert, brothers of Gen. Lord Hill.
Kingston, —., Major, EICS	PA, VE, Lyons	Es on road to Bitche (Di).
McDermot, Thomas, Col.	VE	D 11.9.'09.
Mackenzie, —., Major	VE ?	Es —.
Macleod, —., Col.	VE ?	Of Colbeck, R.
Macmahon, Terence, Major, 53 F	VE	PE ?
Macnamara, —., Col.	Morlaix	R Feb. '04. Perhaps John, of Llangoed, Brecon.
Molesworth, —., Col.	—	R 1804. Perhaps Lieut.-Col. the Hon. W. T.
Moore, —., Col.	Malines	1811.
Murray, Lord John, Col.	VE, PA	1811. Perhaps of the Royal Manx Fencibles.
(d) Omazza, —., Gen.	VE	1811. In PRO. Query spelling? (Possibly O'Meara, D., Major-General of 1810 ?)
Pine, G. H., Lieut.-Col., EICS	VE	1804.
Pye, —., Col.	VA	July 1812.
Reed, Alexander, Capt.	VA	[Es 18.11.'03 (M only)].

Name and Rank	Place	Remarks
Roche, —., Major	Melun, VE, BI, Malines	July 1811: an Irishman.
Ryan, —., Capt.	VE	1811
Sanchey, —., Capt., and family	VE	1811.
(t) Scott, William?, Lieut.-Gen. and family	VE, Versailles	PE. Perhaps not William, but John, father-in-law of Canning.
Sharp, Alexander, Major	VE	PE?
(d) Shipley, Sir Charles, Major-General, RE	VE	R. Query, ever a prisoner?
(t) Stack, Edward, Col. then Major-General.	VE, BI, VE	PE.
(t) Swayne, Henry or Hugh, Col., Royal Irish Artillery	VE, PA	R as Courier, 1806.
Tindal, —., Col.	VE	1804.
(d) Tuggot, —., Paymaster	VE	1811. Query spelling?
Vennell, Henry, Major 89 F (and Mrs)	VE, St Germain	1811.
(t) Whaley, William, Col.	PA, VE, Moulins	PE?
[Wheley, —., Mr	VE	1804 (Di). Perhaps same as last.]
Williams, John, Col.	VE	D 10.4.'12.
Witaker, Samuel, Capt.	VA	[Es 2.11.'03 (M).]

B. CIVILIANS

Name and Rank	Place	Remarks
Addison, —., Dr	VE	Perhaps Merchant Navy. Es, but caught.
(t) Alderson, —., Dr	VE?	Es., but had property confiscated.
Allen, —., Mr, and family	VE	1811. Gentleman.
Amflet, —., Mr	VE	1804. A cook from Brighton (Di).
(t) Anderson, —., Mr	VE	Grocer at Verdun.
Annesley, Gilbert?, Rev.	VE, Geneva	Or William? Perhaps brother of Col. A. (q.v.). D 1807.
Ashford, T.	BE	Merchant (possibly Merchant Navy).
(t) Astley, Philip	VE	Circus proprietor. Es via Italy.
Atkinson, Thomas William	VE, PA	1810. Gentleman.
Atkinson, —., Mr	VE, PA	Medical student.
Aufrere, Anthony, and family	VE, OR	1806. Antiquary and art connoisseur. Editor of *The Lockhart Letters*.
Aytow(?u)n, —., Mr	VE	1811. Possibly Richard A., father of the poet W. E. Aytoun.
Baggott, George	VE	Gentleman: 'taken at sea' (PRO), and not orig. *détenu*. D 11.9.'07.
(d) [Bagu(?e), Antoine	MO	Es 25.8.'10 (M). Merchant.]
Baine, —., Mr	AR	Merchant. Es 29.5.'09 (Bu).
Baird, Andrew, Dr	VE	Probably EICS. [Es 24.4.'09 (M).]
(t) Bance, Augustus	VE?	Business man. Es.

Name and Rank	Place	Remarks
(t) Barklimore, Archibald, Dr	VE, BI	Es 14.9.'08.
Barrington, Richard, Viscount	VA	D 1813.
Barry, Sir Edward	VE	1811.
(t) Bathe, Sir James de	VE	R (interest of the Pope).
Beamish, —., Mr	PA	1811 (PRO). Perhaps one of the two p.o.w.'s Beamish (q.v.).
Beeding, —., Mr and Mrs	VE	Gentry.
Benfield, Paul	PA	Banker. D 1810.
Bentinck, J., Rev.	PA	D 1804.
(d) [Berver, James	VA	Gentleman. Es 18.11.'03 (M).]
Bessborough, Earl of	See Duncannon, Viscount.	
(t) Beverley, Algernon Percy, Earl of	Moulins	PE—from choice ?
Biggar, Charles	VA	[Es 18.11.'03 (M).]
Billings, —., Mr	BI	c. 1808.
(d) [Blackgrove, —., Mr	VA	Es 18.9.'11 (M). May be next.]
(t) Blagrove, Peter	VE	Es to Trieste, 1808 (L). Another version gives 'Playgrove'.
Blake, —.	?	PRO gives 'prisoner' only.
Bland, Robert, Rev.	VE, PA	1811.
(d) [Blankfort, Bartholomew	NI	Es 28.12.'03 (M). Query spelling.]
Blanpied, Daniel	VE	D 16.1.'08. Merchant of Jersey.
Blaquiere, John	PA	PE. 'George' (PRO): became Baron de B., 1812.
Blaxland, —., Mr	VE	1807. Gentleman.
(t) Blount, Charles	VE, Coblenz	Perhaps Baron: perhaps not British
Blount, —.	PA, VE, PA	A student in Paris.
(d) [Blunt, —., Mr	PA	1811 (PRO). Probably same as last.]
(t) Bode, John	VE ?	—
Borel, —., Mr	VE, PA	London merchant: 'Boyel' and 'Bozel' (PRO).
(t) Bouchel, —.	BI	Of Jersey: spy and traitor. Called 'Big Williams'.
Bowens, —., Mr	VE ?, PA	1811. Gentleman ?
Boyd, Walter, Mr	VE, PA	Banker: PE.
Boyle, Lord (and Lady)	VE, PA	1813. Either George, 4th Earl of Glasgow, or his son John (see under Master's Mates).
Bramatyne, Hon. Mr	VE	1811: see above—Bannatyne.
Brodie, —.	VE, BI, Blois	Teacher of English.
(t) Brooks, Thomas, M.P.	VA	For Newton, Lancs. Es 18.11.'04.
Broughton, John	VE, PA	Later Bart. R as a courier.
(d) [Brown, Adam, Mr	VE	Merchant. Es 9.11.'11 (M).]
(d) [Brown, Th., Mr	GI	'Propriétaire.' Es 5.8.'09 (M).]
Brown, —., Mr	PA	1811. May be one of above.
Brown, —., Mr	Gorgnon	7.1811. Perhaps same as last.
(t) Burgh, —., Mr	PA	Or Burke, K.s.
Burney, Fanny (Mme d'Arblay)	Passy	Technically French, but detained till 1812.
Cadogan, Lady	VE, Nancy	Wife (divorced ?) of 4th Earl Cadogan.

Name and Rank	Place	Remarks
Campbell, —., Mr (and Mrs)	VE	1804. Gentry.
Cane, —., Mr	TO	1804 (Ja).
Carey, —., Mr	VA	July 1811
(d) [Casenove, Henry	Geneva	Es 10.12.'10 (M only).]
(d) [Casenove, James	Geneva	Es 10.12.'10 (M only).]
(d) [Cassia, Alexis	Toulouse	Es 28.12.'03 (M only).]
Chalmers, —., Mr	Bordeaux	Merchant: not molested.
Chambers, —., Mr	PA	1811. Gentleman?
Chenevix, Richard	PA	Mineralogist: barely molested, had French wife, and D in France.
Cheyne, —., Mr	VE	Kept brazier's shop at VE: may have been French (El).
Christie, John Harvey	VE	1811 (PRO). [Es 5.1.12 (M).]
Churchill, W. H., Rev.	VE?	Of Colliton, Dorset. R Jan. 1804.
Churchill, —., Mr	VE?	Brother of above. R Jan. 1804.
Clark, Thomas, Dr	VE	[Es 13.5.'12 (M)], but probably tried and failed.
Clarke, —., Mr and Mrs	VE	Gentry: 1804: he might be same as last-named.
Clavering, Sir (John?) Thomas	OR St. Germain, PA	Bart? 1811. Said to have married daughter of an Angers dressmaker.
Clifford, —., Mr	BE	Gentleman. On parole in town.
(t) Clive, Hon. Mr (and wife)	VE	R 1807. Son of Earl of Powis.
(t) Cockburn, Alexander (and wife)	VE	R 1806 (interest of Empress Josephine). Consul at Hamburg. Father of the Lord Chief Justice.
Coghill, Sir John, Bart.	PA	1813. PE.
Colclough, Caesar, Mr	VE?	PE? Later (1818) M.P.
Cole, John	BR	Quaker, of Bristol.
Columbine, Peter	VE?, PA	D 1813. Gentleman.
Concannon, Richard or Lucius? (and wife)	VE	Actor and manager: R (or Es) to Vienna.
Congreve, —., Mr	VE, OR	1811. Gentleman.
Cooper, (Sir?) William, Rev.	VE, Nancy	1811. 'Cooper, S. W.' and not 'Rev.' (PRO).
Cope, Archdall	VE?, PA, VA	1811. Student in Paris.
Cope, —.	VE?, PA, VA	Ditto. Brother of above.
Cotton, —., Mr	St Quentin	1811. Gentleman.
Cowel, —., Mr	AR	Wealthy merchant's son. Teacher in prisoners' school at VA (Wo).
Cra(e?)ighton, Dr	AR	Surg. to depot. Es 29.5.'09 (Bu).
Cramer, F., Mr	VE, TO	1811. Pacifist: allowed anywhere in France.
(t) Crawford, Sir James	Aix-la-Chapelle	Diplomat. Es Sept. '03.
Crawford, Quintin	?	Not molested. Friend of Talleyrand: cousin of last-named.
Crespigny, Philip Champion de	VE, St. Germain	Es May 1811. Gentleman.

Name and Rank	Place	Remarks
Croft, Sir Herbert, Bart. and Rev.	Amiens, PA	Author. R, but preferred to remain in France: D there, 1816.
Cromie, Sir Michael	VE, PA	1811. 'Cromy' (PRO).
(d) Dale (or Daly), Jos.	BI	'On parole in town' (El). 'Navy agent' (O). May be same as Daly, John (Purser, *q.v.*).
(t)(d) [Dalton, —., Mr	VA, BI	(L.) Almost certainly Dutton, *q.v.*]
Daniel, John, Rev.	VE, PA	1811. Ex-Pres. of Douai College.
Darby, Thomas Elde	VE, PA	Es 20.1.'14 (PRO). See Thomas Darby, under Naval *Détenus*.
Darrell, —., Mr	VE	1804. Gentleman.
(t) Davis, John Bunnell, Dr	VE	R. Treated patients at VE free.
Day, George	VA	[Es 13.12.'03 (M only).]
Delivet, Nicholas	AR, AU	Of London, interpreter (Bu). R April '09 for helping with a fire. Query spelling.
Denby, —., Mr	St Germain	1811. Gentleman.
Despard, —., Mr	VE ?, PA	1811. Gentleman.
Devenish, Thomas	VE, BI	1810. 'Sylvester' (PRO). To BI for abusing Napoleon.
Dickinson, William, Mr	VE, PA	Artist and engraver. Remained after war.
Dickinson, —., Mr	VE	Son of above: entered France secretly: R but returned, 1810.
Dillon, Henry Dillon, Theobald Dillon, William	VE and PA	Before 1811. Henry is *not* Col. Henry D. (*q.v.*): and William is not Lieut. W. H. D. (*q.v.*).
(t) Dixie, Sir Beaumont, Bart.	VE, BI, SA, VE	Es, but caught: PE.
Don, Alexander	VE, PA	Son of Scots Bart.: Es 1810 or '11.
(d) Done, Joseph	VE	Merchant. [Es VE 20.7.'10 (M).]
(t) Done, Joshua	VE, BI, BR, etc.	Student. Es 1813.
Donegal, Dow. Marchioness of	VE ?	Arrested '03: R '04.
(t) Drake, W., Mr	VE	Livery-stable keeper and clerk of the VE race-course.
Dring, John, Rev.	VE ? OR	D 1806. Rector of Heathfield, Sussex.
Duff, —., Mr	VE, Nancy	Gentleman. R 1806.
(t) Duke, —., Dr	VE	1810.
(t) Duncannon, Frederick, Viscount	VE	Earl of Bessborough, 1803: R before Nov. 1805.
Dupré, William, Mr	VE ?	Of Jersey. Author of *Lexicographia Neologica Gallia*.
(t) Dutton, (Thomas ?)	VE, BI	Perhaps Thomas D., editor of the *Argus*. L has 'Dalton'.
(t) Eardley, (Hon. ?) (Sampson ?)	VE	R 1807.
Edgeworth, —., Mr	VE, St Germain	July 1811. Not Maria E.'s father, R. L. E., but possibly a brother, Lovell.
Edwards, William	VE, Bruges, VA	1811. Jamaica planter.

Name and Rank	Place	Remarks
Egerton, Hon. Francis Henry, Rev.	VE ?, PA	1811. Later Earl of Bridgewater.
(t) Elgin, Thomas Bruce, Earl of	TO	R 1807.
Ellis, (Felix ?)	VE, Thion-ville, VE	1814. Gentleman. 'Ellice' (Alg).
Erskine, Charles, Cardinal	PA	D 1811. Legally British, and arrested on way from England to Rome.
Estwick, —, Mr	VE	1806. Gentleman.
Eyre, Edmund John	VE	Actor and dramatist.
Fagan, —., Mr	VE	1805. Spy and traitor: ex-Captain of Dillon's Regiment.
Farthing, —., Mr (and wife)	VE (SA ?)	1804. [M has 'Tritisse F.'], Es SA, 9.6.'11.
(t) Ferguson, Robert	VE	F.S.A. R 1805 (interest of Munro).
Fiol, —., Mr	Morlaix	R Feb. 1804.
Fitzgerald, —., Mr (and wife)	VE, PA, St Germain	Very wealthy gentleman. [M has 'Richard, Es May '11'.]
Fitzsimmons, —., Mr	Toulouse	1804.
Fletcher, Edward (?), and family	VE, St Germain	July 1811. Gentleman.
Forbes, C., Mr	TO	Brother of Forbes, J. (q.v.).
Forbes, Eliza, Miss	PA, VE	R 1804. Daughter of next.
(t) Forbes, James	PA, VE	Author. R 1804 (interest of Banks and Jenner) F.R.S.
(t) Forsyth, Joseph	NI, BI, VE, PA, VA	1811. Author of work on Italy.
Fortescue, Robert	VA	[Es 19.10.'03 (M).]
Foster, Augustus	VE ?	R. Gentleman ?
(d) [Fowler, William	AU	Es 25.11.'10 (M). Perhaps a Merchant Captain.]
Fox, —., Dr	VE	Perhaps Merchant Navy.
Fraser, John James	VE	Gentleman. D 19.4.'08.
Frisell, Francis	PA	Author and Francophile. R 1803, but stayed in France.
Fry, —., Mr	AR	D 29.8.'07. Ran Charity Fund at AR.
Galliers, —., Mr	GI	July 1811.
(t ?)Garland, John Watt		One of these—not Nathaniel
Garland, Nathaniel	VE	(R 1807 on interest of Jenner),
(t ?)Garland, Peter		was Wirion's victim.
Gartshaw, —., Mr and family	VE, VA	1811. Gentry.
Gerrard, Alexander, Mr	VE (TO ?)	R. (Gerrard, Capt. of an East Indiaman, was another person.)
Gibbons, Thomas	VE	D 11.8.'10. 'Cuisinier' (PRO).
(t) Giffard, John	VE	1804. Confined later as lunatic.
(d) [Gifford, —., Mr	PA	1811. Probably same as last.]
Gold, Francis, Surgeon	SA	July 1811. Perhaps same as Goold (q.v.).
(t) Goldsmith, Lewis	PA	1809. First editor of the Argus. Perhaps more 'refugee' than 'détenu'.

Name and Rank	Place	Remarks
(t) Goold, Valentine	VE	1812. R (interest of Jenner).
(t) Gorden, W., Rev.	VE	PE. Vicar of Duns Tew. Ran relief fund at VE.
Grant, —., Mr	VE	Gentleman. R 1806 (interest of Lord Lauderdale).
(t) Greathead, Henry	VE	Inventor of lifeboats. R Dec. 1804.
Greatheed, Bertie	VE, Vicenza	Dramatist. R to Italy, 1804.
Greatheed, Bertie (Jun.)	VE, Vicenza	Son of above. D 1804.
Green, William	VE?	Irish M.P.
(t) Green, —	VE	Clerk of the race-course at VE. 'Ex-highwayman' (Ja).
Gurt, —., Mr	VE?, CA	1811. Gentleman.
Haig, —., Mr	VE, SA	1804. Master of British School at SA.
(t) Halpin, John Edward	VE	1811. Actor and miniaturist. 'Edmond' (D.N.B.).
(t) Hamilton, Alexander	PA	Orientalist. R 1808.
(t) Hamilton, Lord Archibald	?	Es January 1804.
Hamilton, Hon. Gustavus	VE	1804. Afterwards 6th Viscount Boyne.
Hamilton, Hon. Mrs	VE?, SA	July 1811. Wife of above?
Harcourt, J(ohn?) S(imon?)	VA	Gentleman. [Es 18.11.'03 (M).]
Hare, Sir Thomas	VE?	R c.1805.
(d) [Harvey, Ives	VE	Es 24.6.'09. Probably same as 'Hurry' and 'Urry' (q.v.).]
Haselfoot, —., Mr	VE, Versailles	1811 [Es July 1811 (M)]. Gentleman.
Hattridge, C. R., Mr	AU	Merchant [Es 5.12.'10 (M)].
Haute(o?)nville, Mr	VE, GI, VE	1811: 'e' (Wo): 'o' (Di): 'Huntenville' (PRO).
Hay, George, Lord	Antwerp	1803. Es '03 or '04? Son of Marquis of Tweeddale: later General.
Hayes, Edward	VE, PA	1811. Miniaturist and painter.
Hayes, Samuel	VE	Detained 10 years, though nearly blind. R as 'invalide', 1813.
Hayne, William	PA	Entered France 1807, and arrested. Lace-maker.
Hearne, John Dillon	VE, Metz	D (Metz) 1807 (Di)? D (VE) 9.6.'08 (PRO). Gentleman.
Heath, James	VE, PA	1810. Engraver.
Hendry, Robert	VE, Jouy	Scottish chemist and calico expert. R by Napoleon, 1806.
Hinds, —., Mr	VE, Brussels	1809. Gentleman.
Holland, —., Mr	TO	July 1811. Gentleman.
Houghton, George (?)	AR	Merchant and banker: Es 29.5.'09.
Houghton, H. P.	AR	Head schoolmaster at AR: perhaps same as above.
Humphreys, —., Mr	VE, PA	1811.
Humphries, William	VE	Business man of Birmingham: D 1.5.'07.
Hunt, —., Rev.	TO, VE?	Chaplain to Lord Elgin.

Name and Rank	Place	Remarks
(d) [Huntenville, —., Mr	VE	1811. Probably same as 'Hautenville', q.v.]
[Hurry, see Urry]		
Hutchinson, Thomas	VE, BI, VE	Language teacher. D 9.4.'12.
Hutchinson, —., Mr	PA	1811. Probably different from above.
Hynds (or Hinds), Montague	BE	Interpreter at BE. Suspected of spying: D 27.12.'11.
Iliffe, —., Mr	BI	1809.
(t) Impey, Sir Elijah	VE ?	Chief Justice of Bengal. R (interest of Talleyrand), July 1804.
[Jackson, James	NI	Es 10.11.'03 (M only).]
[Jackson, John, Mr	VA	Gentleman. Es 3.12.'03 (M only).]
Jackson, (William ?), Rev.	VE	R 1806.
Jackson, —., Dr	VE	Brother of above. D 2.1.'07 (L): 'of a broken heart' (El).

[There may have been three other Jacksons—Edward, Mills (who may have Es), and Richard, but some may be identical with those already listed.]

Name and Rank	Place	Remarks
(t) Jennings, —., Mr (and family)	VE	1811. Horse-dealer.
Jerningham, Sir Thomas, Bart.	PA	1811.
(t) Jersey, Columbine de	?	Es on parole to England.
Jervis, John	VE, PA	1811. Engraver.
(t) Jodrell, Francis	VA	Es Nov 1803. 'Cap. du Commerce' (M). High Sheriff of Cheshire 1813.
Jodrell, Thomas	VA	Es 10.11.'03. Gentleman. (Not the same as last.)
Johnson, William	VE, BI	D there, 18.1.'08.
Johnson, —., Mr	TO	July 1811. 'Ôtage' (PRO).
Kay, Robert	AU	Merchant [Es 5.12.'10 (M).]
Kearney, —., Mr	VE, PA	1811. Gentleman.
Kemp, —., Mr	Montreuil	'On parole: lived with the Mayor' (O'B).
Kensington, —., Mr	VE ?, SA	1811.
King, —., Mr	VA	'Hotelier there for 20 years' (Bo).
(d) [Kinkaid, Pierre	SA	Es 9.6.'11 (M only).]
Kirby, Walter, Dr	PA	D at Paris.
Kirkpatrick, William (and family)	PA	Wine merchant. Detained 1808, with wife, 4 children, and 2 nieces.
Knox, Waring	VE, BI, SA, Melun, VA	D in prison for debt, Dec. 1813.
Kyd, Stewart	VE ?	Radical and Jurist. Es (?) and D (in England ?) 1811.
Lambert, two brothers	?	Freaks with scaly skins: allowed to tour France.
Langley, —., Mr	VE	1807. Gentleman.
Langton, Roger	VE, AU ?	Taken at sea, 1808: PE. [M has 'Richard L., Es AU 5.12.'10'].
Latree, —., Mr	VE, TO	July 1811. Gentleman.
Latte(i ?)n, —., Mr	VE, PA	1811. Gentleman ?

Name and Rank	Place	Remarks
(t) Lawrence, James Henry	VE, TO, OR	'Chevalier.' Es 1.1.'09.
Lawrence, Richard James	VE, Bordeaux, TO	Of Jamaica: father of above. Es October 1808 (or 1809).
(t) Lawson, W., Rev.	VE, AR, BE, VE	PE.
Layton, Richard	VE	Gentleman, of London. D 12.9.'07.
(d) [Learn, Thomas	AU	Es 30.5.'09 (M only)].
Leatham, John	VE, Nantes	Of Madras. D 1811.
(d) [Lebrun, Philippe	VA	Merchant. Es 10.11.'11 (M only).]
(t) Lee, Launcelot, Rev.	VE	1811. See Leigh, Rev.
(d) [Leigh, Philip	AR	Es 18.10.'11 (M only).]
Leigh, —., Rev.	VE	1811. Appears in same PRO list as Lee, L., Rev.
Lempriere, —., Mr (and family)	VE	1811. Probably *not* (*pace* Alger) author of the *Classical Dictionary*.
Lesoeuf, —., Mr (and family)	VE	1811.
Light, William	VE	[Es 5.1.'04 (M only).] Possibly the founder of Adelaide.
(t) Louvaine, George Percy, Lord (and two sons)	Moulins	Later Earl of Beverley and Duke of Northumberland. PE—from choice.
Lovelace, Robert, Mr	VE, VA, PA	1811. Gentleman.
(d) [Lowes, John	AU	'Propriétaire': Es 30.5.'09 (M only).]
(d) [Lucky, David	AU	'Propriétaire': Es. 30.5.'09 (M only).]
Lynch, Edward	VE	'Propriétaire': D 12.12.'10 (PRO).
(d) [Lynch, (J. B. ?)	VE	Es, but retaken at Caen: probably a French subject.]
McCarthy, —., Mr	Bordeaux	Banker. A resident? Not arrested by December 1803.
McCarthy, —., Mr	VE	May be same as last.
Macculloch, James	Brittany	Resident for 35 years, and not molested.
McIntosh, —., Mr	VE, VA	1808.
Mackenzie, —., Mr	VE	1811.
Maclean, Charles, Dr	PA	Arrested while attending Conference, but R 13.12.'03.
Macnab, Henry Grey	Montpellier	Publicist. Scholar. PE, and till death in 1823.
Mainy, Henry	VE	'Étudiant of London' (PRO). D 22.3.'08.
Malisson, W. H., Mr	VA	[Es. 18.12.'03 (M only).] Perhaps 'Malleson'.
(t) Manning, Thomas	PA	Traveller. R 1803 (interest of Carnot and Talleyrand).
Marto(i ?)n, —., Mr	VE	1811.
Masterson, John	Brussels	In French-Irish Regiment before Revolution.
Maude, John Barnabas, Rev.	VE	PE. Fellow of Queen's College, Oxford.

Name and Rank	Place	Remarks
(d) [Maunde, John (later Rev.)	VE ?	R 1807: D 1813. Probably a confusion with last.]
May, —., Dr	VE	1811.
Me(?a)guire, Michael	VE	Coiffeur (?). D 21.1.'08.
Mellish, —. (two brothers)	OR	
Melville, —., Mr	BI	Prisoner there, 1812 (J).
Milne, James, Mr	?	Master cotton-spinner, not molested.
Mingay, —., Mr	TO	July 1811. Query 'Maingay'?
(d) Mocout, —., Mr	VE	1811. [PRO. Query spelling?]
(t) Mogg, —., Mr	AR	Es 1810 unsuccessfully, but R.
Montgomerie, George	VE ? PA ?	R. Gentleman.
Montgomerie, Thomas	VE ? PA ?	R. Gentleman.
(d) [Montgomery, —., Mr	PA	1811. Probably one of the above.]
Moore, John, Mr	VE ?	R.
Moore, —., Mr (and wife)	BI	Es 1810. Wife imprisoned for it.
Morgan, John, Dr	VE, Versailles	[Es 1810 (M only).]
Morshead, Sir John, Bart.	VE ?	R, but D 1813.
Motley, —., Mr	VE	1811.
Mount, —., Mr	VE	1806.
Mount Cashell, Stephen, 2nd Earl of (and Lady)	VE ?	Arrested in Italy, 1803.
(d) Mounteney, Dasci	VE	Merchant [Es 2.5.'09 (M)]. Query 'Dasci': same as next?
Mouteney, De, —., Mr	VE	1807. M probably right as to surname.
Mulvey, Farrell, Dr	VE, BI ?	Attempted Es, but failed.
Murdock, —.	SA ?	'Prisoner' (PRO). Perhaps Patrick, at SA in 1808 (G).
Murton, Thomas Howlett	VE	Painter (London). D 16.2.'11.
Neilson, Robert	VE	Irish gentleman: D 27.8.'07
(t) Newcastle, Dowager Duchess of	TO	R 1807.
(t) Newcastle, Henry Pelham Clinton, Duke of	TO	R 1807.
Newland, (Gideon ?), Mr	Nancy	1804. Gentleman.
Nicholl, John	VE, Lyons	Ex-M.P. for Tregony.
Nicholl, (John ?)	VE, Lyons	Son of above. R to get married.
Nicholls, —., Mr	AR	Hostage, 1808: R 22.4.'09.
(d) O'Byrne, John	Aix	[Es 19.12.'03 (M, who also has 'O'Lyrne').]
O'Connell, Daniel Charles (and wife)	VE, PA	1811. Uncle of the 'Liberator'. PE, a true *détenu*.
O'Kel(l ?)y, John	VE	'Cordonier of Bristol.' D 8.5.'09.
Oliphant, Edward	VE ?	—
(t) Oliver, Richard	VE ?	Ex-M.P. for Limerick.
Onslow, —., Mr	VE ? PA	1811. Gentleman.
Osborn, —., Mr	Weimar	1806. F.R.S.
(d) Ossene, —., Mr	Gorgnon	1811 (PRO). Query spelling?
Owens, Charles S.	VE	[Es 5.1.'04 (M only).]

Name and Rank	Place	Remarks
Pace, Vincent	VE	Hostage, arrested Hamburg, '12: probably a privateer.
Palmer, —., Mr	VE ? PA	1811. Taken at sea in American ship.
Parker, —., Mr	?	Owner of French estate: a resident.
(t) Parry, James	Arles, VE	Ex-editor of *Courier*: cripple. D 1805.
Parry, John	VE ?	R 1809. Gentleman.
Paterson, George Matthew	VA, Lille	Irish by birth, but probably American citizen.
Payne, James	PA	Bookseller. D 1809.
Phillips, —., Mr	VE, PA	1811. Gentleman.
Phillips, —.	AR	Hastings publican, captured by privateer off-shore, 1808.
(t) Pinkerton, John	VE ?	Antiquary and historian. R (interest of Banks and Jenner), 1805.
Plant, —., Dr	BE	1813.
(t) [Playgrove, Peter, see Blagrove, Peter.]		
Poppleton, —., Mr	Caen	Teacher of English.
Potter, Christopher	PA	1811. Introduced printing on porcelain and glass in France.
Powell, —., Mr	Boulogne	Elderly miner (Wi).
(t) Pratt, S. (and wife)	Amiens	1804. Eating-house keeper.
Priestley, —., Mr	BI	*c.* 1808–9.
Quinn, —., Mr	VE, PA	1811. Gentleman.
(d) [Raikes ? Richard, Mr	VA	Es 18.11.'03 (M only, who has 'Raisches')].
Rainsford, —., Mr (and wife)	VE	1811. 'Very wealthy' gentleman.
Ramsey, John (and family)	VE	1811. Gentleman.
Rice, —., Mr	AR	Resident cotton-weaver, Brittany. Arrested '06: D 19.6.'06.
(d) Richards, Benjamin	NI	[Es 18.9.'03 (M only).]
(d) Richardson, Samuel	Marseilles	[Gentleman. Es 18.9.'03 (M only).]
Ritso, —., Mr (and family)	VE	1811. Di: 'Retso' (PRO). Gentry.
Robins, —., Mr	Cherbourg	Tavern-keeper (resident). 1806.
(d) Robinson, Elise (?) (Ellis?)	VE	[Es 17.3.'09. Gentleman (M only).]
Robson, —., Mr	NI	Ex-M.P. R November 1803.
(d) [Rochefort, Granc.	VA	Es 19.10.'03 (M only).]
Roget, Peter Mark, Dr	Geneva	Physician and savant. R July 1803.
Roseve, —., Mr	VE, VA	July 1811.
Rudary, —., Mr	VE	1811.
Rumbold, Sir George	Hamburg, PA	British Minister; seized outside French territory, 25.10.'04, and sent prisoner to Paris. Soon R.
Russell, William, Mr	Ardennes (Normandy)	PE. Merchant and reformer.
St Croix, Edward	VE	Merchant, of Jersey, D 22.4.'08.
Sayer, Augustin	?	Detained 1803, aged 12. Later physician and medical author.
Sayer, John	Spa	Domestic servant. [Es 28.12.'03 (M only).]

Name and Rank	Place	Remarks
Scot(t ?), —., Mr	Morlaix	R Feb. 1804. Gentleman.
(d) [Scott, Stokes J.	NI	Es 18.9.'03 (M only).]
(t) Sevright, (Thomas ?), Mr	Nancy, VE, VA, GI(?)	Brit. agent, Helvoetsluys. R Jan. 1812.
Seymour, Henry	VE, Melun, PA	M.P. R to Switzerland, 1809.
Seymour, —., Mr	VE, PA	1811. Gentleman.
(t) Shaftesbury, Anthony, Earl of	PA	R 1804 (interest of Banks and Jenner).
(d) Sharp, Ch. Jos.	VA	[Es 2.11.'03 (M only).]
Sharp, Cuthbert	VE, PA	Antiquary. R (interest of Regnier) to PA, 1804, and then England.
(d) [Shuten, —.	VA	Es 18.11.'03, but recaptured. (M only: also query name.)]
Slack, —., Mr	VE, VA	July 1811.
Sloper, Granby	VE	Detained 1803: soon R, but re-arrested '06.
Smith, James	PA	Filter-maker: in Temple Prison, PA, 1804.
Smith, James	PA ?	Printer. Not molested. Perhaps the 'Smith, Engraver' allowed to PA before 1811.
Smith, John William	BI	'Hostage' at BI, 1810.
(d) [Smith, Robert, Lieut.-Col.	VA	Es 18.11.'03 (M). Probably same as Smyth (q.v.).]
(d) [Smith, Thomas	VE	Merchant. Es 16.12.'09 (M).]
Smith, Timothy	VE	1806. May well be same as last.
(t) Smyth, —., Mr	VA	Es November '03. Probably Robert, whom M calls 'Lt.-Col. Smith'.
Smyth, Carmichael, Dr	PA	R (interest of French physicians).
Standfast, —., Mr	VA	1803. Merchant.
(d) Stanfurd, C. G. C., Mr	VA	[Es 18.11.'03 (M only).] Perhaps same as last.
(t) Stanhope, John Spencer	VE, PA	R (and Es) March 1813. Gentleman.
Stedman, James John Rousseau	VE	'Propriétaire', London. D 11.10.'10.
Stirling, Sir Walter, Bart.	VE ?	M.P. for St Ives. R before 1807.
Stoddart, Laurence	VE, PA	A paralytic. Allowed to PA before 1811.
Stone, John Hurford	PA	Pro-French printer: naturalized during war.
Stone, Thomas	PA	Refugee from justice. Tried in France for forgery. D 1815.
Stone, William	PA ?	Brother of Stone, J. H. ? Tried in England and fled to France.
Storer, —., Mr	?	Jamaica planter. Es on road to Verdun, 1803.
Story, William (and family)	VE	1811. Chemist. (PRO calls him 'Captain').
(t) Stuckey, —., Mr	VE	Keeper of tailor's shop.
(t) Sturt, Charles	VE, Meaux	Magistrate and M.P. Es 1810.

Name and Rank	Place	Remarks
Style, Lady	St Omer	Widow of Sir Charles Style. D 1803.
(t) Sutton, —., Capt.?	Calais	Commander of Dover packet. Es.
(d) Sweeny, George	BI	Gentleman (from Cork). D 23.6.'06. Query first letter, which looks like 'B' in PRO.
(t) Talbot, Thomas	PA	Committed suicide by carbon poison, 1806.
Tarver, John Charles	—	Aged 13. PE. Educated in France. Later Eton master and author.
Tasbourg, —., Mr	VE ? PA	1811.
Taylor, —.	VE	Founded a club: perhaps Charles T., Ass. Surg., *détenu* (*q.v.*).
Temple, Sir Gre(n ?)ville, Bart.	VE	R to Switzerland and (1810) America.
Thompson, —, Mr	OR	PE. M.P. (for Evesham ?).
Thro(c)kmorton, —., Mr	VE, PA, BI	1812. Gentleman.
Tichborne, Sir Henry	VE, TO, PA	1811.
Tichborne, James, Mr	PA	1811.
(d) Toweley, William	AU	['Propriétaire. Es 30.5.'09' (M).] Query, 'Towneley' ?
(t) Trench, Richard	VE, OR	Barrister, husband of Melesina T. who secured his R 1807.
Tufton, Hon. Charles	VE	PE. Became 10th Earl of Thanet.
Tufton, Hon. Henry	VE	PE. Became 11th and last Earl of Thanet.
(t) Tuthill, George Leman, Dr	VE	Later 'Sir'. R *c.* 1807.
(t) Tweeddale, Marchioness of	VE	D 1804.
(t) Tweeddale, George Hay, 7th Marquis of	VE	D 9.8.'04.
Tyndale, —., Mr	VE	1811.
Underwood, James Richard	VE, PA	PE. Wrote account of taking of Paris, 1814.
Urry, Ives	VE	Founded club at VE. Es 1808 (also called Harvey and Hurry).
Walker, —., Mr	NI	1804.
(t) Wallace, Sir Thomas	VE	1811.
(t) Waller, John	VE, NI	Ex.-M.P. (Limerick ?). R.
Wallop, Hon. Coulson	VE, BI, VE	Son of Earl of Portsmouth. D 30.12.'07.
Ward, William	VA	English swindler. PE, though over 80.
Warwick, —., Mr	VE	1811.
Watson, —., Mr (and family)	VE	July 1811. Gentry.
(d) Weaver, Charles	VA	[Es 2.11.'03 (M only).]
Webb, Sir Thomas, Bart (and Lady)	Lyons	R to Savoy, 1809.
White, William, Rev.	VE	Of Lancaster. D 1806.
(d) [White, W.	VA	Es 2.11.'03 (M only).]
Whiteway, Joseph	BE, BI, BE	October 1810.
Whitlock, —., Mr	VE, PA	1811. Gentleman.
Wickham, —., Dr	VE ?	R (interest of Jenner).

307

Name and Rank	Place	Remarks
Widmer (two brothers)	VE ?	Nephews of Hendry, Robert, *q.v.* R 1811.
Wigney, —., Mr	VE	1804. Of Brighton.
(t) Wilbraham, —., Mr	VE, PA	R 1806. Gentleman.
Wilks, —., Mr	TO	July 1811. Gentleman.
Williams, William Thomas	VE, Nancy	1804. R (interest of Jenner). Gentleman.
(t) Williams, —.	BI	1808. Spy. Probably same as Bouchel, *q.v.*
Willison, —., Mr	Dunkirk	1807. Banker. Perhaps Dutch.
(d) Wilson, Andrew	NI	Artist ? [Es 14.9.'03 (M only).]
Wilson, Edmund	—	Aged 3. Deserted by parents and became French.
(d) Wilson, John	VA	[Es 2.11.'03 (M only).]
(t) Wilson, Stephen, Mr	VE	1804. Gentleman.
Wilson, —., Mr	VE, BI	Sent to BI for turning back on stage, 1807. May be one of the other Wilsons.
Witherden, —., Mr (and family)	VE	1811. Gentry.
(t) Wolfe, Robert, Rev. (and family)	VE, GI	R January 1812.
Wolseley, Charles	Spa	Es 28.12.'03.
Wolseley, Charlotte	VE	Sister of Sir William W., Bart.
Wolseley, Elizabeth	VE	Sister of above.
Wolseley, Henry	VE	1804. Son of Sir William W.
Woodford, John Alexander	VE ?	Son of Sir Ralph W., Bart.
Woodyatt, George	VE, PA	Before 1811. Student, later Dr.
Worsley, Israel	Dunkirk	Unitarian minister. Es 1806.
(t) Wright, William	VE	Student. Es.
(t) Yarmouth, Francis Charles, Lord	VE, PA	R 1806. Son of Marquis of Hertford.

INDEX

INDEX

GEORGE ALLEN & UNWIN LTD

London: 40 Museum Street, W.C.1

Auckland: 24 Wyndham Street
Bombay: 15 Graham Road, Ballard Estate, Bombay 1
Buenos Aires: Escritorio 454-459, Florida 165
Calcutta: 17 Chittaranjan Avenue, Calcutta 13
Cape Town: 109 Long Street
Hong Kong: F1/12 Mirador Mansions, Kowloon
Ibadan: P.O. Box 62
Karachi: Karachi Chambers, McLeod Road
Madras: Mohan Mansions, 38c Mount Road, Madras 6
Mexico: Villalongin 32-10, Piso, Mexico 5, D.F.
Nairobi: P.O. Box 12446
New Delhi: 13-14 Asaf Ali Road, New Delhi 1
São Paulo: Avenida 9 De Julho 1138-Ap. 51
Singapore: 36c Prinsep Street, Singapore 7
Sydney, N.S.W.: Bradbury House, 55 York Street
Toronto: 91 Wellington Street West

NAPOLEON

EMIL LUDWIG

Ludwig was not an historian; he was a master in the art of delineating character. He did not attempt to write either the objective history of a man or the objective history of an epoch. His 'Napoleon' is the INNER history of a man, projected against the background of a tumultuous epoch—which the man did so much to make tumultuous! It is a book more true to life than most histories, and more interesting and readable and vivid than most novels. Those who read it will not only gain a better understanding of Napoleon and his epoch; many of them will gain a clearer understanding of themselves and our own time.

'Brilliantly written. . . . The writer has the supreme art of the biographer.'—*Daily Express*

'A dazzling representation . . . there can be no doubt about the brilliance of it.'—*Liverpool Post*

'A good book admirably translated . . . Ludwig brings the facts home to us more vividly than any other book we can call to mind.'—*New Statesman*

'A marvellous history . . . a masterpiece.'—*Spectator*

12*th impression. Demy 8vo.* 30*s. net*

DAILY LIFE IN PERU UNDER THE LAST INCAS

LOUIS BAUDIN

Translated by WINIFRED BRADFORD

The Inca Empire that was long established in Peru prior to its discovery by the Spanish conquistadors is one of the most astonishing pieces of racial organization the world has ever seen. Louis Baudin, a world authority on this subject, reconstitutes with great vividness every aspect of public and private life in this over-perfect but rather melancholy civilization.

Illustrated. Demy 8vo. 28*s. net*

NAPOLEON'S CAMPAIGNS IN ITALY

R. G. BURTON

5*th impression.* 12*s.6d. net*

DAILY LIFE IN FRANCE UNDER NAPOLEON

JEAN ROBIQUET

Translated from the French by VIOLET M. MACDONALD

When an epoch is crowded with history much of its intimate life is lost to us. During the almost uninterrupted wars of the Consulate and the Empire the great events obscure the little ones; the soldier outshines the civilian, as the epic does the chronicle of manners. In most memoirs of the time we are taken at a gallop across Europe, but we are given no glimpse of what is going on in the houses of the Rue Saint-Denis, under the red umbrellas of the Halles and the elms of the Mall in the provinces.

But since everything in history is interconnected, the infinitely small with the infinitely great, it is not a matter of indifference to know how ordinary French citizens spent their days and nights, dressed, gossiped, amused themselves, tied their cravats and wove their intrigues, enjoyed Frascati's ices and the novels of Mme. Cottin, made fortunes at the Bourse or ruined themselves at *biribi*. We may learn much by following the housewife to market and glancing at the artisan at his bench. From the beginning of the Consulate the evolution of taste, ideas and manners appears closely linked with the fortunes and development of the régime. Domestic comfort, public safety, gaiety of the street, luxury of the drawing-room, all these issued from the hands of the Master, everything seems to have been prepared and directed by him, and on the walls of the home, throughout his reign, the shadow of the little cocked hat is seen to fall.

Demy 8vo. Illustrated. About 25s. net

DAILY LIFE IN EIGHTEENTH CENTURY ITALY

MAURICE VAUSSARD

Translated from the French by MICHAEL HERON

Maurice Vaussard has produced an engagingly realistic account of the conditions of life in town and country, from north to south, and in all levels of society. He describes travel conditions, houses, love and marriage, education, intellectual life, crime and punishment, entertainment and carnivals, religious and military life, the state of industry and wages levels, and the cost of living, amongst many other essential and absorbing topics. The illustrations are almost all by eighteenth century artists.

Demy 8vo. Illustrated. About 28s. net

GEORGE ALLEN & UNWIN LTD